The Late Plays of Tennessee Williams

William Prosser

THE SCARECROW PRESS, INC.
Lanham, Maryland • Toronto • Plymouth, UK
2009

SCARECROW PRESS, INC.

Published in the United States of America
by Scarecrow Press, Inc.
A wholly owned subsidiary of
The Rowman & Littlefield Publishing Group, Inc.
4501 Forbes Boulevard, Suite 200, Lanham, Maryland 20706
www.scarecrowpress.com

Estover Road
Plymouth PL6 7PY
United Kingdom

Copyright © 2009 by Eric Stenshoel

British Library Cataloguing in Publication Information Available

Library of Congress Cataloging-in-Publication Data

Prosser, William, d. 1991.
    The late plays of Tennessee Williams / William Prosser.
        p. cm.
    Includes bibliographical references and index.
    ISBN-13: 978-0-8108-6361-3 (pbk. : alk. paper)
    ISBN-10: 0-8108-6361-8 (pbk. : alk. paper)
    1. Williams, Tennessee, 1911–1983—Criticism and interpretation. 2. American
drama—20th century—History and criticism. I. Title.
    PS3545.I5365Z8237 2009
    812'.54—dc22   2008029331

♾ ™ The paper used in this publication meets the minimum requirements of
American National Standard for Information Sciences—Permanence of Paper
for Printed Library Materials, ANSI/NISO Z39.48-1992.
Manufactured in the United States of America.

Contents

Foreword

$\mathcal{T}$ennessee Williams. I was presumptuous enough to call him Tom; it made me feel like I was part of an "in group" that, in my view at the time, consisted of his sister Rose, an actress and confidante Madame St. Just, his male companion, a knot of male friends living principally in New Orleans and Key West, and his devoted CMA agent Billy Barnes.

Williams was a great playwright and a complex man, and for a short period of time I was able to glimpse both. The playwright was generous in choosing me to direct the Broadway productions of *Eccentricities of a Nightingale* and *Sweet Bird of Youth* (the Irene Worth, Christopher Walken revival), the London production of *A Streetcar Named Desire*, and his last, monumentally brilliant *The Red Devil Battery Sign*.

We discussed *Red Devil* over a period of several months at the Elysee Hotel, his residence in New York City; during many meals at Antoine's in New Orleans; and most conspicuously at his home in Key West, Florida, during an extended period while fashioning the production script. It is this time together in Key West that I remember most clearly.

Starting at 5:00 a.m., Tom tapped feverishly at his typewriter for several hours, a sound that could be heard throughout his walled-in residence—then some two or more hours at pool-side for notes, discussing possible revisions, and finally after 10:00 a.m. we'd start breakfast. His drinking began around noon, he would swim several laps in his pool, and the work would slowly wind down by early afternoon.

During those early morning moments we were alone, and he was an intense and focused listener as I voiced notions for script changes, mostly dialogue. He would smile, think for a moment, and translate my prosaic thoughts into his poetic cadences and images. It was magic—what Williams described as a play for the "Presentational Theatre," a form different from his earlier work, putting aside his previous ways of depicting events, relationships, and scenic environments and seeking more expressive, mystical, and confrontational means of reaching his audience.

The Red Devil Battery Sign is set in Dallas immediately after John F. Kennedy's assassination. It is a morality play. Its metaphor is drawn simply through the characters. The Woman Downtown, the product of an immoral and degrading, inhuman environment, sits alone at a bar, rich and anonymous, representing evil that desires redemption. Her husband, never seen, the Battery Emperor, who, it is hinted, may have engineered the Kennedy assassination, has amassed enormous power and wealth through investments in strategic locations rich in energy resources. He is the Devil. King, the leader of a mariachi band, is a man whose sensitivity, simplicity, and honesty are all that is poetic, human, and redemptive. King has a brain tumor and is slowly dying. His mariachi band is in decline—much as our social order since the Kennedy assassination. La Nina, his daughter, separated from him for over a year, is a flamenco dancer and singer. She returns home with a young business executive who has rejected the false values of his culture and is deeply in love with her. It is to their unborn child that Williams entrusts the future.

I first read the play at Blake's Hotel in London on March 17, 1974. I remember the date well as it was one day prior to the opening of *A Streetcar Named Desire* at the Piccadilly Theatre, in which Claire Bloom starred. *Streetcar* was an immense success and Miss Bloom was brilliant, subsequently earning the Evening Standard Award.

Tennessee's enthusiasm for my work, and my own excitement over the *Red Devil* script, led to an agreement between us for me to direct the play. To me the play was the most important work of the decade, with a clear warning to our society about the destructive force of unbridled corporate power.

The closing of *The Red Devil Battery Sign* in Boston, prior to its Broadway run scheduled at the Shubert Theatre, was a catastrophe for all concerned except the producer, David Merrick, who seemed to take pleasure in its demise.

The reviews were mixed: The *Boston Herald-American*'s widely respected Elliot Norton, conceding the play was overlong and its production not yet ready for audiences, found decided virtues in the script and characters. Thor Eckert Jr. of the *Christian Science Monitor* found the play "a cause for rejoicing" and said that "Williams' touch had not left him" for "creating a haunting theatre piece." The *Boston Globe*'s Kevin Kelly reacted strongly against the play, stating that after many declining years, Williams had declined still further, that *The Red Devil Battery Sign* was "a mess."

Public response was very lively. We were playing to capacity audiences and standing ovations for Anthony Quinn's profoundly moving portrayal of

King. At the closing, the play was first beginning to emerge, not yet right, but so greatly improved from the opening just five performances earlier.

Williams told me he felt devastated and was leaving immediately for Rome. He said he would return if, by some miracle, the play were to continue. Quinn and Bloom went on TV in Boston and talked openly of Merrick's inexplicable behavior in closing the play. They likened Merrick to the evil forces metaphorically portrayed by the Battery Emperor.

After a brief final meeting with the company on Saturday, June 28, 1974, I left to drive my sons to summer camp. The curtain came down on *The Red Devil Battery Sign* for the last time that Saturday night.

The following April, while in Washington to see my wife, Jane Alexander, open in a play at the Kennedy Center, I had dinner with Zelda Fichandler, then the producing director of Arena Stage and currently chair of the graduate acting program at New York University. We discussed Williams' play, and I told her of how my experiences working on *The Red Devil Battery Sign* contrasted so much from my previous experiences as a director. We spoke of the nurturing and tenderness that new material requires and of the consummate faith everyone connected with a new play must have, not only in the regional theater but on Broadway as well.

For a new play, like a new life, is extremely vulnerable, requiring the most careful nurturing. I recalled our work on *The Great White Hope*, done in a completely constructive and creative environment attributable directly to Zelda, and without which the play would surely have failed. With the care that it received it went on to win the Pulitzer Prize.

There is no doubt that *The Red Devil Battery Sign*, Williams' last "panoramic" drama, ranks among his great plays. Its people all resonate the same ache and yearning that can be traced to his earliest characters: neurotic, playful, insecure, loving, needy, sexual, powerful, and oh! so human.

But *The Red Devil Battery Sign* went beyond his other ambitious visions into a world shaken by the assassinations of John F. Kennedy and Martin Luther King Jr. and tumbling into the grasp of an oligarchy of power and greed. A less greedy, less powerful, less cynical man at the helm in Boston, someone who thrilled in the process of creating a masterpiece, would have immeasurably enriched the world of theater as well the final years of Tom's life.

—Ed Sherin

Preface

William Prosser was a theater director who got the opportunity to work with Tennessee Williams when he ran the Tennessee Williams Fine Arts Center in Key West, where he directed the world premiere of the Williams play *Will Mr. Merriwether Return from Memphis?* in 1980. I first met Bill Prosser in 1984 when he moved to New York, took charge of the graduate directing program at Brooklyn College, and became my life partner.

Prosser wrote the manuscript for this book in the mid-1980s after discovering that he was HIV-positive. He was determined to communicate his passion for the late plays of Tennessee Williams while he was still healthy. He succeeded in completing the manuscript before developing any life-threatening conditions and found a publisher, Scarecrow Press, that was interested in publishing it. But Prosser had not banked on the intransigence of Lady Maria St. Just, whom Tennessee had appointed as his literary executor for the benefit of his sister Rose.

Prosser's purpose in writing this book was to help liberate the late plays, most of them then unpublished, from the literary purgatory to which they had been condemned by the critics. But to make his case, Prosser needed to quote from the plays themselves. Because Maria agreed with the negative critical assessment of the late plays and felt that their publication would sully Williams' reputation, she adamantly refused to allow any quotation at all of the unpublished works. Unable to obtain the necessary permissions, Prosser died in 1991 and the manuscript was set aside.

After Maria's death in 1994, I renewed the attempt to get the book published, but to no avail. Finally, a few years ago, Prosser's mentor, the director and playwright Joe Stockdale, called to ask me what had become of Bill's manuscript. After I told him about the previous attempts at publication, he urged me to try again and offered his help. By that time, following the death of

Tennessee's sister Rose in 1996, the literary rights to the late plays were in the hands of either New Directions or The University of the South at Sewanee, who both graciously agreed to grant permission for publication.

In the twenty years since this manuscript was completed, there has been progress. More of the late plays have been published and performed and subjected to scholarly treatment. But Prosser's message is that of a theater director in love with the theatricality of the late plays—a message that still needs to be heard.

—Eric Stenshoel

Introduction: Making Voyages

*K*ey West, Florida, exerts a lawless charm, a contagious raffishness that makes it irresistible as a retreat from the rest of the world. At least this was true in the late seventies and early eighties when I visited and lived there. Now it is starting to look a little like the rest of Florida with boutiques and tourists, motels and pre-fab Disney-mentality resort apartment buildings. Of course, even when I lived there I was told that I had missed the really best good old days. My father, a Floridian, once told me that in the thirties in Key West no one had license plates on their automobiles and that the "conch republic" (as it calls itself) had its own laws, administered by longtime local families and smugglers of whatever was illegal at any particular time. My guess is that Key West will always be a little apart from normal restrictions. I wouldn't be surprised if the new condominiums now going up crumbled early from poor construction, faulty materials, and laissez-faire building codes. It just isn't the right place for progress.

Isolated on a tiny string of bead islands, out in the middle of the Atlantic, Caribbean, and the Gulf of Mexico, it is a never-never land of Oz, a place not only geographically remote but on another plane of consciousness that either immediately seduces or repulses, like some overtly sexual person to whom you cannot be indifferent.

Surrounded by water, water, everywhere—blue, green, bluegreen, grey, sometimes black—one's personal life is enacted against an enormity of ocean. You slow down, become introspective, more physical. If you fit in you slow down. The water reflects yourself back to you. It is a good place for writers needing time and self. And many have lived there. Hemingway, of course. But also in our time, Richard Wilbur and James Merrill. Poets. Key West is good for poets. But especially Tennessee Williams. Key West was where Tennessee lived. And everything that defines Key West was also true of him.

It is not the best place for a professional, regional theater of classical repertory, rehearsal schedules, fund drives, subscription drives, advertising campaigns, and not-to-be-postponed opening nights. But from 1980 to 1983 that is exactly what I attempted to run as both artistic and managing director of the Tennessee Williams Fine Arts Center, a three-million-dollar arts complex located on Stock Island, the island north of Key West where Florida Keys Community College is located. It is also where I got to work with Tennessee Williams and that was why I was there.

As a theater director and teacher who was led to Key West by accidents of career and acquaintances in the late seventies, it was my fortune to meet and work with Tennessee, first at the Greene Street Theatre and later at the Fine Arts Center. I directed six productions of Williams' plays, five of which Tennessee saw, criticized, and quite often praised. It was an exciting time, a kind of fantasy for someone who had always loved the plays of Tennessee Williams. Since my early teens I had admired and been a fan of the man whom I always considered my favorite American playwright.

I first read *The Glass Menagerie* in high school. As a high school misfit in the late fifties involved in theater from age fourteen, it was *my* play. I think I identified with both Tom and Laura. Tom's monologues had a magic, lyrical feeling and I loved to read them aloud to myself. Tom's escape from Laura and his mother promised a new world to an adolescent. But it was an escape that threatened never to find satisfaction in freedom. Like other morbid adolescents I enjoyed both the longing and the pessimism, the aching necessity for movement and the dread that things would not work out. "I descended the steps of this fire escape for a last time and followed, from then on, in my father's footsteps, attempting to find in motion what was lost in space."

There was also in Tennessee Williams a rebellious sexuality that spoke out more courageously than any other playwright of his time. I remember particularly how *Cat on a Hot Tin Roof* seemed daringly explosive with Big Daddy's language, Maggie's overt desire, and Brick's forbidden secrets. For an adolescent discovering himself in the fifties, Williams' plays were an important and honest voice proclaiming the excitement and goodness of sexuality. It also helped that many "grown ups" considered him dangerous. Tennessee expressed most clearly my generation's personal growth and flight from middle class conventionalism with its moral and sexual hang-ups to a freer, more human and humane way of thinking and living.

As a college professor in my forties, I see my students discover Tennessee Williams for the first time. It makes me feel a little like Blanche describing her pupils in *A Streetcar Named Desire*: "And in the spring, it's touching to notice them making their first discovery of love! As if nobody had ever known it before." More often than not the acting and directing students perform scenes from *The Glass Menagerie, A Streetcar Named Desire, Summer and Smoke,* and *Cat on a Hot Tin Roof.* Laura and her Gentleman Caller appear at least once yearly. I haven't got tired of the scenes yet. There is so much to say about them and what tools for teaching actors and directors about intentions, subtext, transitions, communion, and all the other tricks in the Stanislavski bag! It gives me some measure of permanence to know that the scenes that moved me in my teens still move young students. Of course, the pleasures in Williams are not only for the young. Yet perhaps they have changed. Tom in *The Glass Menagerie* seems less romantic and more tragic to me for I am past the days when movement seems glamorous, and I know through long experience that the past is never left. Quite often the scenes now seem as funny as they are passionate. What was once only lyrical and intense has now become more ironic. In other words, the scenes have changed as I have changed.

In 1976 I first visited Key West to direct *Suddenly Last Summer* for the Greene Street Theatre as their opening production. That was when the Greene Street Theatre was really on Greene Street where a video game parlor now resides. One of my students from Virginia Commonwealth University, Roddy Brown, had gone to Key West to start a theater with his friend Jay Drury. The late Peter Pell of Key West Hand Print Fabrics was a third partner. A charming mature lady of many local Key West productions, Janice White, played Mrs. Venable with great style. My talented ex-wife, Roxana Stuart, portrayed Catherine. Other actors included Betty Smith, Jay Drury, and Rita Brown and Gordon Mackey (both students from Virginia).

One late dress rehearsal Tennessee Williams came to watch our efforts. Jay Drury had with charm persuaded Tennessee to see what we were up to. It was a big occasion for us made more exciting by the fact that Tennessee praised our rehearsal. Yet we were not quite ready to open. Peter Pell's donation of blue and orange hibiscus material had not yet covered the old movie house chairs. Tennessee wanted to rewrite the end of the play. Roddy Brown insisted that while the performance was good, it would be better in another week. The Greene Street Theatre must always be dedicated to quality. People would understand if we postponed the opening.

In a week we opened to a Key West first night. Everyone said they loved the production. Peter Pell and Jimmy Russell hosted an opening night party that was elegant and festive. Tennessee declared to a reporter from the *New York Times,* "I'll give them anything!" It was one of those evenings when everyone was elated and as high as the Key West sky.

The next day, nursing hangovers with piña colada and mimosas at the Pier House, we decided we wanted next to do a new play of Tennessee's. He had given Jay Drury the first draft of a recently completed play. It was called *Vieux Carré.* It would be a world premiere. Later in the week we got together to read the play aloud. I remember some of the first draft was written on stationery from a hotel in Hong Kong. For the occasion we cooked a big fish dinner and sat down after the meal to read the play. It was a beautiful poetic drama about Tennessee's early days in New Orleans. We were together then.

Later things fell apart. It doesn't matter why. As in so many collective human endeavors good will gave way to ego, fear, and misunderstanding. It was difficult for all of us to be honest and still sensitive to each other. The Greene Street Theatre never produced *Vieux Carré*. It was produced on Broadway in what Tennessee called "an awful production." The play later went on to London and it had a successful run on the English stage. It was also the last play I directed at the Tennessee Williams Fine Arts Center in March 1983, one month after Tennessee died.

In spring of 1976, after *Suddenly Last Summer,* I returned to New York to finish my doctorate and then moved to Tucson, Arizona, where I headed the Graduate Acting/Directing Program at the University of Arizona. As a tenured professor with a little adobe house, I was securely set up for an Arizona future. That was until Roddy Brown called from Key West in 1979. A new Fine Arts Center was going up in Key West and they were looking for a director. Was I interested? I had been to Key West once more to codirect *Streetcar* with Roddy. It had also been successful and gained Tennessee's approval. Key West was fun as a diversion. But live there? Also, I would be leaving a secure job at a state university to work in a small junior college at a salary cut. From an academic career point of view it was not wise. But I would be able to run my own theater and, of course, there was the lure of Williams. Yes, I would go. After all, if you had lived in Athens in the time of Euripides you would have been a fool not to work with Euripides.

Roxana and I moved to Key West in the autumn of 1979. We found a lovely wood house with a glass ceiling and a tree growing through the bathroom. We moved in during the weekend that Hurricane David was expected. While local residents were boarding up and taping their windows, we carted in box loads of books and records, all of which were later to become victims of tropical mildew.

The Fine Arts Center was to open in January of 1980. Much still needed to be done. I insisted that our first production must be the world premiere of a play by Williams. Tennessee was agreeable and offered us three scripts: *Steps Must Be Gentle* (an unproduced play about Hart Crane); *Something Cloudy, Something Clear* (an early play about a first love); and *Will Mr. Merriwether Return from Memphis?* a fantasy play from 1969. I chose the latter for its potential theatricality and festive use of music. It seemed the best choice for a celebration. Of course, the play was also "late" Williams and bound to be controversial in its experimentation. But I loved the play's wild imagination and poetic theatricality.

The play and center opened in a gala way, a social occasion with champagne and a Dixieland band flown in from New Orleans. *Time* magazine covered the event. It was great publicity for the center and the community college which sponsored it. Said *Time*: "The indisputable triumph belongs to the citizens of Key West, who gave selfless hours and years of effort to build this arts center and who will now be repaid in something sweeter than sweat or money."[1] Tennessee seemed pleased with the production. It had been a rocky and pressure-filled rehearsal period with cast firings and replacements, tension, and some ill will from local theater people who saw professional actors brought in to play key roles. The social aspects of the opening took too much attention away from the artistic concerns of the production. It had been late in the rehearsal period when Tennessee sent me this note:

> Dear Bill:
>
> Sadly the cart has been put in front of the horse. Some lonely island ladies are making an ego-trip out of what should have been just the opening of an unique and interesting unproduced play of mine in a somewhat impractically but touchingly ego type of theater. I do want to do what I can to help you. But things are getting out of hand. I find myself missing the old Greene Street, don't you? Who the fuck wants to drag himself down to the mayor's office at 11 a.m. and get a scroll handed to him.
>
> I am interested in one thing and it's not the "gala" aspects of the coming occasion but a production that won't be an anti-climax.

Of course, Tennessee was right. I had started a local "founders' society" in order to get money and support for the theater but it was a hydra. The opening was becoming a chance for local society to get national recognition. It had been arranged for opening week to be called "Tennessee Williams Week" and Tennessee had to submit to being photographed receiving a proclamation from the mayor of Key West. He was obviously not pleased. Also, in his note he asked me to replace a local actress with a professional. I had to fly to New York, one week before the opening, audition, find a new actress, and get her ready very quickly. Naturally, the actress to be replaced was the wife of an important local personage. What a time! Hardly the "laid back" place Key West was supposed to be.

Somehow the play opened. The local critic of the *Key West Citizen* was scathing in a vitriolic review entitled, "Send Mr. Merriwether Back to Memphis." Fortunately, the *Miami Herald* and *Time* magazine said some nice things about the play and its production. Time passed. That year we produced *The Threepenny Opera* and coproduced three plays with the Greene Street Theatre:

Anything Goes, Equus, and *Twelfth Night.* It was ambitious stuff for a small-town regional theater.

One of my funniest memories is of Tennessee attending *Twelfth Night.* He sat in the center of the fourth row and about one-half hour into the production one could hear gasping coming from his seat. "Help! Get me some medicine! Medicine! Help!"

I thought, "Oh, my God. Tennessee is going to die, right in his own theater!" I rushed down the aisle of the theater. He was with his cousin, Jim Adams, who had played Van Gogh's apparition in *Merriwether.* Somehow, Jim and I got Tennessee out of the theater. Of course, no one in the audience was watching Shakespeare. Jim and Tennessee drove off in their jeep. The next day, much concerned, I phoned Tennessee to see if he was alright. He replied in full health, "Oh, you know baby, I never did much like *Twelfth Night.*" The devil had been *acting*! He had been dying all right. Dying to get out of the theater and couldn't wait until intermission. I don't know, maybe he didn't want to walk out in full view of the audience. Perhaps he was afraid they would think he didn't like our production.

I have many memories of Tennessee from the next three years. The memories have no order, no time sequence, but flash in quick succession from image to image. I remember Tennessee with his sister, Rose, one night when he and Rose (who had been silent during dinner) together recited quite spontaneously the twenty-third Psalm, "The Lord is my shepherd." I remember Tennessee holding court many times at the Pier House frequently treating many people to drinks and meals. One time I was reciting some personal woes to Tennessee when he handed me an unopened bottle of bourbon. "Here," he said. "That's the only thing I can give to help you!"

During the time we were in Key West, my wife, Roxana, and I parted, getting a divorce. Roxana returned to New York, and Tennessee let her use his Manhattan Plaza apartment for over a year. He could be very generous.

The last year of his life I watched his house for him and fed his animals while he was away. He wanted to keep his animals—a bull dog, cat, and parrot—but had no one to feed them during his many absences. He had plans to go to Europe. I agreed to stay in the house and try to take care of the animals. I was not the best person for this job as I had to be at the theater for many hours and could not spend much time at the house. One late afternoon I returned to Tennessee's to find the back gate open and Cornelius, the bull dog, gone. A pool man had been at the house earlier to clean the swimming pool and may have left the back gate open. I don't really know what happened. Cornelius was never found, in spite of an all-island search and radio and newspaper articles. Rumor had it that Cornelius had been seen on one of the outgoing shrimp boats, having taken up with one of the local fishermen.

Who knows? Anyway, I had to tell Tennessee about the dog's disappearance. But Tennessee was very resigned. "It would have happened sooner or later."

When I read accounts of Tennessee's life that stress dissipation and neurosis, drugs and promiscuity, I feel as if I were reading about a stranger, or looking at an unfinished portrait. Of course, his most desperate drug and mental problems were probably over by the late seventies and early eighties when I knew him. And it is true that he was often temperamental while "in his cups," but important things are missing from this popular tabloid picture. What's missing is Tennessee's love of work, his love of poetry, and his great love for the theater. Williams' humor is missing from books like Donald Spoto's *The Kindness of Strangers.*

When I knew Tennessee, everything in his life seemed a preparation for, or respite from, the four or five hours he spent almost every day in writing. I spent the night several times at his house while he was in residence and witnessed the ritual of his life at that time. Tennessee would retire fairly early, usually by midnight, and awake very early in the morning, five or six o'clock, in order to write. You could hear the sound of the typewriter throughout the house. Coffee had been made the night before for him, and he always had a bottle of white wine in the refrigerator to get him going. One bottle usually lasted a few days, so I don't think he drank that much in the morning. But it had to be there. He would then go back to sleep until early noon at which time he would emerge from his room for lunch. The rest of the day included socializing, swimming, often painting, and other things, but this was only time passing until he got back to writing. Time passage and, of course, observation of life.

Williams loved to read aloud or have others read aloud, and some of my most pleasant memories were hearing Tennessee read his own work or the poems of Hart Crane. More often than not Tennessee and I talked about poetry and drama but not in any deeply analytical way. Usually he loved or hated the work of other writers, getting intense, almost physical, pleasure out of poetic writing.

I believe that Tennessee's love of theater extended into the creation of dramatic scenes in his own life. He would sometimes bait people in order to get reactions out of them. Domestic crises often seemed to be brewing or in climax, usually centering on a friend's perceived betrayal, a current secretary or lover or secretary/lover, or some pined-for object of affection. I have also seen him laugh in the middle of the most seemingly serious confrontation, calling into question his real feelings. He could "break" out of one mood into another the way actors sometimes "break" out of character and you are reminded that they are only acting.

Tennessee "dressed" for dinner, and it was at dinner that some of the best conversations occurred as well as some of the most explosive scenes. One time he appeared at a local costume ball dressed as Yasser Arafat. He like to provoke responses, he enjoyed confrontations. He also loved to imitate people and was often hilariously cruel in his imitations. But then he could become quickly depressed and express sorrowful empathy for the object of his ridicule. Political opinions often escaped with expletives—strongly expressed, almost as strongly as he expressed hatred of perceived theatrical enemies and vicious critics.

I never found Williams' theatricality to be distasteful or an indication of insincerity. The theater was lifeblood to him. I have seen the same habitual explosiveness in many people from difficult family situations where "domestic" scenes were commonplace outlets for problems. I think that for such people the theater with its releasing climaxes can be helpful therapy in impossible circumstances. Of course, theater with its catharses can also become an addiction. Life is often forced into dramatic structures. For many theater people, theater is more than an occupation. It can be the model for all experience in which a love for heightened experience is more important than reality, truth less important than the vitality of passion. Blanche DuBois in *A Streetcar Named Desire* cries out, "I don't want realism. I want magic!" I think Tennessee was always trying to make his life into magic. What a tragic, doomed ambition. Easy to misunderstand but ultimately worthy of understanding and a certain admiration. More than anything else in his life, Tennessee's art permitted that magic and it was his greatest addiction.

The last times I saw Tennessee were at a dinner party at his house and for a reading of *Vieux Carré* by some local actors, also at his house. At the dinner he was very depressed and at one point said, "Let us talk about death shall we?" He said he wasn't afraid of death but only of dying, its possible pain. He also read a poem entitled "Arctic Light," which he had recently written. It was about death as a going toward light. There is no question that death was much on his mind that evening. But a few days after, at the reading of *Vieux Carré*, he was gracious and helpful. He complimented the actors and seemed genuinely interested in our production. It didn't matter to Tennessee where a production was. It was work, work "the loveliest of all four letter words, surpassing even the importance of love, most times."[2]

I was in New York to cast a final role in *Vieux Carré* when Tennessee died. I hadn't known he was also in New York. A good friend of mine informed me of Tennessee's death. Impulsively, we both got in a cab and drove to the Elysee Hotel where Tennessee had died. In the bar where frequently Tennessee had sat, people were toasting him and offering drinks in his honor. Everywhere I went, restaurants, elevators, lobbies, one heard the name Tennessee Williams. A truly national figure had died; multitudes of people were touched by his death.

That evening Betty Williams of the *Key West Citizen* called and asked what I felt. I was angry with sensational reports coming out stressing Tennessee's loneliness and misery, his personal habits, the suggestion that a decadent life style had destroyed him. Tennessee was seventy-one years old. When he lived in Key West he swam twenty laps a day in his swimming pool. His body and soul had suffered shocks. But he was incredibly strong for all that he had experienced. I said to Betty, "He had a full, happy life." It seemed ironic, I am sure, to call Tennessee Williams' life happy, but it is now Tennessee's incredible laughter I best remember. I remember it coming from the middle of the theater named in his honor, at rehearsals, at dinner tables, sitting around his living room. Tennessee *roared* when he laughed; he cackled and *roared*. He was the best audience for his own plays and often laughed riotously at what others considered his sad plays. It was this combination of laughter and sorrow, which like Anton Chekhov, his favorite playwright, were his particular vision and tone. Nor was his laughter polite or nice. It could be cruel and demonic, but more often he laughed at what could not be helped. He often laughed at himself.

All this introduction is to warn the reader that this book, this critical work, this defense, has a strong personal bias. Tennessee Williams was my friend, "faithful and just to me." As a theater director, critic, and theater historian, however, I think I am qualified to defend the late plays with special qualifications and some knowledge. As his friend I believe I am even better qualified to understand him. Perhaps love is the best adjunct to understanding. Or if love makes us blind, then all great art must be suspect as it is usually acclaimed "great" by those who love it best. I believe all critical work has a bias, recognized or not, and perhaps the beginning of knowledge is the admission of one's personal bias, in so far as one understands oneself.

During my time as director of the Tennessee Williams Fine Arts Center, I always wanted to direct new plays by Tennessee, or at least the less well-known later plays. Some of them had been unsuccessfully produced, others never produced or published at all. Certainly Tennessee's greatest interest in those years was his most recent work. I found myself consistently responding to the late work as a theater director and wanted to do productions of many of them. Yet, as manager of the theater, I was in the necessary business of selling tickets. The pressure on a theater manager to do well-known commercial plays is enormous, especially when the survival of the theater depends upon income from ticket sales. Even in Key West audiences prefer to see musicals, comedies, and stars. Most submitted themselves to one Williams play a year but even his best-known plays did not sell as well as *Annie Get Your Gun* or *Hair*. Eventually this manager–artistic director schizophrenia convinced me I could not do both jobs, and so I left Key West in the summer of 1983. It had been a good trip and I had been taught limits, limits to myself and Key West. I hope this book will convey the enthusiasm I feel for Williams' "late" plays in my desire to direct them. In a way, each chapter may be seen as a director's research and analysis for potential productions. Of course, I did direct *Will Mr. Merriwether Return from Memphis?* and *Vieux Carré* in Key West and those experiences hopefully give the chapters on those plays special insight.

I see Tennessee Williams' late plays as experimental artistic trips, visits to new lands by a habitual traveler, experiments in new forms by a restless mind. Tennessee was always taking trips. Any of us would love to have been the places he went and known the people he knew. He could never stay in one place for long. You could never pin him down. For two months before his death, I didn't know for certain where he was. He was "away" somewhere on a trip.

One of my favorite passages in Williams is from *Camino Real*. It talks about making voyages. The poet Lord Byron is leaving *Camino Real*. For him, it has become a confining and stultifying place.

> There is a time for departure even when there's no certain place to go!
>
> I'm going to look for one, now. I'm sailing to Athens. At least I can look up at the Acropolis, I can stand at the foot of it and look up at broken columns on the crest of a hill—if not purity, at least its recollection . . .
>
> I can sit quietly looking for a long, long time in absolute silence, and possibly, yes, still possibly—
>
> The old pure music will come to me again. Of course on the other hand I may hear only the little noise of insects in the grass . . .
>
> But I am sailing for Athens! Make voyages!—Attempt them!—there's nothing else.

Key West and Tennessee Williams took me on artistic and personal voyages. I hope this book will be a tour guide for others to places not yet totally explored.

—W. P.

NOTES

1. T. E. Kalem, "Apparitions and Cakewalkers," *Time*, February 4, 1980, 61.
2. Tennessee Williams, *Memoirs* (Garden City, NY: Doubleday, 1975), 241.

• 1 •

Tennessee Williams and the Critics

*M*ugged in the spring of 1979 in Key West, Florida, Tennessee Williams said, "Maybe they weren't punks at all, but New York drama critics." It was not the first time Williams employed humor in the face of humiliation. Seldom has an artist endured so public a condemnation as Williams faced in the last twenty years of his life. Also, seldom has an artist responded so publicly to that drudging, time after time alluding to his critical reception in occasional articles and interviews published almost as continually as his plays fared badly before the public. I know of no other writer who has received such publicity, such fascinated ghoulishness, such anatomizing of his perceived failures. It is almost as if Williams in his late commercial theatrical failures were enacting some national tragedy of the once successful, now failed artist. In a country where commercial success endows value and failure takes it away, Williams' pattern of early success and late failure has the tragic pattern of a publicly en- acted drama with the playwright as sacrificial icon. The artist fails for us, does it in our behalf, acts out our private fears of failure. This failure is particularly sat- isfying to the culture if it follows great success, reaffirming once more our faith in a democratic and homogeneous populace in which no one is better than anyone else. Elia Kazan once summed up the pattern and the theme, prophetic of his own career as well as descriptive of that of Williams: "In America you're a success or you're a failure. Any half-way ground . . . isn't recognized." I once asked a prominent casting agent if he knew who a certain director was. The casting agent replied, "Oh, yeah, *him*, he used to be somebody." Or as F. Scott Fitzgerald said, "There are no second acts in American lives."

The nadir of Tennessee Williams' critical reputation was probably reached on June 10, 1969, when Time-Life, Inc., ran a full-page advertisement in the *New York Times* excoriating Williams in the most aggressive manner for the

1

recent failure of his play *In the Bar of a Tokyo Hotel*. The ad was part of a daily campaign used to convince newspaper readers that *Life* magazine was a no-nonsense truth giver of tough opinions. A picture of Tennessee was accompanied by large bold type saying COME TO LIFE. To the side of the large type was written the following:

> Played out? "Tennessee Williams has suffered an infantile regression from which there seems no exit . . . Almost free of incident or drama . . . nothing about *In the Bar of a Tokyo Hotel* deserves its production."
>
> That's the kind of play it is, and that's the kind of play it gets in this week's Life.
>
> From a theatre review that predicts the demise of one of America's major playwrights to a news breaking story that unseats a Supreme Court judge, we call a bad play when we see it.
>
> And it's that kind of strong stuff on Life's pages that gets us a major play from 36.5 million adults. Every week.[1]

This "macho" advertisement is extraordinary as a cultural document. Probably never before had a negative review of an artist been used to "sell" a product in such a dramatic way. Madison Avenue must have felt that the news of Williams' disaster would bring enjoyment to readers of the *New York Times* and serve as an inducement to buy *Life*. This "toughness" proved the magazine's credentials and would sell more subscriptions.

The extraordinary fact is that Tennessee Williams went on writing for the next thirteen years, went on trying to have his plays produced. Some of these plays were produced, mostly with negative critical responses. Many of those plays have never been published and some of them are totally unknown.

Interestingly, during the last years of Williams' life the playwright was given numerous national honors such as the Commonwealth Award and the Presidential Award of Artistic Merit. Honorary doctorates were offered and given but few of the late plays earned audience or critical approval. Enormous royalties flowed in from the early plays so in no way was Williams financially uncomfortable. It was simply that no one seemed to want his new plays and little else mattered to him.

The saga of Williams' relation to his critics as well as to the public is a fascinating story, spanning nearly forty years of creative output. It tells much of changes in taste, manners, and morals of American culture while it also reveals certain constants in our society. Seldom has an artist in our country been so popular and respected at the same time he was dismissed and vilified.

It is the mission of this book to advocate Williams' late plays, to stimulate reevaluation, to introduce unfamiliar works, to suggest interpretations, and finally to encourage the publication and production of works by a playwright whom even his most serious critics concede a major talent in the American theater.

Part of the work must confront Williams' critics. Plays sometimes endure, criticism seldom is remembered. However, when a critical opinion is as pervasive as that surrounding Williams' late plays, productions, perusal, and even consideration are seldom undertaken. For many it is a critical *given* that the late work is bad and unworthy of consideration.

Nevertheless the work must be undertaken, if only to show how a major talent changed. Of course, it is my contention that the talent was *not* destroyed, but indeed, that it went on in different directions to produce extraordinarily unpopular and misunderstood works. Lack of popularity is not necessarily proof of artistic failure. Perceptions of works of art change as times change. Criticism itself is undergoing such major changes that judgments made twenty years ago may no longer seem true. Basic principles of criticism are everywhere under attack. Deconstructionism and postmodernism are but two radically provocative movements in contemporary thought that challenge the way we look at all works of art.

Judgments in art constantly change. One year Beethoven is "in" and seems the supreme composer, another year Mozart seems the only necessary and true expression of the complete human experience. Oscillation, correction, assertion, and reaction—these are the only constants. Artists often undergo a period of disfavor late in their careers. If they are major artists, their reputations usually return. Cultural history swings back and forth from the classical to the romantic temperament, and artists return to vogue when their prevailing temperament once more coincides with its corresponding historical moment. Tennessee Williams was primarily a romantic writer, and by this is simply meant that he put emotion above intellect as the primary quality of his art. This is not to say that Williams' works are devoid of thought. Indeed, I hope to challenge that oft-repeated assertion. But if one had to award a prevailing combatant primacy on the human battlefield of emotion/intellect, then in Williams one would see man as primarily motivated by emotion rather than by reason and objectivity, or rather, in Williams knowledge comes through the emotions. We know things because we feel them. That this view of man may seem true today may be proof that Williams' historical moment is once more upon us in the continuing but shortening oscillation of history and human consciousness.

The story of the critical response to Williams' plays is also a chronicle of American response to sexuality in drama, and perhaps to sex in general. Williams' popularity after *The Glass Menagerie* was often tied into a response to what was considered "sensational" in his plays. This was certainly the case in the late forties and fifties when honest sexuality was fairly bursting at the seams to find expression in American culture.

Looking back one sees how much sexual frustration was excited and expressed in the drama of that time. Theater, year after year, dared more than any other art form to openly discuss the undiscussable, sexuality certainly, but really all social taboos. Remember the censorship imposed on all Williams scripts when they became films? Only the theater in those days was relatively free. But censorship was not totally unknown there either. Williams had to cut a slightly off-color joke from *Cat on a Hot Tin Roof.* One went to the theater to hear controversial subjects discussed, to be shocked, to vicariously and pruriently "get it off." Can one believe today that about fifty years ago the Catholic church forbade its members from seeing *Baby Doll?* For a certain part of the population, Williams was a daring speaker of the unspeakable. For a perhaps larger majority he was scandalous and, yes, dirty.

Attitudes, especially toward bodily functions, die slowly, or rather, they probably do not die at all but fester underground when they become intellectually indefensible. They lie waiting for a chance to emerge again in some guise. Williams' critical disreputation in the sixties gave closet Puritans the chance for which they were waiting. And they didn't even have to discuss sex. Williams was no longer considered a good playwright by the critical establishment. There is a vehemence in Williams' reviews in the sixties that goes beyond critical objectivity. Revenge was taken on him; the enjoyed destruction of a reputation. Idol smashing can be an outlet for the repressed Puritan sensibility and Puritanism never totally disappears in America. This attitude, this tendency in American history and culture, was one of the primary targets of Williams' art and it is partly because of that art's power that Williams needed to be debunked.

Of course, there are many other reasons for the demise of Williams' reputation as a playwright. Actually in the sixties he turned away from sensational subjects in his plays. Old defenders who had enjoyed his daring may have become disappointed that the playwright's new work no longer gave the same old "kick." New interests in the drama were mistaken for fatigue, especially since intensity had been one the earmarks of Williams' plays. So, stored-up resentment of sexual frankness and violent theatricality joined with disappointment over the lessening of sex and violence in the late plays. What was left? Actually, a great deal, as I hope to show.

It is amazing to see how much criticism of Williams in the fifties centered on the discussion of his sexual content. The most sophisticated criticism usually did not attack Williams directly for his sexuality but rather attacked him under the guise of "immaturity" and "adolescent" sentimentality. A perceived tendency to shock was often criticized as manipulative theatricalism that had little to do with real life.

The following comments by Signi Falk are typical of this line of criticism. She begins by ridiculing recurrent character types in Williams:

These (brute animal man, Mama's boy, frustrated unmarried female) are the character types which keep reappearing in the world of Tennessee Williams. Most of them according to the discriminating critics have been more deeply affected by the theater than by life. It is generally recognized that this writer has a talent for penetrating human character, for describing frustrations and various forms of escapism, as well as catching the spirit of joyous living. However, when he obscures this special insight by indulging in theatrical lies, and creates scenes dripping with sentiment or relying on shock and violence for effect, then he deserves the ridicule he has received.[2]

What veiled connotations, what niceness of consciousness rebelling against vulgarity! This criticism could almost be spoken by one of Williams' characters reproving another for lack of manners. Miss Alma could be speaking to John ("discriminating critics") in *Summer and Smoke*. What "various forms of escapism"? Are they so terrible they can't even be mentioned? What does she mean by "the spirit of joyous living"? Perhaps the critic has secretly been reading D. H. Lawrence or Ibsen's *Ghosts*. But the great give away is "indulging in theatrical lies." For this critic, theater is a sensual experience in which one "indulges." Like food, drink, sex, and all the other Puritan abominations, theater is suspect and dangerous. It is not *true* because it is not lifelike; it is a lie, extraordinary. By this criterion nearly all dramatic literature would have to be condemned. Is Macbeth "lifelike"? Have you ever met a Medea, a Phaedra, or a Lear? By Miss Falk's condemnation all, *all* the Greeks and Elizabethans would be guilty of the sin of theater. Theater *is* a lie. Most of drama is composed not of the ordinary but the extraordinary and the greatest interest is created not by realistic dramatization but the conflict of archetypal characters. Nor should Williams be condemned for using certain kinds of characters repeatedly. Most artists have obsessive and recurring concerns. Chekhov wrote repeatedly of the Russian provinces, Strindberg was obsessed with vampiric women, and Renaissance painters endlessly painted Italian Madonnas. These repetitions in themselves should not be subject to criticism, especially when the types are universal and develop in interesting ways as they did in Williams' late work.

The academy has seldom been approving of Williams any more than the "moral majority." I can remember no defenders of him in the English department of my undergraduate school. Theater professors often venerated Williams, but they were always considered intellectually suspect by professors in the humanities as if centuries of theatrical prejudice and doubtful integrity still clung around people who really worked in the theater. Interestingly, few professors in my Ph.D. program in theater had much regard for Tennessee Williams either. It has always been largely unfashionable for intellectuals to endorse Williams. In my experience theater *practitioners* have been his main supporters.

The general criticism of the academy has usually been that while Williams was theatrical and talented, he lacked the maturity to be taken seriously as an intellectual. The general view was that he also lacked the craft to fashion a structurally unified drama held together by a consistent and intellectually defensible point of view. Of course, critics have consistently compared American drama to European and often found American drama lacking in this regard. Richard Gilman, a well-known American critic, dramatically stated this point of view in *Tulane Drama Review* when he lamented, "The American drama is almost mindless; we weep for the intellectual deficiencies of Miller and Williams."[3]

This point of view seems to have been more prevalent among American than European critics. O'Neill, Miller, and Williams have curiously been more often more admired abroad than in their own country. It is almost as if American intellectuals suffered from an inferiority complex when comparing their culture to Europeans'. It seems one proves one's international intellectual credentials by separating oneself from one's own culture. Robert Brustein, the self-styled critic and consistent opponent of commercialism in the theater, perhaps summed up a prevailing academic attitude to Williams in his review of *Sweet Bird of Youth* printed in the *Hudson Review*: "In *Sweet Bird of Youth*, Tennessee Williams seems less concerned with dramatic verisimilitude than with communicating some hazy notions about such disparate items as Sex, Youth, Time, Corruption, Purity, Castration, Politics and the South . . . Cavorting through the forest of his own unconscious, Williams has taken to playing hide and seek with reality in a manner which he does not always control. *Sweet Bird of Youth* . . . frequently looks less like art than like some kind of confession and apology."[4] What really is being said here is that Williams, a disturbed individual, is adolescently stunted and his compulsions make him intellectually remiss. Williams is not serious, but "cavorting," and "playing hide and seek." He should grow up and not use his art as his personal therapy. What "growing up" means in this kind of dismissive criticism is never clear, nor does it recognize the confessional nature of much art, not least that of August Strindberg, one of Brustein's heroes described with adulation in Brustein's book *The Theatre of Revolt*.

I believe there is in much of this criticism an implied accusation of softness, of femininity, of, well, homosexuality as an arrested state of psychological development in the artist. It is *male* to be consistent; it is female to be muddled. Remember George Burns and Gracie Allen? Mature male artists have cohesive, all-encompassing visions. Women get fixed on details, can't quite put things all together. Men build structures, women feel things. Williams' homosexuality was a well-known-but-never-alluded-to fact in the 1950s. Much criticism often implied as much. But this kind of criticism never quite stated its prejudices, nor am I sure was even quite conscious of them. Homophobia and sexism are so a part of our culture that they are often unconscious to the homophobic and the sexist. Behind all of this lies a male distrust of emotional intensity as a female and inferior trait. By implication the homosexual artist is closer to the female sensibility and therefore deficient in the same way.

Williams was probably distrusted by the academy for another important reason. He was enormously successful financially and had enjoyed great public popularity. At one point in his career he could claim to be "one of the three wealthiest writers" in America. Our society may venerate wealth, but the intellectual establishment rarely participates in the rewards of money. Indeed, to be financially and commercially successful in our country is to be artistically suspect. Segregated from large financial rewards by an anti-intellectual culture, the intelligentsia automatically suspects any financially successful artist to be de facto anti-intellectual. It is an understandable prejudice born out of defensiveness in a society that gives little prestige to intellectual contribution. In other words, most artists, critics, and members of the intelligentsia had good reason to be envious of Tennessee Williams.

While the academic establishment seldom approved of Tennessee Williams, he was lauded greatly for nearly twenty years by daily critics writing for the major New York newspapers. Critics of established reputations like Stark Young, Brooks Atkinson, and Walter Kerr all praised his work and helped to create a large audience for the plays. One of America's greatest critics, Stark Young, prophetically evaluated Williams after *The Glass Menagerie*, noting the playwright's originality:

> The author is not awed by the usual sterilities of our playwriting patterns.
> On the other hand he is too imaginative, genuine, or has too much good
> taste, to be coy about the free devices on which his play is built, a true, rich
> talent, unpredictable like all truer talents, an astute stage sense, an intense
> quivering clarity, all light and feeling once the intelligence of it is well
> anchored—a talent too, I should say, that New York will buy tickets for
> in later plays, especially if enough of the sexy is added to things, but will
> never quite understand.[5]

The "sexy" was indeed added and New York did buy tickets and no, they didn't ever "quite understand."

The years of greatest acceptance for Williams on Broadway consistently found him receiving accolade reviews along with careful commendation. Reviewing *A Streetcar Named Desire*, Brooks Atkinson praised Williams for qualities that remained the playwright's greatest gifts: "it [*Streetcar*] reveals Mr.

Williams as a genuine poetic playwright, whose knowledge of people is honest and thorough, and whose sympathy is profoundly human."[6]

After *Cat on a Hot Tin Roof* opened, Walter Kerr gave the play this summary eulogy: "Mr. Williams is the man of our time who comes closest to hurling the actual blood and bone of life onto the stage; he is also the man whose prose comes closest to being an incisive natural poetry."[7]

During the fifties Williams received his worst reviews for *Camino Real*. Kerr, abandoning the playwright, called the play "hopelessly mired in his new love—symbolism"[8] and Eric Bentley (never an admirer of Williams) facetiously quipped, "The unreal which crept up on us furtively, now meets us head-on."[9] It is interesting to note that *Camino Real* is the play of Williams most frequently compared to the late plays in reviews of the sixties, seventies, and eighties. Presumably the "unreal" nature of much of the late work harkens back to *Camino Real*. For many, of course, this comparison served as proof of the waywardness of the new work. However, it is interesting that *Camino Real* has received many revivals at prestigious theaters since its first production. It seems to have gained a succès d'estime and is a favorite Williams play, especially among theater people.

Generally reviewers abandoned Williams after *Night of the Iguana*. The apogee of Williams' popularity probably came when *Time* magazine ran a cover story on the playwright in 1962, placing Williams in the "dark tradition" of American letters represented by such undisputed greats as Melville, Hawthorne, and Poe. But seven years later *Time* called *In the Bar of a Tokyo Hotel* "more deserving of a coroner's report than a review."[10]

It is here my subject begins: the late plays of Tennessee Williams. The late plays, for practical purposes, may be defined as those plays coming after *Night of the Iguana*, those written during Williams' long years of disfavor with most of the critical establishment. The division however is more than practical. It is my belief that starting with the second Broadway production of *The Milk Train Doesn't Stop Here Anymore*, Williams' writing underwent a profound change that may have been predicted in some of his earlier work but that only became dominant as a new direction for the playwright in the early sixties after *Night of the Iguana*. Many influences caused this change and it is not easy to ascribe the change to one cause. It was rather the confluence of many currents, some personal but also artistic and cultural.

My work deals with ten major plays and several shorter works of Williams' late period. The plays will be analyzed using Aristotle's guidelines: plot, character, thought, diction, music, and spectacle. It is my feeling that while Aristotle has been destructive to much drama as a prescriptive critic, his abilities as a descriptive and clear thinker on drama have seldom been equaled. Actually most of Aristotle's damage seems to have been committed by medieval and French neoclassic critics interpreting Aristotle for their own purposes. My work assumes a knowledge of Williams' most famous dramas through *Night of the Iguana*. They will be referred to continually as assumed knowledge. Late works will be discussed in detail, some of which are published, others not. Their discussion is often aimed at piquing the curiosity of readers to read and see these plays. Part of what I am doing is attempting to catalog the late work.

A special problem arises when dealing with the plays of Tennessee Williams, especially the late plays. When analyzing late Williams one must specify which version is being discussed. Many of the plays were extensively rewritten. Sometimes there are published editions of several versions; other times the published version represents Williams' last work on a play. In order to study Williams' development in the late plays, it is necessary to look at as many versions of a single play as possible. They often changed radically. Sometimes the changes were responses to criticism of a previous version; sometimes they represented further thinking on the plays. Whatever the reasons, the rewrites often produced *different* plays. In many cases the changes represented further dramatic experimentation, radicalization; other times the rewrites returned to more conventional means of drama, attempting to make experimental impulses more commercial. I do not believe that the publication record of these different versions necessarily represents Williams' wish that earlier versions of certain plays be permanently forgotten. He was always too involved with *current* thought on his plays to worry much about destroying past versions. Ideally, all versions of each play would be published so the reader could compare for himself. I have sought to investigate as many drafts of the plays discussed as possible. They are a fascinating study of the dramatist at work, particularly since Williams was an indefatigable rewriter. In general, I have tried to resist a temptation to evaluate different versions of the plays but have sought rather to show their differences and hopefully illuminate their various beauties.

A few more critical points. One of the most controversial allegations that has been leveled at Tennessee Williams is an accusation of dishonesty arising from the well-known homosexuality of the writer. The accusation usually asserts that Williams' female characters are "men in drag" and the heterosexual males in his plays are homosexual fantasies. There is the suggestion that this is a way in which the homosexual writer can "have" the idealized heterosexual males. There is also quite often the suggestion that Williams hated women and that his portrayals of disturbed women are a kind of vengeance on the female sex. This hatred of women, it is implied, is also another aspect of his homosexuality. Gordon Rogoff in his essay "The Restless Intelligence of Tennessee Williams" brilliantly attacked this line of criticism and I cannot argue the case better: "This style of criticism, carried to its logical ends, yields a howling multitude of fallacies. No writer, be he major-minor-homo- or hetero, could truthfully escape censure. Shakespeare, who (arguably) revealed something of homosexual attachment in his sonnets, must perforce have given much of his energy to masking his homosexuality in his plays, helped psychologically, it is true, by having his women played by boys in drag anyway . . . The crisis of veiled homosexuality is, then, one of those decoys invented by a critical fraternity which is itself in crisis."[11] Gore Vidal in his introduction to Williams' *Collected Stories* also fires strong ammunition at the allegation of homosexual dishonesty:

> Let us now clear up a misunderstanding about Tennessee and his work. Yes, he liked to have sex with men. No, he did not hate women, as the anti-fag brigade insists. Tennessee loved women, as any actress who has ever played one of his characters will testify. Certainly he never ceased to love Rose. But that makes him even *worse* the anti-fag brigade wail, as they move to their fall-back position. *He thinks he is a woman.* He puts himself, sick and vicious as he is, on the stage in drag; and then he travesties all good, normal, family-worshipping women and their supportive, mature men. But Tennessee never thought of himself as a woman. He was very much a man; he was also very much an artist. He could inhabit any gender; his sympathies, however, were almost always with those defeated by the squares or by time, once the sweet bird of youth has flown—or by death, "which has never been much in the way of completion."[12]

More, however, is in question than the kind of criticism that Gore Vidal characterizes as coming from the "anti-fag brigade." The question really is this: Does the homosexual artist have a different kind of consciousness from the heterosexual artist? Is there such as thing as a homosexual sensibility? Are heterosexuals one kind of person and homosexuals quite a different sort? Can they ever participate in each other's worlds, or are they forever cut off from one another, exclusive and separate? Obviously some critics feel they are irrevocably separate. When John Simon complains of "fag directors" in *New York* magazine he typifies Gore Vidal's "anti-fag brigade."[13] The implication always is that the homosexual artist is in some way limited, indeed is an inferior artist because of his sexual preference. Fag art by implication is bad art.

There is another possibility that may be true. Perhaps all human beings line up somewhere on a male/female, homo-hetero spectrum that is defined by its two polarities. Perhaps most artists fall somewhere near the center of this spectrum and are more able to empathize with and understand both male and female consciousness. Homosexuality in this description becomes not a liability but an asset.

The answer to this debate is not really known. In a time of great scientific exploration we still do not understand human sexuality, its origins and effects. However it is not only incorrect to assume a separate homosexual consciousness, it is somehow inhumane and immoral. It is also a very shaky critical supposition and should not be the basis for the denigration of artists who happen to be homosexual.

Theater is a collaborative art and its highest achievement consists in the creation of a *Gesamtkunstwerke*, a total art in which all of the elements come together to make a total effect. Theater is literature but it is also music and painting, dance and sculpture. It exists today and is gone tomorrow and so must make its effect in a limited period of time. Since there are so many component parts to a theater piece, there are many opportunities for things "to go wrong." It is amazing that there is ever any good theater.

The ideal theater critic would be a man of few prejudices who responds to all the arts in equal measure, with all senses equally excitable to visual and auditory beauty. Too often theater critics have literary backgrounds and respond to theater as illustrated literature. A great deal of the most exciting theater is happening today in that area where visual art takes its place beside literary art as an expressive component. I maintain that Williams in his plays envisioned this new theater of all the senses; theater that occurs at the meeting place where all of man's potential pleasures—visual, auditory, intellectual, emotional, sensual—create an overpowering experience. People who love theater love the immediacy of being totally alive in the ephemeral present, of being overpowered by something larger than themselves. This work hopes to illuminate those areas where Williams' sense of total theater aspires to that kind of overpowering experience. This is surely what Williams meant in the afterword to the printed version of *Camino Real* when he wrote:

> The incontinent blaze of a live theater, a theater meant for seeing and feeling, has never been and never will be extinguished by a bucket brigade of critics, new or old, bearing vessels that range from cut-glass punchbowl to Haviland tea-cup. And in my dissident opinion, a play in a book is only the shadow of a play and not even a clear shadow of it. Those who did not like *Camino Real* on the stage will not be likely to form a higher opinion of it in print, for of all the works I have written, this one was meant most for the vulgarity of performance. The printed script of a play is hardly more than an architect's blueprint of a house not yet built or built and destroyed. The color, the grace and levitation, the structural pattern in motion, the quick interplay of live beings, suspended like fitful lightning in a cloud, these things are the play, not words on paper, nor thoughts and ideas of an author, those shabby things snatched off basement counters at Gimbels.[14]

I submit that this is one of the best definitions of theater I have ever read and an aesthetic toward which Williams always aspired. We must read then the late plays as blueprints for live performances, performances that probably have not yet taken place in any realized fashion.

NOTES

1. *Life* magazine advertisement, *New York Times*, June 10, 1969.

2. Signi Falk, "The Profitable World of Tennessee Williams," *Modern Drama*, December 1958, 179.

3. Richard Gilman, "The Drama Is Coming Now," *Tulane Drama Review*, vol. 7, no. 4 (Summer 1963), 29.

4. Robert Brustein, "Williams' Nebulous Nightmare," *Hudson Review*, vol. 12, no. 2 (Summer 1959).

5. Gordon Rogoff, "The Restless Intelligence of Tennessee Williams," *Tulane Drama Review*, vol. 10, no. 4 (Summer 1966), 78–92.

6. Brooks Atkinson, "First Night at the Theatre," *New York Times*, December 4, 1947.

7. Walter Kerr, *New York Herald Tribune*, March 25, 1955.

8. Eric Bentley, *The Dramatic Event: An American Chronicle* (New York: Horizon, 1954).

9. Bentley, *The Dramatic Event*, chapter 2, note 7.

10. T. E. Kalem, "Torpid Tennessee," *Time*, May 23, 1969.

11. Rogoff, "The Restless Intelligence of Tennessee Williams."

12. Gore Vidal, introduction to *Tennessee Williams Collected Stories*, by Tennessee Williams (New York: New Directions, 1985), xxiv.

13. John Simon, *New York*, March 8, 1985.

14. Tennessee Williams, afterword to *Camino Real* (New York: New Directions, 1953), xii.

· 2 ·

Milk Train to Byzantium

 $\mathcal{T}$ he generally accepted, prevailing view of Tennessee Williams' career is that his best work for the American theater was done before the 1960s. *Night of the Iguana* opened on Broadway December 28, 1961, and was indeed his last critically well-received, commercially successful Broadway production. Broadway success for Williams had always been the true sign of final accomplishment. *The Glass Menagerie* premiered in 1945 on Broadway and it was from there that his plays made his international reputation. Theatrically, Broadway was his home. Lack of success on Broadway in his late career was a painful exile for Tennessee Williams.

The perceived diminishing quality in Williams' artistic output is generally attributed to a destructive lifestyle that included drugs, alcohol, promiscuous sexual activity, and parasitic friends who gave the playwright bad advice. This certainly is the view of Donald Spoto's biography, published shortly after Williams' death, *The Kindness of Strangers*. The concurrently published *Tennessee: Cry of the Heart* by Dotson Rader, for all its loving remembrance of a personal friend, also shows us a man out of control, a victim of addictions. Along with the addictions, it is generally thought that the death of Frank Merlo in 1962 had a catastrophic effect on Williams both as a man and as an artist. The implication is that Frank Merlo, Tennessee's lover of longest standing, had offered the playwright a personal stability that enabled him to create his masterpieces. All of these assumptions take a romantic and simplistic view of the artist. It is a view that Tennessee himself had promoted in his *Memoirs*, describing love affairs and one-night stands along with embarrassing social scenes born out of alcohol and drug abuse. Of course, these are the tales that sell books. Nowhere is there documented the artistic process, the thinking, the perceptions that lay behind the continuous output that counters the view of Williams as an incapacitated human being and failed artist. This is not surprising. Williams, like many artists, disliked talking about his work. He believed that writing was an intuitive process that suffered from too much analysis. Often accepting the critics' view of his late work, Williams once told Gore Vidal that he had slept through the sixties, to which Vidal replied, "You didn't miss a thing." If Williams slept, it was an enormously active sleep, producing play after play.

The Milk Train Doesn't Stop Here Anymore opened at a pivotal moment in American drama as well as a time of crisis in Tennessee Williams' personal life. In the autumn of 1962 Edward Albee's *Who's Afraid of Virginia Woolf?* opened on Broadway and made an enormous impression. Here was a commercially successful, serious new play by an American playwright who went beyond the realistic traditions of American drama to write in symbolic and thought-provoking terms. George and Martha, Albee's main characters, were more than a university town couple. They were the father and mother of America turned into a childless, brawling, frightened pair of cruel monsters. Living a lie, they constructed a life for an imaginary child and finally blamed each other for that child's death. What was to be made of it? Perhaps it *was* possible to write a commercially successful play outside the strictures of realism and get away with it. During the 1962–1963 theatrical season, it was certainly *the* play to see and discuss.

Tennessee Williams had been a successful playwright for nearly twenty years at this point. His previous play, *Night of the Iguana*, was a commercial and critical success, winning the prestigious New York Drama Critics Award. The fifty-two-year-old playwright was considered by many to be the preeminent dramatist of his day. Edward Albee acknowledged this stature in *Who's Afraid of Virginia Woolf?* by having George quote a line from *A Streetcar Named Desire*. Throwing flowers at Martha, George declaims, "Flores, flores para los muertos." In *Streetcar* this line is spoken by a Mexican street vendor who terrifies the distracted Blanche. A private joke between playwrights, the line was also a kind of homage from the younger playwright to the older. Albee was often written of as Williams' successor in serious drama. Williams was now the old garde, and it is doubtful whether it was a role that he enjoyed, particularly since he had tried to write a symbolic fantasy with *Camino Real* in 1953. It was his biggest post-*Menagerie* commercial failure. Albee may have seemed to Williams to have been successful where he himself had failed. But, then, neither had Eugene O'Neill achieved much commercial success with his experiments outside realism. It was an old problem for American playwrights: how to write an artistically successful commercial drama that departed from realism. Perhaps with Albee's success it was time to try again. Maybe the American public would finally accept a poetic drama that augmented realism with pure symbolism unaided by causal exposition.

Other theatrical currents may have encouraged Williams to depart from realism with greater experimentation. European dramatists of poetic vision and experimental dramaturgy were making their mark on American theater. The late fifties and early sixties was the period when American audiences were first exposed to what the critic Martin Esslin, in an influential book, had called the "Theatre of the Absurd." Esslin described a new kind of theater that embodied an existential world changing dramatic structures to mirror a new philosophical vision. Most importantly this meant that traditional linear dramatic structures with actions based on cause and effect were no longer found to be accurate models of a universe considered to be without purpose, subject to accident, and ultimately without any absolute meaning.

Samuel Beckett in *Waiting for Godot, Endgame*, and *Krapp's Last Tape* substituted circular, entropic structures for traditional plays with beginnings, middles, and climactic ends. His plays raised more questions than they answered and certainly offered audiences no easy affirmations. Eugene Ionesco showed the emptiness that lay behind human language in plays like *The Bald Soprano* and *The Lesson*. In *The Maids* and *The Balcony*, Jean Genet saw life as an erotic theatrical performance that only violence could integrate. The English playwright Harold Pinter, whom Tennessee Williams greatly admired, eschewed exposition, refusing to answer questions of history or motivation. Characters in Pinter's *The Caretaker* or *The Birthday Party* reveal few of their secrets. All of these playwrights broke Aristotelian rules of dramaturgy. The effect was refreshing to some; confusing and threatening to many. No person seriously interested in theater during this period could have been left uninfluenced by these writers. They challenged everything the theater had been, even making inroads into the commercial American theater. One could not discuss serious theater without debating the absurdists in the early sixties.

The Milk Train Doesn't Stop Here Anymore, like many of Williams' plays, had its first germ of idea in a short story. Entitled "Man Bring This Up Road" and written in 1953, it simply relates an encounter between an enormously wealthy widow, Flora Goforth, and an itinerant young poet who is broke and looking for a free meal. The story deals satirically with the rich woman and ends with her turning out the poor poet. In the short story Flora is not dying nor is she writing her memoirs. The poet, called Jimmy Dobyne, offers no spiritual solace. He is simply hungry.

Rewritten as a play that premiered during the summer of 1962 at the Festival of Two Worlds in Spoleto, Italy, the simple short story became a symbolic fable of death. It is deceptively tempting to read the play as a dramatization of Williams' grappling with Frank Merlo's death. However, news of Merlo's illness reached Williams in Europe shortly after the play's premiere, and Merlo finally died after the play's first Broadway production. Merlo's illness and death may have been on Williams' mind during the period he worked on *Milk Train*, but Flora (the dying celebrity in the play) is more like Tennessee than she is like Frank Merlo. It is she who is famous and writing memoirs. To further confuse the biographical connection, the other main character in the play also contains elements of both Merlo and Williams. Chris, the itinerant poet, acts as a subservient character to Flora. Merlo certainly played a subservient role to Williams during his life, but he is not Chris any more than he is Flora. It is Tennessee who was a poet not Merlo. Who is which character? Williams and Merlo are both characters and neither. The characters also contain other people Williams knew. Anna Magnani had died of cancer in the late fifties. Countless young men often sought out employment from Williams or he sought them out. In other words, Williams' characters are amalgams, combining all he knew of himself and others. Finally, the characters are themselves—original creations who never lived until Williams created them. They are fictions, not representations of real people. If we take a simple biographical approach to understanding the play we are stuck. *Milk Train* may have been influenced by Merlo's dying and death, but Tennessee had always been preoccupied with death. *Streetcar* was written during a time when the playwright was sure he was dying.

Art does not have a simple cause and effect relationship with the events in an artist's life. That is too simple an explanation. Nor does knowing the circumstances under which a work was created ever explain that work. Much more is needed because art always transforms life into something else. It is the something else that is important, not the facts of an artist's life. Let us look at the plays.

The only published edition of *Milk Train* is the second and last Broadway version, which premiered in 1964 starring Tallulah Bankhead and Tab Hunter. It seems to represent Williams' preferred last thoughts on the play. However, to understand the radical shift in Williams' work at this point in his career, *both* Broadway versions must be compared. The first Broadway production, which starred Hermione Baddeley, had opened in January 1963 and is basically the same script presented in Spoleto during the summer of 1962.

The movement of the action in both plays is essentially the same. The differences come in the beginnings and ends of the two plays, in their theatrical "framing," and in their treatment of Flora's death. However, the *action* of both versions begins with Flora Goforth dictating her memoirs to her secretary, Blackie, on the veranda of her mountaintop villa on the *Divina Costiera* of Italy. She is in a hurry to finish her work: "We're working against time, Blackie. Remember, try to remember, I've got two deadlines to meet, my New York publishers and my London publishers, both, have my Memoirs on their Fall list. I said fall. It's already late in August. Now do you see why there's no time for goofing, or must I draw you a picture of autumn leaves falling."

Chris Flanders, an itinerant poet and mobile maker, arrives on the mountain, sending up a book of poems. He asks to see Mrs. Goforth. Interested but wary, Mrs. Goforth puts the intruder in the "little pink guest house." She may grant him an interview later. In both versions of the play a scene follows between Mrs. Goforth's secretary and Chris. Blackie seems attracted to Chris and the possibility of a liaison is suggested. Blackie frankly tells Chris that her employer is dying:

Chris: She doesn't know she's—

Blackie: Dying? Oh no! Won't face it! Apparently never thought that her—legendary—existence—could go on less than forever!

The next major scene in both versions is a hilariously bitchy scene between Flora and an old acquaintance; the Contessa Vera Ridgeway in the first version, simply called the Witch of Capri in the rewrite. The basic purpose of this scene is to let the "witch" tell Flora that Chris has a reputation as a free loader who latches on to old women who are dying. He has been called "the angel of death." The two women pay a visit to the pink villa, getting a closer look at Chris as he sleeps on pink silk sheets. Flora's interest in Chris does not seem lessened by the witch's "dirt." She wants to know more: "Did he sleep with that old Ferguson bitch? or was he just her Death Angel?"

The major plot question is clearly set up. Will Flora seduce Chris? Will she "get him"? It is perhaps Williams' oldest plot device. Who will get whom? Will anyone get anyone? Laura and the Gentleman Caller, Blanche and Mitch, Stanley and Blanche, Alma and John, Serafina and Mangiacavallo, the Princess and Chance Wayne: the list is long and the plot device of endless fascination. Williams' plays continually portray the mating *bugaku*. But in *Milk Train* the action is so delayed, Flora's move so unlikely to succeed that the old device has less interest, less power than usual. It almost seems like a gratuitous act practiced out of habit in the face of something stronger than sex, namely, her death.

A short scene late at night on the veranda strengthens the alliance between Chris and Blackie, but they are interrupted when Flora awakens in terror to dictate the memory of her first husband's death. She rushes in panic onto the terrace of her white villa. The memory of his death has forced a middle-of-the-night realization of her own situation: "I see lights blazing under the high, high terrace but not a light blazing as bright as the blaze of terror I saw in his eyes! Wind, cold wind, clean, clean! Release! Relief! Escape from—I'm lost, blind, dying! I don't know where I— . . . Blackie! Blackie, don't leave me alone!"

The next scene, played in the theater after an intermission, begins in both versions of the play with a discussion of "the meaning of life" before moving on to the first interview between Chris and Flora Goforth. They get on with each other, perhaps more so in the second version. (In the second version Chris tells us more of his past.) Flora confides in Chris her fear of death: "I still go to bed every night wondering if I'll wake up the next day." She makes a subtle sexual overture to Chris, who retreats. He is more interested in giving her companionship and a spiritual acceptance of fate. She distrusts him, suspects him of being an adventurer. The scene is interrupted when a coughing fit brings up blood from Flora's lungs.

There is a final confrontation between Chris and Flora in both versions of the play. She invites him into her bedroom where she receives him naked under her open robe. Again he declines her invitation. He tries once more to give her a religious acceptance of her condition. Furiously Flora confronts him: "Did somebody tell you I was dying this summer? Yes, isn't that why you came here, because you imagined that I'd be ripe for a soft touch since I'm dying this summer."

Chris answers honestly but ambiguously: "Yes, that's why I came here."

A major question in both versions of the play concerns Chris' motivations. Is he spiritually motivated or merely an opportunist? A purely symbolic death figure or a real person? All interpretations are possible. Williams refuses to answer the question simply. However, the emphasis on possible answers is different in the two versions as I shall discuss later.

The two endings of *Milk Train* differ greatly. In the first Broadway version Flora's death was merely suggested, not shown. At first, she sends Chris away convinced that he is a fraud. But then she has an eruptive change of heart. Finally she calls out to Blackie: "Catch the mobile constructor, stop the poet! He's on his way back down the road. Tell him to come back up and tell him, tell him . . . Yes, tell him that he would touch the heart of a stone and he has touched my heart, and I hope—I hope that I can touch his too, Blackie!"

Chris does not return to the scene. Flora stares at the hanging mobile Chris has left for her. The final stage directions dictate a final calm for the end of the play:

"(The mobile makes a barely audible delicate sad music as it turns. Mrs. Goforth automatically raises a hand to her pain. But she keeps her eyes on the mobile. She speaks one more time.) 'Well, finally, maybe—after all, in the end.' (And then the stage lights dim out.)"

This reversal, or peripeteia, suggests some resolution of the problems the play has presented. The heart can still love, human feeling for another is still possible even at the threshold of death. Unclearly articulated but nonetheless suggested is a serene acceptance of death by Flora. Chris has given her something after all.

The revised published *Milk Train* meant to represent Williams' final thoughts on the play (and possibly on death as well), is quite different. Flora does not send Chris away. As she lies dying Chris removes rings from Flora's fingers. But the old woman does not seem to mind. She says to him, "Be here when I wake up." Flora never accepts that she is dying; she thinks that she will wake up. A brief scene between Chris and Blackie ends the play.

Blackie: Did she say anything to you before she—?

Chris: She said to me: "Be here when I wake up." After I'd taken her hand and stripped the rings off her fingers.

Blackie: What did you do with—?

Chris (giving her a look that might suggest an understandable shrewdness): Under her pillow like a Pharaoh's breakfast waiting for the Pharaoh to wake up hungry . . . (Blackie comes up behind him on the forestage and offers him the wine goblet. A wave is heard breaking under the mountain.)

Blackie: The sea is saying the name of your next mobile.

Chris: Boom!

Blackie: What does it mean?

Chris: It says "Boom," and that's just what it means. No translation, no explanation, just "Boom." (He drinks from the goblet and passes it back to her.)

The positive calm of the first *Milk Train* is replaced in this last version with an ironic, cryptic ending. Things have not added up. Mysticism is replaced by a cold epilogue after the fact of death. But our opinion of Chris is still not certain. Of course, the emphasis is more sinister. It is strongly suggested that Chris stripped the rings off the dying woman for his own profit. But even this is not certain. Perhaps the rings *did* cut her fingers. His look to Blackie *might* suggest shrewdness. In the face of Flora's death, Chris' motivation does not seem very important. Balancing his possible callowness is an elegiac sadness in his description of Flora's death: "You always wonder afterwards where it's gone, so far, so quickly. You feel it must be still around somewhere. But there's no sign of it."

Williams does not want us to know the "truth" of Chris. Nor does he wish to give any resolution or reversal in Flora. She dies unconscious with no understanding of Chris or her situation. What does it mean? Boom! That's all.

The most noticeable and commented upon change in the second version of *Milk Train* was the addition of a theatrical device much ridiculed when the play was restaged in 1964. Williams added two figures who function as Chinese prop men at the play's beginning and near its end. They comment upon the play like an ironic Greek chorus and also make Brechtian announcements of the action to take place. We first encounter them at the beginning of the play before the realistic action begins:

> One: We fetch and carry.
>
> Two: Furniture and props.
>
> One: To make the presentation—the play or masque or pageant—move more gracefully, quickly through the course of the two final days of Mrs. Goforth's existence.

After introducing themselves, these theatrical characters perform a flag raising ceremony, flying Flora Goforth's personal standard embroidered with a golden griffin. They speak again in the final moments of the play concurrent with the last moments of Flora's life. Lowering the flag they pay a kind of tribute to the protagonist.

> One: Flag-lowering ceremony on the late Mrs. Goforth's mountain. (A muted bugle is heard from a distance.)
>
> Two: Bugle. That's not Taps, that's Reveille.
>
> One: It's Reveille always, Taps, never for the golden griffin.

The griffin, half lion and half eagle, stands not only for Flora but for a divided human condition as well. Man is earthbound by his ferocious lion-like nature but aspires to the free flight of his eagle half. Torn by this split nature individual men may die, but the human condition seems never to change or end. Reborn in every individual, the tortured struggle is continually renewed.

In the printed version of the play, Williams wrote an apologia for his Chinese stage managers: "My excuse, or reason, is that I think the play will come off better the farther it is removed from conventional theatre, since it's been rightly described as an allegory and as a 'sophisticated fairy tale.'"[1]

We are not meant to look at this play as realism or to seek realistic explanations for events and characters. Something more formal, more dance-like, ancient, and universal is intended. Also, the prop men have the effect of distancing an audience from the action of the play. In their interruptions, by their presence they remind the audience that it is watching a theatrical performance. Students of dramatic literature will immediately recognize a Brechtian *Verfrem-dungseffekt*, or alienation device. Brecht often used this technique to cool off the empathy of an audience. In their announcement of the play's action, "the final days of Mrs. Goforth's existence," they also use Brecht's forecasting technique. We are told what will happen so we do not get too involved with the plot of the play. What "happens" is not meant to generate any suspense. We are always to remember that we are watching a ritual of death. What is important is how the main character conducts herself in the ritual. Style in death, not the possible escape, is all. More importantly we are asked to question the meaning of the ritual. How does Flora face death? Can she face it? Can any of us? What is the play's final view of life and death? What may human beings give to one another? Is love possible? How do we know one another? What is the meaning of the ritual that is life?

It is on these questions that Williams wants us to concentrate. Indeed, much of the play is discussion of these enormous questions. The emotion we feel from this play ultimately comes from our personal interest in the answers to the questions. We all enact the same ritual; we all must die. The play asks us to share our humanity in this universal drama in which we all play a part. The impulse for the play is religious but the answers give no theological comfort.

Key speeches in *Milk Train* remained the same in both versions. The following monologue begins scene 5 (first scene after intermission) and it is the same in both versions:

"I've often wondered, but I've wondered more lately. Meaning of *life* . . . Sometimes I think, I suspect, that everything we do is a way of not thinking about it. Meaning of life, and meaning of death, too . . . *What in hell are we doing?* Just going from one goddamn frantic distraction to another, till finally one too many goddamn frantic distractions leads to disaster, and blackout? Eclipse of, total of sun?"

This question is the heart and spine of both plays but the answer in the two versions is different. In the first version of *Milk Train* Williams suggests a possible sharing between human beings that gives life and death meaning. It is the same kind of nonsexual love Hannah Jelkes gives Shannon in *Night of the Iguana*. Facing death alone, we reach out for love, indeed must create some form of God for ourselves. Late, difficult, and perhaps unheard, the heart sheds it tough skin and becomes vulnerable once more. This is a kind of triumph, perhaps the only one possible.

Chris seems to propose this possible salvation for Mrs. Goforth when he offers his care of her:

Chris: Caring for somebody gives me the sense of being—sheltered, protected.

Mrs. Goforth: "Sheltered, protected" from what?

Chris: Unreality!—lostness? Have you seen how two little animals sleep together, a pair of kittens or puppies? . . . All day they seem so secure in the house of their master, but at night, when they sleep, they don't seem secure of their owner's true care for them. Then they curl up against each other, and now and then if you watch them, you notice they nudge each other a little with their heads or their paws, little signals between them. The signals mean we're not in danger . . . sleep: we're close. It's safe here . . . We're all of us living in a house we're not used to . . . a house full of—voices, noises, objects, strange shadows, light that's even stranger— . . . Then it gets to be dark. We're left alone with each other and give those gentle little nudges with our paws and our nuzzles before we can slip into sleep and rest for the next day's playtime . . . and the next day's mysteries.

Sentimental? Perhaps. The imagery of the kittens and puppies *is* cloyingly reminiscent of childhood greeting cards but it is nonetheless accurate and appropriate for an itinerant pseudo-poet whom we never quite trust. It is also affecting in spite of itself. It certainly affects Flora. But her needs and desires are sexual as well. As she tells Blackie at one point:

"I do need male company, Blackie, that's what I need to be me, the old Sissy Goforth, high, low, jack and the game!" She is clearly not talking about platonic love. Sex is life for Flora and its absence is death. Even in her last hours the old woman wants Chris to make love to her.

Thematically, Williams is showing opposing forces of sex and death, eros and thanatos. He had dramatized the same agon in *A Streetcar Named Desire*. This time the possibility of personal relations, *caritas*, is suggested as a possible meaning in the face of personal extinction. A kind of spiritual exchange between human beings may ameliorate the pain of death. In the first version of *Milk Train* Williams affirmed that possibility while in the final play the answer seems to be uncertainty, negation, and despair.

The characters in the published, rewritten version of *Milk Train* are crueler, more grotesque. Flora tells us less of her amusing Follies-girl past. Chris has a more specific past but he is also hungrier and more materialistic. The servants of the house are shown to be thieves. A sadistic groundskeeper is added to the play. Blackie is more neurotic and hysterical, and we know less of her past difficulties. The entire atmosphere is darker and more bizarre.

The language in both versions of *Milk Train* is repetitive, using key words repeatedly in long structures of incomplete sentences. This style is even more pronounced in the second version. Dashes, multiple periods, ellipses continually interrupt thoughts as words elude characters searching for ways to complete their sentences. The style is byzantine in its attempt to describe what is difficult to express, in its uncertainty of being understood. This speech to the Witch of Capri is one example:

Has it ever struck you, Connie, that life is all memory, except for the one present moment that goes by you so quickly you hardly catch it going? It's really all memory, Connie, except for each passing moment. What I just now said to you is a memory now—recollection. Uh-hummm . . . (She paces the terrace.)—I'm up now. When I was at the table is a memory, now. (She arrives at the lighted area downstage right and turns.)—when I turned at the other end of the terrace is a memory, now . . . Practically everything is a memory to me, now, so I'm writing my memoirs . . . (She points up.) Shooting star: it's shot:—a memory now. Four husbands, all memory now. All lovers, all memory now.

The ending short nonsentences in the above passage give climax to the speech, the commas serving as caesuras, breathing spells while energy is running out. The dashes and ellipses (— or . . .) indicate pauses in the speech, searchings for words. Normally they are a sign to an actor that subtext must fill the pauses for transitions made. Here, more often than not, they indicate the mind coming up against a blank wall. Only the return to a previously used word, "memory" keeps the voice going at all.

Words are becoming suspect for Williams, a threatening development for a poet. If all is memory, as he says in the passage, reality itself is fragile. Passing moments may be real but they cannot be held. Williams in this play is beginning to question the basic nature of reality, its insubstantiality and elusiveness. It is a thematic concern that informs more and more of his late work as he goes on for the next twenty years. It is perhaps the ultimate theme of any theater artist since theater itself is a metaphor for that which is both real and unreal. As for Shakespeare, the theater for Williams is both craft and metaphor, form and content. All is used to express a vision of a precarious reality. This does not mean that Williams himself has become unbalanced. One need not be unbalanced to question the ultimate nature of reality.

Nearly as important as language, sound effects make an enormous contribution to the poetic and theatrical effect of *Milk Train*. The most insistent sound used is the loud crash of the sea breaking below Flora's villa. Boom! Indeed this sound effect has such symbolic importance to Williams that he renamed his screenplay of *Milk Train*, shortening the long title to the exclamatory *Boom!* Interestingly, the sound effect is not in the original version of the play. Along with its increased theatricalism, this sound effect is used to communicate what is difficult to express in words. The sound effect, tricky to successfully achieve in the theater, should sound an indomitable musical note of doom and fate, meaningless in its content but irrefutable in its power. It constantly relates the human actions of the play to something larger in nature over which the characters have no control.

Similarly Flora's buzzer, which insistently summons Blackie to service, has an irritating effect in the play. Tense and grating, the buzzer expresses Flora's desperation, translated into mechanical sound. Its jarring sound jolts the audience as it summons Blackie to her stressful task. Properly used, the buzzer should also create dramatic tension in the play, the atmosphere of stress.

Flora's voice electrically magnified over a loud speaker has a similar effect. Many of her orders and some of her dictation are heard by the audience in this manner. The effect is unreal and theatrical, again distancing us humanly and at the same time creating a bizarre and fascinating sound. How much this device is used would be at the discretion of a director, but Williams requests it quite consistently in the second version of the play.

An enormously powerful use of stage sound as an expressive element in both versions of the play comes in a climactic moment of the final interrogation of Chris by Mrs. Goforth. In response to Chris' offering of "something to mean God" Flora wildly rings her servant's bell:

> Mrs. Goforth: I heard what you said *God*. My eyes are out of focus but not my ears! Well, bring Him here, I'm ready to lay out a red carpet for Him, but how do you bring Him? Whistle? Ring a bell for Him? (She snatches a bell off her desk and rings it fiercely.) Huh? How? What? (She staggers back against the desk gasping.)

In the hands of a good actress this could be an extraordinary moment in the theater.

Scenic effects of color and space also create poetic effects as in all of Williams' plays. The predominant white of the villa is contrasted with "cascades of bougainvillaea," red and orange and pink blossoms, vibrant blood colors. Similarly Chris' pink villa contrasts sensually with the blank whiteness of the dominating villa. Backing the stage is a huge cyclorama on which a sensitive lighting designer must project delicate poetic effects. The following description of the beginning of scene 5 evokes the mood of reflection Williams' desires:

"Coins of gold light, reflected from the sea far below, flicker upon the playing area, which is backed by a fair sky."

A true man of the twentieth-century theater, one cognizant of the expressive capabilities of stage lighting, Williams demands a designer capable of giving a visual equivalent of his stage directions. Nothing less will realize the potential beauties of his play on the stage.

The floor plan for the action is not specifically directed. It is not always clear how the playwright wants us to move from the white villa to the pink villa or to the various bedrooms depicted. A cinematic effect is obviously desired and an easy accommodation of scene changes. In the second version of the play, the Chinese prop men help accommodate fluidity in scene changes by simply shifting screens. At one point a screen is turned "perpendicular to the proscenium" to allow us a different view of the library we have already seen. This perpendicular screen allows Flora and Chris to stand on either side, seen by the audience, and to play a scene. The screen separating them becomes a visual metaphor for their human separateness. In all of the scenic elements it is difficult for the audience to realistically know where they are in relation to Flora's villa or any of its rooms. We never get a clear picture of the stage design as real space, and I believe this is an intentional part of the play's means. Williams does not want us to have the comfort of spatial orientation. This is not a world in which people know where they are.

Costume, in both versions of *Milk Train*, is garish, theatrical, and symbolic. This aspect is more exaggerated in the second version. In the later version Chris wears a Samurai robe to complement Flora's Kabuki costume. Relics of Mrs. Goforth's travels, they obviously heighten the ritualistic aspect of the plays. The Witch of Capri is similarly fantastic in costume, looking like something out of a children's pantomime: "She looks like a creature out of a sophisticated fairy tale, her costume like something that might have been designed for Fata Morgana. Her dress is gray chiffon, paneled, and on her blue-tinted head she wears a cone shaped hat studded with pearls, the peaks of it draped with the material of her dress. Her expressive, claw-like hands are aglitter with gems."

What on earth does Williams mean by this? Often in the late plays, fantastic creatures appear dressed in the most outlandish fashion. Usually, they are "possibly" human as in this extraordinary case. There are such creatures in heaven and earth and, while they are fantastic, they may also be real. The fantastic and the real often refuse to stay in their respective worlds in the late plays and this is an important part of the vision of those plays.

Our last view of Mrs. Goforth in her death bed garments is that of a dying monarch: "She wears a majestic ermine-trimmed robe to which she has pinned her 'most important jewels,' and rings blaze on her fingers that clench the chair arms."

Williams creates grotesque lyricism with these bizarre costumes. I know of no other playwright in American drama who dares such effects except perhaps Rosalyn Drexler or Charles Ludlam and his Theatre of the Ridiculous. Actually the "camp" of Ludlam's theater is not far removed from these costumes. Costume for the love of its theatricality, masks created to hide and illuminate at the same time, joy in artifice—all of these elements of costuming express what Flora calls "the hard shell of my heart, the calcium deposits grown around it." It is not accidental that she opens her robes to Chris, tries to strip off her costume. It is her fate that he does not wish to see what is underneath, further proof of the necessity for costume.

One is left chilled, disturbed, by the "Kabuki" *Milk Train*. The vision is dark, grotesque. Williams could not have written a play less likely to "work" with a Broadway audience than if he had consciously determined to do so. All elements of commercially successful American drama (plot, realism, empathy, and affirmation) have been largely abandoned. They have been replaced with poetry, philosophical discussion, theatricalism, and despair.

The first *Milk Train* was not universally damned. It is true that its reception was not as enthusiastic as *Night of the Iguana*, Williams' previous Broadway play, but many of the critics saw beauty in his song of death. John Chapman writing in the *New York Daily News* said, "Once again, Williams gives the theater great excitement."[2] Robert Coleman called the play "the most ambitious work the dramatist has attempted since *Camino Real*. It is shocking, moving, and downright disturbing."[3] The critic Walter Kerr mainly complained of the play's lack of plot and Chris' lack of definition as a character: "The evening is two hours old before Miss Baddeley [playing Flora] actually makes the sensual proposal she has planned from the beginning . . . The young man is not defined at all."[4]

John McClain was also largely negative: "The play is as meandering as its title, and doesn't get any closer to a resolution— . . . These are odd and often outrageous people he writes about, and there is some doubt that it is worth spending an evening with them."[5]

These complaints would become common in criticism of Williams' late plays: lack of structure and lack of empathy. Richard Watts saw something in the play while calling it "one of Tennessee Williams' lesser plays": "The plays of Tennessee Williams may be roughly divided into two categories. There is the so-called block-buster type with its smashing dramatic effects . . . then there is the quieter, more brooding and introspective kind. It is to this second school, less sensational and rather more mature, that his latest work belongs."[6]

In a clumsy way Watts is perceptive of a shift in Williams' work away from sensational subjects in the plays of the late fifties *(Sweet Bird of Youth's* castration and *Suddenly Last Summer's* cannibalism) toward quieter but no less turbulent concerns. In the late plays, violence is internalized, repressed, resulting in cracked visions of reality. Violence in the material world is replaced with psychic violence, deeply felt disturbances resulting from epistemological and metaphysical concerns of reality and eternity.

The *Village Voice* reviewed the play with sensitivity and insight. Michael Smith, then critic, wrote: "At its best 'Milk Train' is a profoundly cynical, corrupt, and disgusted play. The production seems to obscure what Williams is getting at—but the intensity and insistence of Tennessee Williams' vision is everywhere behind it, still developing and unmistakable."[7]

Smith understood that Williams was going through a change in his writing while acknowledging the recognizable voice of the playwright. The play's cynicism was seen as one of its strengths, the vision noted without value judgment.

While many critics applauded Hermione Baddeley's stage presence and comic abilities in the difficult role of Flora Goforth, the character's vulnerability, her fears and loneliness seem not to have been properly communicated. This is an old problem in the playing of Williams' female characters. Amanda and Blanche, as well as Flora, can seem comic caricatures. Audiences laugh *at* Amanda and Blanche if actresses of honesty and emotional reserves are not cast in the roles. We may laugh at these characters but in key dramatic moments we *must* also weep for them. This is largely an actress' responsibility but it is also a problem of casting and stage direction. Directors must be in sympathy with Williams' vision and make demands on actresses that go beyond acceptance of a serviceable surface reading of a role. All must ask more of themselves in playing Williams, especially in the exhausting search for emotional truth and depth. This may be even more important in the later plays, which do not have solid plot structures to keep audience interest. *Menagerie* and *Streetcar* can still be successful evenings in the theater without *great* performances in the female roles. *The Milk Train Doesn't Stop Here Anymore* must have a great performance to make clear Flora Goforth's vulnerability as well as her comic grotesqueness.

Henry Hewes writing in the *Saturday Review of Literature* saw the first production as lacking in its ability to communicate the play's subtlety. Like Michael Smith he was sensitive to the play's special qualities and difficulties:

> Of all the plays Tennessee Williams has written, his latest is perhaps the most ambiguous and subliminal . . . [Williams] is less interested in fulfilling the dramatic potential of his play than he is in creating the contemporary atmosphere of life as it is illuminated by the proximity of death . . . the milk of human kindness has dried up . . . the potential greatness of this work lies in its achievement of total human mystery in Chekhovian moments of communication suddenly reached unintentionally by people moving in many directions. For some reason, this production rushes right past these. Although an occasional distant bell or strain of music reminds us that they were intended. Like people at a train stop we watch disappointedly as our train races by. The milk train turns out to be an unscheduled express.[8]

It must never be forgotten that Williams' favorite playwright was Anton Chekhov and his favorite play, *The Sea-Gull*. Subtextual subtlety is as much a need in the acting of a Williams play as in Chekhov and may be as difficult to achieve and as rarely seen as in productions of the great Russian playwright.

Perhaps the most negative review *The Milk Train Doesn't Stop Here Anymore* received came from the critic Richard Gilman writing in the respected *Commonweal* journal. Entitling his review "Mistuh Williams, He Dead," this may have been the first of many "obituary" reviews Williams was to receive in the years ahead. No longer even worthy of respect, Williams is characterized as a hysterical child by the critic:

> Why, rather than be banal and hysterical and absurd, doesn't he keep quiet? Why doesn't he simply stop writing, stay absolutely unproductive for a long time in Key West, or the South of Spain, or the corner of any bar and just think? We know that this is what he has been trying to do, but how is it possible in the midst of that self-created din, the clatter of the somersaults he keeps turning in front of us, like a spoiled child who needs to have his existence continually justified, indeed ascertained by our glances, which show admiration, fear, disgust and troubled love?
>
> How many plays in how many years? How terrifying it must be to feel that a season cannot pass, as for that child an evening cannot, without your name being on clucking tongues and your reflection in the encircling eyes. But Williams seems unable to let go; he is wedded to his fear and compulsion, which are bringing about his creative suicide because they are the very things that make a silent, fertile period in the desert, his possible salvation, so impossible.[9]

It is fascinating the way reviews of late Williams plays became the occasion for character assaults and diatribes against the playwright. The critic in his parental and superior role castigates the child he hates, fears, and loves for his perceived failures. His solution is to tell the erring child to "keep quiet." But if Williams is the child, could not Gilman conceivably be accused of child abuse?

The reception of the first production of *Milk Train* may have been a disappointment to Tennessee Williams, but the vitriolic response and the total fiasco of the second Broadway production the following year must have been devastating to him. Starring Tallulah Bankhead in a "come back" performance and Tab Hunter in his first Broadway appearance, this production of *Milk Train* seems to have been a travesty of the play.

The Kabuki stage techniques were not understood and there is some indication that the English director Tony Richardson got carried away with the oriental influence, especially in the use of an intrusively cacophonous Kabuki-influenced musical score by Ned Rorem. Several critics wondered if the play took place in Italy or Japan. Bankhead, Tab Hunter, and even the audience came in for particularly harsh critical comment. Often the comments verged upon bitchery as the production itself seems to have verged on camp. John Chapman's comments were typical: "The setting didn't stimulate my imagination much, and neither did Miss Bankhead. She could roar the old Bankhead roar once in a while and get loud laughter from one of the queerest audiences since the early days of the Ballet Russe de Monte Carlo. But she did not arouse in me the pity that Williams originally wrote into her part, and she was unintelligible."[10] Walter Kerr likewise panned the production. Of Bankhead he wrote, "This is not a performance, it is an appearance." Tab Hunter came in for even greater ridicule. "What energy he brings with him is born of the gymnasium."[11]

The production was one of the great disasters of the American theater, a laugh-provoking fiasco. But it was more than that. It was the beginning of a general treatment of Tennessee Williams as a destroyed playwright. It was open season and the critics responded for the next twenty years with the special vitriol that is reserved for that which is on the downslide of American popularity, especially reserved for those artists who have been previously loved and praised.

But *The Milk Train Doesn't Stop Here Anymore*, both versions, should be looked at anew. It is clear that even a good production of the rewrite would probably have been unsuccessful in 1963. *Who's Afraid of Virginia Woolf?* for all its ultimate experimentalism still "feels" like a realistic play in the theater. George and Martha live in a realistic house, the play has climactic plot revelations, and the characters although unattractive in their cruelty are comic and ultimately sympathetic. George and Martha do "love each other." Cradled in each others arms at the end of the play, facing a frightening future they "have each other." Albee has it both ways in *Virginia Woolf*. No one should have taken his success in 1962 (especially not Albee) as a sign that the Broadway audience was ready for experimentation in the commercial theater.

There have seldom been commercially successful American dramas that were not realistic, plotted, and with empathic characters of clear motivation. Thornton Wilder's fantasies, exceptions to the norm of realism, used archetypal characters of universal appeal, "normal" types who were basically good and well meaning. The commercial failure of *Camino Real* should have warned Williams of his response. Nor did he rewrite *Milk Train* to make it more palatable. What had been ambiguous and mysterious in the first version became cruel and grotesque in the second.

Williams probably had little choice in the way he wrote. Never calculatedly commercial, his darkening vision dictated a new direction. It is not his fault that audiences and critics did not go along with him. The sadness is that he never seemed to understand their abandonment. Like every artist, Tennessee wanted to write the truth as he saw it and he wanted to be loved for it. Of course, the less he was loved, the more surreal, the darker his vision became.

A word on the subject of audience empathy: I have noted how the second *Milk Train* distanced audiences from Williams' characters. It is a tricky subject this question of empathy, especially in our time of antiheroes coexisting with conventionally melodramatic television good guys. What may touch one man's heart may leave another quite cold. Probably no other critical judgment, except perhaps sentimentality, is as subject to a critic's subjectivity as is empathy. Brechtian alienation often backfires as Brecht himself discovered with *Mother Courage*. Sometimes, the tougher a character, the more sympathetic. The cuddliest of creatures can become loathsome while we may weep for the death of monsters. Ultimately, probably, we weep for ourselves and the loss of what we value and love. It has everything to do with who we are and who we would like to be. Of course, sometimes we confuse the latter for the former.

I find the second Flora Goforth to be more moving because I find her more honest. I do not believe in sudden character reversals as much as I might wish for them. I do not believe in the healing grace of single interviews; therefore it is more touching to me when Flora's last words are "Be here when I awake." The grotesque vision of an old woman on the verge of death making a sexual overture seems to me to be laughable but also touchingly real and in some ways heroic. Most touching and universal is Flora's fear of death. Some subjects are so inherently emotional that distance is necessary even to discuss them. This I believe is the real purpose of Williams' distancing devices in the rewritten *Milk Train*. Not cruelty, nor diminishing humanity, rather honesty and deep care caused Williams to increasingly use dramatic techniques that distanced and puzzled his audiences. Pity informed by contempt, love informed by honesty. We are always in a double relationship of involvement and detachment. Alienation and lack of empathy are not just experimental theater techniques; they are the condition of a large part of our lives. Occasionally, once in a while, we may feel genuine empathy for someone or a character in a play. How exciting and moving that triumph in spite of our separateness. But if it is to be honest, the triumph is never easy, for all human beings are a mixture of that which is admirable and that which is monstrous. Empathy in the face of that mixture is the most moving thing of all.

NOTES

1. Tennessee Williams, author's notes to *The Milktrain Doesn't Stop Here Anymore: The Theatre of Tennessee Williams*, vol. 5 (New York: New Directions, 1963), 3.

2. John Chapman, *New York Daily News*, January 18, 1963.

3. Robert Coleman, *New York Mirror*, January 18, 1963.

4. Walter Kerr, CBS News broadcast, January 18, 1963.

5. John McClain, *New York Journal-American*, January 18, 1963.

6. Richard Watts, *New York Post*, January 18, 1963.

7. Michael Smith, *Village Voice*, January 24, 1963.

8. Henry Hewes, *The Saturday Review of Literature*, 1963.

9. Richard Gilman, "Mistuh Williams, He Dead," *Commonweal*, February 8, 1963.

10. John Chapman, *New York Daily News*, January 3, 1964.

11. Walter Kerr, *New York Herald Tribune*, January 2, 1964.

· 3 ·

Down and Out in
New Orleans and Cocaloony Key

$\mathscr{M}$arch 1966 brought Tennessee Williams' *Slapstick Tragedy* to Broadway and New York. Probably not since Samuel Beckett's *Waiting for Godot* opened on Broadway had a play sought a less hospitable or more unlikely home. Williams himself knew that the plays comprising *Slapstick Tragedy* (*The Mutilated* and *The Gnädiges Fräulein*), would probably not be a commercial success. In May 1965 he had given an interview stating, "*Slapstick Tragedy*. I don't think they'll work. The plays are in the same vein as *Camino Real* and *Camino Real* didn't go over well."[1]

In another interview Tennessee referred to the plays as "way out." Perhaps Williams was hoping that the contemporary interest in "theater of the absurd" might create an audience for his experiments.

While Williams often eschewed theater of the absurd, he admired Edward Albee's *Who's Afraid of Virginia Woolf?* and sought as the director of *Slapstick Tragedy* Alan Schneider, the director most associated with American productions of Beckett and Pinter. Schneider, not ordinarily a commercial director, had directed *Who's Afraid of Virginia Woolf?* and so had won Broadway acclaim as well as artistic commendation from the off-Broadway audiences who normally welcomed absurd plays. Perhaps Williams too could have it both ways.

The sixties was a rich period of contending labels for different genres of drama: absurdist, black comedy, gallows humor, tragicomedy, theater of cruelty. All of these were consistently discussed concepts in newspapers, magazines, and journals. Williams usually avoided labeling his plays. In interviews he frequently contradicted himself and was seldom interested in reaching generalizations about the genres of his work. However, the very title of these two one-acts, *Slapstick Tragedy*, recognized the question of genre that was sure to be discussed when the plays were produced. Williams created his own genre at the same time that he bowed to the fashion of categorization.

What does it mean? Not content to simply call the plays "tragicomedy," Williams according to his title wanted to combine "slapstick," the lowest form of cruel physical comedy, with the most exalted and ennobling of dramatic forms, the tragedy. Williams, then, is attempting to reconcile, contain, show coexistent the lowest aspects of human behavior with the highest. Nothing less will make his vision complete.

Fantasy elements in *The Mutilated* and *The Gnädiges Fräulein*, the two one-act plays that comprise *Slapstick Tragedy*, are in some ways reminiscent of the fantasy in *Camino Real*. However, what was romantic in *Camino Real* has turned grotesque, what was poetic is more bizarre, or rather the poetry has changed from the lyrical and the lofty to the ironic and bitter. There are few "soft" moments in *Slapstick Tragedy* without parody or "camp." Former lyricism is glimpsed through the reality of a cartoon present. What was romantic has turned laughable. Lord Byron has left Camino Real, leaving its inhabitants quite threadbare. Casanova has been replaced by anonymous sailors and the inarticulate Indian Joe. Marguerite Gautier is mutilated though still surviving but Kilroy's heart has died years before.

The Mutilated and *The Gnädiges Fräulein* are united by their theatrical experimentation. Both plays are marked by a departure from realism, indeed are special because of these departures which make them important in Williams' ever-broadening use of theatricalism in the late plays. *The Mutilated*, though the more conventional of the two plays, moves into theatrical fantasy at its conclusion and in a good production should be informed from its first few moments by this same fantasy. *The Gnädiges Fräulein* performed as the second half of the evening moves the audience into its own demented world. That world becomes inhabited by the audience, experienced from the inside, not merely observed in troubled characters but a world seen from within its own madness. An evening of *Slapstick Tragedy*, properly experienced in the theater, is a wild journey that becomes more adventurous and bizarre as the evening progresses.

The situation and plot of *The Mutilated* can be described rather easily. Once more we are in the old French quarter of New Orleans. Most of the play takes place in the "Silver Dollar Hotel on South Rampart Street." The play occurs on Christmas Eve and Christmas morning and revolves around two female characters, Celeste and Trinket. Celeste, at the play's beginning, has just been released from the Women's House of Detention where she has served a short sentence for shoplifting. Her brother has bailed her out but wants nothing more to do with her. She returns to the Silver Dollar Hotel hoping to get her old room. But she has been thrown out and her few possessions have been locked away in lieu of payment of back rent. Broke, she has only one possible salvation—to revive a former friendship with Trinket Dugan, another inhabitant of the hotel who is financially better off. Celeste must seek and obtain Trinket's protection and support. However, Trinket is furious with Celeste for publicizing to the world Trinket's private affliction, namely, that she has had a mastectomy and has been left with one breast, that she is "mutilated" as Trinket calls herself. Christmas Eve finds Trinket at a turning point in her life. After years of seclusion without a man, she is determined to find a partner this evening and bring him back to her room. She can no longer bear her solitude, for "in life there has to be *two*." The objectives of these characters create the plays action and plot. Will Celeste win over Trinket? Will Trinket find a man? Both characters are desperate. Both desperately need a "miracle."

As characters Celeste and Trinket are a familiar comic duo. It is a duo that Williams uses often in the late plays. Celeste is a loud, brawling, busty, healthy, strong-willed animal, mostly concerned with her own physical needs. Trinket is more sensitive, more fragile, a poetic, frail type more used to the finer things in life. She uses more refined language and is more sensitive to insults. A variant on the body/soul split, they have relatives in Hannah and Maxine in *Night of the Iguana*, Molly and Polly in *The Gnädiges Fräulein*, Bessie and Flora in *A Perfect Analysis Given by a Parrot*, Gogo and Didi in *Waiting for Godot*, Hamm and Clov in *Endgame*, not to mention Laurel and Hardy or Abbott and Costello.

Williams gives both characters unexpected moments of character depth and strength. Celeste can be both philosophical and poetic when she needs those qualities to give her strength. "When you're lost in this world you're lost and not found, the lost and found department is just the lost department, but I'm going in that lobby like I've just come back from the biggest social event of the Goddam season, no shit." Ultimately it's her guts that makes Celeste admirable. Her refusal to be humiliated by the most humiliating of circumstances.

Trinket exhibits unexpected courage as well as comic sexuality in her handling of a young sailor named Slim whom she manages to snare back to her room. Talking to Slim's buddy, Trinket brazenly gives orders: "Now! Quick! Find your buddy! It's him I want for Christmas . . . Tall, crowned with gold that's so gold it's like his head caught fire, and I know, I remember the kind of skin that goes with flame-colored hair it's like snow, it's like sunlight in snow, I remember, I know!" An idealized fantasy of a male? Yes, of course, but that is exactly what Trinket requires. And she gets him! The actual seduction scene is both sad and funny and completely anticlimactic. Drunk, Slim knocks over coffee and demands money from Trinket. His comments punctuate Trinket's poetic utterances with a satiric refrain: "There's somethin'

Goddam wrong here, peculiar, not natural, morbid." Slim passes out and starts to snore. There will be no consummation of love tonight. Trinket consoles herself, "Well, anyhow, I have somebody here with me. Celeste's alone, but I'm not. I'm not alone but she is." In her qualified happiness Trinket compares herself to Celeste, unable to escape their relationship even in her moment of quasi-triumph. Celeste's imagined misery makes Trinket's partial happiness sweeter to savor.

The plot is resolved Christmas morning after Trinket's abortive liaison. Celeste has slept on the hotel lobby sofa and is about to be kicked out when Trinket offers a reconciliation telephoned through the desk clerk on duty: "Bernie, tell her to come on up to my room and have a glass of wine with me. I want to bury the hatchet." Swallowing her pride Celeste visits Trinket in her room and the two women are reconciled in a Christmas morning communion of forgiveness. Celeste invokes a mysterious presence into the room, and the play ends with a religious experience for the two women. Celeste explains the phenomenon to Trinket: "There was an elderly sister at Sacred Heart Convent School that received invisible presences, and once she told me that if I was ever cut off and forgotten by the blood of my blood and was homeless alone in the world, I would receive the invisible presence of our Lady in a room I was in."

Williams theatrically dramatizes this subjective experience through a dramatic use of light: "There has been a gradual change of light in the room; it now seems to be coming through stained glass windows—a subjective phenomenon of the trance falling over the women." Both women kiss the hem of the invisible "Our Lady's" garment. Trinket experiences a cessation of physical pain, "The pain in my breast is gone!" The play ends with a chorus of singers and a mysterious "Jack in Black" who sings a Christmas carol not unmixed with irony and dread:

Chorus:

> A miracle, a miracle!
> The light of wonder in our eyes.

(Jack in Black crosses through them, smiling and lifting his hat.)

> But that's a dream, for dream we must
> That we're made not of mortal dust:
> There's Jack, there's Jack, there's Jack in Black!

Jack in Black: Expect me, but not yet, not yet!

Chorus:

> A miracle, a miracle!
> He's smiling and it means not yet.

What is to be made of all this? Has Williams gone religious? Isn't it all sen-timental and manipulatively precious? I think not, if one reads the play as an uneasy Christmas ceremony, an unrealistic act of faith arising out of the needs of the destitute. It is, after all, miracle as subjective experience.

If we look at the beginning of the play, we remember that the chorus is introduced at curtain rise. This is done less in Brechtian fashion than as a kind of religious choir that invokes a repeated prayer: "A miracle, a miracle." The play is a Christmas religious service, a candlelit service of soft outlines. In his production notes to the published play, Williams requests a nonrealistic physical production embodying suggested realities: "The sets are as delicate as Japanese line drawings: they should be so abstract, so spidery, with the exception of Trinket Dugan's bedroom, that the audience will accept the nonrealistic style of the play."

Changes in locale from Hotel to Jackson Park and the Cafe Boheme move the play through time and space, but these locales must not be hard edged nor clearly defined. The set must seem to be fading—reality itself per-haps fading as the play progresses. Only Trinket's room, secure and her own, has much definition. Little wonder that Celeste wants to share it.

The play moves into subjective experience, the fantastic, as it progresses, and while it has a romantic aura to it there is much in the play to make its positive ending a Pyrrhic victory. The chorus' carol makes clear that the mercy shown Celeste and Trinket in the play is both rare and unusual, something that is most often gone without:

> I think the strange, the crazed, the queer
> Will have their holiday this year
> And for a little while, a little while
> There will be pity for the wild.

This carol is as much a hope, an invocation, as anything else. The Christmas setting invites comparison with the miracle of Bethlehem when shelter was given to the newborn son of God, but this carol is for the homeless, the des-titute, social outcasts; in fact, all those whom traditional Christianity professes to be the recipients of its prayers and good deeds but who more often than not go without any good fortune. For a "little while" there may actually be sanctuary. The play then is a reworking of the Christmas story, a Christmas ceremony with music and lights but one specifically for the miserable and the unfortunate. It is, if you will, an act of faith, performed by the destitute for themselves. Faith often commences when human pain can turn nowhere else. Theater itself may offer sanctuary for the wild for a little while.

The presence of Jack in Black is a most un-Christian reminder of death's ultimate power:

> I'm Jack the Black who stacks the deck,
> Who loads the dice and tricks the wheel
> The bell has stopped because I smile.
> It means forget me for a while.

Theater, faith, love are all momentary illusions that offer refuge but ultimately are unreal. The play recognizes spiritual need and perhaps comes out of a habit of faith that persists long after a rational belief in the transcendent power of religion dies. In his *Memoirs*, Williams unequivocally stated his religious beliefs: "I am unable to believe that there is anything but permanent oblivion after death. It is a dreadful apostasy with which to live a human life."[2] And yet of course, Williams "converted" to Catholicism in the late sixties, undoubtedly an act of public theater yet surely momentarily felt. He wore a cross around his neck in later years and was often given to personal reminiscences of his grandfather, an Episcopalian minister. His religious position was totally absurd, with his actions often contradicting his stated beliefs. But *that*, Williams seems to be saying in *The Mutilated*, is the split human condition. Crucifixion is not such a powerful symbol for nothing, and its pain is perhaps more frequently experienced than the miracle of Christmas.

Williams' affection for his characters in *The Mutilated* is an act of charity. Critics often accused him of sentimentality, and they certainly saw little to identify with in *The Mutilated*. Martin Gottfried's scorn in his review of *Slapstick Tragedy* is typical of the general ridicule heaped upon the plays: "Mutilation, along with various other physical violences, bizarre animals and discards, rejects, and parasites, is a standard part of the Williams' song and dance. And while his concern with the pained and lonely was once moving and true, it has since become a great cliché—the most honest of compassion will suffocate with repetition."[3] Whose compassion has suffocated—Williams' or Gottfried's? Is there no longer any need for compassion? Or have the conditions that caused Williams' original sympathy for the "pained and lonely" disappeared? Perhaps Gottfried is just tired of hearing about it and wishes it would go away. Of course one can understand how news of the "mutilated" might be depressing in a newspaper like *Women's Wear Daily*.

Williams' poetic gifts have not abandoned him in the play. The lyric side of Williams' muse remains but also changes into something more humorous and purposefully excessive. Trinket often speaks with this kind of extravagant lyricism both appreciative and satiric of Southern speech: "I pity transients at Christmas. This hotel is full of derelicts, Bernie, lost, lonely, homeless at Christmas. Heaven knows what secret sorrows they carry with them! And very few care!" Of course we have heard this voice before in Williams. It is the rhythm and accent, the vocabulary of Amanda and Blanche.

Celeste speaks with the earthier side of Williams' music, percussive and bitchy: "I see there's been a Christmas celebration. Was it organized by Trinket Dugan? Did she put on her Santie Claus suit and ring a cow bell under that sorry tree? I never seen a worse-decorated tree, broken ornaments on it and needles already shedding, it sure looks sad.—Sample bottles of cheap perfume for the ladies and dime-store ties for the gents? Ha ha! Christmas is something you got to do big or don't do it." This kind of down-to-earth dialogue balances the flights of lyricism and creates a cruel comedy. It is reminiscent of the rhythm and vocabulary of Maggie the Cat. Characters in the play often use language to hurt each other. Words are a major weapon for these powerless people. Trinket and Celeste are not diminished in their vocabularies. Indeed, much of the play's humor comes from the ingenuity with which the two women use cruel language to wound each other. Celeste calls Trinket, among other things, a "Fink, Mutilated Fink," and Trinket is not above a good retort: "SHE SPITS—Where's the toad? Wherever a witch spits it produces a *toad*!"

The play's "slapstick" qualities come from its physical farce as well as its verbal exchanges. While Trinket is alone with Slim in her room, Celeste storms up and down the street, up and down the stairs, "yowling at the moon" like a dog. She throws Trinket's stolen purse into the orchestra pit. She is so extreme as to be an object of comic derision but then in a magnificent coup de théâtre the tone changes dramatically: "Celeste runs down the stairs. At bottom, she stops and looks up at the sky, weeping like a lost child. There is a pause, a silence. Celeste approaches the orchestra pit, stoops, her hand extended. The purse is handed back to her from below. She returns sobbing to the bottom of the outside staircase; she removes the rosary from Trinket's purse and begins, to 'tell her beads,' sobbing." Not in the lines but in the "business" this theatrical moment turns the play from slapstick to possible tragedy. In effect, Celeste's cry is a tragic outcry to the heavens at the injustice of the universe. Perhaps not as warranted as Hecuba's or Lear's, Trinket's pain at this moment, her anger and indignation, is nonetheless as great as any tragic image of "unaccommodated man." Pain does not ask if it is warranted to be expressed nor does compassion debate the worthiness of the object of its pity.

There is also cruel comedy in Trinket's affliction. Her "mutilation" is not only a personal sorrow; it is her source of exaggerated self-pity and therefore an object of scorn and laughter. There is something of a "sick joke" in this play. The sick joke is that form of explosive laughter that comes from using personal (usually physical) affliction as a source of laughter. Paraplegics, the blind, lepers have all at some time been the source of that most taboo, most socially reprehensible of all humor, the sick joke. It is the taboo itself that makes it so explosive, saying the unsayable. The sick joke, cruel as it may be, is perhaps a kind of healthy laughter, cutting across social restrictions and manners, which joys in its own health and survival while exorcising possible illness. If the worst of things can be laughed at, they can somehow be kept at bay. It is this cruel laughter that is most new in Williams' work at this time and that will reach its most outrageous expression in *The Gnädiges Fräulein*. It is also this cruelty that links Williams to the concurrent black comedy and theater of cruelty, simultaneous phenomena of the late sixties. This is not to say that Williams imitated other writers of the time. These tendencies were present in the zeitgeist and Williams like most artists was sensitive to the times.

To combine the sick joke with the tragic—is such a thing possible? Does not the sick joke preclude empathy for its object of scorn? May cruelty and compassion coexist? They certainly do in life. Why do mixed genres, commonplace in many great writers of the twentieth century, seem so difficult in the theater? Perhaps because they are difficult to perform. Far too often one aspect of the mixed genre takes precedence in performance. Theater exists in time, and perhaps we can only feel one thing at any given time. The switching from cruelty to compassion, from laughter to tears, required by the mixed genre is difficult to control in an audience that cannot pause to reflect during performance. How to switch from comedy to tragedy, from distance to empathy, from laughter to tears—this is one of the greatest challenges for contemporary theater performers. The best plays of the twentieth century demand that ability. Occasionally productions are successful in fulfilling that challenge. But it is very difficult.

The Gnädiges Fräulein moves *Slapstick Tragedy* into an almost totally disoriented world in which waiting, idle chatter, and survival out of habit rule an elemental animal world. Set in the isolation of Cocaloony Key, "the southernmost bit of terra firma" of the "Disunited Mistakes," Cocaloony Key is Oz, a natural zoo of animals in which human beings compete with and are threatened by giant Cocaloony birds that swoop down upon them out of the sky. Even in this reduced world, however, there exists Polly, a "gossip columnist and society-editor of the Cocaloony News Gazette" and Molly, the socially pretentious owner of a local flop house called "the big dormitory." Polly uses her position on the Gazette to gain power over Molly, a tight-fisted business woman seeking free publicity for her guest house. Much of the play features these old combatants in ridiculous sparring, non sequiturs, and jokes. The few moments of peace and shared friendship between them occur when they "turn on" to "Mary Jane" and rock together in marijuana bliss in their respective rockers.

> Molly: Let's synchronize rockers! Hold yours till I count to three. OK?
> Polly: Count away!

Molly: One! Two! Three! *ROCK!* (They rock with pelvic thrusts as if having sex.)

Polly: WHEEE!

Molly: Now we're rocking in beautiful unison, Polly!

Polly: In tune with the infinite, Molly!

Molly: In absolute harmony with it!

Together: Huff, Huff, Huff. WHEE!

This is only one of many outrageous moments in the play but it is perhaps the most incongruous: two aging ladies, pretenders to prestige, smoke marijuana together and go out of their minds in ecstatic exercise. Of course, it goes nowhere. Rockers for all their motion make no progress. But they have a wonderful time. Once it is over, they return to their parasitical, manipulative selves. Molly threatens to remove her advertisement from the Gazette unless Polly writes a complimentary article about the big dormitory. The parodic moments of romantic transcendence in the rocking chairs are the only peace offered the comic duo. Most of their time is spent bickering or competing for the attention of Indian Joe, a blond Indian with "Caribbean blue eyes." The only plot these characters embody is the possibility of a write up for the big dormitory. Will Molly get a story from Polly? The story most likely to sell is the story of the Gnädiges Fräulein, a totally destitute, barely surviving old circus performer who at one time was "a personage."

> Molly: Take the Gnädiges Fräulein, one instant for an instance, there's a personage for you, internationally celebrated for yea many years on this earth if not on other planets, yes, I've got the Fräulein to mention only a few of the more or less permanent guests of the big dormitory under the rooftree of God.

Down on her luck the Fräulein is forced to compete at the fish docks with Cocaloony birds for discarded fish from the boats. Molly demands three fish a day from the Fräulein for her rent. This absurd situation poses the play's main plot question. As Molly puts it, "The Gnädiges Fräulein is required to deliver three fish a day to keep eviction away from the door, and now that the co-caloonies have turned against her will she have guts enough to fight or will she retire from the fish-docks like she did from show business under pressure!?" The Fräulein is a fantastic sight. "She wears a costume which would not be out of place at the Moulin Rouge in the time of Toulouse-Lautrec. One eye is covered by a large blood-stained bandage. Her hair is an aureole of bright orange curls, very fuzzy." Already deaf in one ear, she responds with song whenever anyone shouts at her. Pitiful and laughable, the Fräulein supplies degraded suffering upon which Polly and Molly comment with cold detached observation. Three times during the play we see the Fräulein respond to the boats' whistles, heading toward the docks to fight for her daily toll of fish. Each time she returns from the docks more battered than before.

Perhaps the most moving moment of the play occurs when, totally blinded, the Fräulein gives way to despair, which is coolly observed by Molly and Polly. The Fräulein starts with a song: "Her costume is the same except that her tulle skirt, or tou-tou is spangled with fresh drops of blood that glitters like rubies and her legs, bare from mid-thigh to ankle are likewise streaked with blood . . . She is transfigured like a saint under torture."

After the song, the Fräulein holds up her scrapbook and pretends to read through a lorgnon while reciting her press clippings from memory. Polly and Molly provide comic-cruel commentary:

> Molly: She always holds up her lorgnon when she reads her press clippings.
>
> Polly: But she can't read her old press clippings.
>
> Molly: That's not the point.
>
> Polly: Then what is the point in your opinion, Molly?
>
> Molly: Habit! Habit! Now do you get the point?
>
> Polly: Do you mean it's a habit with her to hold up her lorgnon when she is reading her scrapbook.
>
> Molly: Absolutely. It's a custom, a habit, a—now look! Now, look. And listen! She is expressing the inexpressible regret of all her regrets.
>
> Fräulein (regretfully): AHHHHHHHHHH!
>
> Polly: Saddest soliloquy on the stage since Hamlet's . . .
>
> Fräulein: AHHHHHHHHHHHHHHHHHHHHHH . . .
>
> Molly: I hope she don't repeat it.
>
> Fräulein: AHHHHHHHHHHHHHHHHHHHHHHHHHHHHHHHH . . .
>
> Molly: Tell her not to repeat it.
>
> Polly (to Gnädiges Fräulein): Don't repeat it.

The scene in its double tone of suffering and coolness recalls Gogo and Didi in *Waiting for Godot* as they observe the sufferings of the blind Pozzo and his servant, Lucky. Suffering is never really felt except by those who directly experience pain, and at some point a person's pain becomes tiresome to others. Empathy only goes so far and is eventually replaced by indifference. The Fräulein's anguish is like Celeste's cry to the sky in *The Mutilated*; it expresses the tragic in "slapstick tragedy" while Polly and Molly's comments supply the cruel slapstick.

By the end of the play, the Fräulein is blind in both eyes, her hair has been pulled out, her garish costume stripped, and she is only wearing blood-stained, torn tights. Polly and Molly have taken a captured fish from her and have retired into the house for supper. The Fräulein alone on the forestage hears the boat whistle: "The boat whistles again. She assumes the starting position of a competitive runner and waits for the whistle. It's delayed a bit for the interior pantomime. Indian Joe pushes one lady to the left and one to the right and seats himself at the table picking up the fish. Polly holds out the wine bottle to him. The parlor dims as the third whistle sounds—the Gnädiges Fräulein starts a wild, blind dash for the fish-docks."

The characters in *The Gnädiges Fräulein* are bizarre cartoon figures, with Molly and Poly as a clown team. Even the Fräulein comes from a clown tradition, the clown who gets dumped upon, "he who gets slapped." The circus world of the Fräulein's past did not die when she left "show biz" but continued into a larger arena. Indian Joe is a glamorized circus Indian, all body and no brain, the circus muscle man. Williams tells us that "he doesn't have to be anything but an erotic fantasy in appearance." (This admission beats his critics to the punch.) Two other characters appear briefly: a "permanent transient" and a Cocaloony bird. Another resident of the big dormitory, the "permanent transient" with his derby hat, evokes Emmett Kelly's sad-sack clown in his speechless but gentle drunkenness. Most fantastic of all is a large Cocaloony bird who appears big as life to threaten all the inhabitants of Cocaloony Key. His appearance is like some obscene cartoon but in this play, the outrageous is the norm.

The dialogue in *The Gnädiges Fräulein* is frequently absurd and often seems unmotivated. While sometimes funny, Polly and Molly are frequently inane. Poetry in the play mocks itself with self-conscious parody:

> Molly: Yep, the Dark Angel has a duplicate key to the big dormitory and faithfully every night he drops by to inspect the sleepers and check their dog tags. He wanders among the two and three decker bunks and never leaves without company, nope, never leaves unattended and no one grieves when he leaves.
>
> Polly (lisping): Between the dark and the daylight—
>
> Molly: When the gloom of doom is in flower—
>
> Together: Comes a pause in the night's occupation Which is known as the Angel's Dark Hour.

"Camp" may be the best description of this dialogue and indeed the play has a strong camp element, ridiculously parodying excessive sentimentality.

The play is nevertheless enormously musical. There are arias and duets, counterpoint and antiphony. Cacophony of the birds and violence create musical climaxes. Cries and unarticulated sounds often express more than words. "Arias" within the dialogue such as Polly's opening speech and Molly's long expositional speech about the Fräulein's past contain long run-on sentences in which characters sound like perpetual motion machines until they abruptly stop in mid-sentence, run out of steam, have nothing more to say, lose concentration.

> Polly: Yais, everything's southernmost here, like southern fried chicken is southernmost fried chicken. But who's got a chicken? None of us southernmost white Anglo-Saxon Protestants are living on fish and fish only because of thyroid deficiency in our southernmost systems: we live on fish because regardless of faith or lack of it, every day is Friday, gastronomically speaking, because of readjustment of the economy which is southernmost too. OOPS!—Did I lose concentration? No . . . it's nice not to lose concentration especially when you've got to deliver an address to the Southernmost Branch of the Audubon Society on the vicious, overgrown seabirds which are called cocaloonies, and are responsible for the name and notoriety of this—OOPS! particular Key.

During the preceding speech, Polly is being attacked by Cocaloony birds, which accounts for her cries of "OOPS!" but her rambling, hilarious speech has great difficulty sticking to the point, which, of course, is the point. It is "stoned" rap, carefully sculpted by Williams to communicate the off-center quality of life in Cocaloony Key. The only motion is wind-down or sudden stop, loss of concentration in which the mind encounters its own pointlessness.

Another important quality of "absurdist" dialogue is present in *The Gnädiges Fräulein*. Quite often in absurdist plays, characters say things out of character that give evidence of knowledge of the absurdity in which they find themselves. Absurd characters are often both "in" and "out" of their situations at the same time. Their vocabulary is frequently ironic and self-aware. Molly, for example, is periodically given to philosophic remarks that seem beyond the vocabulary of a simple hotelier. "All of us, Polly, sally forth once too often. It's an inexorable law to which the Gnädiges Fräulein seems not to be an exception." One is reminded of similar parodies of "home truths" satirized in *Waiting for Godot* and other famous absurd plays. Aphorisms beyond the realistic abilities of bums or a Cocaloony landlady suggest that absurd characters have fallen from higher social situations, have experienced all that education can give, have pasts more elevated than their present conditions.

Absurd characters are glimpsed "after their fall," and despite their largely petty dialogue, they are occasionally capable of profundities that are usually spoken with self-mockery and irony.

Other characters react to absurdity with silence, which is perhaps a more logical choice. This seems to be the case of the Fräulein, who has very few lines and mostly sings old sentimental songs on cue. Her silence, however, is eloquent. After all, what is there to say?

In spite of its experimental theatricality, Williams has a simple theme in *The Gnädiges Fräulein.* Of course the play is partially about the victimization of the artist in our society, but I think this theme is less important than was originally thought when the play was first produced. The play is more than a veiled metaphor for Williams' (as the Fräulein) treatment at the hands of the New York critics, although many Williams reviews do read more like bird attacks than carefully reasoned evaluations. But remember, Polly and Molly are also victims of the economic depression that has hit Cocaloony Key. Parasitism is the natural human condition, and it is shared by all the characters in the play. As Molly says, "Nothing is more intolerant, Polly, than one parasite of another." Cruelty comes less from individual meanness than from necessity; the law of the jungle dictates that all animals, human beings included, must compete for survival. Men and women will always find a way to be cruel as they struggle to maintain themselves against all odds. Of course, some are better equipped for the struggle than others. The Gnädiges Fräulein has been severely incapacitated by disappointment in love. In the play we learn that the Fräulein's present situation, her retirement from show biz, is the result of an unrequited love for a circus seal trainer. In her pain she has transferred her masochistic affections to Indian Joe, who readily takes advantage of her servitude. Love, then, nearly incapacitates one for life's struggles. Williams mocks the unrequited nature of love. "He couldn't stand her because she adored him." Love has caused the Fräulein to lose her balance: "She lost her sense of reality and she drifted." Personal sorrow may cause a loss of reality but as we see in the play an off-center reality is an accurate picture of the larger world as well. Not only the Fräulein but all the inhabitants of Cocaloony Key are demented. Personal madness can become a necessary defense against a more universal disorder, and all the characters in the play seem to have created their own mad defense systems. Polly's self-importance and Molly's social pretensions are as mad as anything we see in the Fräulein.

Above all, the play is a tribute to the human capability for survival in the most impossible, cruel, and absurd of situations. "Anything havin' a leg to stand on can sleep standin' up if it has to." The Fräulein's response to the boat whistles may be Pavlovian in its animal response, but it is also noble and tragic as well as funny and absurd. Tragedy tells us that life is most magnificently heroic only in the most reduced of human circumstances. At the end of his *Memoirs* writing of his sister Rose, Tennessee wrote this final sentence: "After all, high station in life is earned by the gallantry with which appalling experiences are survived with grace."[4] A successful production of *The Gnädiges Fräulein* would express that grace as well as the play's grotesqueness. After all, *gnädiges* is a German word meaning gracious and merciful.

Theatrically *The Gnädiges Fräulein* introduces elements not seen before in Williams' work. While symbolism and fantasy had been present in *Camino Real*, *The Gnädiges Fräulein* creates a more completely illogical world than any other play Williams had written up to this time. His production notes call for a "totally unrealistic arrangement of porch, assorted props, steps, a yard, and picket fence." This mixed-up environment has nothing in its right place, "as if Picasso had designed it." The set Williams describes is to be a "subtle variety of grays and grayish whites that you see in pelican feathers and clouds." These grays, common in the Florida Keys, produce a washed-out look as if years of rain and wind have bleached them. The only bright colors in the set are a "particularly incongruous Victorian Parlor," which is inside Molly's guest house. Not much action occurs there. It is seen as a bright location just a little beyond the central action of the play, which takes place mostly on Molly's front porch and in her disoriented front yard. This is not the usual Williams world of scrim and dissolving backgrounds. What is there is quite present, if in illogical relationships. Edges are hard and cartoon-like. The Cocaloony bird who appears in the play is not a symbolic suggestion but rather a larger-than-life-size vicious version of Sesame Street's Big Bird, a cartoon, and very much "there." Costumes in the play, especially those of the bird, Indian Joe, and the Fräulein, are circus costumes, theatrical and overstated. They give color and humor to the cartoon.

One particularly absurd element in the production is the seemingly endless supply of illogical props that are at Molly's disposal throughout the play. Sometimes she speaks through a megaphone, other times she looks through a telescope; finally she accompanies herself on a big drum for theatrical emphasis as she tells the story of the Fräulein's life. Where do these props come from? What is a megaphone doing on the front porch? Of course they are for spontaneous comic effect, illogical in the way circus clowns carry incongruous props. Theatrically, *The Gnädiges Fräulein* is a slapstick circus clown show in which audiences are made aware of the cruelty of the circus.

Most of the New York critics responded negatively to *Slapstick Tragedy*. Many were puzzled by the play and this puzzlement in most cases expressed itself in hostile derision:

> Frankly, there is nothing more bizarre on Broadway . . . There are times when this outlandish play is uproarious. By contrast it eventually becomes

embarrassing to watch Miss Leighton's gracious lady [the Fräulein] deteriorate into something too pitiful for humor, and too strange for pity.[5]

It is as if Mr. Williams had dredged through a garbage can and come up with a Madonna . . . I would say that this is Mr. Williams' bid for High Camp and Pop Art . . . a feckless and unrealized ambition.[6]

This brilliant talent is sleeping . . . Mr. Williams has neither grown nor changed . . . What promises to be a farce of Steinbeckian raffishness drags on pointlessly because the author did not know how to finish it. This has not deterred him from presenting it.[7]

They are grotesques, although comic, and also are outside normal society . . . The second play, in a sure enough vein of slapstick is quite funny at times, but it is all the more bitter beneath . . . This overlay of horror on comedy does not however produce genuine tragedy, or comedy either. The poor Fräulein is too inhuman to elicit sympathy . . . It is as though Mr. Williams had been viewing the painted monsters of Hieronymus Bosch before sitting down to write "The Gnädiges Fräulein."[8]

It seems to me that what has happened to Tennessee Williams is the saddest thing that has happened to the current theater in the last decade. For reasons obviously his own he has decided to devote his talents to the Out and the Abstract and they have reached full flower in the two one-acts presented . . . irritatingly vague and formless vignettes . . . *The Gnädiges Fräulein* defies description. I haven't the foggiest idea of what Mr. Williams has to tell us but it must be reported that it is extremely funny much of the time . . . I know Mr. Williams is trying to do something ambiguous and ambitious but, gee, I wish he would give us something old and square like "Streetcar Named Desire"![9]

The previous comments fall into obvious patterns. First there are the "philistine" remarks, the "I don't get it" comments. At least they are honest responses. One can hear this kind of comment any day at any modern art gallery or at any concert of "modern" music. Another category of comments falls into the implied "moralistic" remarks where a critic has failed to respond to characters because the critic has found them distasteful, immoral, and therefore outside his powers of empathy. Critics have made remarks of this kind as long as there have been artists and critics. One need only think of *La Dame aux Camelias, La Boheme, Carmen, Ghosts, Mrs. Warren's Profession, Desire Under the Elms,* or *A Streetcar Named Desire.* One would think that the embarrassment of history would teach critics something. Moralistic criticism is perhaps the most reprehensible of all in that it not only implies moral judgment on the artist and his creation but shows a lack of humanity on the part of the reviewer.

The more serious comments discuss the problem of mixed genre. This is a serious artistic debate and one worthy of discussion. Can a work of art be both comic and tragic at the same time? Unfortunately, this discussion often embodies both a philistine and moralist subtext. Sometimes a reviewer will react negatively to a mixed genre because the play does not follow prescriptions of past experience. The unsettling power of mixed genre can be confusing to the philistine who prefers repetitions of past experiences. The moralistic objection to the mixed genre is more difficult to explain. However, if we remember Aristotle's description of tragedy as the imitation of actions of "good" men and comedy as the imitation of the actions of "bad" men, we may understand that a mixed genre causes a moral confusion unsettling to the moralist who demands a clear picture of good and bad.

More substantive criticism came from the weekly critics, but it often also embodied predetermined critical assumptions as well as philistinism and moralism. Michael Smith of *The Village Voice*, Robert Brustein in *The New Republic*, Wilfrid Sheed in *Commonweal*, Henry Hewes in *The Saturday Review of Literature*—these are among the most respected critics of their time.

> In both of them Williams has tried tricks with form and style and the result has been to diffuse the emotions and muddle the themes . . . the pervasive desperation has afflicted the plays as well as the characters . . . Williams lost control of his technique, aesthetic distance vanished . . . the feeling I got from the evening [is] that both of these plays are direct metaphorical enactments of Tennessee Williams' concern for his own life. The author's erratic control over the tone of the plays and evident lack of perspective suggest that he can't quite distinguish these "mutilated" characters from his own self-image.[10]

Clothed in critical jargon we get here the "biographical" critical error. How does one get from a play the feeling that its playwright is in personal crisis? What proof is there of such an assumption? Williams' subject matter in all of his plays could have suggested that. What Smith perceives as a lack of control and aesthetic distance may simply be the result of Williams' complex attempt at a mixed genre. Of course Williams' very public image at the time often gave the impression of a man out of control and many critics confused that image with the plays. One wonders if the same feeling would have been received had Smith known nothing of Williams' personal life. Doubtless Van Gogh's neighbors, who experienced the painter in the throes of occasional madness, saw his paintings as little more than the ravings of a lunatic while today we see them as controlled expressions of something quite new.

Slapstick Tragedy opened on Broadway in the same month as William Inge's *Where's Daddy?*—another established American playwright who was having difficulty with the critics. In his *Commonweal* review Wilfrid Sheed castigated both playwrights for "trying to keep up this season with the younger set." Besides impugning the playwrights' integrities, this remark suggested not only foolishness on the part of the two established dramatists but that they were somehow "over the hill." Their worst sin perhaps was they were not "new." Sheed writes in the most condescending manner:

> Since the *Gnädiges Fräulein* has already been savaged almost as much as its heroine . . . by the nation's critics, and has gone limping into limbo, we shall content ourselves here with a last playful kick in the teeth. The short of it is that *Gnädiges Fräulein* is a comedy heavily dependent upon wild black gags and these gags are not very good. The audience laughs for a while out of expectation . . . but every cheap laugh has to be paid for in the theater and a kind of dumb agony sets in as we realize the jokes are bad and getting worse . . . Comedy requires a consensus of myth and we have to be reminded first why it is funny for a woman to have her eyes pecked out.[11]

Of course the "gags" aren't merely funny nor are they really "gags." Sheed reviews the play as if it were attempting to be a Neil Simon comedy but didn't get laughs. Most annoying of all is the glee with which Sheed chronicles his disdain for the play. Why are critics always at their wittiest when they write bad reviews? Possibly because as well as requiring a "consensus of myth" (whatever that means in these mythless days), comedy is often most successful when it is most cruel, a truth that *The Gnädiges Fräulein* embodies in its central vision. A critic has the greatest opportunity for wit when a work of art is negatively reviewed. Parasitism is not confined to Cocaloony Key.

Surprisingly, Robert Brustein, always a loner in his opinions, found some complimentary things to say about the expiring corpse of *Slapstick Tragedy*, noting "flair and humour and a brave attempt at novelty." Recognizing the play as a "farce-fantasy in the absurdist manner," Brunstein claims it "has undeniable weaknesses in tone and theme and doesn't run the stretch; but it also has a little daring and even a certain degree of charm."[12] How careful Brustein is in his praise of a playwright he had always found lacking!

Henry Hewes did not love *Slapstick Tragedy* but in his characteristically generous spirit wrote, "Above all one appreciates Mr. Williams' originality of conception." He also noted that "Broadway is notoriously inhospitable to any bill of unrelated short plays."[13] He might also have said that Broadway is notoriously inhospitable to experimental plays by its greatest playwrights who are perceived as past their prime. O'Neill, Miller, Inge, and Albee all experienced the same indignities.

There was really only one positive review for *Slapstick Tragedy* by a man who was primarily a theater artist and an occasional critic. Harold Clurman, one of America's great theatrical directors, used the event of his review in the *Nation* to make general comments on Broadway and it critics: "Tennessee Williams did himself an injustice by having his two one-act plays produced on Broadway. They might have gained considerable esteem had they been given in a more modest manner . . . A second injustice, almost as great, is the plays' critical response. *Slapstick Tragedy* is not the author's 'top drawer' work but he has struck a new note in at least the second of the two plays and both have a peculiarly personal stamp that merits attention."[14]

Clurman is particularly eloquent in noting that *The Mutilated* is not really sentimental but "is savage." He recognizes that the final moments of the play are "bitterly ironic" and the play's style contains "deliberate bitchiness." As if to answer the critics who found *The Mutilated* unfunny, Clurman writes, "The play requires its jokes to be horrible; its horror funny." *The Gnädiges Fräulein* came in for even more praise, "farcical fantasy altogether new for Williams." Filled with "sardonic mirth," the play is an "effective mixture of gallows humor and Rabelaisian zest." Finally Clurman makes a prediction that has as yet not come true: "Both plays are sure to be seen and acclaimed in future productions at universities, community theaters and on foreign stages."[15] I know of few productions of these plays. Universities and community theaters seldom produce plays that are either not classics or not successful in New York. Our universities and our community theaters (yes, even our regional theaters) mostly follow the guiding lights of Broadway, and that is the shameful truth of most of our theatrical institutions.

Critics have been quoted at length here because they are so important in understanding the story of Tennessee Williams' late plays. I do not know whether Tennessee read all of these critics. I suspect he read a fair number. He always referred to them in general as "the New York critics." Williams' paranoia about the critics was not without justification. The reviewers, critics, created an environment that made it more and more difficult for Williams to get the kinds of productions he wanted for his plays. As his "stock" went down, producers and directors became less interested in putting on his plays. In his later years Williams was often in the position of having to seek out theaters, to "audition" his scripts for approval. To many producers he was that most despised of all American types, the "has been." His critical reputation certainly made it easier for directors and producers to make demands for changes in the scripts, to temper his more experimental instincts, to demand changes that were thought to make the plays more commercial.

Of course this situation affected his work. Of course he became more bitter. Sometimes Williams wrote plays that he thought would be more commercial; sometimes the plays got wilder and more personal but always, the commerce of theater art, the victimization of those on the "outs," influenced his vision. The angrier Williams became, the more the system ridiculed him.

Martin Gottfried used his review of *Slapstick Tragedy* as an occasion to write a summary view of Williams. His view seems to have been the majority view in 1966. It is a devastatingly cruel description full of malice, the kind of review that almost seems to ask for the artist's death, a verbal murder: "Tennessee Williams is a playwright in trouble. Having years ago abandoned his natural inclinations to write money-making self-parodies, he finds himself wandering in pathetic circles. Left within the skeleton of his own poetry, he roams mistaken streets with no direction, no sense of himself, his instincts themselves confused."[16] Why so much hatred? Why this venom? It is difficult to understand this kind of review except as an act of vengeance. What could it possibly achieve? But Tennessee, like the Gnädiges Fräulein herself, while bloodied, would get up many times from such blows, his instincts never confused in the necessity to continue writing.

The Gnädiges Fräulein was a radical departure stylistically for Tennessee Williams. It was an attempt to introduce the freedom of theatrical experimentation of European absurdists into the commercial Broadway theater by a major playwright who had proven himself a commercially successful writer as well as an artist. It is a clown show, among other things, with bizarre one-dimensional characters in an unrealistic setting. Characters sometimes speak "out of character." Bizarre actions replace "believable" events. The play refuses to take itself seriously, at the same time asking the audience for tolerance and sympathy. It is small wonder that many thought Williams had gone off the deep end, a feeling sometimes substantiated by the often theatrical behavior of his personal life.

What is most original in these plays is new cruelty wedded to ultimate sympathy, two simultaneously possible relationships to the world. *Slapstick Tragedy* shows the universally predatory nature of all men, parasitism bred into the necessity of existence. Extreme situations blown out of proportion create cruel cartoons in these plays. Ionesco in *Rhinoceros* comes to mind as well as Beckett's *Waiting for Godot*, in which a clown duo fight and banter as they coolly observe the pain of others around them. The Fräulein is perhaps reminiscent of Lucky in *Godot*, the victimized fall guy, forced to continually perform for his supper. Instinct, habit, and survival at all costs are all that remain.

Williams in *The Gnädiges Fräulein* sees love as sexual enslavement that motivates extreme behavior. We all look for love in impossible and unworthy places. The Fräulein remembers her Viennese lover and seeks his substitution even with the inarticulate Indian Joe. The comic is that which equates the noble with the animal. The need for food and sex, the survival of the species, obliterates all nicer chimeras of civilization, and each must fight for his own share or more. But what an appalling situation is the human condition as seen in these plays! Slapstick comes from cruelty but tragedy from the desire for transcendence. Courage and grace may be the only admirable qualities possible to animal-like men. "After all, high station in life is earned by the gallantry with which appalling experiences are survived with grace."

NOTES

1. Quoted in John Gruen, "The Inward Journey of Tennessee Williams," *New York Herald Tribune*, May 2, 1965.

2. Tennessee Williams, *Memoirs* (Garden City, NY: Double Day, 1975), 248.

3. Martin Gottfried, *Women's Wear Daily*, February 23, 1966.

4. Williams, *Memoirs*, 252.

5. Norman Nadel, "Bizarre, Grim 'Slapstick Tragedy,'" *New York World-Telegram and Sun*, February 23, 1966.

6. George Oppenheimer, *Newsday*, February 23, 1966.

7. Stanley Kauffmann, "Theater: Tennessee Williams Returns; 'Slapstick Tragedy' at the Longacre Margaret Leighton and Kate Reid Star," *New York Times*, February 23, 1966.

8. Richard P. Cooke, *New York Post*, February 23, 1966.

9. John McClain, "The Out and the Abstract," *New York Journal-American*, February 23, 1966.

10. Michael Smith, "Theater Journal," *Village Voice*, March 3, 1966.

11. Wilfrid Sheed, "The Stage," *Commonweal*, April 8, 1966.

12. Robert Brustein, "A Question of Identity," *New Republic*, March 26, 1966.

13. Henry Hewes, *Saturday Review of Literature*, March 16, 1966.

14. Harold Clurman, "Theatre," *Nation*, March 14, 1966.

15. Clurman, "Theatre."

16. Gottfried, *Women's Wear Daily*.

· 4 ·

Mississippi and Tokyo

Slapstick Tragedy played on Broadway for four performances. Never before had a Williams play had such a short run. But Williams was not to be defeated by this failure. In two years he was "back on Broadway" with a new play, *Kingdom of Earth*. It was produced by the producer of mammoth musicals, David Merrick. Doubtless Tennessee was anxious to "bounce back," but it is doubtful that in former days he would have considered letting David Merrick produce one of his plays. Merrick was anxious to show himself a producer of serious plays, but he was also famous for interfering in the creative process.

The history of *Kingdom of Earth* is fascinating in its evolution. The play is based on a short story of the same name first published in 1954. During the fifties, the title emerged several times as a "work in progress." At one point it was even announced as a play for Maureen Stapleton. In February 1967 a one-act play was published in *Esquire* entitled *Kingdom of Earth*. The full-length play finally opened on Broadway on March 26, 1968, under the title *The Seven Descents of Myrtle*.

During stormy rehearsals and tryouts in Boston for the play, Williams consistently resisted Merrick's insistence that the title of the play be changed from *Kingdom of Earth*. It is further evidence of Williams' slipping "clout" that Merrick won the battle, and the play opened in New York under a title that Williams admitted made no sense.

In all versions, *Kingdom of Earth* involved the same simple story. Taking place in a backwater Mississippi farm community, Lot and his wife, Myrtle, arrive at their farm during an impending flood disaster. The farm is managed by Lot's half brother, Chicken, who hopes to inherit the farm after Lot's death. Since Lot is tubercular, this death is expected to be soon. To foil Chicken, Lot has married Myrtle in the hope of passing the farm on to his new bride.

52

During the action of the play, Chicken seduces Myrtle and Lot dies. The play ends with flood waters imminent. Chicken and Myrtle climb up to the roof of the farmhouse for safety. Chicken is obviously triumphant.

The play is a parable of sexuality, Lawrentian in its view. It sees a world in which the survival of the fittest rules. Chicken sums up the play's theme: "life just plain don't care for the weak." It is also a ringing espousal of the superiority of heterosexual love as life's one solidly positive value: "There's nothing in the world, in the whole kingdom of earth, that can compare with one thing, and that one thing, is what's able to happen between a man and a woman, just that thing, nothing more is perfect."

Granted, this speech is given by Chicken and is not necessarily the author's point of view. However, Lot is drawn so epicenely in the play that Chicken looks like a hero in comparison. The action of the play, Myrtle's "happiness" after sex with Chicken, and indeed the survival of Chicken and Myrtle, endorses Chicken's philosophy as the true one.

The genesis of *Kingdom of Earth* reveals radical shifts in Williams' attitude to his simple situation and characters. The short story is told in the first person from Chicken's point of view. It is a ribald, sexually explicit earthy comic tale of vitality and healthy sexuality. The last line of the story gives a clear idea of the story's theme and tone: "It's earth I'm after and now I am honest about it and don't pretend I'm nothing but what I am, a lustful creature determined on satisfaction and likely as not to get my full share of it." This is the Williams of *The Rose Tattoo*, an earlier Williams, still concerned with the conflict between spiritual and physical values, the body versus the soul. As in *The Rose Tattoo*, the answer is affirmatively physical. The Cavalier casts out the Puritan.

After the critical failure of *Slapstick Tragedy*, Williams went back to earlier material perhaps hoping to find what he may have felt had been lost. The first result was the one-act play, *Kingdom of Earth*, as published in *Esquire* magazine. The one-act is a brutal, fast-moving, nightmarish depiction of copulation in which mating occurs oblivious to suffering. Lot, the brother, dies offstage. He is not given much specificity. The tone is ironic. Ultimately, Myrtle is a figure of pity as she cries after capitulating to Chicken: "Oh, God, have mercy on my—puzzled—soul, my lost, sinful puzzled, soul!" The play shows heterosexuality as a triumphant force of nature but the tone is terrifying, with cruelty mixed in with the triumph. It is a more ambiguous and richer statement than the later, more sentimental, full-length play.

In the Broadway version, "fleshed out" for a full evening, all the characters except Chicken are given more specificity. Conceptually the characters are schematic stereotypes, but the play gives more detail to the stereotypes. Myrtle becomes more likeable and less elemental. This is one case where a fuller characterization makes the characters' actions less believable. Lot, a very present character, is so effeminate and cruel that his death is desirable and necessary. In addition, Lot's appearance, dressed in transvestite drag, just before his death, makes him a ludicrous figure, laughable and unsympathetic. What was horrible becomes oddly just, taking out any terror and also any pity for the characters. We feel that Myrtle has been saved from a terrible fate by Lot's death and by her tryst with Chicken. The play becomes a "positive" statement about heterosexuality. But it is not convincing. Surely, calculated to please a Broadway audience, the play has neither the celebratory sensuality of the short story nor the nightmarish horror of the one-act play. One wishes the more effective one-act version would be performed. It is a piece of true sixties Williams: strong theater without pandering. As the characters evolved, the play shifted focus. The grotesqueness with which Williams drew the character of Lot confused the play. The play is neither early nor late Williams but an unconvincing child born out of the desire to be commercially successful, the desire to be accepted. At the same time the playwright was caught in a new vision that could never be acceptable to a majority of the audience. Lot's obscene portrayal is a product of late Williams grotesqueness, but it is not informed with the compassion Williams gave his other grotesques in the sixties.

At first look, *In the Bar of a Tokyo Hotel* seems obviously autobiographical and perhaps confessional. One of its main characters is an artist facing a personal breakdown because of his entrance into a new phase of his art. The parallel is inescapable. The reviews of the play noted this in a generally disparaging way, and Williams himself seems to have understood the play in this personal way. In a note to the cast of the production, Williams explains the "meaning" of *Tokyo Hotel*:

> It is about the unusually early and peculiarly humiliating doom of the artist. He has made, in the beginning of his vocation, an almost total commitment of himself to this work. As Mark truthfully says, the intensity of his work, the unremitting challenges and demands that it makes to him and of him (in most cases daily) leave so little of him after the working hours that simple comfortable *being* is impossible for him . . . His youth passes. The health of his body fails him. Then the work increases its demand from most of him to practically all of him. At last it seems to him like an impotent attempt at making love. At that point, he is sentenced to death, and as death approaches he hasn't the comfort of feeling with any conviction that any of his work has had any essential value.[1]

Of course, Williams is talking in a personal way about himself to his cast. But Tennessee always understood his characters in terms of himself. Aspects of

Mark are obviously autobiographical, but Williams is also Miriam, the artist's wife, as well as the play's detached Bar-man. If we can separate the artist's personal life and look at the play freshly, another play, one far more universal, emerges. That is the salvation of all art that may start as personal therapy but occasionally ends as something that transcends the personal.

In the Bar of a Tokyo Hotel is a simple "still" play of oblique dialogue that nonetheless contains plot questions of some interest. In a way, the greatest drama of the play, Mark's confrontation with his art, takes place offstage. We are in an antechamber attendant on Mark's fate and await, as does his wife, the outcome of his solitary offstage battle. The play is a play of "waiting" that takes place in a near-empty bar in Tokyo. The Tokyo bar setting establishes a rootless, distant, hermetic world in which little occurs. There should be an unreal air-conditioned quality to the bar that, while "real," is also a kind of limbo, strange and foreign.

At rise of curtain a rather exotically dressed woman is sitting in a bar alone except for the Japanese Bar-man. She is "cruising" him. This aggressive and neurotic woman pursues the anonymous Bar-man, who rebuffs all advances with polite yet detached irony.

> Miriam: How many hours of sleep do you need a night?
>
> Bar-man: Thank you for being interested, but why are you interested?
>
> Miriam: I'm always interested. For me, only four hours of sleep are necessary.
>
> Bar-man: You waken in the dark?
>
> Miriam: Not usually, you see, I go to bed late.
>
> Bar-man: You mean excursions at night?
>
> Miriam: Yes, I'm restless at night. What's your name?
>
> Bar-man: I am the Bar-man.

Miriam's sexual quest leads nowhere. Describing herself as a woman of "vitality" ("I have enough and a little more than enough"), Miriam smokes a pipe of marijuana to ease her anxiousness and also to discomfort the Bar-man.

> Bar-man: You are smoking a pipe of marijuana.
>
> Miriam: A pipe of Panama Red.
>
> Bar-man: The pleasure of a guest is usually my pleasure, but will you do me the kindness?
>
> Miriam: I will put it out for you. Put it out means extinguish.
>
> Bar-man: Thank you.

The possibility of a diversionary trip is considered by Miriam who with self-irony imagines a brief lyrical vacation to Kyoto:

> Miriam: I've been told I shouldn't miss Kyoto. The person, the acquaintance, the man that mentioned Kyoto to me said that Kyoto is a place of lovely old pagodas and flowering trees in flower at this time of.
>
> Bar-man: Yes, go to Kyoto.
>
> Miriam: Yes, I'll go to Kyoto on an evening train. I love the clackety-clack of the wheels and the cool wind through the window. I hope there's a train leaving at.
>
> Bar-man: The concierge can give you the schedules.
>
> Miriam: I'll go this evening.
>
> Bar-man: It is possible to go more early.
>
> Miriam: I prefer an evening train. Kyoto. To absorb Kyoto wouldn't take me long. A woman of my vitality absorbs a place quickly. I could absorb a pagoda in a minute.

Of course, she won't go to Kyoto. Miriam has more than a little self-dislike mixed in with her boorishness. A futility of travel seems to have been reached long before. "I look. I absorb. I go on." She is proud but also unutterably bored, with herself as well as with all else. Sex is a possible diversion, but she is not likely to get "present action" out of the Bar-man. She decides to send a telegram to her husband Mark's art dealer, which reveals to the audience the crisis in her personal situation. Her husband, a famous painter, is undergoing a breakdown. The telegram demands help from the art dealer. She reads aloud: "Dear Leonard. I'm sorry to tell you that Mark has suffered a total collapse of the nervous system. Hmmm. Mental and physical, too. With most situations I am able to cope but not this one. I mean not alone. Mark is your most lucrative property. Please fly to Tokyo at once to protect it. Otherwise I will be forced to." Mark enters the bar. In attempting to bring a chair to Miriam's table, he "stumbles to his knees." Miriam confronts him with his condition but Mark says that tension from his new work is causing his nervous state. She insists that he needs to return for care in the United States. His "Aunt Grace" and Leonard, his art dealer, will care for him.

> Miriam: They'd meet you at the airport. They'd see your condition. It's their problem from there. I can't let it be mine.
>
> Mark: Miriam, you don't mean you want me to fly back alone?

Miriam wants to leave Mark, to continue alone, to be free of him. Mark leaves the bar for a toilet where he may be sick. Left alone again Miriam and the Bar-man confront each other over a flower vase.

Bar-man: I've been instructed to be sure that a vase containing a flower is on each table. The purple flower on the red table is. (He returns the vase and flower to the table.)

Miriam: Not wanted by a hotel guest in the bar. (She hands the Bar-man the vase and flower.)

This small struggle will be won by Miriam in the second scene of the play when she finally smashes the vase. In this first scene the Bar-man replaces the vase and wins a first round. In the world of the Tokyo bar such minimal actions become dramatic. When Mark returns Miriam says that she is having lunch with a friend to discuss "marital difficulties" and that gentlemen are not permitted to attend. Mark promises he will wash and dress well; he does not want to be left alone. But Miriam will not hear of it.

Miriam: Even if I weren't having lunch with Elaine I wouldn't with you today.

Mark: I have an immaculately clean summer suit.

Miriam: It would do nothing for your disequilibrium on the.

Mark: After a quick, cold shower, I.

Miriam: You don't hear what I say. It's useless talking to you.

Mark: The loss of balance comes from the.

Miriam: I said that she said that.

Mark: I can't be left alone now. I have a clean summer suit and after a cold shower, I.

Miriam: For God's sake, can't I be allowed some freedom of?

Mark: Yes, of course. It's only that.

Miriam: Tyrannical dependence.

Their scene climaxes with Mark accusing Miriam of infidelity, which she obliquely acknowledges. She has slipped out at night and returned near daybreak. "She offers the compliment to me of waiting until she thinks I'm asleep." In a rage Mark ends their interview bringing to crisis their difficulties but offering no resolution: "Go on, you cunt, to this, this lunch with a gentleman named Elaine. I'm sure you'll be on time . . . As for me, the man that you married is still a living man with no broken bones, and if later on I feel hungry, I'll have lunch alone, but not in my room with canvasses demanding what I can't give them yet, no, but as for flying back, we'll fly back together, or. (He seizes her shoulders. She staggers to her knees; he lifts her and flings her through the arch, out of the bar.)" This scene is worthy of August Strindberg at his most intense; a man and woman locked in a painful relationship only death can resolve. The Bar-man offers to help Mark back to his room but Mark wants to stay in the bar. His line ends the first scene:

> Mark (crossing to center table and sitting in a chair): I think that I will stay here till my wife returns from.

The second scene, called "Part II," occurs several days later. We are still in the bar. The Bar-man is "washing glasses in a cloud of steam." Miriam enters and continues an innuendo-filled badinage that the Bar-man continues to resist.

> Miriam: You're supposed to take the drinks to the tables.
>
> Bar-man: I know that I am, and I have told you that I am engaged and not faithless.

Leonard arrives. He has seen Mark and diplomatically avoids judging the artist's new work. He speaks with Miriam:

> Leonard: If I said that I've never seen so much torment expressed in canvasses before, your response would be "crock" I suppose.
>
> Miriam (hurling the flower vase at the bar): There. That's my response.

This violence is followed by Miriam's insistence that Mark is insane: "The man is mad. He is mad." She needs to separate herself from Mark. However, Leonard feels that Mark's instability is the result of Miriam's slow withdrawal from the painter. Soon Mark enters the bar with "bloodied bits of tissue paper scattered over his face." He has cut himself shaving. "His appearance is ravaged and fantastic; yet he has a childlike quality." They can no longer get any service in the bar. The Bar-man has withdrawn. Breathless, Mark complains that his vision has been affected. He speaks mysteriously about Michelangelo who painted "the creation of the creation of the creation." He recalls one single moment of happiness: "A crowded lively party was in progress and I burst out of the star-chamber, my studio, bare-assed as when I first added my cry of protest to the. Shambled dizzily to the. Opened the sliding-glass doors, noticed the presence of no one but my wife. Shouted to her, 'Goddamn but I think I've done a painting!' I never did more than *think* I'd done one, you see." Ultimately, Mark is most tortured by the suspicion that all his work is a "crock" (Miriam's favorite word). More than anything, he needs the faith of his own worth as an artist. Miriam's critical eye always denies him that approval. That is the source of their need for each other as well as their power over each other. He needs her approval and she needs him to need it. Leaving the bar once more to wash his face, Mark "staggers and falls to the floor." He is carried out and Leonard follows. Soon Leonard returns with the never quite stated news that Mark is dead.

> Leonard: The concierge is making the. Arrangements.
>
> Miriam: Released!
>
> Leonard: Yes, he's released from.
>
> Miriam: I meant that I am released.

Miriam refuses to pretend to cry. She refers to an aforementioned "circle of light" that is her defense against chaos. "The circle is narrow. And protective. We have to stay inside. It's our existence and our protection. The protection of our existence. It's our home if we have one." Leonard does not understand. Miriam tries to explain that Mark "made the mistake of deliberately moving out of the." She offers a tempered eulogy for Mark. "It would be strange but possible if later I discovered that I cared for him deeply in spite of. He thought that he could create his own circle of light." Released, yes, but also destroyed by Mark's death, Miriam no longer has any purpose to her life. This line ends the play:

> Miriam: I have no plans. I have nowhere to go. (With abrupt violence, she wrenches the bracelets from her arms and flings them to her feet. The stage darkens.)

Not grief, but fury at the joke of her existence, creates emotion more horrible than simple tears can express or release.

There are really only two characters of any substance in *Tokyo Hotel*. Miriam and Mark, two separate characters bound to each other (parasitically or symbiotically?), they are two poles of a relationship that might create one human being:

> Miriam: Are we two people, Mark, or are we—
>
> Mark (with the force of dread): Stop there! (She lifts her hands to her face but the words continue through it.)
>
> Miriam: Two sides of!
>
> Mark: Stop!
>
> Miriam: One! An artist inhabiting the body of a compulsive—
>
> Mark: Bitch!

One might see the play as having only *one* character, Miriam and Mark representing the divided parts of a single personality. Miriam is the sensual body but also critical intelligence. Mark is emotion but also artistic commitment and spirituality. Miriam is will; Mark is intuition. The play does exist on this symbolic level, yet the two of them are also fascinating and believable characters in their own right.

Perhaps the most multifaceted character in the play is Miriam. Her acid tongue and aggressive behavior brand her an "ugly American." At first look she is an unattractive character, insensitive to the delicacy of Japan and the Japanese. But we gradually see behind Miriam's mask. She is the veteran of many personal wars with Mark. Serving as the attendant to an artist has hardened and exhausted her.

> Miriam: I have clipped flowers outside your studio and heard you talk to your work as if you were talking to another person in the studio with you.
>
> Mark: No. To myself.
>
> Miriam: And I was clipping flowers. It's natural that I felt a little excluded, but I never spoke of it, did I?
>
> Mark: The work of a painter is lonely.
>
> Miriam: So is clipping flowers. I'm afraid that loneliness has become a worn-out thing to discuss.

In spite of Miriam's claims to vitality, she is spiritually exhausted. Long, futile struggles with lovers, with parts of oneself, leave one bitter—and it is bitterness and sadness that lie behind Miriam's sarcasm, her bitchery, her emptiness. She is ultimately to be pitied, perhaps more so than Mark. Mark has his art. Miriam waits for Mark.

Vulgar and insensitive, Miriam wants to appear sure of herself: "Where I'm headed is something I always know." She is actually far from sure of herself, and at the end of the play has no idea of where she is going. Her whole life is bound up with Mark's needs. She desperately wants to be free of that responsibility and yet is also paralyzed with fear of losing him. A kind of Hedda Gabler, Miriam is a fascinating combination of strength and weakness. Perhaps her most attractive feature is the candor that makes her so formidable. This Dragon Lady is awesomely honest. She can also be devastatingly funny. Her cat-and-mouse game with the Bar-man, full of self-irony, gives the play its few moments of humor.

Mark is simpler and at first more sympathetic. A victim of his vocation, Mark suffers the artist's agony of creation and self-doubt. He is totally absorbed in himself and his art. His commitment to art is religious and never to be doubted. On that altar he sacrifices himself and all others. His involvement with his art causes a selfishness that denies Miriam's needs.

Both roles are difficult—Miriam in its multifacetedness, Mark in its intensity. Both parts demand actors of the greatest abilities, genius actors. We must care about Miriam, understand her long journey; what living through another does to one. Her particular kind of incompleteness is savage. Mark is a suffering raw nerve on the verge of both possible collapse and possible enlightenment. We must not only observe his symptoms but understand the cause of his suffering. Notoriously few portraits of artists have been successful in drama, perhaps because the internal artistic process is devilishly difficult to dramatize. Williams describes Mark brilliantly, but the actor playing Mark must also participate in Williams' understanding.

The other characters in *Tokyo Hotel* are less fully drawn. Leonard is sympathetic but he functions primarily as a confidant. Out of his league, he is a businessman, a placater incapable of giving real help. He just does not participate in Mark and Miriam's world. The Bar-man offers comic observation and is a kind of Japanese stage manager. He is a God, an enigmatic Buddha who observes the bar's dramas with detachment and irony. There is a Hawaiian woman in the play who passes through the bar twice. With no lines, she is a little more than movement, color passing through. There is a world outside the bar; we just don't know much about it.

In the Bar of a Tokyo Hotel has the effect of an agonized scream. It is among the most despairing of all Williams' plays. Its general difficulty and relative inaccessibility may be a result of the special nature of its characters, who at first may seem unsympathetic. Their problems may seem rarefied, not experienced by a large audience. The problems of the artist are not universal, yet if looked at more sympathetically, the characters in *Tokyo Hotel* are universal in their divided human natures. Thematically the play is not only a portrait of an artist but of all as incomplete and unfinished. We need not be a king to care for a king in a play. The artist, like a king, is quite often an "overreacher" involved in universal tragic struggles. Their suitability as dramatic heroes is warranted by their specialness.

The separations of the self, its divisions and fragmentation, extend in all directions: to one's relationships, to one's work, to parts of one's self, and certainly to the infinite beyond. Everywhere is separateness. This is what the play is most about. It is perhaps the most difficult voyage of all. Connection. It doesn't seem possible in this play.

Tennessee Williams' conception of the artist is undeniably romantic; one might almost say religious. For Williams, creation is a subjective experience in which the artist does not consciously or intellectually create so much as he opens up the barriers to his subconscious in order to allow whatever images, sounds, colors, words that are there to emerge. In this way whatever emerges will be unique, special to the subconscious from which it comes. Control must eventually come, but there is always a battle between (contact with, permission of) freedom within and control without that creates art. Improvisation must meet form; however, if the art is to be fresh and new, improvisation must always threaten form. To many observers, a new phase in art may seem uncontrolled ravings. That is the hazard, the danger every artist faces. Nothing good comes from that which is not spontaneous. In Williams' view the artist may sacrifice himself to the process and a price is paid in personal health and comfort. The process may leave the artist exhausted, an insomniac, needful of drugs and alcohol, hungry for the forgetfulness of sex. At its most extreme the process may take the artist very near breakdown. This view of the artist, while self-dramatizing to some extent, is hardly without precedent or historic support. Plato saw the poet as a rhapsodist whose poems were produced in trance-like states that took him "out of his mind." Of course, in Plato this bred a kind of distrust. The artist as inspired madman has existed as long as the view of the artist as a craftsman creating order. Dionysus never lives very far from Apollo, and both are venerable inhabitants of the "house of art."

In the experience of the creation of his art, the artist may experience a disappearance between the subjective self and its creation: "I've understood the intimacy that should, that has to exist between the,—the painter and the—I! It. Now it turned to me, or I turned to it, no division between us at all anymore! The one-ness, the!"

The onrush of this experience must be handled carefully. It seems to have a will of its own. "Sometimes the interruption of work, especially in a new style, causes a, causes a—loss of momentum that's never recovered!" The process is as frightening as it is exhilarating: "I feel as if I were crossing the frontier of a country I have no permission to enter, this, this! I tell you, it *terrifies* me!" Eventually the artist must take control of his new inner world: "In the beginning, a new style of work can be stronger than you, but you learn to control it. It has to be controlled. You learn to control it." But if the work is to be good, chances of a loss of control must be encountered. One must come very close to disaster to be really good: "An artist has to lay his life on the line."

The greatest fear is that the work will be no good. Leonard, Mark's art dealer, expresses his view of new work: "The, uh, the very early, exploratory phase of a new technique is not for exhibition." This is a commercial and practical point of view. The question of exhibition is not a consideration of the artist during his work, indeed, it may be a totally inhibiting factor. The artist does what he does and hopes it may be understood and liked. The danger always exists that the further he gives permission to the subconscious, the more remote from any possible audience the artist may become.

One remarkable aspect of *Tokyo Hotel* is the coolness and control with which Williams observes the demonic artistic process. He seems to be forcing himself to be as detached as possible in describing Mark's battle with his offstage canvasses. Indeed, every time we see Mark, we see a man trying desperately to control himself. We hear the artistic process described by him but we never witness it. We see the ravages of Mark's battles in his falls, his incomplete sentences, his bloodied face. But never can the actual artistic battle be witnessed; it is a solitary drama of the soul, perhaps totally elusive to dramatic presentation. Miriam, in her detachment, greatly aids the play's cool tone. She is the icy antidote to Mark's suffering, strangely necessary to both Mark and the play. The setting of the bar also influences the play's detachment. Painful scenes are subsumed by public indifference and the Bar-man exerts an omnipotent coolness over all events in his domain.

In describing the solitary process of artistic creation Tennessee Williams uses extensive symbolism. No symbol in the play is more important or pervasive than the "circle of light" described by both Miriam and Mark. At the play's start Miriam is sitting in "a small area of intense light." This circle of light is a major motif and exerts not only mystery but perhaps some confusion. Like most good symbols it operates on several levels. It suggests divine grace, but more importantly the "circle of light" is symbolic of the limits of self, consciousness trapped inside itself. It is the "solitary confinement" of every individual. This is an old Williams' theme going back to his first full-length play, *Battle of Angels*. In that play the itinerant Val tells Myra, the lonely store lady, "We're all of us locked tight inside our own bodies. Sentenced—you might say—to solitary confinement inside our own skins." *In the Bar of a Tokyo Hotel* dramatizes this confinement, showing separateness not only between people but between parts of one's self. Integration of self may be as difficult to achieve as communication with another person or the outside world.

The play's theme of incompleteness is most totally embodied by *Tokyo Hotel* in Williams' use of language and dialogue. Certainly the most novel aspect of the play is the way Williams uses many incomplete sentences followed not with ellipses (. . .) but with a period. This idiosyncratic device is used throughout the play.

> Mark (slowly): I've always approached my work with a feeling of frightened timidity because the possibilities are.
>
> Miriam: You are making an effort to explain a mystery that I.
>
> Mark: The possibilities of a canvas that presents itself for.
>
> Miriam: The assault of a madman. You're destroying.
>
> Mark: I suppose I might say it's.

Miriam: Crock.

Mark: Adventure.

At first this technique may seem artificial, a self-conscious artistic device calling attention to itself. This is especially true when reading the play. But how
are these lines to be performed? Should the periods be stressed? Followed by
pauses? Should last words be down or up inflected to suggest ends or that
something is to follow? Should actors interrupt or dove-tail their lines? Williams does not tell us nor does he use pause indicators in the text in the way
that Beckett and Pinter do in this kind of dialogue.

There are several reasonable possibilities. First of all, in the play sentences
quite often end when completion is really unnecessary. In other words we get
what a character is saying without the character saying it.

> Mark (slowly): I've always approached my work with a feeling of fright-
> ened timidity because the possibilities are [infinite, limitless?].
>
> Miriam: You are making an effort to explain a mystery that I [do not un-
> derstand, do not want to understand?].
>
> Mark: The possibilities of a canvas that presents itself for [the artist, paint-
> ing?].
>
> Miriam: [She corrects his thought.] The assault of a madman. You're de-
> stroying [yourself, your art, me?].
>
> Mark: I suppose I might say it's. [?]
>
> Miriam: Crock. [She completes his sentence.]
>
> Mark: Adventure. [He corrects her and completes his sentence.]

There is enormous variety here. In some cases the character *knows* how
he would finish a line, but the line's outcome is almost too obvious to speak.
There is communication *fatigue*. The actor here would think the unfinished
part but either consciously or unconsciously decide not to verbalize the end.
Perhaps the character is aware on some level of the obviousness of what he
(she) is saying. Conventional language, conversation in life, lives most of the
time in cliché. (Remember Ionesco.) To be aware of this is to be disenchanted
with language, bored with words. What's the use?

Other times in this dialogue, the mind might simply stop in mid-sentence
as if the characters suddenly became aware of the absurdity of their words or
as if the mind suddenly confronted a blank emptiness that totally absorbed
the character. Sentences order reality in totally arbitrary ways. Perhaps these
characters see the abyss before the ends of their sentences.

Sometimes a sentence ends because a character does not know how to finish it. ("I suppose I might say it's.") Another character may try to enter the first character's world by finishing it for him ("Crock"). But they seldom get it right. Their entrance into the other's sentence is actually an act of aggression, not really meant as understanding or help. Sometimes a character may discover a way to finish his own previous thought ("Adventure"). These are climactic moments and usually the end of a "beat."

In rehearsal, the director and actors would specifically decide in each instance what is going on. This decisive specificity would take out a self-conscious artiness in the playing of the lines. The subtext needs to be very exact. The actor must not think of the lines as "stylistic" devices any more than the good Shakespearean actor calls attention to the fact that he is speaking iambic pentameter. The style must be felt and subsumed into the character's inner life.

Another point should be made about this dialogue. It is extremely musical. In the before-noted dialogue we have a contrapuntal duet ending in two climactic high notes ("Crock"; "Adventure"). Again in the playing this must not seem self-conscious. Each character is singing his own musical line, enormously rhythmical, seeking its own separate completion.

Williams' language in *In the Bar of a Tokyo Hotel* is stripped, lean, and minimal. He has curbed himself almost entirely of long sentences and multiple clauses. It is perhaps the least lyrical, least "Southern" speech in any of his plays.

Mark: Too soon after work.

Miriam: Much.

Mark: I was afraid. You'd.

Miriam: I wasn't waiting for you.

Mark: I'm glad I came down in time.

Miriam: Time for what?

Mark: To catch you.

Miriam: I can't be caught.

This might also be called "Zen dialogue," cryptic and communicative in what is absent. It also shows the rhythmic influence of Beckett and Pinter. Short repetitive phrases have replaced longer sentences.

Occasionally Williams uses longer, lyrically descriptive writing. These moments invariably describe a fantasy or remember some happy moment from the past.

Bar-man: Go to Kyoto. Go to Kyoto today.

Miriam: Oh, I'll go to Kyoto . . . Lovely old pagodas with clear pools to reflect them and the flowering trees in flower. Perhaps after that I'll absorb the Uzu Peninsula with you.

The vowel sounds in the above passage ("Go to Kyoto") exert a pacifying influence like some momentary narcotic. These moments do no last long in the play. Miriam returns with frustration to her more usually percussive voice: "Yes. Kon-nichi-Wa. That's the word for hello. Hong-Kong, Singapore, Bangkok—what a name for a city! Hmmm. I think I'll skip India where on the streets they drop dead of starvation. Misfortune doesn't attract me." Mark's one short passage of lyrical freedom occurs near the end of the play when he tells Leonard and Miriam of the day in which he felt he had really achieved something with his painting: "It was one of those diaphanous afternoons in August. You know that seem to drift skyward to some clearer space and then to another space even higher and clearer."

In keeping with Williams' asceticism in this play, there is almost no played music. The lean dialogue creates its own music, and there is little of Williams' traditional use of music or sound effects to create theatrical effects. The sole exception to this is a set of wind chimes, which occasionally sound throughout the drama: "From time to time a wind sweeps through the bar. Ornamented glass pendants—suspended from the arch of a door leading off-stage—chatter musically when the wind blows through. This is used as a way of underlining or punctuating." Quite often the wind chimes will play on the entrance or exit of a character. This is reminiscent of some Oriental theatrical device, an artificial and unrealistic formality. But generally no music reaches the confines of the bar. It is a quiet place.

Visual spectacle is likewise negligible in the play. Williams does not describe the room except to say that the bar itself is "of polished bamboo." Only two visual aspects of the production are specifically requested: Miriam's costume and her lighting. "A smartly and exotically dressed American woman is seated at a small round table in a small area of intense light. She is glossily handsome. She wears a hat crowned with blue-black cock feathers."

Miriam's theatrical costume (a sexy male bird) is a vivid image made more outstanding with the strong light. This, of course, is the symbolic circle of isolation that figures so dominantly in the play. The Bar-man is also separately lit in "a pin-spot of light." The two circles of light do not converge. Williams does not say when or if the lighting in the bar ever changes. Presumably, by the time Mark enters, the general light levels are higher in the bar. However, Williams wants, I think, an overall dimness to pervade the bar except for the intense light on Miriam's table where almost all the action of the play occurs. The table, in fact, is a painfully confining area. Paralysis as well as separation are aspects of this Tokyo bar. This is not a world of many objects, nor much action, music, or color. Occasional outbursts of violence break the atmosphere, but they are short and do not radically affect the general environment.

The critical reception of *In the Bar of a Tokyo Hotel* was far worse than merely bad. The play was an occasion for conjecture and analysis aimed at the playwright's personal life. If ever a play became confused with a dramatist's life, it was this one. The main target of criticism was Williams' life in the sixties. Granted, Williams had sometimes made a public spectacle of his life, appearing on television talk shows when he was not in the best of conditions. But the reviews were an almost universal funeral, an assumption that the artist's death in the play was a ironic prediction of Williams' own artistic death. Forgotten almost entirely was the fact that regardless of how personal the source material of a work art, the work is changed; artist and work are always separate. Ironically, in many ways, this is the subject of the play. Comment upon comment in the reviews mentioned the "personal" nature of the play.

> The play seems almost too personal and as a result too painful to be seen in the cold light of public scrutiny. Mr. Williams has, perhaps, never been over reluctant to show the world his wounds—but in this new play he seems to be doing nothing else.[2]

> The play is an unabashed confession. Having had it produced may serve the playwright as therapy. There are things an artist feels he *must* deliver himself of no matter how "tasteless" the display may appear to his friends and critics.[3]

> Like Eugene O'Neill before him, Tennessee Williams in his later period appears to be turning to more personal material. His most recent work, *In the Bar of a Tokyo Hotel*, seems concerned with expressing Williams's agony both at the specter of old age, waning sexual magnetism, and death.[4]

> What is most terrifying is the public shedding of the playwright's emotional skin. I am inclined to be tough about this—the self-indulgence is rampant, almost blubbering. But my heart isn't in it. Williams' problems are no secret and if they were, they aren't anymore.[5]

In the Bar of a Tokyo Hotel is far less autobiographical than *Long Day's Journey into Night* by Eugene O'Neill or *After the Fall* by Arthur Miller. After all, Williams was not (primarily) a painter. He was not "married." Mark's artistic concerns and his emotional health were not problems peculiar to Williams alone. The question of an artist's relationship to his work and his pain over the question of its ultimate value are surely problems for all serious artists with long careers. Mark, in part, is based upon the painters Mark Rothko and Jackson Pollock, both the victims of breakdowns and resulting deaths. The personal nature of a work of art does not by itself necessarily discredit that work of art. *Long Day's Journey into Night* is generally recognized as one of the very greatest American plays. What is more to the point is *what* is being shown. *In the Bar of a Tokyo Hotel* is not sexually autobiographical; it does not show drug addiction. The painter is not even an alcoholic, although several reviewers mistakenly claimed he was. The play shows a man out of control, at the point of emotional breakdown, perhaps madness. This is what is so painful—what is so unbearable. Loss of control may be the greatest of all sins and it will not be borne for long. Mark in the play is desperately trying to control himself, but he is not successful. A self-indulgent actor could go far in making the character even more unbearable. Some things cannot be watched for long. They are too threatening. The suggestion of loss of control, perhaps more than anything, makes an audience uncomfortable. But this is the drama Williams has chosen to show. Mark's loss of control in the play, I believe, became confused with the playwright's perceived lack of control over his play. The play is complex and mysterious but it is not uncontrolled. If anything the play's tone is cool and detached as it watches Mark's pain. It may well be that whatever was not understood or liked in the play was seen as the result of Williams' publicized lack of control in his own personal life. Mark's breakdown was seen by many as personal exhibitionism and self-pity by Williams. This was an easy assumption, far easier than dealing with the play on its own merits.

As usual Williams' perceived failure brought out the cleverness, nay, even the poetic talents of the critics. But then Williams had always stimulated critics to write their most colorful stuff.

> Tennessee Williams is lying on the sickbed of his formidable talent. Ever since *The Milk Train Doesn't Stop Here Anymore*, his work has become increasingly infirm—so grave that *In the Bar of a Tokyo Hotel* seems more deserving of a coroner's report than a review.[6]

> For some time now, any number of epigones have been turning out better imitation Tennessee Williams plays than Williams himself has written lately. As a result, Williams was forced to abandon self-imitation for self-parody and produce several, rather unsuccessful, Williams pastiches. But *In the Bar of a Tokyo Hotel* does not even qualify as poor parody: It makes *The Seven Descents of Myrtle* look, by comparison, like a triumphal ascent of Parnassus. It is a play by a man at the end of, not his talent (that was long ago), but his tether—a man around whom the last props of the dramatic edifice have crumbled, and who, in an impotent frenzy, stamps his feet on the few remaining bricks.[7]

Stefan Kanfer, in a *Life* magazine review entitled "White Dwarf's Tragic Fade-out," was perhaps the most cruel:

> The sky is full of lies. Many of the stars we see no longer exist: Their light still travels toward earth but they have been burned out for eons. Astronomers call the ones with a faint rusty glow Red Giants. Their fires grew huge just before death. The stars that merely shrank and faded are given a less flattering label: White Dwarves. Yet an astronomer would be derelict in his duty to history if he did not record their extinction.
>
> Tennessee Williams appears to be a White Dwarf. We are still receiving his messages, but it is now obvious that they come from a cinder.[8]

The "White Dwarf" metaphor is so personally insulting in its physical connotations of smallness and ugliness that one almost forgets the presumption of the critic in making himself an "astronomer" who has a scientific responsibility to tell the "truth," as if value judgments in art can ever have any objective proof in the same way that one might prove the death of a far distant star. How may a critic ever assume an artist to be dead? Or are we not to take this review seriously but see it only as "entertainment"? Kanfer, of course, goes beyond his judgment on *Tokyo Hotel* and calls all of Williams' earlier work into question with his metaphor. What appeared to be a "Red Giant" is really a "White Dwarf." "The sky is full of lies." Defenders of Williams are left sputtering in rage.

It was Kanfer's review that served as the source of *Life*'s advertisement in *The New York Times* boasting of *Life*'s toughness.[9] Tennessee's picture was blown up in the full-page ad with a boast from *Life* that it "predicts the demise of one of America's major playwrights." If it is true that audiences and critics cannot bear the vision of an out-of-control character on the stage, it is curious that they should respond to the possibility of such destruction of a human life with such enthusiasm. There is such exuberance in these negative reviews, such joyful bashing, that one must question the motives of the critics. The cruelty seems so excessive.

Some of the critics adopted an elegiac, sad tone in writing of *In the Bar of a Tokyo Hotel*:

> It is sad to have Tennessee Williams, to whom the American theater owes so much, offering us this inferior little drama.[10]

> The failure of *In the Bar of a Tokyo Hotel* is unimportant compared with our concern for its author. Tennessee Williams need never write another line to be assured of his supremacy as a playwright. And he can write as many unsuccessful works as he wishes. His quest for the creation of his own

circle of light may be painful, but we will rejoice in his determination to follow it.[11]

One must never forget that, despite his present esthetic humiliation, Tennessee Williams is a thoroughbred.[12]

Even Martin Gottfried, a consistently strident critic of Williams, found pity for the devastated playwright: "It is dreadful, of course, but worse, it is pitiable."[13]

Of course, many of these comments are more insulting in their sympathy than are the outright assaults. This became a tendency in many critics during the next decade. Accepting as axiomatic that Williams was "finished," reviewers often applauded him for earlier achievements as if to personally make up to the playwright for their inability to find value in his current work. This kind condescension must have been as enraging to the playwright as the more savage attacks. Perhaps more. Pity from critics may be the greatest insult of all.

A few critics actually dealt with the play. Walter Kerr felt the characters were abstractions rather than the flesh-and-blood portraits needed to make a compelling drama: "I had the feeling I was attending to theoretical people— . . . two articulate blanks kept gnawing at each other meanly . . . the secret knowledge we must all have [of the characters] was not present."[14] Williams' unfinished sentences came in for a good deal of mockery. Kerr in his Sunday piece in the *New York Times* wrote that Williams had "made a fetish of the unfinished sentence."[15] And John Simon did not miss the opportunity to satirize with panache this idiosyncratic technique: "Unfinished sentences . . . are the stock in trade of this play; there are scores of them lying around supposedly pregnant and tremulous with the burden of the unsaid. Actually a platitude with its tail chopped off is nothing more than a bleeding platitude."[16] One can see how this technique, if heavily underlined in performance for symbolic significance, could cause pretentious affectation, and this apparently is what occurred. Harold Clurman, an excellent observer of actors, significantly wrote of the actress playing Miriam: "Anne Meacham as his wife *italicizes* every line she utters."[17] The actors were unable to make their characters sufficiently sympathetic as a help to the play. Richard Watts' description of Miriam makes it clear that Anne Meacham probably played the surface bitchiness of the character without communicating the character's inner pain: "[Miriam is] a noisy demanding and neurotic woman with no visible redeeming qualities, she is waiting, apparently with eagerness, for the death of her ailing artist husband, and although she talks a lot, she has really no interesting confidences to offer us."[18] Similarly, Donald Madden's performance seems to have stressed Mark's hysteria rather than the character's attempts at control. Ross Wetzsteon's description of the performances makes painful parody of a performance that surely did not serve the play well. "'These visions, these visions. I've got to get them on canvas!' he cries out, his face in his hands, his jaw quivering with the last twinges of whimpering Romanticism."[19] Actually, Wetzsteon is not accurately quoting the play. What Mark actually says is "The images flash in my brain, and I have to get them on nailed-down canvas at once or they." However, one can imagine a performance of the line that might leave memories of a more melodramatic line. This may have been true of Madden's performance.

Alone of all the reviewers, Jack Kroll in *Newsweek* saw power in the play:

> Like a fighter who has taken too many roundhouse rights, Williams has plenty of scar tissue— . . . In this latest one he has allowed his real concerns to appear in stark and raw form . . . It is terror that activates the play—the terror of a mind that sees the stations of life as mere consolations for the inescapable reality of death, of dissolution, of the central betraying illusion that is woven into the fabric of life itself . . . the play itself rattles with melodrama; but in the age of the heartless *avant-garde*, it is good to see how Williams still has the touch, how he can cut situations and dialogue on biases and bevels, to produce a play rather than an ego-freakout . . . Perhaps the play is little more than charade illustrating the cry Williams gives to his painter, "An artist has to lay his life on the line!" but one can hear the echo of depth in it.[20]

More than in any other of Williams' plays, *Tokyo Hotel* shows no positive life force to counter the despair of the playwright's vision. Even in *The Gnädiges Fräulein*, the Fräulein "goes on." This play ends with death ("the black needle") and Miriam's last line, "I have no plans. I have nowhere to go." Impasse. Relationships offer no solace, not even momentarily, and one is irretrievably cut off not only from others but from parts of one's self. It is a totally bleak work in which the one possibly redeeming value (art) is shown as a possible "crock." The play is a scream of terror, made more horrible by the play's coolness. The scream occurs in a vacuum. This is not what anyone wants to believe about life. Perhaps critics shriveled as much from the play's vision as its execution. It is, after all, an unbearable vision of life.

The play's reception may in part also be understood as a reaction to its interest in the artist as its central concern. There is a common impatience with art that depicts the agony of the artist. Artists are privileged people in our society who choose their vocations. Envy of artists is a common phenomenon among nonartists. Dare one say critics? Few are interested in the pain of the artist. It is rather like hearing the woes of the wealthy. After all, artists choose what they want to do, have more freedom, and, occasionally, great adulation. So how bad can it be? Audiences have little patience with anguish that cannot be understood materially. Everyone can identify with Tom in *The Glass Menagerie*. He is a would-be artist, a worker in a shoe factory who must reenact

universal rites of passage in leaving his home. Mark is a financially successful and critically recognized artist. Few of us have experienced that kind of
success. In a democratic society, great success is suspicious and perhaps even
resented. Mark's misery is perhaps deserved. But at age fifty-eight, Mark's
agony was what Tennessee Williams most knew and understood. What else
could he write about?

The personal autobiographical implications of *Tokyo Hotel* are obvious but
the play can be understood without any reference to Tennessee Williams' life.
It is not necessary to know the details of Williams' life. They are temptingly
accessible as an explanation of the play, but they only give us superficial tabloid
understanding. It is true that Williams was hospitalized late in 1969 in St. Louis.
He was hospitalized for three months. But this fact alone does little to help us
understand the play. It may enable some to dismiss the play as the product of a
sick mind, but such dismissal shows little understanding of the complexity and
strengths of the human mind. One of man's greatest achievements is that even
in periods of great stress and personal pain, works of art can be created. In point
of fact *Tokyo Hotel* was written before his hospitalization. It premiered in May
of 1969 and Williams was hospitalized in September 1969.

Williams himself participated in dismissive self-criticism calling *Tokyo
Hotel* a play "from my stoned age." It is easy to understand this kind of remark
as a defensive avoidance, and Williams, like Mark, may have been haunted by
the possibility that his work was a "crock." But that does not mean the play is
incomprehensible. Indeed, I hope to have shown that it is all very understandable. Of course, in this case, understanding is most painful.

A few words should be said about the "theater of the absurd" and Tennessee Williams' relationship to it. Martin Esslin's influential book *The Theatre
of the Absurd*, published in 1961, had given its name to a large group of widely
different playwrights who first came to prominence in the mid-fifties. Its
members, as identified by Esslin, included Samuel Beckett, Eugene Ionesco,
Arthur Adamov, Jean Genet, Harold Pinter, Fernando Arabal, and Edward Albee. While recognizing their various differences, Esslin wrote that this group
had in common a basic philosophical attitude, but even more importantly they
were investigating new structural approaches to the drama as influenced by this
attitude. The philosophical attitude of the absurdists might broadly be termed
existentialist: "The hallmark of this attitude is its sense that the certitudes
and unshakable assumptions of former ages have been swept away, that they
have been discredited as cheap and somewhat childish illusions. The decline
of religious faith was masked until the end of the Second World War by the
substitute religions of faith in progress, materialism, and various totalitarian
fallacies. All this was shattered by the war."[21]

Disillusionment following World War II was experienced more totally in Europe than in the United States, which, while participating in World War II, did not experience war on its own ground. It was possible for the United States to emerge from World War II believing in itself as the "good guys," heroes in the progressive march of history in which things could only get better for all. It took the Vietnam War in the sixties to shake our fundamental belief in ourselves as heroic figures.

The term "absurd" is taken by Esslin from Albert Camus' essay *The Myth of Sisyphus*, which saw man's relationship to himself and to the world as one which makes no rational sense:

> Of whom and of what indeed can I say: "I know that." This heart within me I can feel, and I judge that it exists. There ends all my knowledge, and the rest is construction. For if I try to seize this self of which I feel sure, if I try to define and summarize it, it is nothing but water slipping through my fingers . . . This very heart which is mine will forever remain indefinable to me . . . Forever I shall be a stranger to myself . . . all the knowledge on earth will give me nothing to assure me that this world is mine.[22]

This divorce from the world, this schism within the self, creates an emotional reaction that is the feeling of absurdity. As Camus describes it, absurdity is more than an intellectual stance; it is the complete intellectual and emotional response of a man's whole being, a revolt and "nausea" that changes forever the way one looks at the world and the self. Absurdity is both unavoidable and unbearable to the rational man since the mind insists on truth but also demands order and unity from its experience. In a sense, man is always tortured by the split between his needs and the impossibility of their fulfillment. Stretched on the rack of an absurd universe, man whips himself with his need for order. It is a kind of cosmic joke.

As Esslin points out in his book, the absurdists go beyond philosophic discussion of the absurd. Camus and Sartre had done that in their plays, writing traditionally structured, clearly rational articulations of the absurd. While discussing history as nonprogressive, they maintained dramatic structures built upon progressive conceptions of time. Traditional dramatic structure with its beginnings, middles, and ends, its expositions, crises, and climaxes, suggests that reality has shape and order. Dramatic climaxes and resolutions mirror a reality with moments of clarifying cleansing action that resolve conflicts for better or worse. This model for dramatic structure is deeply satisfying to man's need for order; to the absurdist, however, it is a lie. A rationally ordered universe existing within a linear time structure is no longer believable. It may be pleasing to dream about but it is not true.

With nearly all of Aristotle's elements of drama, the absurdists posed new possibilities. Plot, causal in its implications, is replaced by situations. Characters are not necessarily consistent or understandable. Indeed quite often characters are mechanical or simplistic; other times they are unfathomably mysterious. Exposition does not explain character. Thought is seldom embodied in argument, and conclusions about the actions of the plays are firmly resisted. Summations are eschewed. The theater of the absurd has renounced arguing *about* the absurdity of the human condition; it merely *presents* it in concrete stage images. Language is suspect for the absurdist. Sometimes it becomes truncated; other times it is mocked. Self-consciously lyric poetry is usually avoided although occasional moments of lyric poetry sometimes create a nostalgia for "the old style." "Poetry *of* the theater" replaces "poetry *in* the theater." For the absurdists, spectacle is more than entertaining ephemera. It often embodies the very meaning of the play. To change the stage setting of a Beckett play is in some way to radically change the heart of Beckett's meaning since that meaning is embodied as much in the stage picture as it is in the play's words.

The plays of the absurd movement reached America mostly in the late fifties. *Waiting for Godot* premiered on Broadway in 1957. It was not well received. It was really off Broadway that the absurd movement made its greatest impact. Productions of Beckett, Genet, and Ionesco were among the most admired theater of the period by artists and intellectuals. Edward Albee was one of the few American writers to participate in the movement, and he was critically acclaimed with his off-Broadway productions of *The Zoo Story* and *The American Dream*. University and college theaters soon began producing absurdist plays and by the mid-sixties they were familiar to anyone seriously interested in theater.

Williams, of course, first made his mark in an earlier period. In a sense the theater of the absurd challenged the foundations of Williams' dramaturgy. The dramaturgy of the forties and early fifties in America was solidly realistic and Aristotelian. For Williams to adopt absurdist techniques in his writing would have been a major change in his fundamental aesthetic. Actually, it is extremely doubtful whether Williams ever consciously set out to become an absurdist. Temperamentally he was too romantic to feel at home with the theater of the absurd's cool European cynicism: "I can't really work in the theater of the absurd. I can work in fantasy—in romantic fantasy—and I can work in very far out plays. But I could never make a joke out of human existence."[23] Williams said this in 1965. Yet Williams was never the most articulate spokesman about his plays. He disliked literary conversations about style and genre. It is not clear what he meant by "far out" plays. He was an intuitive writer, and his intuition led him to explore techniques of the theater of the absurd quite uncalculatedly. It is doubtful that he ever would have used that label, but labels are mostly important to critics, seldom to artists. The fact is that in the plays of the sixties and later, Williams intuitively explored absurdist techniques: static or cyclical plots, situational dramas, "flat" characters, mysteriously symbolic characters, absurd dialogue, and fantastic "unreal" settings.

Perhaps no play of Williams is more absurd than *In the Bar of a Tokyo Hotel*. Despite its "bar" setting, the play really takes place in a kind of limbo. The Tokyo bar is anyplace far from home without purpose. The play's truncated language reveals fatigue with language, a distrust and recognition of its limitations. Most importantly, Williams refuses to answer questions of characterization. It would have been easy to make Miriam and Mark more sympathetic with long Williams' monologues about the past. How they got where they got. *A Streetcar Named Desire* gives Blanche most of her sympathy through this device. But Williams here, rather like Harold Pinter, refuses to give causal explanations. This is the situation. We must fill in the blanks. Nor does Williams really sum up the drama in Miriam's last speech about the "circle of light" ("it's imperative for us to stay inside of.") Miriam's last speech does not really give us a clear message, but rather adds to the play's mystery. Nor is Mark's death a carefully prepared climactic moment. It is instead an arbitrary event. It happens offstage and in no way allows a catharsis. Certainly Tennessee Williams was too compassionate a man to ever make a joke out of human existence. On the other hand he was always honest enough to recognize a good joke.

Several critics have seen Williams' supposed artistic demise as a result of his experiments with new forms. It is often suggested that Williams' sallies into new areas were not natural for him. Indeed there is the implication that Williams was in some way dishonest with himself, that he was trying to keep up with a younger generation. Martin Gottfried expressed this opinion in his negative review of *In the Bar of a Tokyo Hotel*: "In a foolish and self-destructive attempt to throw out his old style for a modern one, he turned away from what he could do so beautifully and began bouncing frantically from one style to another. With each successive play, control over materials slipped until he finally lost his greatest strength—language."[24] Williams never really lost his ability to write beautiful language. He controlled it for his particular purposes, which became different as he became older. Style changes as vision changes. One would have to have been totally insensitive not to realize in the 1960s that the world was radically changing, even for Americans. The Vietnam War with its nightly television horrors, the unsolved Kennedy assassinations, drug experimentation, the escalating threat of nuclear war—all these contributed to an obviously insecure world of little clarity and rationality. The world was expanding into a world of multiple realities. To write realistic plays of clear motivation, beautiful language, and resolving climaxes would have been not only unaware; it would have been supremely dishonest. The external chaos of the world wedded to an aging mind as it confronted death and eternity demanded a new style of writing in Williams. No great artist repeats himself stylistically. Picasso's blue period may have been more accessible and popular, but that did not stop him from entering cubism. Absurdism in the modern world is more than a literary movement; it has become the core of our reality. We can never be the same. Absurdism may be avoided, shunned, forgotten but it remains always there, ready to assert itself whether we like it or not.

NOTES

1. Quoted in Richard F. Leavitt, *The World of Tennessee Williams* (New York: G. P. Putnam & Sons, 1978), 146.

2. Clive Barnes, "'In the Bar of a Tokyo Hotel': Williams Play Explores Decay of an Artist," *New York Times*, May 12, 1969.

3. Harold Clurman, "Theatre," *Nation*, June 2, 1969.

4. Henry Hewes, "Tennessee's Quest," *Saturday Review of Literature*, May 31, 1969.

5. Martin Gottfried, "Theatre: *In the Bar of a Tokyo Hotel*," *Women's Wear Daily*, May 12, 1969.

6. T. E. Kalem, "Torpid Tennessee," *Time*, May 23, 1969.

7. John Simon, "The Eighth Descent of Tennessee," *New York*, May 26, 1969.

8. Stefan Kanfer, "White Dwarf's Tragic Fade-out," *Life*, June 13, 1969.

9. *Life* magazine advertisement, *New York Times*, June 10, 1969.

10. Richard Watts, *New York Post*, May 12, 1969.

11. Hewes, "Tennessee's Quest."

12. Kalem, "Torpid Tennessee."

13. Gottfried, "Theatre."

14. Walter Kerr, "The Facts Don't Add Up to Faces," *New York Times*, May 25, 1969.

15. Kerr, "The Facts Don't Add Up to Faces."

16. Simon, "The Eighth Descent of Tennessee."

17. Clurman, "Theatre."

18. Watts, *New York Post*.

19. Ross Wetzsteon, *Village Voice*, May 22, 1969.

20. Jack Kroll, *Newsweek*, May 26, 1969.

21. Martin Esslin, *The Theatre of the Absurd* (Garden City, NY: Anchor Books, 1961), xviii.

22. Albert Camus, *The Myth of Sisyphus* (New York: Vintage Books, 1955), 14–15.

23. Tennessee Williams, quoted in interview with John Gruen, *New York Herald Tribune*, May 2, 1965.

24. Gottfried, "Theatre."

In an Unknown State

$\mathcal{T}$he *Two-Character Play*, or *Out Cry* as it was called for several years, may be the most revised, multi-versioned play in the entire Tennessee Williams canon. It is certainly one of his most difficult plays, both difficult to understand and difficult to "like." This difficulty may be one of the reasons for its many rewrites. Williams always had a hard time accepting the fact that any of his plays might be "caviar to the general." Some democratic American strain in him always looked for acceptance of his most complex visions. Part of his self-justification seemed to reside in his need to make what he considered his deviant self understandable to some presumed "norm" in the population. All versions of the play, however, kept certain aspects that were sure to make the play unpopular with any widespread audience.

The play is unrealistic, has "special" characters, lacks a clear plot, has little humor, is lacking in Southern color, has no sex and no "external" violence, and is a despairing view, among other things, of the impossibility of knowledge. However, the play was obviously important to Williams and its many versions attest to his obsession with the play and his desire to finally "get it right."

The first mention of the play of which I am aware comes from an interview in the *New York Times* (October 26, 1966) announcing the drama as a one-act play to be performed with another one-act play, *I Can't Imagine Tomorrow*. In the interview Williams described the one-act play: "It concerns a brother and sister performing in a play that becomes confused with their lives. The action weaves back and forth between reality and non-reality."[1] This premise remained constant in all versions of the play as did nearly all the elements of the dramatic situation.

The play had its first production on December 12, 1967, in London, England, at the Hampstead Theatre Club. It featured Peter Wyngarde as Felice (the brother) and Mary Ure as Clare (the sister). The play was then published by New Directions in 1969 in a "special" edition at the Spiral Press. It was a beautifully printed book, 350 volumes all signed by the author. The American premiere occurred on July 8, 1971, at the Ivanhoe Theater in Chicago. Directed by George Keathley, it featured Donald Madden as Felice and Eileen Herlie as Clare. Williams changed the title to *Out Cry* for its American premiere.

Out Cry finally opened in New York on March 1, 1973, after playing "on the road" in Philadelphia, Washington, and Boston. This production was directed by the English director, Peter Glenville, and starred Michael York as Felice and Cara Duff-MacCormick as Clare. It received mostly poor press in New York and closed after ten performances. The play subsequently resurfaced in off- and off-off-Broadway productions during the seventies and early eighties. It was once more revised in 1976 as *The Two-Character Play* when it appeared in volume 5 of the New Directions series entitled *The Theatre of Tennessee Williams*.

There is no definitive edition of *The Two-Character Play/Out Cry*. I have read six versions of the manuscript in addition to the three published versions. (*Out Cry* was published after its Broadway run apparently somewhat changed from the Broadway script.) There were also productions after the last published version in 1975 when Williams continued to change and cut the play. I have no doubt that if he were still alive and attending rehearsals of another production of the play, he would continue to change the script. *The Two-Character Play* was never really "finished." This fact is entirely appropriate to the vision of the play(s) and may even be an expressive adjunct to its (their) existence. This last statement will become clearer with our discussion.

For the purposes of this chapter I will refer mainly to the published versions of 1969, 1973, and 1976. That should be enough to show the play's journey, the differences, problems, and strengths. One could write a close analysis of the textual changes in all the versions. It would offer a fascinating study of the playwright's mind over a ten-year period. But that would be an entire book and is not my aim here. However, it must be mentioned that Williams' continuous work over this period reveals a playwright dealing with practical problems of craft and not some "freaked out" artist who is out of control. The play is difficult, but the solutions Williams explores in its different versions are not irrational excursions into arbitrary paths.

The basic situation in all versions of the play remains the same. Felice and Clare, a brother-and-sister, actor-actress team have arrived at a theater to perform a play. The theater's staff has disappeared and the pair receive a telegram from their company, which has abandoned them, accusing the two of insanity. But the audience is arriving; the show must go on. Felice pressures Clare into a performance of a special play they have played many times before. It is entitled *The Two-Character Play* and only requires the two of them to perform it. Clare tries to escape but cannot. She cannot remember the lines. Felice tells her to improvise. She can't remember the end of the play. They must find it in their playing. The play-within-the-play also features a brother and sister named Felice and Clare. The actor and actress must play children (or adults playing children). The children are afraid to go out of their house. They are parentless. The father has killed the mother and shot himself so the children must go outside to obtain their life-sustaining provisions. They must convince Mr. Grossman at the market that the Acme Insurance Company is sending them a check that will pay their grocery bill. This is the only way they can survive. Actually the insurance company has refused payment because the father's death was a suicide, and it is questionable whether he qualifies for insurance. However, the "children" must lie in order to live. Playing on a stairless set surrounded by overgrown sunflowers, the brother and sister taunt each other with their fear of leaving the house as well as their fear of "confinement." The very word "confined" is a forbidden word that they nonetheless use. Finally, Felice pushes Clare out of the house. But she eventually gets back in. Felice declares that he will himself leave. But he also cannot bring himself to really leave. The two characters bring up the possibility of using their father's gun with "real" bullets in order to end their lives, but before that possibility is explored, the play-within-the-play ends. The audience has left the theater in disgust. The actor and actress are deserted and alone once more. They try to leave the theater but cannot. They have been locked in. What can they do? Felice suggests they perform *The Two-Character Play* for themselves. Their imaginations can create a warm sunny day in the cold, dark theater. They start the play. Felice rushes them to the end of the play when they must deal with the gun.

Endings of different versions are different but the above outline is true for every version of the play I have read. The basic situation is a brilliant conceit, an Escher image in which perceived reality changes before the eyes. A fascinating conundrum, it is easy to understand why Williams returned to the play again and again. The situation is like a recurring bad dream, full of possible interpretations yet always elusively inconclusive. Question follows question as we analyze the situation. We know that the "inside" play is frequently interrupted by the actors "breaking" character. But we never know for sure what is interruption or what is part of the play-within-the-play. How much of the play "within" is improvised? Have the characters really just arrived at a new theater? Is the telegram real? Was there ever a company? Is the setup with its theatrical situation "real" or is it too a play? Did the mother and father really die? The possibility exists that we are in a mad house and are watching the playacting (mad antics) of characters (people) who imagine themselves to be actors. Which play is the frame play? Did the events in the play-within-the-play really happen to the actor and actress? Is there a real gun? Real bullets? Can the actors really not get out of the theater? At every step in the play, in every beat, the truth of the situation may be questioned. This, of course, is the point. The dramatic situation is obviously a metaphor for reality as theater, a precarious reality that may not be distinguishable from madness, a reality about which we may know very little.

The dramatic metaphor is certainly intriguing but can a metaphor be a play extending over an evening of theater? What action may occur within the metaphor? Do we care about these real/unreal characters? Why should we care? Once recognized can the metaphor develop, keep our interest? Does it not create too much distance by the very nature of its questioning of its own reality?

The first and final published versions of the play resolve these problems in different ways while the second published version of *Out Cry* is less satisfying in its attempt to find conventional answers to this most unconventional of plays. But let us deal with each of these three versions, one at a time.

The 1969 published edition of *The Two-Character Play* is the most uncompromising in length and texture. Divided into three parts, it has no intermission, no escape for the audience. The three parts are entitled "Part One: Before the Performance," "Part Two: The Performance," and "Part Three: After the Performance." Of course, this neat division of performance and reality is compromised by the interruptions within "the performance" as well as our questioning of the ultimate reality of the conditions "before" and "after" the performance, but the division is a starting place for understanding, even if it will finally be destroyed as an anchor for reality.

The set "onstage" is specifically identified as a "Southern interior" surrounded by tall sunflowers. It will be brightly lit in contrast to the surrounding backstage areas, which are always present but lit in "a dusky violet lighting." One of the backstage props is a "statue of a giant, in papier-mâché, which has a distinctly ominous look." This unexplained presence will appear in every version of the play as will the sunflowers that surround the onstage setting. The effect must be something like a collage of realities, the magic of a theater with its multitudes of evocative props and unrelated images within which sits a realistic living room.

In this version Felice is specifically described as "youthful without being young." Alone, onstage at curtain, he speaks the first lines of a monologue that is destined for several incarnations in various versions: "To play with fear is to play with fire. No, worse, much worse than playing with fire. It's possible to play with fire and get away with it as a flame-swallower does. Yes, and fire has limits. It comes to a river or sea and there it stops, it comes to stone or bare earth that it can't leap across, and there is stopped, having nothing more to consume. But fear—" Felice is both writing and speaking his mind. The speech serves several purposes. It states a major subject of the play (fear) and also creates a metaphor comparing fear to fire. Felice's sensibility as a poet still in command of language is established. "To play," of course, also means "to act in the theater," and this first line immediately suggests the double nature of everything in the play. Felice continues with a description of his current condition: "Where did it begin, where, when? This feeling of confusion began when I can't think where." The subject changes back to fear, "the fierce little man with the drum inside the rib cage," and then moves on to the difficulty of love. Fear destroys love, too. "Oh, never catch hold of and cry out to a person you love or need as deeply as if you loved. 'Take care of me, I'm frightened, don't know the next step!'" The person so needed would not respond, would see the fear as "blackmail": "Yes, and then the next morning you have to make your own coffee, your own phone calls, and go alone to the doctor to say: 'I'm afraid I'm dying.'" What may at first seem like a rambling confused monologue is really an exegesis on the varieties and effects of fear. It is set up, rather clearly, as the topic of the play.

Clare calls from offstage. She is lost in the dark reaches of the backstage area calling out for Felice's help. Her frightened voice makes certain demands on Felice: "She's going to ask questions, questions that I can't answer, but I mustn't let her know how little I know till after the performance. A performance seems impossible but we've got to give one and its got to be good. What I have to do now is keep her from getting too panicky to give a good performance in this state theater of a state unknown, but she's not easy to fool. If I show any confusion about things here, she'll catch it and go to pieces." Felice's fear of Clare's panic is obviously also fear of his own panic. Clare, at her entrance, seems fairly relaxed, even capable of humor: "After last season's disasters we should have taken a rest instead of touring these primitive, faraway places . . . Do you know how I woke up? A squeaky noise and a flopping about of wings somewhere up toward the invisible ceiling. I said to myself: 'It's probably a bat,' but I wasn't scared, I wasn't even surprised. (They both laugh, sadly and lightly.)"

In this early version of the play, Clare has a sweetness to her, and Williams notes her "deceptive quality of youth." There is a shared kindness between the two. Her refrained question, "Where is everybody?" has a plaintive quality to it. She is also the more practical of the two. "I like to know what I'm playing and especially how a play ends." However, given their circumstances, Felice is the stronger, prompting Clare on to a performance she fears she cannot give. "Clare, you're going to play Clare." She is also afraid Felice will leave her, but he assures her, "Neither of us will ever abandon the other."

Felice steps before the curtain to announce the play. Clare threatens to leave for her dressing room. From the audience we hear "guttural-sounding speech with, above it, someone's mocking laugh." At this laughter, Clare "throws off her coat as if accepting a challenge." She will act tonight. "Do I enter first or do you?" Felice makes an announcement, "The performance commences."

The first part of the play sets up the characters' intentions and the dramatic action. They must play the play and they must not panic. They must keep control. The play is their way of coping. At one point Felice admonishes Clare not to look at the audience. "When you look at an audience before a performance, you play self-consciously, you don't get lost in the play." Getting "lost" in the play clearly is a salvation. Will they be able to do it?

"The Performance" ("Part Two") begins. Williams describes the tempo he wants. "The performance is feverishly erratic. Is it meant to be that way? Perhaps it is." In view of this kind of "high pitch," "Part One" should probably be played with as much control as possible. There is nothing in "Part One" to disallow that. Fear becomes panic in the play-within-the-play; the play seems to release what is controlled and subtextual in "Before the Performance." Williams also gives the actors an important direction at the start of "The Performance": "in spite of their wild playing, it should be apparent that Clare and Felice are gifted performers." In other words, like all good performers, Clare and Felice must create a believable reality, not "indicate" that they are "acting." This will make the play-within-the-play seem magical and believable in its own right.

The play begins with Clare on the telephone and the basic problem of the play-within-the-play is immediately stated. Clare asks Felice what they would do if the phone were dead. (It actually is as they will later discover.) He answers his own question, "We'd have to go out of the house . . . We'd have to dare to because we'd have to unless we preferred starvation." Soon the play-within-the-play is interrupted when Clare (the actress) sees the telegram from the deserting company on the set. Felice throws it off the set reassuring her, "There now, it never existed, it was just a moment of panic."

As the play-within-the-play continues it becomes clear that panic for the actors is mounting. It becomes impossible for the audience to tell what is an interruption and what is "in the play," or what is being newly improvised at this performance. Perhaps sections that seem improvised have always been "in." The better the acting, the more difficult it should be to tell where the two worlds separate and where they merge.

The performance becomes manic. A prop revolver is discussed. Lines become confused. Clare calls out repeatedly for "Line!" She declares: "Felice, this isn't a performance, this is an exhibition of panic." He replies: "Panic is the play's subject. And the style of the play." They sing a song. They shout out the windows for help. Together they try to leave they house but Clare runs back in saying, "I have a pain in my heart." Felice threatens to leave her. "When I go out of this house I'll never come back." He "exits" the house and walks down and speaks to the audience. "No, I can't leave her alone. I feel so exposed, so cold. And behind me I feel the house. It seems to be breathing a faint warm, breath on my back . . . Yes, I'm already defeated." Felice returns to the house. They stare at each other. He speaks: "The silence between us lasts much longer than it does in the play." A signal is given that Felice, as he says, is "about to speak a new line in *The Two-Character Play*." They discuss "father's revolver." Felice brings the revolver out "from under the sheet music on the piano top." He puts it on the table and begins to mime "the action of blowing soap bubbles." A lovely shared moment ends the play-within-the-play.

> Felice: Now I turn to my sister who has the face of an angel and say to her: "Look! Do you see?"
>
> Clare: Yes I do, it's lovely and it still hasn't broken.
>
> Felice: Sometimes we do still see the same things at the same time.

The "inside" play ends abruptly with no resolution. Lights are dimmed and Clare breaks the spell starting "Part Three" ("After the Performance"). "Well, that's that. Put on your coat Felice." The audience has walked out on the performance but Felice hasn't noticed. "I was lost in the play." Their panic seems to have subsided. Clare wants to leave the theater. Felice is enraged that the audience left. Clare tries subtly to make a point: "Felice, about the play, *The Two-Character Play*. I wonder sometimes if it isn't a little too personal, too special for most audiences." They will go to the hotel. But Felice returns from offstage with terrible news. The doors are locked. They can't get out of the theater! Clare shouts: "Out, out out! Human outcry!" but then she becomes strangely resolved. "I've always suspected that theatres are prisons for actors." Felice wants them to go back into the play. "If we can imagine summer, we can imagine more light." He takes the revolver off the table and puts it under a sofa pillow. They "go into the play." They rush to lines about the sunflowers:

> Clare: Felice, look out the window. There's a giant sunflower out there that's grown as tall as the house.

Felice: Oh, yes, I see it. Its colors so brilliant that it seems to be shouting!

Clare: Keep your eyes on it a minute, it's a sight to be seen.

The final stage direction has Clare lifting the pillow under which the revolver lies: "She draws an audible breath." The end. Lights are dimmed out.

No resolution, no death, just the possibility of a gun shot. Is this the way every performance ends? Is this the first time the actors have found themselves locked inside a theater? Doubtful. Perhaps this is the way the performance goes every night. Maybe they've never been outside this theater. How long has this been going on? How much longer will it go on? No answers.

The progression of the action in *The Two-Character Play* is the same as the movement of the characters' consciousness from controlled fear to panic. The panic is finally exorcised in the course of the play-within-the-play. The climax of the play-within-the-play is the characters' acceptance that they will never get out of the house, and this climax, this recognition, is repeated in the actors' realization that they will never leave the theater. The only possible solution—suicide—is not dramatized.

The shape and rhythm of the play has the form of classic tragedy that attempts through pity and fear (terror) to cause a catharsis in the audience. Whether or not this attempt succeeds depends largely upon the audience's ability to empathize with Felice and Clare. However, that is the playwright's intention in the play. Williams is attempting to write a tragedy within the limitless confines of an absurd vision. His characters must gain their stature from their artistic ambitions and the use of their art to achieve overreaching goals. As for so many modern characters, art replaces religion and politics as the object of the tragic character's ambition. The failure of art to supply satisfying answers is no less painful than the cruelty of the gods in classic tragedy.

More controversially, Williams' characters achieve stature through their neuroses. I believe he sees the neurotic, the deviant, as more sensitive to life's cruelty and therefore more deserving of our sympathy than ordinary characters. Needless to say, Williams' admiration for the artistic and the deviant is not a universally shared value, which in part accounts for the lack of acceptance many of his plays have experienced. Once, when asked to describe this play, Tennessee said, "It is a tragedy. It is about two people who have suffered a lot. But you could say there is a catharsis at the end."[2]

In this first version of the play, Felice and Clare serve as a double protagonist who work together to overcome their fate. Their destruction, their nemesis, their inability "to stay in the play," the audience's abandonment of them is as inexorable a fate as Oedipus' prophecy or Phaedra's falling in love with the wrong person. In a sense, the audience has taken the place of the gods and their rejection of Felice and Clare is not subject to appeal.

Another problem with the play as tragedy (besides the problem of audience empathy) is that there is no clear climax in which the catharsis may be effected, no shattering moment of external violence to incite terror and purge our emotions. *Waiting for Godot* has the same problem. Its pattern of cyclical waiting seems to have no outlet. Yet, I can imagine in a good production of *Godot* or *The Two-Character Play* a catharsis of sorts. It would come out of the characters' recognition and emotional contact with the impossible absurdity of the human situation. A cry of anguish at life's injustice would arise so spontaneously from deep inside the characters (and actors) that all in the audience would recognize the pain and be cleansed by its expression. The opportunities for these moments exist in these plays, and I believe were envisioned by their authors. Emotional pain coming from philosophical despair—a unification of mind and emotion that cries out in its ignorance, unbearably painful. "Out, out, human outcry!"

In the published 1973 version, *Out Cry* begins rather differently. Felice is once more onstage alone but the play begins more actively. The actor is trying to move the huge prop statue. Beginning in action, Felice calls out, "Is there someone, anyone, back here to help me move this please? I can't alone." More desperate and less contemplative, he expresses a certain hostility toward Clare.

> Felice: Act one, scene one. At rise of curtain I am discovered alone since she never enters on cue and in a condition that I can predict anymore.
>
> Clare (in a strangulated cry, at distance): Felice!
>
> Felice: I know what that cry means. She's rising reluctantly to the surface of consciousness.

Whose consciousness? Her own or that of Felice? The possibility that Clare is a part of Felice's "consciousness" is suggested.

Felice is more frantic in this version. A struggle between the siblings is set up. They are less allies, more combatants. The monologue is also longer. Felice comments ironically on his powers as a writer; he speaks directly to the audience: "Of course, you realize that I'm trying to catch you and hold you with an opening monologue that has to extend through several—rather—arbitrary transitions, only related in a general way to—" This new monologue confuses the start of the play in several important ways. Is the audience there from the beginning or are they coming in to see the play-within-the-play? Felice's manic mood starts the play on too high a plane of desperation. It also suggests an interpretation of the play's action (Clare as a part of Felice's consciousness) before we have accepted the first level of the play's reality: namely, that two actors have come to perform a play. In addition, the lines about fear are scattered throughout the monologue with less logic so that we do not really understand the thematic importance of fear as it will relate to the whole structure of the play. The transitions between thoughts are less logical, making Felice less controlled, his thoughts more confused, more unfinished. The length of the monologue also diminishes Clare's importance in the play. She is more an adjunct to Felice's consciousness. The play is more "the one and one-half character play."

When Clare finally enters, she, too, is in an excited mood: "I'm on fire with panic." The play will stay on this high level of emotion for the entire evening. The play-within-the-play progresses similarly as in all versions, but the hostility between Clare and Felice is more strongly emphasized, culminating in the two characters taunting each other with the forbidden word "confined."

> Clare: You shouldn't have spoken that word! "Confined!" That word is not in the—
>
> Felice: Oh. A prohibited word. When a word can't be used, when it's prohibited, its silence increases its size. It gets larger and larger till it's so enormous that no house can hold it.

The importance the characters give this word strongly suggests an interpretation of the play. The play's "secret" may be that Felice and Clare are inmates, "confined" in a mental institution. This possibility is further suggested later in the play when Clare reveals that Felice has previously been institutionalized.

> Clare: You've been obsessed with locked doors since your stay at State Haven!
>
> Felice: Yes, I have the advantage of having experienced, once, the comforts, the security, the humanizing influence of—
>
> Clare: Locked doors!
>
> Felice: At State Haven!

The addition of this information to the play, not in the first version, permits the audience to see the plays as the possible ravings of a lunatic. The problem with this interpretation, certainly a possibility, is that while it seems to give "answers," it also allows the audience to dismiss the play's vision as "madness." It lets the audience off the hook too easily, suggesting that the play is not relevant to "normal" people. What is not easily understood is too easily dismissed as insanity.

Clare's use of the word "confined" produces violence in Felice, which, rather arbitrarily, gives "Part One" a climax and intermission.

(He turns to face her, furiously. She smiles and forms the word "confined" with her lips; then she says it with a whisper. He snatches up a pillow.)

Clare: Confined, confined!

(He thrusts the pillow over her mouth holding her by the shoulder. She struggles as if suffocating. Suddenly she stops struggling and looks toward the audience.)

Clare: Felice, there is a gunman out there. A man with a gun pointed at me.

Felice: Clare! Please.

(Felice stares at her helplessly for a few moments, then turns to the audience and says:)

Felice: I am afraid that there will have to be an interval of about ten minutes while my sister recovers. You see, she is not at all well tonight.

(An Interval of Ten Minutes.)

One imagines the audience clambering out of their seats, up the aisles of the Lyceum Theatre (where *Out Cry* played in New York), out into the relative security of the Times Square area where a cigarette or drink could offer temporary relief from Williams' inferno vision of madness. How many came back for the second act? I don't know, but it is doubtful whether the play should be given an intermission. After all, there is no intermission to consciousness. I would also be afraid to let the audience out of the theater. Should they not be "confined" along with the actors?

The real madness, of course, is that the play ever played on Broadway at all. It could never be commercial. Giving the play an interval could only compromise the play's vision, not make the play more palatable. It's supposed to be unbearable.

"Part Two" of *Out Cry* starts at the continuing high pitch: "There is evidence of a struggle between them during the interval." The pace of the play increases. Williams, at one point, calls for "Lightning pace: the effect of a Mass recited in a church containing a time bomb about to explode." The play-within-the-play resolves the same way as the first version. Neither Clare nor Felice can leave the house. However, their acceptance of their fate includes a new element: "She takes several faltering steps toward him: then rushes into his extended arms like two lovers melting after a long separation." This rather melodramatic moment not only suggests the end to their hostility, but it implies blatant incestuous eroticism. Broadway will have its sex.

The final scene of *Out Cry* follows the main outline. Locked in the theater they go back "into the play" to the sound of "distant explosions." Once more they end looking at sunflowers, after Clare has tried to take the revolver from under the pillow. Felice seems to want her to shoot him.

> Felice: Hurry, it won't hold! (She crosses to him and touches his hand.)
>
> Clare: Magic is a habit—
>
> Felice: Magic is the habit of our existence.
>
> (The lights fade, and they accept its fading, as a death, somehow transcended.)

Lovely last line. What does it mean? That there is no escape except the magic of theater? Life itself is an act of magic? The final "transcendence" somehow seems an unwarranted if pleasant affirmation. An upbeat ending? Perhaps the commercial theater is once again asserting its need for affirmation. But nothing will really make Williams' torture of his audience less painful. *Out Cry* attempts to unify and create dramatic action through the movement in Felice and Clare's relationship from hostility to love—a reaffirmation of their union. But the movement is not totally convincing. It is a technique that will be more successful in the last published version of *The Two-Character Play.*

Out Cry is most marked by its divided attitude toward its audience. On one hand Williams is trying to make the play more accessible and dramatic, but at the same time he barely disguises his assault on the audience. The real attitude of *Out Cry* toward its audience is anger and contempt. Clare's description of the audience leaving the theater is perhaps prophetic of not only Broadway's abandonment of Williams but also the death of serious theater on Broadway.

> Clare: The house is completely empty.
>
> Felice: Walked? Out? All?
>
> Clare: Yes, yes, were you unconscious? One stood up down front with a grunt and the others all followed suit and shuffled out en masse! And I'm glad the torture is over!

Perhaps *Out Cry* is most distinguished by its desire to torture the audience at the same time it seeks their approval. Sad endeavor, almost an elegy for the theater.

In his *Memoirs* Williams clearly states his dissatisfaction with *Out Cry* on Broadway. "I considered *Out Cry* a major work and its misadventure on Broadway has not altered that personal estimate of it . . . My feelings toward the director became very bitter because of his autocratic behavior . . . At the interval on opening night at the Lyceum, I heard someone descending from the balcony with me observe that the play had been better in its Chicago tryout the year before, and I turned to the stranger and said, 'Thanks, I agree.'"[3]

Interestingly, after *The Two-Character Play* was revised and published in 1975, *Out Cry* was withdrawn from publication by New Directions Publishers. Williams clearly preferred the later version. However, it is fascinating to study *Out Cry* as a document giving evidence of the playwright's struggle to give dramatic shape to his difficult material. It is also evidence of the effect of Broadway commercialism on an uncommercial play.

The Broadway production of *Out Cry* starred two young actors, Michael York and Cara Duff-MacCormick. Presumably it was thought that the younger attractive performers would add commercial value to the production. However, central to the drama of *The Two-Character Play/Out Cry* is a sense that this brother and sister have been together a long time. All versions include this climactic speech by Clare: "Oh, what a long, long way we've travelled together, too long now for separation. Yes, all the way back to sunflowers and soap bubbles, and there's no turning back on the road even if the road's backward; and—"

In the last published version of the play (1975), Williams makes more specific his characterization of Felice and Clare as older actors. "He [Felice] has a quality of youth without being young." But it is Clare who changes most in her characterization. Several critics had called the characters indistinguishable from each other, and Williams is obviously addressing this "problem" in the new portrayal of Clare. "Her condition when she appears is 'stoned' and her grand theatre manner will alternate with something startlingly coarse . . . Both of these aspects, the grand and the vulgar, disappear entirely from the part of Clare in 'The Performance' when she will have a childlike simplicity, the pure and sad precociousness of a little girl." This characterization affords some theater-type humor and also permits more transition and progression in the character. The play-within-the-play becomes the device by which Clare recaptures her younger, purer self at the same rediscovering her love for Felice—and Felice for her. They begin at opposite poles: "We never hear the same thing at the same time anymore, *caro*." Felice is exhausted. "Oh Felice, you look so terribly tired!" He doesn't know if he can make it through the play, if he can remember the lines. In this version Clare is the stronger. Drugs and alcohol have made her less panicky, more numb. But she wants to know if the play has been cut. "I told you that I would not perform again in *The Two-Character Play* until you had cut it." No, he has not. She tells him she will cut as she goes along in the performance. They build to a fight with Felice screaming at her: "You castrating bitch, you drunk slut! . . . I can't bear the sight of your—eyes, they're eyes of an old demented whore! Lewd, degenerate, leering!" They whip themselves into a frenzy, getting up energy for the performance, which immediately commences with a subtext of performer hostility.

Williams keeps an interval after "Part One," once again ending with Felice trying to "suffocate" Clare, who is truly shocked. "They stare at each other silently for a moment. She has forgotten the next bit of business." The interval comes from a need to rest and repair the damage rather than an artificially induced "tag ending" for an act. Also the hostility is so clearly set up at the beginning of the performance that it evolves more naturally to a climax.

More information is given about the father and mother in the last published version. The father was an astrologer who gave "psychic reading and astrological predictions." He was also a ward at State Haven mental hospital. We see the children as repeating the lives of their parents. Clare relates more details of their mother's murder. Both Felice and Clare fondly remember a time when their father took them "to the sea coast." In an uncharacteristically lyric speech (for this play) Felice recalls the event: "Away from the Municipal, past the lighthouse tower and into the sand dunes where he tore off his suit and looked so much more elegant without it that we tore off ours, and he carried me into the water on his smooth gold shoulders and I learned to swim as if I'd always known how to." In this version we see how the past interacts with the present. It is the greatest source of the characters' confinement. Somehow they are forced to reenact the past as the source of their pain as well as their joy and love. Their inability to leave the house is their inability to leave the past. But as they recapture the past "in the play," they also recapture their love for each other.

The climax of the play after they have discovered their imprisonment within the theater is more dramatic than in any other version of the play. The gun is brought out and they both try to shoot the other. "She quickly retrieves the revolver from beneath the sofa, and resolutely aims it at Felice, holding the revolver at arm's length. There is a pause." She can't do it. Clare drops the gun "as if it had scorched her hand." Felice picks it up and aims it at Clare. "Felice tries very hard to pull the trigger: he cannot." He drops the revolver to the floor. "In both their faces is a tender admission of defeat. They reach out their hands to one another . . . As they slowly embrace, there is total dark in which: The Curtain Falls." This is a touching ending that permits no easy transcendence. However, an honest love does emerge in the characters' defeated togetherness. The performance has moved the characters closer together. It has become a vehicle of love and panic has been subsumed.

The first and third published versions of *The Two-Character Play* seem to me to be successful in different ways. In the first, the two characters act as one protagonist (two parts of the same consciousness). They confront both chaos and confinement acting out a therapeutic catharsis. In the third version, two old friends at odds find their love through the performance of the play. Both versions allow for natural affirmations in the face of the dying light. In the first version art is the answer, and in the last it is love.

Having compared three version of *The Two-Character Play/Out Cry*, shown their differences but also similarities, it may be possible to make some generalizations about this composite/hypothetical work. All versions operate with certain plot questions. Will Felice and Clare be able to perform the play? Once inside the performance will the brother and sister be able to leave the house? And finally, what can Felice and Clare do once they have discovered they are locked inside the theater? All of these questions are raised in all versions. The success of this potentially static play resides in a production's ability to make these questions seem important and real. However, the "plot" is largely vitiated by the unrealistic, improbable nature of the situation. Generally, audiences are only interested in what happens to characters in believable, probable situations. In order to become involved in a plot, audiences must forget they are watching a play and believe they are watching "real things happening to real people." The real "plot" in all versions of *The Two-Character Play* deals more with the characters' psychological problems. May panic be controlled and exorcised? Will Felice and Clare reconcile their differences and achieve unity of vision once again?

Audience acceptance of the situation is further complicated by the possibility that the two characters are really polarities within one consciousness and what we are really watching is a split personality trying to control its own hysteria as it seeks some form of integration. Williams never spells this out for us, but as in *In the Bar of a Tokyo Hotel*, we see two characters, mysteriously joined, who represent two aspects of one consciousness.

In the first published version, the two aspects represent traditional male and female roles. Felice is the reasoning, ordering artist while Clare represents emotion and practicality. Felice is the parent, Clare the child. Together they seek to exorcise panic.

In the final printed version the characters are further apart. They represent fatigue (Felice) and dissipation (Clare) as well as intellect and emotion. Time has taken its toll on them. They are older and more war torn. Also, they sound different and are more individualistic. The earlier Felice and Clare often sound alike, taking their tone from each other. On this symbolic level of interpretation, the real movement of the play is psychological, representing a kind of therapy. The plot questions of the play's performance, and the possibility that they may leave the house (or theater), are academic and unimportant. They must perform the play (no real choice) and they can never leave either the house or the theater until they die. Suicide *is* a possibility and it may be the only real question, present in the entire play's subtext, but only dramatized at the play's end. This question, left unresolved in the first version, is answered negatively in the final published version. They love each other too much to murder each other, or if we see the characters as one, to commit suicide.

One of the most fascinating aspects of *The Two-Character Play* is its discussion of theater and dramaturgy as it struggles throughout the various versions to find its form. In all versions Felice speaks to Clare before the performance about improvisation. "Tonight there'll have to be a lot of improvisation, but if we're both lost in the play, the bits of improvisation won't matter at all, in fact they make the play better." Improvisation, change, may stimulate more honest playing. In some ways, Williams' many changes in the play constitute a form of improvisation. His compulsion to rewrite evidences a restless mind struggling to give shape to his play at the same time recognizing there may be no possible unity for the "play." Clare resists Felice's love of improvisation: "I like to know what I'm playing and especially how a play ends." Clare represents that part of Williams' mind that seeks classical order in the drama. Felice is more romantic, excited by and open to experimentation. The question of "endings" is especially relevant to the difficult task of the dramatist. Endings summarize a play and dictate the way an audience is to feel about a play. They are literally the playwright's last thought in the play. Clare criticizes *The Two-Character Play* for having no ending. "Felice, is it possible that *The Two-Character Play* doesn't have an ending? . . . It never seems to end but just to stop, and it always seems to stop just short of something important when you suddenly say: 'The performance is over.'" Felice replies with an answer that describes his purpose in *The Two-Character Play* (and surely that of Williams as well): "It's possible for a play to have no ending in the usual sense of an ending, in order to make a point about nothing really ending." Clare refuses to let the question rest there: "Things do end, they actually have to." Presumably she means death. Williams' series of endings for his play show the playwright struggling with this question. Near the end of the play before entering the play-within-the-play again (finally?), Clare adds this insight to the discussion: "When a play works out inevitably, it works out well."

Williams' long rewrite history with *The Two-Character Play* reveals his search for that inevitability. The ending of the play changed frequently. (In one unpublished version the final moment used gun shots in the dark to signal the characters' deaths.) The last published version feels the most inevitable in its consideration of murder and suicide but also the rejection of both as a possible ending. Things will obviously go on. The actors will continue to play *The Two-Character Play* until death. But when that death occurs will not be their choice. Williams may have found his "inevitability" in the final published version.

The language in all versions of *The Two-Character Play/Out Cry* shows variety and beauty. If not as lyrical as some of his early writing, the poetry is chiseled and increasingly succinct. The language in the 1969 version is more baroque, using longer sentences with more imagery. The 1976 version is leaner, more cut, more considered. In the 1969 version Clare says,

> All I remember about this last trip—I must've had a fever—is that it would be light and then it would be dark and then it would be light or half light again and then dark again, and the country changed from prairies to mountains and then back again to prairies again and then back to mountains, and my watch froze to death, and I tell you honestly I don't have any idea or any suspicion of where we are now except we seem to be in a big ice box of a theatre somewhere that seems like nowhere.

In the final published version this long, breathless sentence is greatly simplified: "All I remember is that it would be light and then it would be dark and then it would be light and then dark again, and mountains turned to prairies and back to mountains, and I tell you honestly I don't have any idea or suspicion of where we are now." The youthful rush has become more measured, more straightforward. Williams has edited out all he doesn't need, and while the result may be less musical, it is surely more powerful.

There is no played offstage "music" indicated in the first published script of *The Two-Character Play* and very few suggestions for lighting effects. The production elements are far more minimal in comparison to most Williams plays. The Broadway production of *Out Cry* did use offstage music and symbolic images were projected on a backdrop. These elements apparently were meant to give a dream-like subjective feeling to the play. These effects are noted in the published 1973 version so Williams apparently approved of their use. The offstage music and projected images were abandoned in the 1976 published version. The only music comes from an onstage tape recorder that Felice turns on in certain lyric moments such as the description of their childhood memories of their father at the beach. The offstage music and projected images may have been considered too sentimental. By having Felice turn on a tape recorder in view of the audience, the sentiment is muted and becomes partly ironic.

The stage of the theater is the most important visual metaphor in all versions of the play. Williams makes this very clear in the set descriptions of the last published version: "About the stage enclosing this incomplete interior are scattered unassembled pieces of scenery for other plays than the play-within-the-play which will be 'performed.' Perhaps this exterior setting is the more important of the two. It must not only suggest the disordered images of a mind approaching collapse but also, correspondingly, the phantasmagoria of the nightmarish world that all of us live in at present, not just the subjective but the true world with all its dismaying shapes and shadows." The presence of the theater with its cluttered emptiness and potentiality for magic must dominate all the events of the play. Nor is this clutter only an expression of a disturbed mind. Williams insists that the play's "subjective" confusion is a true mirror of the "objective" world, an honest and sane image of an obviously irrational world, the natural response to uncontrollable chaos.

It would be endlessly lengthy and ultimately fruitless to quote many critics over the twenty-year life span of *The Two-Character Play/Out Cry*'s existence. The charges against the play can be imagined. Snippets of some of the criticisms follow:

> *Outcry* is static, unmoving and immovable, an inscribed tombstone of a play that goes quickly to its death.[4]

> No doubt Williams is giving vent here to the interaction of the two sides of his nature but to conduct one's unsuccessful psychoanalysis in public and call it theater is, to say the least, unfortunate.[5]

> Here the man who suffers and the mind which creates are no more separate than a drunk and his crying jag.[6]

> I spent the whole first act fearing abusive shouts from the audience to the play . . . and left at the intermission relieved that if such a possible and awful thing was to happen, at least I had not witnessed it.[7]

> None of the maundering, continuously self-interrupted dialogues . . . aroused my sympathy, much less my interest. I was bored to the point of indignation.[8]

> Lamentably, Williams has turned a theater into a prison for audiences.[9]

Over and over the complaints are the same. The play is too personal. It does not let the audience "in." They don't know how to take it, feel nothing, and are ultimately bored. But this response has by no means been universal. Perhaps the most enthusiastic notice the play ever received came from its first production in London when the playwright/drama critic Frank Marcus wrote in *London Magazine*: "It generates great tension, because it is written with an urgency, with a heartfelt compulsion, that transcends theater. Williams' plays have sometimes seemed self-consciously baroque, and, hence, decadent, but here the writing is muscular as well as poetic. I think *The Two-Character Play* is his masterpiece."[10] Some critics even found the play worthy of praise in its Broadway production:

Puzzling, maddening, wordy, inconclusive and finally disturbing.[11]

A beautiful, baffling play.[12]

A complete puzzle to me . . . I thought his enigma . . . was almost steadily interesting—a fascination of its own.[13]

It is an annoying, pretentious, slightly maudlin piece of work, but I found it impossible to dismiss it entirely; there is something haunting about it.[14]

Perhaps in one of his finest moments Clive Barnes reviewed the Broadway "scene" as well as the play: "Undoubtedly 'Outcry' is a very brave and very difficult play. It is not ordinary Broadway fare, and seen in the context of Broadway show business its situation and its poetry, its demands on ears and minds, may seem . . . pretentious. Yet this is an adventure into drama at which many, perhaps the majority, will scoff, but some will find stimulating. Minorities, needless to say, are not always wrong."[15]

The reviews quoted above mark an important change in the press' treatment of Williams. First there are no personally abusive reviews. Anger at Williams seems to have been replaced with sadness or, worse, embarrassment for him. Second, there have begun to be champions, who, in defending Williams, implicitly attack the commercial American theater. This trend will continue to grow until the late eighties, when the Broadway theater will have virtually disappeared as a producer of serious theater. This trend had already started in the sixties during which time Williams wrote his most difficult late works. The erosion of Broadway as a place for art did little to help Williams in his quixotic attempts to find success on the "great white way."

It *is* difficult to like *The Two-Character Play* or to identify with its characters. Some of the play's problems are better solved in the first and last published versions of the play than in the *Out Cry* Broadway script. But part of the problem must also be addressed in the direction, casting, and acting of the play. The play's director must work very carefully for optimal variety in tone and rhythm, not letting the play start on too hysterical a level. Humor must be found wherever possible but not forced where it does not exist. The play must find a natural progression to an organic climax. Fear to panic, climax, and final acceptance. Hostility to fury and then love. But without the right actors, nothing will work.

The actors should not be too young; they must be able to convince an audience that they have lived through a good deal. They must also project a certain timeless innocence that will make them attractive to an audience. They must be grand but not too elegant. They must be able to let their emotions rip, yet recover dignity. They must have a special chemistry with each other. The actors who play Felice and Clare must be very intelligent. They must understand the despair that comes from life's unanswered questions; they must be capable of asking the questions and capable of caring that there are no answers. There are few such actors yet the play will not work without them.

A word about Pirandello. Nearly every critic writing about *The Two-Character Play* has noted its thematic debt to the Italian playwright Luigi Pirandello whose overriding concern was the elusive relation of illusion and reality, the theater and life, madness and sanity. One might also mention the debt to Shakespeare. After all, it is Shakespeare who wrote about man as a "poor strutting player" destined to act on a "stage of fools" in a universe in which "all the world's a stage." *The Two-Character Play* has also been described as influenced by Samuel Beckett with his absurd universe in which two characters spend their lives in futile endeavors. Strindberg may also be recognized in the play's vision of male/female combatants, and on and on.

Many have seen these influences in Williams as a sign that he had somehow "lost contact with his roots," as proof of his waning talents, loss of originality. But Williams had always been influenced by other writers: Chekhov, Hart Crane, D. H. Lawrence, to name a few. His identity was partially forged by his openness to the art of his time. But no one could ever have mistaken Williams' plays for those of other writers. His voice, though metamorphosed, was always recognizable. No one would mistake *The Two-Character Play* for a play by Pirandello or Beckett. Seen another way, Williams' awareness of the most influential dramatists of the twentieth century is evidence of his awareness of his age and the unmistakable way in which those artists have changed our perceptions of reality.

Something must be said about madness and the biographical background of the play. It is tempting to read *The Two-Character Play* as a play about madness. The suggestion persists in all versions of the play that Felice and Clare are "insane." Tennessee himself often explained the play as a product of his own mental problems during the ten years of the play's creation: "I wrote it when I was approaching a mental breakdown and rewrote it after my alleged recovery . . . Not that I wasn't crazy. I was thoroughly freaked out. I think all artists are freaked out under the skin. Some of them appear to have a very normal facade. I've always been mad."[16] Tennessee liked to characterize himself as "mad," and he preferred personal biographical explanations of his plays to academic discussions of the plays' meanings. He actually loathed such discussions but rather enjoyed the personal drama of his own life.

"Madness" as an explanation of the play's content is dismissive and easy. I think it exists more as a description of society's opinion of Felice and Clare rather than a true description of the characters' state of mind. Fear of madness rather than madness motivates much of the play.

More than anything *The Two-Character Play* raises philosophical questions that account for the play's power. How do we know "the other"? Perhaps the other, our knowledge of the other, is only a projection of our own ego. Are Clare and Felice two characters but one person? Does Felice "create" Clare? How do we know what we know? Is there love? In what ways are all men "confined" in prison? In aloneness ("solitary confinement within our own skins")? Does the past confine us? Our parents? Time? History? Do our natures confine us? Our bodies? Our ignorance of our purpose? All are possible sources of our confinement.

In what ways is our life theater? Probably lies are necessary to our existence. We pretend we know what we are doing in order to get on with our lives, in order to bear our confinement. We act and our actions make us forget their futility in the face of death and our ignorance. We play many roles that have no relationship to each other. We act "as if" and in our imaginations create moment to moment realities. Few of them are lasting. The ephemerality of theater may be the truest experience of our lives.

Is *The Two-Character Play* a good play? I do not know. Possibly the question is meaningless. It *is* a haunting and disturbing play. Disturbing because it makes one question the acceptance of the theater of one's life. One cannot "like" the play. It is too frightening. But fear is the play's subject. Once I see that the questions the play raises are universal I begin to identify with the characters. I understand their pain. The play becomes less intellectual and more immediate. Catharsis becomes possible.

Most importantly *The Two-Character Play* is a complex and rich play. It may ultimately be that its density will allow it to outlast simpler works of art that seldom hold our interest past a single season on Broadway. Smash hits often disappear when they have exhausted their sensation. Complex works have ways of revealing themselves with time.

NOTES

1. Tennessee Williams, quoted in Sam Zolotow, "'The Rose Tatoo' to Continue Run,"*New York Times*, October 26, 1966.
2. Tennessee Williams.

3. Tennessee Williams, *Memoirs* (Garden City, NY: Double Day, 1975).

4. Kevin Kelly, *Boston Globe*, March 11, 1973.

5. John Simon, *New York*, March 1973.

6. T. E. Kalem, "The Crack-Up," *Time*, March 12, 1973.

7. Martin Gottfried, *Women's Wear Daily*, March 5, 1973.

8. Brendan Gill, "And Still Champion," *New Yorker*, March 10, 1973.

9. Jack Kroll, "Prisoner's Base," *Newsweek*, March 12, 1973.

10. Frank Marcus, "A Masterpiece," *London Magazine*, February 1968.

11. Douglas Watt, *New York Daily News*, March 2, 1973.

12. Hobe Morrison, *Variety*, March 7, 1973.

13. Richard Watts, *New York Post*, March 17, 1973.

14. Julius Novick, "Honest or Merely Disarming," *Village Voice*, March 8, 1973.

15. Clive Barnes, "Stage: A Static 'Out Cry,'" *New York Times*, March 2, 1973.

16. Tennessee Williams, quoted in *Courier-Journal and Times*, Louisville, KY, June 6, 1971.

· 6 ·

The Longest Distance

$\mathcal{A}$fter the failure of *Out Cry* on Broadway in 1973, Williams took a long voyage to the Orient on a ship called the *Oronza*. "My agent booked me onto this Cherry Blossom Cruise—it turned out to be a geriatric cruise. Everybody on it was 80 or over, and they had huge stabilizers to keep the ship from rocking . . . and yet these old people were breaking hips right and left. The doctor's office was always full of them. And three died before we hit Yokohama."[1] It was in this environment that Williams wrote the first draft of *Vieux Carré* and, with the play, took an even longer journey, for as Tom says in *The Glass Menagerie*, "time is the longest distance between two places."

The play's imaginative voyage took Williams back to New Orleans, 1938–1939, to the time when he was twenty-seven years old and a struggling writer. A "memory play," *Vieux Carré* may have been a consciously decided return to New Orleans in order to heal wounds from the *Out Cry* experience as well as an effort to restimulate his creative imagination with the past. As he had often done, Williams used an earlier short story as a starting place for the play. It is fascinating to read in the short story "Angel in the Alcove" the following lines written in 1943.

> New Orleans and the moon have always seemed to me to have an understanding between them, an intimacy of sisters grown old together, no longer needing more than a speechless look to communicate their feelings to each other. The lunar atmosphere of the city draws me back whenever the waves of energy which removed me to more vital towns have spent themselves and a time for recession is called for. Each time I have felt some rather profound psychic wound, a loss or failure, I have returned to this city. At such periods I would seem to belong there and nowhere else in the country.

So, on a boat bound for Yokohama, Williams imaginatively traveled back to New Orleans, as it existed in the late thirties, and began work on a play that is one of his most important late works, a great play, and a turning point in his career. It was a partial return to aspects of earlier forms and style, but Williams was now quite transformed by his experiments in the sixties and early seventies.

At the time of the first Broadway production of *Vieux Carré*, much was said about Williams' return to naturalism in the play as if the prodigal son had returned home from errant wanderings in the evil land of experimental theater. Martin Gottfried, a particularly vitriolic critic of Williams in the sixties revealed this attitude in his *New York Post* review. "It is good after so long a spell, to be able to follow a Williams narrative and note a Williams character. His effort, despite the tremendous success of his early plays, to change and grow was daring and courageous but I think, mistaken. Poetic naturalism is in Williams' blood."[2] How little Gottfried understands *Vieux Carré*, or for that matter the earlier plays of Williams. *Vieux Carré* is only partially naturalistic. Since it is a "memory play," all that the audience sees and hears exists only in the mind, consciousness, and imperfect recollection of the narrator. As such it is subjective interpretation and suspect as "truth." The same could be said of *The Glass Menagerie*, in which all exists in Tom Wingfield's memory. The relative truth of all in *The Glass Menagerie* as well as in *Vieux Carré* is easily forgotten, so strong is the appeal of naturalism to audiences.

The evolution of *Vieux Carré* is a fascinating story, revealing Williams in early drafts still exploring the Pirandellian experimentation of *The Two-Character Play* and using the theater as a metaphor for reality. The original drafts of *Vieux Carré* were less naturalistic than the Broadway or even the final published version. One cannot say that *Vieux Carré* was conceived as a decisive return to "poetic naturalism." The script evolved in that direction due to commercial as well as artistic considerations but the obviously uncommercial aspects of the earlier drafts still informed and influenced the final version of the play.

It would be wrong to produce *Vieux Carré* as naturalism and that may have been one of the problems with the original Broadway production. Also, what is "poetic naturalism"? Aren't "poetic" and "naturalism" opposite terms? "Poetry" assumes subjective expression while "naturalism" pretends objective reportage. Of course, "poetic realism" was a commonly used label for much of early Williams. However, the term is a misnomer. Williams' plays had always been far more "poetic" than they were "realistic."

Now this chapter must become more personal than previous chapters, for my experience of the early drafts of *Vieux Carré* is firsthand. It is, I believe, an untold story and one that would be helpful to a fuller understanding of the play. The published *Vieux Carré* (the *only* published version), is the one produced on the English stage in 1978. It was a major rewrite and an enormous improvement over the Broadway version. However, it was also a very different kind of play from the one originally envisioned by Williams in his first drafts. Those early drafts were more theatrically adventurous than either the Broadway or English versions. Williams retreated from that experimentation for various reasons but found in his final version an alternative solution that served his original intention in a less controversial, but highly successful, way. However, the vision of those early drafts could and should inform any good production of *Vieux Carré*, for the vision of life as theater (or dream) is essential to any successful production of the play.

Let me be more specific. In March of 1976, after I had directed *Suddenly Last Summer* for the Greene Street Theatre in Key West, Williams gave me (and the three producers of the theater) the first draft of *Vieux Carré* to read as a potential production for the theater. (This much is discussed in my introduction.) The play consisted of two parts. Part 1 was entitled "The Angel in the Alcove" after the short story of the same name and relating the same basic incidents. Part 2 was called "I Never Get Dressed till after Dark on Sundays" and was set in a different New Orleans apartment with totally different characters.

Part 1 was the memory play of a writer looking back at his younger self. Williams was very specific about the Writer's identity: "He is, of course, myself, at twenty-eight."[3] The Writer lives at 722 Toulouse Street, "the first place I stayed when I entered the Bohemian world that I was never to totally leave for the rest of my life."[4] In the course of the play the Writer encounters a homosexual tubercular painter as well as Mrs. Wire, a landlady as tenacious as her name. The Writer also remembers two destitute old crones living in the same boarding house who meet starvation with aristocratic manners. Essentially, the plot of the play in its first draft is slight, wandering, and anecdotal. It tells of the Writer's sexual "coming out" and narrates the eviction of the tubercular painter by Mrs. Wire. The first part seems to end with the Writer preparing to leave 722 Toulouse Street. The Writer had been comforted by an apparition, "an angel in the alcove" that resembles his dead grandmother, "Grand." But by the end of the act she no longer appears to him. "I had prepared for departure but I lingered for a last look at the Angel in the alcove. She—didn't appear. And I felt that this delicate old lady angel—my name for her was 'Grand'—had already abandoned the place . . . Angels warn you to leave a place by leaving it before you . . . I knew that if I ever was visited by her again, it would be in another time at a another place—which I still haven't reached . . . and wonder if I will ever." The Writer exits, but then from the audience comes a voice, "Hold curtain! Worklights, please!" It is a director's voice and we have been watching a dress rehearsal for a Broadway play. Everything witnessed up to this point has been a play-within-a-play.

Part 2, "I Never Get Dressed till after Dark on Sundays" begins in a "one-room slave quarters apartment in the Vieux Carré of New Orleans." Jane is trying to wake Tye from "an unnaturally deep sleep." She slaps his face with a towel, which finally rouses him. He reacts, "Some men would beat a chick up for less'n that, y'know." But then, the actor playing Tye "breaks character" and speaks to the Director and Playwright.

> Tye (in a cultivated voice): May I speak?
>
> Director: Is that a line in the play?
>
> Tye: It's a request to make a comment on a line in the play that always sticks in my craw, it's pointlessly cheap and offensive, it's not what I'd ever say to a girl of her class that I cared for.
>
> Playwright (aside to himself): Should never have southern gentlemen in my plays.

Not only are we watching a rehearsal, but the Playwright (a self-portrait of Williams at an older age) is present. The atmosphere is very tense. The actor playing Tye is antagonistic and offensive to the Playwright. He calls the Playwright "an arrogant old mother." The Director is a condescending Englishman who sarcastically sides with the actor.

> Director: Mr. Tysdale [the actor playing Tye], of course you are playing the boy in the play but you are not personally the boy and since the author's still living—
>
> Playwright (from the aisle): Thanks.
>
> Director: I'm afraid until the line is deleted by the author, it will have to be delivered by the actor.
>
> Playwright (at back of house): Hear, hear!
>
> Director: Regardless of our mutual distaste. (Then in a loud whisper.) Of course you might forget it opening night.

What emerges from this "inside" picture of a rehearsal is a bitchy, funny, bitter portrait of "show biz" in which nearly all the participants are at war. It is particularly jarring after the atmospheric environment of part 1 portraying New Orleans in the thirties.

One cannot help but remember that the director of Williams' previous Broadway play, *Out Cry*, had been Peter Glenville, an Englishman. The portrait of Mr. Leigh-Bowes (the director's name) as more interested in social engagements than in the play he is directing is a scathing portrait that might be interpreted as a therapeutic act of vengeance. Of course, no one ever saw this version on the stage.

Only the actress playing Jane is truly dedicated. She and the Playwright share a rapport. The rehearsal continues. The play-within-the-play reveals a sensual, psychologically sadomasochistic relationship between Jane, an educated young lady of artistic ambitions, and Tye, who is a barker for a French Quarter strip show.

Their affair is strained because of Tye's undependability, his late-night drunken returns. There is evidence on his arm that he has used hard drugs. Jane expresses a need to break away, but Tye dominates her sexually in a kind of rape.

In the next scene Tye explains his need for a "needle" the previous night with a description of a horrible murder of the striptease headliner, the Champagne Girl, by a mobster named Fat Charlie. The Champagne Girl threatened to leave Fat Charlie, who had his lupo dogs attack and kill the girl. Sickened, Jane wants Tye to leave. She tells him she is going to have a visitor, a wealthy Brazilian who is interested in "buying her." A climactic moment occurs when we are to hear the footsteps of the Brazilian. Once more "Tye" breaks character: "Hey isn't this bit [the Brazilian] cast and we preview Monday?" The producers want the stage manager, Hilary, to play the small part. But the Playwright uses the crisis to suggest an alternative solution. He asks them to "stay in character and describe the action." Tye reluctantly agrees. The actors describe an imagined dispelling of the invisible Brazilian. Later Tye is to smoke a marijuana cigarette. The actor complains of a lack of props. The Playwright asks the actor to "mime" the action and Tye quips, "All very Pirandello."

Tye (the character) initiates a serious conversation as he smokes his imaginary joint. "Jane, you're thinner, ain't you?" It is revealed that Jane is very ill, dying from blood cancer. "I don't remember the name of it, some—blood thing—progressive, rather fast at my age, and no cure—I think I had a remission when I met you." Truth told, no more to say, Tye gently tries to retreat from the scene: "Jane, it's after dark. I got to get dressed now, Babe." He must go to work but promises to return later with "pizza and a bottle of vino." Jane ends the play-within-the-play:

> Jane: How presumptuous of me, how—conceited of me to think that I, Jane, out of everybody living isn't scared of—can't even speak the word!
>
> Playwright: Downstage.
>
> (She moves quickly forward.)
>
> Jane: —Death.

The rehearsal is over. The Director dismisses the actors, "Now children, let's have a fifteen-minute breather at Sardis from the fetid atmosphere of the Old French Quarter."

The original draft of *Vieux Carré* had four alternate endings. In two the Playwright has the final line, "Please leave the worklight on till I start that stroll to the Picadilly Bar" and then the stage direction: "The worklight is immediately turned off."

In another, the Playwright, who has been quietly drinking from a pint bottle throughout the rehearsal, falls into the orchestra pit but then "climbs out of the pit" saying, "Old cats know how to fall." In another ending the Playwright, unhappy with the curtain line of his play, discusses the problem with Jane: "About that curtain, it may be effective, could be, but it's just a curtain and we can't settle for that. Can we, Jane . . . A play's not stopped by a curtain, I mean if it's a true thing, it continues after the curtain the way life does after sleep, it comes out of the night stop and goes into the next day. And maybe it goes on in the minds and hearts of the audience after, so—look."

Once more, we see Williams, as in *The Two-Character Play*, wrestling with the problem of "endings." Of course, more is carried over from *The Two-Character Play* than the issue of endings. Williams is still obsessed with metaphors of illusion and reality. The whole rehearsal setting of the two parts using stereotyped theater types seems so less "real" than the play within. Which *is* real?

Reading the first draft of *Vieux Carré* was an exciting experience. One felt present at a very early stage of creation. The several levels of reality and the fact that Williams was going back to his New Orleans roots at the same time made it obviously important in Williams' work. The rehearsal setting added complexity to the New Orleans memories, as if Williams wanted to go back to something from which he was irrevocably separated.

The black humor provided by the crone characters marked a return to the madcap comedy of *Slapstick Tragedy*, while the Southern setting returned Williams to his easily recognizable poetic voice as well as great theatrical potential. This was also Williams' first depiction of a homosexual assignation, an open fact, dramatized in actual scenes rather than being reported or discussed. In *Vieux Carré* the accusation of "veiled" homosexuality could not be leveled against the Playwright.

There exist in the two parts of *Vieux Carré* (in this first draft) two separate self-portraits: Williams as a young man and Williams as an older, successful, but battle-scarred playwright. The impulse for the play necessarily seemed to me the meeting of these two selves, the older man's search for his younger self, not just for youth but for the vulnerability of youth. The play did not quite say that yet. In this early draft the vision of the older Playwright as an abused member of the theatrical world verged on self-pity. But the humor of the situation seemed a mitigating ingredient. Also, this was only a first draft. However, to my mind the obligatory scene of this first draft should have been a "meeting" between the older Playwright and the young Writer. This scene was not in the play.

The Greene Street Theatre expressed enthusiasm for *Vieux Carré*, and it was agreed that they would produce it the following year. All of this, of course, was without any discussion with Tennessee's agent, Bill Barnes. It was really rather inconceivable that a small company in Key West would premiere a major Tennessee Williams play, but after seeing our production of *Suddenly Last Summer*, Tennessee had been quoted in the *New York Times* as saying, "I'll give them anything. I thought for Key West, after all those revolting productions, to see a vigorous, semi-professional production it's marvelous."[5]

The next summer I received from Tennessee a rewrite of *Vieux Carré*. Major changes had occurred. The most important change was that he had removed the older Playwright in part 2 as well as the Director and the Stage Manager. His substitutions were disappointing. The two plays were still framed by a rehearsal setting, but now a final dress rehearsal was taking place in extremely odd circumstances. "It is a winter day . . . The Director has been 'snowed in' at his home in, Nyack, New York. The PLAYWRIGHT, who is not mentioned by name and is as absent as the Director, is bedridden in his hotel with Hong Kong flu. The ACTORS have valiantly shown up—to be received by a decrepit OLD MAN who has been engaged in a sort of unspecified assistant capacity." In this draft, the rehearsal situation is set up right from the start. There is no surprise revelation at the end of part 1. The Old Man, named Ferguson, is a mysterious creation only cursorily explained—a kind of J. M. Barrie elderly elf full of theater lore and unlimited wisdom. An unconvincing convention that allows for the rehearsal setting and certain statements about the theater without the possibly embarrassing presence (to Williams) of the Playwright or Director, Ferguson is given to saying things like "Mr. Tysdale, forgive me for indulging in reminiscence, but—I knew some of the great ones, like Alice Brady. This you'll hardly believe but I—directed Miss Alice Brady in her last play." Tye is still difficult, but Jane is supportive of Ferguson and the rehearsal, even after Tye reveals to the company that Jane was named "co-respondent in Mrs. Leigh-Bowes divorce suit last year." At the end of the play the lines from the first draft about "curtains" are given to Ferguson. The two "New Orleans" plays are basically the same but with fewer rehearsal interruptions in part 2.

I received this rewritten draft of *Vieux Carré* in the summer of 1976 prior to my move to begin work at the University of Arizona. The draft was disappointing. Ferguson seemed a contrived character created to offset possible criticism of the personal autobiographical view of the obviously angry Playwright. My hope of progressive and unifying self-portraits of the Playwright in the two plays had to be discarded. I no longer saw any connection between the two plays except that they were set in New Orleans and framed by a rehearsal situation. What to do?

I was and am primarily a teacher/director who made (makes) his living in academia. I had directed professional productions in regional theaters, but I was by no means a seasoned professional theater director. Part of me wanted to write Williams my honest reaction to the rewrite but another part was afraid to do so. He might interpret my remarks to him as presumptuous, arrogant, or insensitive. Finally, I reasoned that if we were to work together I would have to be "honest" with him. I wrote Tennessee a long letter, fearfully dashing off my thoughts on the play. It was not carefully considered, well-written, nor particularly diplomatic, but I hoped Williams would respect my candor. I quote here, with some embarrassment, portions of this letter.

> I have just read rewrite of *Vieux Carré* and don't know what to make of it. The play originally seemed to me about the nature of reality and time. I like the complexities of its multilevels of reality. What in all of this is real? What can the audience or anyone hold onto? I think the answer in the original draft was in the Angel and whatever she represents. In a strange way, the most real, the most vital life that the play describes is the play within the first part (in Mrs. Wire's boarding house). Sometime in the past, even when things were most destitute, when the writer's pain was most acute, there was a blessed event—a visitation of an angel—THAT WAS REAL. It seems to me that the rest of the play is a search for that visitation again. It may not have been "real" (it may have been a scene within a play), but at the time it happened the young writer was CONNECTED and therefore it was real. Middle-aged, the writer, the narrator, looks back because he needs that visitation again. He NEEDS the inspiration and strength given by that visitation. The last vision we have (or had) of the artist was as the disillusioned alcoholic, spiritually destitute, older playwright, still trying, through his work to find some connection, even when all around him seems vanity (theatrical vanity *in vanitas*).

How I loved the word "real"! How obsessed with CAPITAL LETTERS, how like an undergraduate English major thrilled by his insights!

The above letter should be an object lesson to young directors dealing with fragile playwrights (and they all are). Be careful! Be careful of what you say and especially of what you write. My worst gaffe may have been to call Ferguson a "cliché death symbol." How did I ever see that? Cliché yes, and a poor substitute for Williams' self-portrait, but how did I get "death symbol" out of him?

On July 19, 1976, I received from Peter Pell (one of the three Greene Street Theatre producers) a letter enclosing a photocopy of another letter from Tennessee withdrawing *Vieux Carré* from the theater. Tennessee had also sent my letter to Peter. The following is an excerpt from Tennessee's letter:

> I enclose a letter from William Prosser which I found waiting for me here [the Elysee Hotel in New York]. I know you'll agree with me that this intellectualizing into extinction is no premise on which to approach a new work. I hope you will understand what he is talking about better than I did. I work from emotion only and could not possibly contend with the barrage of intellectualization that would attend the production. He's a lovely guy but I think if I am presented once more at the Greene Street Theatre it will have to be once more with a play which has already been established.

Peter Pell was furious, inviting me to "enjoy Tucson,—indefinitely." I was angry at myself, hurt, and above all despondent that I had not understood Williams' vulnerability. I was also afraid that my academic education had stunted me artistically. Perhaps I was too "intellectual." *But* I still felt I was right about the play.

Frantically, I called Tennessee after receiving Pell's letter. I apologized for any unintended rudeness. He was kind but admonished me, "Don't write me, baby. If you wanna tell me somethin', just call me on the telephone." Letters are dangerous. They do not have the advantage of a tone of voice which may be solicitous while saying "difficult" things.

Soon after this, *Vieux Carré* was announced as a Broadway production with Allan Arthur Seidelmann as director. Surely this production had been a possibility during the summer of 1976. Perhaps my letter gave Williams an out from a commitment he had unwisely and impetuously made out of his enthusiasm for *Suddenly Last Summer*.

The Broadway production of *Vieux Carré* opened at the St. James Theatre on May 11, 1977. It starred Sylvia Sidney as Mrs. Wire, Richard Alfieri as the Writer, Tom Aldredge as the Painter, Diane Kagan as Jane, and John William Reilly as Tye. It ran for ten performances after playing nearly a month in previews. Originally scheduled to tour out-of-town, prior to its Broadway opening, the large set was impossible to tour so the play stayed in New York. During late previews the entire framing of the play as a dress rehearsal was discarded, as was the character of Ferguson. When it opened the play was essentially two one-act plays, "The Angel in the Alcove" and "I Never Get Dressed till after Dark on Sundays." All that united the two plays was their New Orleans setting. Any Pirandellian complexity was totally removed.

The Sunday before the play opened Tennessee wrote of his "late" work in the *New York Times*. Perhaps responding to critics who were always admonishing him to write in a different way, Williams explained that his way of writing was necessary to him and not a matter of choice.

> Of course no one is more acutely aware than I that I am widely regarded as the ghost of a writer, a ghost still visible, excessively solid of flesh and perhaps too ambulatory, but a writer remembered mostly for works which were staged between 1944 and 1961.
>
> Once his critics, his audience, and the academic communities in which his work is studied have found what they consider a suitable term for the style of a playwright, it seems to be very difficult for them to concede him the privilege and necessity of turning to other ways. He truly must make these departures from his past ways, for just as his life has encountered a sudden deviation from its previous course, as if he'd encountered a sudden deviation from its previous course, as if he'd suddenly confronted a wall of fire, his work must follow him in the frantic efforts he makes to go past this flaming barrier.
>
> If his motive impulse in writing is the root-impulse of expressing the present conditions of his life, his world, his work must either be abandoned right there or it must take the dangerous course of reflecting his private panic, and cry it out to all who will listen and try to understand.
>
> I wonder how many of you will feel that I'm indulging in self-pity and how many of you will feel that I am simply trying to tell you how it is.[6]

Ironically, many of the critics reacting to *Vieux Carré* castigated Williams, this time not for new departures but for repeating himself without his former vigor. John Simon led the brigade with his customary facility for venom:

> A man who would steal and resteal from himself is the saddest of failures. Reprehensible as it may be to steal from others, it is at least enterprising: a sign of awareness that the outside world exists. Williams, however, as his part-time friend Gore Vidal has reminded us (though we hardly needed reminding), has not kept up with anything: books, events, currents of thought. He is manifestly content to live the rich, sensual life of success, spiced here and there with a little agonizing about failure, being unloved, and the approach of death. Whatever fund he had for attending to the life of people and ideas around him, he has long since dissipated. When he does write a play, it is perforce a rehash, or at the utmost a replay of youthful memories.[7]

After *The Two-Character Play/Out Cry*, Williams had been accused of stealing from Pirandello and Beckett. Many had thought he had veered from his natural roots. Now he is criticized for "rehash." One really wonders if the accusation of replay is a proper criticism of an artist. (Of course, I do not think

Vieux Carré is "rehash" or "replay"—especially as it was originally conceived and was ultimately realized.) The passage of time softens the impatience with artists who seem to be repeating themselves. We are more forgiving to artists we have not grown up with in our demand for variety. Perhaps critics, especially as consumer reporters, are too demanding of novelty, too hungry for this year's rage, too intolerant of yesterday's insights. Also, Gore Vidal notwithstanding, Williams did read widely and also followed current events. He had a large library and listened to the news every night. I often heard him express political opinions. He saw films and went to other writers' plays. He admired Pinter and Albee and Joe Orton. He was not an intellectual nor was he analytically critical. He did not have Gore Vidal's love of history, but it is untrue to say that he was unaware of his external world.

Nor can we quite leave Simon's review without noting several subtextual connotations that lurk under Simon's clever, cute, bitchy prose. Surely the portrait of Williams living "the rich, sensual life of success" contains Puritanism and envy. It suggests that anyone who is rich, sensual, and successful cannot have anything of value to say to us. Hedonism is a priori proof of worthlessness. Simon knows many of his readers will share that American prejudice as well as that American attraction. There is also the suggestion of dismissal of not only Williams but also Gore Vidal as a "part-time friend." That leering oxymoron (part-time friend) directed against another well-known homosexual writer further prejudices the reader against Williams. Gore Vidal, as part-time friend would presumably know how Williams spends his private time. Simon gets two "fags" with one stone.

John Simon was not alone is accusing Williams of self-imitation, though few others made that accusation an umbrella for so many other vices.

> A playwright has every right to imitate himself, I suppose, but what is shocking is the ineptitude, the inexactitude of the imitation.[8]

> The dialogue has some of the usual felicities of Williams' writing, though there are signs of a weakening in precision. There is a certain wretched honesty and boldness in several of the scenes but they also seem tired: the tune has too often been replayed.[9]

While many critics recognized the Williams voice, almost none questioned the difference in the voice except to see it as somehow weaker. It is *not* as strong, as virile, as in *Streetcar* or *Cat*. It is an older man's voice with the attendant merits and weaknesses of age. The voices in *Vieux Carré* must be heard as echoes, as if from some distance. The ghost-like, almost ethereal nature of much of the writing is a proper expression of its view of the past as insubstantial dream or remembered theater.

In his Sunday piece for the *New York Times,* Walter Kerr spoke of the distinctive beauty of the Williams voice and used the occasion to generalize about Williams' great stature in the American theater: "Tennessee Williams's voice is the most distinctively poetic, the most idiosyncratically moving, and at the same time the most firmly dramatic to have come the American theater's way—ever. No point in calling the man our best living playwright. He is our best playwright period and let qualifications go hang."[10] Kerr, however, criticized the overall structure of *Vieux Carré* as lacking "urgencies," comparing it to *The Glass Menagerie,* which, "for all its smoky aura of reminiscence, moved angrily, sorrowfully, grippingly": "Here [in *Vieux Carré*] there are no such energies at work. The tubercular painter will cough his life away and simply disappear from the play. The girl will be unable to penetrate the stupor of her man. The others will go their noisy or flighty rounds. Echoes have been recorded; no dynamic pattern has been arranged to house them."[11] What Walter Kerr senses in the Broadway version was its lack of any overall raison d'etre, caused by cutting the rehearsal framework and the underdeveloped role of the Writer as the unifying consciousness of the entire play. Late in the previews of *Vieux Carré,* Tennessee must have decided that the rehearsal setting and the character Ferguson did not work. But he had no time to organically discover another way of unifying the two parts. Broadway pressures dictated that the play open once it was in previews. The play needed a longer gestation period. But that is not possible in New York. It would take another production, another director, to permit an organic development of the material.

The problem of linking the two parts of *Vieux Carré* as well as the failure to find a solution in the Broadway production was noted by Brendan Gill in the *New Yorker:* "I'm sorry to report that the gesture is a shaky one, for Mr. Williams has chosen to write the play in the languidly discursive style of his recent experiments in autobiography. The two acts are like two chapters in a longish book: one follows the other and yet has no necessary connection with it."[12]

Williams' *Memoirs* had been published in 1975. In many ways *Memoirs* predicted *Vieux Carré* in both its frankness about homosexuality and in its non-linear sequence of chronology. Both in *Vieux Carré* and *Memoirs,* Tennessee was dealing with the problem of how one organizes memory. Traditionally, autobiographies start in the beginning ("I was born in . . .") and end with self-evaluation and the considerations of one's lifetime achievements. They posit self-knowledge. In his *Memoirs,* Williams started in the year of composition, 1973–1974, and then randomly darted back and forth between the present and the past. Truths were the truths at the day of composition. While many reviewers saw the organization of *Memoirs* as haphazard, others recognized in it an attempt to express the way memory really works. Jack Richardson, a fellow playwright, understood Williams' intent: "A raw display of a private life that has come to no pat conclusion about itself, a mixture of incongruous incidents and associations remembered in the way most of us remember our past when we are not coercing it into the shape of a finely wrought *Bildungsroman*. In such a remembrance, events make random appearances, moments that have long seemed of no consequence suddenly usurp the privileges of significance and thought turns doughty, sentimental, and somewhat self-pitying."[13]

But how to organize this concept of memory into a play that must occur within three hours' playing time? This intent, not achieved in the Broadway incarnation, *is* something new, hardly rehash, to create a memory play that remains dramatically interesting. *The Glass Menagerie* had been dramatically exciting but one usually forgets that it is memory while watching it. Amanda and Laura take on a reality apart from Tom's memories of them. We forget that they are *Tom's* Amanda and *Tom's* Laura. In *Vieux Carré* Williams wanted to do something more difficult: to present the past clearly as memory in a theatrical present and to continually remind the audience that they are watching memory.

The circumstances surrounding the Broadway production of *Vieux Carré* were such that it was apparently badly designed and poorly directed. It is a sad testament that a great playwright in his late career no longer had the clout or respect to demand the best. The producers had difficulty financing *Vieux Carré*. Williams was no longer prestigious or "bankable." No Elia Kazan or Jo Mielziner was available to Williams in the late seventies. Many reviewers noted with sadness the amateurish quality of the production: "What was potentially strongest in this chamber music play of time, place and memory has been botched by inept direction, wretched lighting, and dissonance of mood. In some future productions, the sense of Chekhovian stasis—lapsed yesterdays, foreclosed tomorrows—will be recaptured."[14]

One "future production" that better realized Williams' intention both in production and rewritten script occurred the next year in England, produced first by the Nottingham Playhouse, and later in the West End. Directed by Keith Hack, it starred Sylvia Miles as Mrs. Wire and played in London for over six months receiving a mostly favorable press. It is embarrassing and disgraceful that a great American playwright had to go to England to receive a good production. It is also sad that the English critics were more appreciative of Williams with fewer grinding axes, fewer scores to settle, fewer memories of past promise, less anger, and less disappointment.

The rewritten English version, which became the only published version, is one of the triumphs of Williams' late career. Undoubtedly the excellence of the finished play owes much to the unpressured rehearsal conditions in Nottingham as well as the intelligence and sensitivity of the director, Keith

Hack. It is significant that Williams dedicated the published version to Hack. But then, much of Williams best work had emerged, as is usually the case, in the rehearsal cauldron with good directors. Kazan and Clurman to be sure but in this instance Keith Hack. Unfortunately there weren't that many who had the opportunity.

Williams' solution to the structural problems of *Vieux Carré* was to combine the two plays into one whole, making the young Writer's developing consciousness the organizing unifier of the play. The young Writer confronts and learns from not only Nightingale and Mrs. Wire but also Jane and Tye. They are *all* memories as well as lessons in the education of the young man as an artist. The different stories, different worlds of the painter, Mrs. Wire, Jane, Tye, the "crones" alternate musically in counterpoint to each other, a pattern that may at first seem arbitrary but is actually well organized in thematic, musical, and psychological progression. The Writer switches from world to world in the way memory really works but with a subconscious drive toward illumination.

Williams is still very specific about the time and place of his memories. It is 1938–1939, and the setting is the boarding house at 722 Toulouse Street, "a poetic evocation of all the cheap rooming houses of the world." Jane and Tye now live here as well as Nightingale and the others. In order to simultaneously show several playing areas, doors and drapes denote the specific locations of the Writer's room with its alcove, the painter's cubicle, Tye and Jane's room, plus Mrs. Wire's kitchen. But Williams wants the designer to use his imagination in creating this remembered space: "a realistic setting is impossible."

At the start of the play the Writer announces the play as memory. We are to understand that all the characters are "unreal"; they exist only in recollection:

> Writer: Once this house was alive, it was occupied once. In my recollection
> it still is but by shadowy occupants like ghosts. Now they enter the lighter
> areas of my memory.

Scene 1 introduces all the major characters of the play, like some symphony or concerto grosso in which all the instruments are heard. Characters are also given chief concerns, identifying attributes, like musical motifs. Each is different. Each has a different problem, each his or her own voice. Mrs. Wire is obsessed with policing her tenants. The young Writer is unformed: "I have no plans for the future." Jane is marked by her disdain for her surroundings as well as her honesty. Nightingale's attempt to bring a "pick up" into the house brands him as an experienced homosexual and therefore an adversary of Mrs. Wire. When she denies admittance to Nightingale's "cousin," the painter spits at her, "Fuck off, you old witch." The two starving crones, Miss Carrie and

Mary Maude, are seen carrying "greasy, paper bags" containing food they have secured from the garbage pail. They pretend it is leftover food from an elegant restaurant. Tye, drunk, stumbles onto the scene carrying boxes of stolen merchandise. Tension between Tye and Jane is established at the end of the scene with Tye imploring Jane, "Come to bed" and Jane responding, "Don't lean on me." All of this is in the first scene.

If scene 1 is an introduction, *allegro ma non troppo*, the second scene is a *largo*, given its tone from the sound of rain, the coughing sounds of Nightingale, and the sounds of the young Writer alone crying in the night from his solitary cubicle, "a sound of dry and desperate sobbing which sounds as though nothing in the world could ever appease the wound from which it comes: loneliness, inborn and inbred, to the bone."

Hearing the young Writer's crying, the painter Nightingale enters the Writer's room to console him. The scene is a combination seduction and "sharing" scene. The Writer tells Nightingale he is remembering his dead grandmother but is embarrassed because "I was taught not to cry because it's . . . humiliating." Nightingale replies with affectionate humor: "You're a victim of conventional teaching which you'd better forget." The painter makes a direct sexual overture to the young man:

> Nightingale: You don't seem experienced yet . . . but, are you . . . excuse my blunt approach . . . but are you . . . ?
>
> (He completes the question by placing a shaky hand on the writer's crumpled, sheet-covered body.)
>
> Writer (in a stifled voice): Oh . . . I'm not sure I know . . . I . . .
>
> Nightingale: Ain't come out completely, as we put it?
>
> Writer: Completely, no, just one—experience.

The Writer relates his "one experience" to Nightingale, recounting meeting a young paratrooper at a party. The paratrooper took him into another room where they had sex. Quite ingenuous in response to Nightingale's question, "You did *him* or—," the Writer replies, "I told him that I . . . loved . . . him. I'd been drinking." But Nightingale understands, rejects this dismissal by drinking, and replies, "Love can happen like that for one night only." Nightingale presses for sexual contact, "This would help you . . . You are alone in the world and I am, too." Over the Writer's protests and to the sound of outside rain, the painter subdues the young Writer as the lights go out.

The scene resumes with the Writer, once more alone. In a monologue he describes the visitation of an apparition resembling his dead grandmother, an "angel in the alcove": "I wondered if she'd witnessed the encounter between the painter and me and what her attitude was toward such—perversions? Of longing? . . . I felt that she neither blamed nor approved the encounter. No. Wait. She seemed to lift one hand very, very slightly before my eyes closed with sleep. An almost invisible gesture of . . . forgiveness? through understanding? . . . before she dissolved into sleep." This "aria" with its ghostly imagery ends the scene on a mystical, "airy" note, appropriate to the second *largo* or *adagio* movement of a large symphony.

Scene 3 brings Jane and Tye more directly into the Writer's world, a scene in which Jane, out of loneliness, invites the Writer into her room, the room where Tye is sleeping. Tye wakes up and a conflict ensues as Tye baits the Writer with homophobic remarks: "Faggots, they all do something artistic all of them." The scene is further charged with the Writer's conflicting embarrassment, attraction to Tye, and desire to be Jane's friend. Tye finally evicts the Writer from his territory with a pointed story of a transvestite.

Jane confronts Tye with his unkindness. She needs friends—"Frankly, I am frantic with loneliness!"—but she also concedes that Tye gives her physical pleasure: "Of course you pleasure me, Tye . . . Silk on silk is lovely . . . regardless of the danger."

The scene ends with the sound of typing as if to remind us of the Writer's continual presence as the consciousness of the play. We are seeing both the source, process, and product of the Writer's art. The scene has been an *allegro* movement with mounting tension ending in brassy sexual heat, a contrast to the rainy submission of the previous scene.

Scene 4 presents Mrs. Wire's relationship with the Writer, threatening eviction but leading him into her employ as a means of paying his rent. Macabre comedy enters with the two "crones" responding to the smell of Mrs. Wire's gumbo. Miss Carrie and Mary Maude tell fantastic stories of wealthy relatives in the Garden District as they attempt to "panhandle" gumbo from the totally aware Mrs. Wire. Cruel humor comes from the contrast of the crones' pretensions with Mrs. Wire's honesty and earthiness. Mrs. Wire pretends to spit in the gumbo before serving some to the ladies: "I always spit in a pot of gumbo to give it a special flavor, like a boot black spits on a shoe."

The scene accelerates with Tye's drunken entrance. The Writer puts Tye to bed in the Writer's own room. He then continues his interview with Mrs. Wire and agrees to advertise a restaurant Mrs. Wire intends to open: "Meals for a quarter in the quarter." Nightingale sneaks into the Writer's room and starts to unzip the fly of the sleeping Tye. Tye awakes in a fury: "No goddamn faggot messes with me, never. For less'n a hundred dollars." Hearing the ruckus Jane rushes in and takes Tye back to their room. The Writer confronts Nightingale in anger. The scene has built with all its major characters (instruments) playing in tandem.

A long mime sequence ends the scene, a kind of choreographed dance, in which each character goes his own way, yet is simultaneously visible to the audience.

> The Writer enters his cubicle. Nightingale's face slowly turns to a mask of sorrow past expression. There is music. Nightingale puts out his cigarette and enters his cubicle.

> Jane undresses Tye. The Writer undresses. Nightingale sits on his cot. Tye and Jane begin to make love. Downstairs, Nursie [the black maid] mops the floor, singing to her self. The Writer moves slowly to his bed and places his hand on the warm sheets that Tye has left.

A kind of mimed quintet, the scene's ending is in marked contrast to its previous violence. The different characters in their own concerns, in their isolation, offer a moving contrapuntal commentary on each other.

Scene 5 is relatively short, an angry duet in which Nightingale once more seeks a liaison with the Writer. This time the Writer fiercely rejects the painter. "I don't want to catch your cold"—to which the rejected Nightingale replies, "And I don't want to catch your cold, which is a cold in the heart, that's a hell of a lot more fatal to a boy with literary pretension." Responding with a "cold rage he has never felt before," the Writer confronts Nightingale with his tuberculosis. "Don't call it a cold anymore or a touch of the flu!" Convulsively, Nightingale retreats as Mrs. Wire's voice adds to the scene's already high volume. "You watch out, I'll get the goods on you yet!" Nightingale ends the scene with an anguished cry, "The persecution continues."

The next scene (sixth movement), in marked contrast, takes its mood from a lighting note that asks for "daylight tinged with rain." A short quiet scene between Jane and the Writer in which the Writer brings a letter to Jane. The letter is from "Oschner's clinic" and, from Jane's response to its contents, it obviously contains bad news. The two share a drink together while Tye sleeps nearby. They discuss the young man's writing, and Jane is sympathetic to a rejection of one of his manuscripts. At the end of the scene the Writer asks directly:

> Writer: Jane, what was the letter, wasn't it about you?

> Jane: Let's just say it was a sort of a personal, signed rejection slip, too.—

The Writer leaves. Lights out on Jane as she is "fiercely tearing the letter to bits." The *adagio* scene ends in this eruption of denial.

The last scene of part 1 (scene 7) is a long tour de force that begins in a comic, *presto* mode. Mrs. Wire is boiling water to pour through the cracks in the floor in order to roust a party in a basement apartment she rents to "Mr. T. Hambleton Biggs." Mr. Biggs is a photographer described by the Writer as a "very effete man . . . who had somehow acquired a perfect Oxford accent in Baton Rouge, Louisiana." He is at present entertaining several male "models," and Mrs. Wire hopes to stop what she describes as an "orgy" by raining down boiling water on the party in progress.

Matters come to a climax when the photographer and models run out of the basement. Screams build. All inhabitants of the boarding house converge on the kitchen. Sirens, screams from the two crones, punctuating comments by Jane and Nightingale, Mrs. Wire's shouted accusations, the photographer's protests, and finally the police shouts and banging, all create a comic cadenza. All of the instruments (characters) get into it. The black maid, Nursie, hums a church hymn. Jane comments, "It's like a dream."

> Photographer: Right up there! Burns like this could disfigure me for, life!
>
> (A patrolman bangs at the door . . . Miss Carrie and Mary Maude have clung together. Their terrified whispers maintaining a low-pitched threnody to the shouting and banging. Now as the two patrolmen enter, their hysteria erupts in shrill screams. The screams are so intense that the patrolmen's attention is directed upon them.)
>
> Patrolman: Christ! Is this a fuckin' madhouse—

This wild scene, almost like the second-act climax of a Kaufman and Hart comedy, must be "conducted" by the director of the play. So totally is the effect musical and auditory, great care must be taken in rehearsal to insure that each voice remains clear and distinct while the overall scene builds to a crescendo.

After a blackout, a short scene follows in night court. Only the Writer is seen, lit by a spot light. We hear voices of both the Judge and Mrs. Wire. The Judge directly asks the Writer if Mrs. Wire poured "boiling water through the floor of her kitchen into the studio of Mr. T. Hamilton Biggs?" The Writer hesitantly replies "I, uh . . . think it's unlikely . . . a lady would do such a thing." Laughter is heard in the night court. Mrs. Wire is judged guilty and given a fine of fifty dollars.

The last section of this three-part scene, the coda, is a quiet scene in which Mrs. Wire asks the Writer to share a drink with her. Surprised, the Writer agrees, telling her that he has never seen her drink before. In a beautiful speech (aria) Mrs. Wire reveals her motive for drinking. It is a speech that also thematically sums up all we have seen in the first part of the play.

> Mrs. Wire: I only touch this bottle, which also belonged to the late Mr. Wire before he descended to hell between two crooked lawyers, I touch

it only when forced to by such a shocking experience as I had tonight, the discovery that I was completely alone in the world, a solitary ole woman cared for by no one. You know, I heard some doctor say on the radio that people die of loneliness, specially at my age. They do. Die of it, it kills 'em. Oh, that's not the cause that's put on the death warrant, but that the *true* cause. I tell you, there's so much loneliness in this house that you can hear it. Set still and you can hear: a sort of awful—soft groaning in the walls.

Writer: All I hear is rain on the roof.

Mrs. Wire: You're still too young to hear it, but I hear it and I feel it, too, like a ache in ev'ry bone of my body. It makes me want to scream, but I got to keep still. A landlady ain't permitted to scream. It would disturb the tenants. But sometime I will, I'll scream, I'll scream loud enough to bring the roof down on us all.

The Writer retreats to his cubicle leaving Mrs. Wire, once more, truly alone. Nightingale passes through on his way to his separate room. He is laughingly appreciative of Mrs. Wire's misfortunes in court. The scene and part 1 end with a shattering note.

(The light builds on Mrs. Wire, and she rises from the kitchen table and utters a piercing cry. Music appears.)

Nursie: Mizz Wire, what on earth is it? A bat?

Mrs. Wire: I just felt like screaming, and so I screamed! That's all. (The lights dim out.)

Part 2 (scene 8) accelerates the drama of the play with the possibility of two crises. The Writer meets a young drifter named Sky who invites him to travel west. Obviously attracted to both the idea and the drifter, the Writer weighs the possibility much to the concern of Mrs. Wire, who has become attached in a motherly way to the Writer.

The other crisis arises out of Mrs. Wire's insistent avowal that she will evict Nightingale. She considers him a "health threat" to the house: "I got that TB case spitting contagion wherever he goes, leaves a track of blood behind him like a chicken that's had its head chopped off."

Scene 9 continues the possibility of more departures. Jane tells Tye that she is leaving him. It is the "day of our parting." Contrapuntal to their scene is the sounds of tourists outside in the courtyard, part of the city's Azalea Festival, admitting visitors to old homes. "Edwina, Edwina, come see this dream of a little courtyard. Oh, my, yais, like a dream." This line, echoing Jane's earlier "like a dream," also reminds us of Nina's curtain line in the second act of Chekhov's *The Sea-Gull*. Tennessee often said *The Sea-Gull* was his favorite play. But more importantly, the musical refrain reminds us once more of the play as unreal memory, dream and memory being related to each other in their insubstantiality.

The scene accelerates into a rape when Tye refuses to accept Jane's decision for parting. Mrs. Wire adds her tensile voice to the situation: "You all quit that loud fornication in there!" Nursie enters with news that the sick Nightingale needs an ambulance. Hysterically, Mrs. Wire calls the hospital ending the scene with a note of panic: "The nightingale is violent with fever—"

Scene 10 is a tender scene between the dying Nightingale and the Writer who narrates that "for the first time, I returned his visits." The Writer helps Nightingale to put on make up and admires the painter's most precious possession left him by his "sainted mother": "a tortoise shell comb with a mother of pearl handle and her silver framed mirror." But it is really too late to give much help to Nightingale, who calls the Writer a "boy with soft skin and stone heart." They listen to the rain. A strain of music and "the angel enters from her dark passage" but Nightingale cannot see her. "I don't receive apparitions. They're only seen by the mad."

Leaving Nightingale alone, the Writer looks for the comforting presence of his grandmother's apparition in his alcove, but "her image was much fainter than it had ever been before." He starts to pack his things for departure but then begins to write. "I worked the longest I'd ever worked in my life, nearly all that Sunday. I wrote about Jane and Tye, I could hear them across the narrow hall. Writers are shameless spies."

Scene 11 begins with Jane sobbing on the bed and Tye "rolling a joint." Blues music, "bye-bye blues," sets the tone and continues the elegiac mood of the previous scene. Tye tells Jane the story of the Champagne Girl's murder using violent imagery, cruel percussive music: "Lupos are those big black dawgs that're used for attack. The man has three of 'em, and when he patrols his territory at night, they sit in the back seat of his Lincoln, set up there, mouths wide open on their dagger teeth and their black eyes rollin' like dice in a nigger crapshooter's hands. And night before last, Jesus! he let 'em into the Champagne Girl's apartment, and they well they ate her—Gnawed her tits off her ribs, gnawed her sweet little ass off."

Tye seeks consolation from Jane who is revolted by the story. He needs her but she tells him "the situation's turned impossible on us." She tells Tye she is expecting a Brazilian "customer." Furious, Tye refuses to leave. Footsteps are heard. Jane rushes out thinking it will be her visitor, but it is hospital interns entering with a stretcher to remove the dying Nightingale from the house.

The Writer reappears as narrator describing the actions and movements of Jane and Tye. We are seeing the scene reenacted as he describes it, remembers it, creates it.

Writer: It was getting dim in the room.

Tye: It's almost getting dark.

Writer: They didn't talk. He smoked his reefer. He ended his reefer. He looked at her steady in the room getting dark and said . . .

Tye: I see you clear.

Tye says that Jane has gotten "sort of skinny." He wants her to "level" with him. She tells him she is dying. "She stares at him; he averts his face. She moves around him to look at his face; he averts it again. She clasps it between her hands and compels him to look at her. He looks down." After this "choreographed" moment, Tye retreats, "Jane, it's getting dark and I better get dressed now—"

The last scene, (scene 12), follows immediately as Mrs. Wire enters. She imagines her son, Timmy, in a kind of sleepwalking "mad" scene, mistaking the Writer for her lost son. The Writer tries to disentangle himself from her embrace. Finally he is able to flee to his room where he "sinks onto his cot"; and "the angel of the alcove appears in the dusk." He shouts out to her, "Grand!" but she leaves him, and the Writer notes, "I guess angels warn you to leave a place by leaving before you."

We cut back to Jane and Tye's room. He is dressed and leaving for work. He promises to return, "We got love between us!" He leaves. The Writer, also starting to leave, hears Jane frantically crying out for her cat, "Beret!" He enters her room and seeing that she has fallen on the floor "lifts her from the floor." He tells her he is leaving, "a trip to the west coast with this young vagrant." But he feels she needs him to stay with her. They start to play chess. "Each of us abandoned to the other," as Jane says.

But soon "there is a distant sustained high note from Sky's clarinet." It is a signal to the Writer that he must leave. At first the Writer tries to ignore the sound knowing that Jane needs his company. But soon it can no longer be ignored. Jane, sensing the Writer's conflict, shouts down to the courtyard, "Your friend's coming right away, just picking up his luggage." The Writer leaves Jane. Nursie brings her Beret the cat, "visible, white, and fluffy as a piece of cloud." The Writer meets Mrs. Wire on the stairs. She warns him, "Be careful of the future." As he leaves the house all the play's characters emerge from the shadows "in dim spots of light." A dramatic sound effect climaxes the Writer's exit: "As he first draws the door open, he is forced back a few steps by a cacophony of sound: the waiting storm of his future—mechanical racking cries of pain and pleasure, snatches of song. It fades out. Again there is the urgent call of the clarinet. He crosses to the open door." The last speech of the play, spoken by the Writer, reminds us of the insubstantiality of all we have seen: voices remembered in a now empty house. "They're disappearing behind me. Going. People you've known in places do that: they go when you go. The earth seems to swallow them up, the walls absorb them like moisture, remain with you only as ghosts; their voices are echoes, fading but remembered."

Williams solved the former lack of unification in *Vieux Carré* in two basic ways: through musical structure and the growth of the Writer's consciousness. The play's characters alternate their "stories" in symphonic structure somewhat reminiscent of the way Anton Chekhov gives motifs to characters within a group protagonist. Williams alternates worlds and "tempi," using characters like instruments, illustrating common themes. In part 1 the play's dominant theme is loneliness, a fact of life shared by every character in the play. This theme is brilliantly illustrated in Mrs. Wire's conclusive "aria" on loneliness.

In part 2 the main theme becomes departure and death, or one might say just departures, since death is also a kind of departure. Death is everywhere in the play. Jane's imminent death echoes Nightingale's, and the whole play is dominated by the memory of Grand's death. Everyone leaves everyone: the Writer, but also Tye as well as the angel. This musical organization of various voices not only gives the play variety and links all its various parts, but it is a particularly appropriate representation of memory, music being a common evocation of past events. In hearing sounds, music, or voices, we often have emotional memories unattached to their situational causes. The play's gossamer fabric is well served by this musical structure.

Perhaps the most important organizing device adopted by Williams is using the young Writer as the clear consciousness of the play. Everything we see and hear is part of the developing sensibility of the young Tennessee Williams as remembered by the older artist. In a way, the play is about the education of an artist. It chronicles important moments in the development of the Writer's consciousness. An older writer (Williams in his sixties) remembers his younger self at critical point in his career, and one suspects the process of sensitizing reoccurs for the older artist as it occurs for the younger man for the first time.

What is the nature of this critical moment, and what is the nature of this growth? *Vieux Carré* is a coming-out play both sexually and artistically, and the two processes mirror each other both humanly and artistically. It is very important that the Writer change and develop in the course of the evening. At the beginning of the play we see him alone, frightened, vulnerable, crying in the night, submitting to a liaison with the tubercular painter out of loneliness. As the play continues the Writer becomes harder. Mrs. Wire points this out:

> Mrs. Wire: This I'll tell you, when you first come to my door I swear I seen and recognized a young gentleman in you shy shaky, but . . .

Writer: Panicky! Yes. Gentleman? My folks say so. I wonder. I've noticed I do have some troublesome little difficulties in my . . . negotiated truce with life. Oh, there's a price for things, that's something I've learned in the Vieux carré. For everything that you purchase in this marketplace, you pay out of here. (He thumps his chest.) And the cash, the stuff you use in your work can be overdrawn, depleted like a reservoir going dry in a long season of drought.

What is this young man talking about? Writer's block in so young a man? Yes, partly, but it is also the older Williams talking about what he considered a block in the mid 1970s. The experience of drying up. The sense of hardness that is a protection against vulnerability is seen in the play as part of the growth process the young writer has to experience and get through in order to grow. Nightingale notes this hardness in the young Writer:

Nightingale: You know, you're going to grow into a selfish, callous man. Returning no visits, reciprocating no caring . . .

Writer: Why do you predict that?

Nightingale: That little opacity on your left eye pupil could mean a thing like that happening to your heart.

Writer: You have to protect your heart.

Nightingale: With a shell of calcium? Would that improve your work?

Later, Nightingale accuses the Writer of having a "cold in the heart." The Writer needs to learn self-protection in order to survive. But that growing hardness may take its toll on the artist's work, his ability to feel and experience. What is the solution?

In the course of the play, the Writer experiences love and death, sexual awakening of his "true" (homosexual) nature, and finally learns that he and everyone in the world is "alone." Williams' first great memory play, *The Glass Menagerie*, is about the need to escape the family, a necessary initiation for a man and an artist. *Vieux Carré* is what the artist learns once he has escaped. There is no more family and he is on his own. People are lonely and sometimes they die of loneliness. The climactic moment of the play comes after he has escaped the mad dreamings of Mrs. Wire, who imagines him to be her lost son, Timmy. The Writer declares: "Mrs. Wire, I'm not your child. I am nobody's child. Was maybe, but not now. I've grown into a man, about to take his first step out of this waiting station into the world."

At this point, the Writer runs to his room and in his loneliness calls out for the protective love of his grandmother's apparition. She, too, has disappeared.

And the advice is clear: "I guess angels warn you to leave a place by leaving before you."

The knowledge is hard and painful. People suffer and die. What the Writer is left with, however, is not hardness or coldness. He travels through that stage to a tragic understanding of human aloneness and the inability of humans to save each other. He gains compassion for Nightingale, whom he finally "visits"; Mrs. Wire; and, most of all, the dying young Jane. He is open, vulnerable, in pain, and alone, a conscious human ready now to become an artist. He is ready to graduate, to leave, which is a "desperate undertaking."

The play has no real plot. Or rather it has many plots. Will Nightingale seduce the Writer? Will Jane leave Tye? Will Mrs. Wire evict the Writer? Will she evict Nightingale? Each character has a series of plot questions, but the plots do not hold us the way they do in a realistic play. All, as memory, has already happened; therefore the illusion of volition necessary to a good plot is missing. Events occur with dream inevitability and dream-like helplessness. The important "plot" is within the young Writer. Will he grow? Will he become what he wants to become? The answer is yes, but he pays a terrific price in knowledge and pain.

The play's characters, while not stereotypes, do have certain identifying signatures. As memory, they are not remembered as well-rounded characters with many facets. They have major colors that largely define them, but that, too, is the way we usually remember people. This is not to say that the characters do not surprise us. One of the master strokes of Williams' English rewrite is the dimensionality given to Mrs. Wire. In the earlier drafts Mrs. Wire is a harridan, a close copy of her strident characterization in an early one-act play entitled *The Lady of Larkspur Lotion*. Of course, Mrs. Wire is still unkind, but she also suffers loneliness and we see behind her metallic surface. Nor is Jane a victimized Southern belle. She is not Blanche DuBois nor even Stella. If anything she is unique among Williams' women as a consciously liberated young woman who uses Tye almost as much as he uses her. Nor is Tye an unredeemed insensitive stud. He does need Jane and she is attracted to something innocent about him that raises him above his job and background. It is a role that must be carefully cast, as much for vulnerability as attractive masculinity. Nightingale is a great creation, funny and pathetic, perhaps a vision to Williams of what he might (might have) become if he is not (were not) successful. The minor characters of Mary Maude, Miss Carrie, and even the photographer are Williams' eccentrics, members of his specially populated menagerie, affectionately treated for their bizarre theatricality.

The most underdeveloped character in the play is the young Writer. He hardly exists as a character at all. But after all, he *is* Williams and not observed from the outside by the playwright. Like all of us who experience ourselves as amorphous consciousness, the Writer thinks and feels but he is not defined. How could he be? He is in the act of discovering himself. He is a first-person observer like most first-person narrators in novels, able to see others and describe events but unable to see himself. The role is the most difficult to cast, for the character must be sensitive without being soft, capable of both fury and strength yet obviously an artist.

One thing more must be said about the characters in *Vieux Carré*. Of course, they *are* reminiscent of other Williams' creations, echoes of other characters: Stanley, Tom, Maggie, Maxine, and on and on. But these characters make up an expansive mosaic of the Williams work. *Vieux Carré* is a summation play containing within it both the promise of plays to come and the echo of plays remembered. Future characters are suggested and that, too, is part of the play's richness. Variety and change but also lifelong obsessions define most of us.

This chapter has been filled with examples of Williams' magnificent language and the play is an encyclopedia of his verbal powers. It is true that there are occasional lines that make one wince. Jane's line, "I've been betrayed by a sensual streak in my nature," is possibly embarrassing, but a good actress could deliver the line with irony and even get an intentional laugh. There are some anachronisms of period. Jane's feminist talk, for instance, sounds vaguely out of place. And Tennessee's newfound use of words like "prick" and "fuck," while inoffensive, does not evoke the period of the play's memories. Williams is beginning to get a little sloppy in the late plays, but like Picasso's late "messy" drawings, he is impatient with details, anxious to make the main points, aware that time is running out. After all, Shakespeare was full of anachronisms too. Neither playwright was primarily concerned with accurate external reports of events.

Music is used theatrically and extravagantly in *Vieux Carré*. After the claustrophobic spareness of *In the Bar of a Tokyo Hotel* and *The Two-Character Play*, one almost wallows in the expansive sensuality of *Vieux Carré*. Lighting, too, is used expressively, making possible the cinematic dissolves required by the play's memories. Costumes, also, must evoke the period with color and wit, all colors that express the poetic and sexual ambience that defines New Orleans, "desire, and early sorrow." The play requires great designers with poetic temperaments and could be ruined by unimaginative and insensitive artisans.

The English critics, in general, welcomed *Vieux Carré* to the British stage and their care, generosity, and affection for the American playwright is as obvious as the occasional mockery, superior disdain, and sometime pity of many of their American counterparts.

Do you know what it means to miss New Orleans? Tennessee Williams does and over the years the public have come to share his feelings. We have all wished him a return to the quality of *A Streetcar Named Desire* and if the quality, then why not the locale? *Vieux Carré* returns us to both: and there has hardly been a more satisfying evening in the West End since the revival of *Streetcar* at the same theatre.[15]

In *Vieux Carré* Tennessee Williams engages in every known form of excess and yet gets away with it—or nearly enough—in the way that only an old magician could.[16]

The play is about growing up, but growing up in a pretty idiosyncratic way. It is about discovering that the world consists of Tennessee Williams people and Tennessee Williams situations, the embryonic data for a dozen Tennessee Williams plays . . . His compassion for his walking wounded has tended to become a bit woozy and maudlin of late, so it is nice to be able to report that the chronological distance, combined with the distance he has programmed into the play's structure brings its rewards. For Williams, this is a hard-nosed, tough minded piece, full of sour laughter and measured pain, demanding a cool, acerbic production and getting it from director and designer at Nottingham.[17]

In Tennessee Williams' latest play there is a sense of the writer reaching a new period of maturity, and a feeling of newly found liberation. It is a very fine piece indeed.[18]

To be sure, there were some negative comments in some of the English reviews. Peter Jenkins, quoted previously, enjoyed the evening but also called the play a "sentimental extravaganza and bad taste farrago." Yet he also wrote that "it should not work but work it amazingly does, at least it did for me." It must also be stated that the New York critics' first viewing of the play was in a vastly inferior version in an (apparently) vastly inferior production.

The English rewrite of the play finally did play in New York in 1983 at the off-Broadway W.P.A. Theatre. Opening two months after Williams' death, it was generally well received though not so widely reviewed as the Broadway production had been. Clive Barnes, who had been one of the few critics to like the original play, now mixed no reservations in his praise. "I have no doubt about it, a major play and destined to be regarded as a play at least as important as *The Glass Menagerie* . . . To say that Williams overwrites is about as perceptive as saying the iceman cometh. They both do. *Vieux Carré* is not your normal organized play. It was ripped from the guts of a dying man trying to remember what ripping meant . . . *Vieux Carré* is once again alive and well. It is a tumultuous evening in the theater."[19] The W.P.A. production directed by Stephen Zuckerman sold out its relatively brief run. There was discussion of moving it to Broadway. It never happened.

Not all the critics were convinced. Accusations of "rehash" resurfaced. "The triptych-like balancing of *Vieux Carré*'s three stories doesn't solve all its problems, chief of which is the fact that the material looks like reworked scraps of situations familiar to us from other and stronger Williams plays . . . The structure of *Vieux Carré* is workable, the southern atmosphere and life are often beautifully evoked but the general effect the evening leaves is one of the artist's fatigue and wear."[20]

One wonders how two people can be so differently affected by the same play and same production. Obviously, it has a great deal to do with the critic's agreement with the artist's vision, his receptivity to the point of view. Feingold is sympathetic to political theater, a lover of Brecht. Barnes is older, a balletomane (and another Englishman), someone who often compares theater to other art forms. The musical, choreographed nature of *Vieux Carré* would attract Barnes. Also, Barnes is closer to Williams' age; Feingold is a younger Turk, bred in the testy competitiveness of New York, suspicious of emotion and sentiment. Critical judgments often tell us more about critics than they do about the works discussed.

What can be said in summary? *Vieux Carré* is a major milestone in the Williams' canon. Not only is it a great play, qualifications be damned, it records the moment when Williams' vision turned from the anger and despair reflected in the previous plays to a more compassionate and forgiving view of the world. Compassion does not mean moral approval of cruelty. The play records that as well. Rather compassion here means understanding and "forgiveness through understanding." In the same way that the Angel in the play is perceived as forgiving the homosexuality of the young Writer, Williams forgives life and maybe himself as well.

One would like to have seen how *Vieux Carré* would have developed if Williams had continued to develop the play as a play "in rehearsal." One would also like to have seen how he might have developed the first draft's vision of the Playwright as an older man. Commercial considerations as well as fear of accusations of "self-pity" may have influenced Williams' abandonment of these ideas, but it is also possible that rediscovery of his past reawakened more tender feelings; love for his characters, which made the bitchery in the theater setting and the alienation of the Pirandellian structure irrelevant to his vision. His view is that the world is still ephemeral, but it is not unkind. This change is a great triumph in Williams' career and not unlike Shakespeare's view in his late plays, away from the bitter negation expressed in plays like *Troilus and Cressida* and *Timon of Athens* to the sublime acceptance and forgiveness of *The Winter's Tale* and *The Tempest*.

Finally, *Vieux Carré* is an act of love to remembered people who influenced and changed a young man into an artist. There is a sense of sorrow at the ephemerality of human relationships and their inability to defeat death or aloneness. But art—the act of writing, the creative process in which we participate by watching *Vieux Carré*—finally becomes an act of love and defense against life's crushing realities. Art, in the end, becomes compassion more lasting than relationships, which must always be defeated by time.

In September 1982 I went over to Tennessee's house to do a tape-recorded interview with him for the season's program of the Tennessee Williams Fine Arts Center in Key West. Our annual Williams production was to be *Vieux Carré*, and I wanted to talk about the play with him. He hated discussing his work, but our interview did reveal some of his real feelings.

Me: I think *Vieux Carré* is a beautiful play.

Tennessee: I must say Keith Hack, the English director, was enormously helpful.

Me: I know you inscribed the play to him.

Tennessee: Yeah, he made me work twice a day. It nearly killed me, but it made a good play out of it. I'm bad at talking about my plays.

Me: The Writer as a young man is a pure, vulnerable human being.

Tennessee: Yeah.

Me: As he goes on do you see him getting harder?

Tennessee: I think he gets a little harder, yeah.

Me: Do you want to know what I think the impulse for the play is?

Tennessee: What?

Me: I think the impulse for this particular play is your desire to recapture that innocent pure part of yourself exemplified by the young Writer in the play. There's a part of you that tries to keep that sacred, totally innocent, and loving. As one gets older it becomes hard to keep.

Tennessee: I think finally it becomes very easy again.

Me: Really.

Tennessee: Yeah.

Me: Why?

Tennessee: You have no reason to be otherwise.

Me: What does purity mean to you?

Tennessee: Now that sort of thing stumps me altogether.

Me: You write about it.

Tennessee: Honesty, I would say, and truth to one's principles.

Me: I don't think you've ever violated that.

Tennessee: My life has been very helter skelter.

Me: I mean artistically.

Tennessee: Never willingly.

NOTES

1. "Orpheus Holds His Own: William Burroughs Talks with Tennessee Williams," *Village Voice*, May 16, 1977.

2. Martin Gottfried, *New York Post*, May 12, 1977.

3. Tennessee Williams, quoted in Craig Clinton, "Finding the Way: The Evolution of Tennessee Williams's *Vieux Carré*," *Resources for American Literary Study*, vol. 26, no. 1 (2000), 49–63.

4. Williams, quoted in Richard F. Leavitt, *The World of Tennessee Williams* (New York: Putnam, 1978), 158.

5. Tennessee Williams, quoted in Leavitt, *The World of Tennessee Williams*, 158,

6. Tennessee Williams, "I Am Widely Regarded as the Ghost of a Writer." *New York Times*, May 3, 1977.

7. John Simon, "Warmed-over Vice and Innocence," *The New Leader*, June 20, 1977.

8. Alan Rich, "Morpheus Descending," *New York*, May 30, 1977.

9. Harold Clurman, "Theatre," *Nation*, May 28, 1977.

10. Walter Kerr, "Stage View: A Touch of the Poet Isn't Enough to Sustain Williams's Latest Play," *New York Times*, May 22, 1977.

11. Kerr, "Stage View."

12. Brendan Gill, "Consolations of Memory," *New Yorker*, May 23, 1977.

13. Jack Richardson, "Unaffected Recollections: Memoirs," *New York Times Book Review*, November 2, 1975.

14. T. E. Kalem, "Down and Out in N.O., " *Time*, May 23, 1977.

15. Robert Cushman, "Back to New Orleans," *Observer*, August 26, 1978.

16. Peter Jenkins, "Summer Treats," *Spectator*, August 26, 1978.

17. Benedict Nightingale, "Tuition Fees," *New Statesman*, May 19, 1978.

18. Sally Aire, "*Vieux Carré*," *Plays and Players*, March 1978.

19. Clive Barnes, "Tennessee Is Alive and Well in 'Vieux Carré,'" *New York Post*, April 4, 1983.

20. Michael Feingold, "Small Craft Warnings," *Village Voice*, April 19, 1983.

$\cdot$ *7* $\cdot$

Night Flight from Dallas

$\mathcal{T}$he years 1975–1976 were a busy and prolific period for Tennessee Williams. *Memoirs,* as well as a novel entitled *Moise and the World of Reason,* were published in 1975. The first production of *The Red Devil Battery Sign* opened and closed in Boston in June 1975. It was then rewritten and produced in Vienna in January 1976. *This Is (An Entertainment)* was also produced in January 1976 in San Francisco at the American Conservatory Theater. *The Eccentricities of a Nightingale,* a rewrite of *Summer and Smoke,* was presented first in Buffalo, New York, and then at the Morosco Theatre in New York City in November of 1976. New versions of *Kingdom of Earth* and *The Two-Character Play* were produced. And it was also the period during which *Vieux Carré* was written and readied for Broadway.

This enormous output represents work from previous years stretching back to the sixties. However, it is difficult to make a simple chronology of what was written when since Williams worked on several works at the same time, going from project to project as necessity and desire dictated. He obviously worked hard and wrote constantly. The output, apart from any judgment on the work, is evidence of an enormously disciplined artist. There is no way Williams could have produced this body of work if he had not been alert and aware.

Nor is it easy to see a simple thematic or stylistic development in his work at this time. In the previous chapter I suggested that the earliest drafts of *Vieux Carré* were a reaction to the Broadway failure of *Out Cry* in 1973 and continued some formal experiments in form of the previous play as well. This may be true. What is extraordinary, however, is that in the same period Williams was working on another major play, *The Red Devil Battery Sign,* which is very different from either *The Two-Character Play* or *Vieux Carré.*

128

The Red Devil Battery Sign is a large, sprawling, ambitious play that attempts no less than a major statement about "moral corruption" in the United States in the approach of the last quarter of the twentieth century. It has neither the absurd claustrophobia of *The Two-Character Play* nor the gentle lyricism of *Vieux Carré*. It is a "big" play painted in vibrant colors on a much larger canvas than either of those plays. It is remarkable that Williams worked on it while he was also writing other major plays, attending rehearsals, and creating all the other work he produced during this period.

Donald Spoto in his biography of Williams, *The Kindness of Strangers*, tells us that as early as 1960 Williams was working on a play for Diana Barrymore entitled *Poem for Two* and that "the material resurfaced years later in *The Red Devil Battery Sign*." The play as described by Spoto, has a "vaguely political thesis" and is "set in a penthouse suite in a Houston hotel."[1]

A "first draft (revised)" of *The Red Devil Battery Sign*, bearing the date August 1973, exists in the Billy Rose Theatre Collection at Lincoln Center Library. It is the earliest draft of which I am aware. The manuscript describes the action of the play as occurring "in Dallas, at the Yellow Rose of Texas Hotel, shortly after the Kennedy Assassination." The portrayal of its main female character, simply called "Woman Downtown," bears some resemblance to what is known of Diana Barrymore as someone with a drinking problem given to extrovert public behavior. It makes sense that *The Red Devil Battery Sign* evolved out of *Poem for Two*. Edwin Sherin, director of the Boston production of *Red Devil*, remembers Tennessee telling him that the play was originally written for Barrymore, who was a close friend of Williams.[2]

Called "A Work for the Presentational Theatre" on its title page, the first draft of *The Red Devil Battery Sign* begins in the bar of the Yellow Rose of Texas Hotel. A drunken woman, Woman Downtown (hereafter simply called the Woman) is making loud comments about the Kennedy assassination, Jack Ruby, and a large corporation that manufactures batteries. She speaks with aggressive, sexual frankness: "Ah, fuzz and pigs over-run the world today, all trigger happy, yeh, all armed with weapons that burn to kill because they don't have—you know what I mean!—*Natural—born—cojones*." She hints at knowledge that is dangerous to know. A drunk man in the bar makes a pass at her and she kicks him in the groin. King del Rey, a handsome middle-aged Mexican American, enters the bar and gets the woman out of the developing hassle. She takes him to her penthouse and despite protests that he must be home early, they end up in bed.

> Woman: Will you put my fire out? It's blazed for many moons. It would be a very merciful act of extinction of fire . . . might even induce some hours of natural sleep.

The scene ends passionately. In bed together, after she has taken a pill she calls her "Sandman special," she begs him:

Woman: Hold me! Hold ME! HO-O-OOLD ME!

King: Christ!

Woman: Yes, that's the name of it, Christ and God and the Holy Ghost and their mother! Tighter! Tighter!

In scene 3, post-coitus, King tells his story. He has been the band leader of a mariachi group called "the King's Men." He also reveals a deep love for his daughter, Nina, a former singer and flamenco dancer with the group. Now retired, King is dependant upon his wife, Perla, for support. An accident has left him dangerously ill. "It happened that night at the Sheraton Lane in San Antone. We just finished a set and started to leave the bandstand, and I felt a stab in my head, I stumbled off the bandstand, fell on my face, blackened out. They broke a popper under my nose but I—didn't get up. The doctor said 'I think it might be a good idea to run you through some tests, just to eliminate some possibilities.' Well, they found this—accident—in my head."

King must leave to get back home to his wife with whom he has "an endurable marriage." The Woman tells him their sex has "gone into my heart." She asks him if he has "ever felt what I mean." He replies "Yes" and turns to kiss her again. Her response is passionate and desperate: "Kiss me deep, deeper, mouth open, before you abandon me again to the special hell I live in." As he starts to leave, the Woman grabs a bottle of gin to wash down a Nembutal. King tries to stop her drinking in bed. This infuriates her. Angrily, he warns her of her future: "You're going to wind up not a lady with some habits that don't fit a lady but you're going to wind up not young anymore but middle-aged and going to liquor, fat, and a cunt. That's right, just a cunt, the kind that is picked up by any stranger and banged in alleys and back of trucks and that finally surfaces in a, in a—yes, a bloated cadaver that surfaces in a polluted river or canal somewhere off a rotten wharf close to a—garbage disposal plant." She answers him with a call for comfort. The scene fades as they begin to make love again.

A highly sexual love affair develops. The Woman becomes wildly possessive of King. Finally, King demands to know more about her. "You take me up here and I might as well come into the bedroom of a hotel prostitute, no name, no past, no future, no knowledge of who you are but a naked female body on a big bed with a smell of gin on her breath." Throwing her out of their bed and into a chair, he interrogates her. "What made you what you are, a woman that can't give her name?" The Woman interprets his demands as a sign that he is through with her but he reassures her, "I will never be through with you till I . . . die."

He forces her to tell some of her story. It is a sordid tale full of break-downs, suicide attempts, and a marriage to a man she calls "Scout Master," a millionaire who owns a worldwide conglomerate of enormous power, the Red Devil Battery Corporation. She is now separated from him and black-mailing him with incriminating pictures: "In the safe deposit box downstairs I've got naked pictures of boy-scouts, one of which died mysteriously of a heart condition at age fifteen without previous history of any cardiac trouble." King calms her and she describes their meeting as the beginning of her life, "beautiful meaning, begun just one month ago on that bed there!" Once again the scene ends in an embrace as she "seizes his body against her."

In scene 6 (still in act 1) King informs the Woman that his daughter is coming home to visit and they must "cool it for a little while." She accuses him viciously of having "an incestuous feeling" for his daughter. She also warns him that she will pick up another man: "You've put my cunt on fire and if you don't satisfy it, a strange man will, a man at the next bar stool." A battle ensues. He tries to leave but she holds onto him. He promises to stay with her until a sleeping pill puts her out.

Suddenly through the window she sees a Red Devil Battery sign, blink-ing on and off, invading the Penthouse room: "His sign grinning in my win-dow." King explains that the "Red Devil Battery Building, tallest building in town was formally opened today." The red neon sign has just been turned on for the first time. He cradles her in his arms again as the scene ends.

The last scene of act 1 is a short scene in which a housekeeper enters the Woman's bedroom. It is Perla, a Mexican woman, who is King's wife. The Woman guesses Perla's identity when she tells her that she is in a hurry to meet a daughter at the airport and must quickly clean the room. Perla also mentions that she has "an invalid husband to support." The Woman gives Perla a large tip, which the Mexican woman hesitantly takes. In this first draft Perla does not suspect the Woman's identity nor her connection with King.

Act 2 is set in and around King's house, "interior and exterior of a small, almost oppressively small, frame cottage on the outskirts of the city." The Woman "floats" throughout the scene as she talks to King on the telephone. This device is important to Williams, and it remains in all versions of the play. In the first draft Williams makes the personal comment that the device "will be vulnerable to attack, say, by Mr. Martin Gottfried of W.W.D." Obviously Williams *did* read his critics and was affected by them. However, this does not change the playwright's intent. "I want this scene to have a mobility that could not be had by keeping the WOMAN DOWNTOWN in a single set area of the stage. Once the interior of the house has been established I would like her to seem to be wandering across the shimmering profile of the city, the menacing, fulminous 'wasteland' and the night-sky on which clouds may be projected."

The act starts with a long phone conversation between the Woman and King. It is clear to the audience that King has suffered an accident; "a gauze bandage" is wrapped around his head. The Woman is desperate to see him. Scout Master is threatening to withdraw alimony from her, "claims that I'm living a life of debauchery here, the life of a tramp, a whore!" She senses something is wrong with him. "King, your voice *is* different." He tells her he has suffered a "cut on my forehead." She presses him to "come downtown." Perla appears and King hangs up pretending to talk to a card-playing friend: "No, no, Charlie, no game of cards tonight."

At this point in the first draft the focus shifts entirely to the domestic drama in King's household. Tension between King and Perla erupts preceding the entrance of Nina with her lover, McCabe. Perla warns King that McCabe is a "married man she's living with unmarried in Chicago!" Perla also tells King that Nina "looks like a *tramp!*" It is further established that McCabe has a gun and has "threatened to shoot himself if she [Nina] makes any objection to him coming down here with her."

Nina and McCabe enter. King interrogates McCabe and then threatens him with a knife. King demands the gun from McCabe: "My weapon's in my hand pointed at your crotch, ready for surgery on it if you don't surrender to me this un-licensed firearm right now."

A phone call from the Woman interrupts the scene. She has a doctor with her who she hopes can help King. King hangs up. A short scene between the doctor and the Woman follows. It is a scene that was subsequently cut from all versions, but it is a touching scene making clear King's probable fate.

> Doctor: If his history's what you told me, it has come back and—Oh, you could possibly operate on him again but the result would be no more than a little prolongation in a vegetable state.
>
> Woman: *Don't you understand? All I want is him here!*
>
> Doctor: What good would that do you or him, Miss?
>
> Woman: Mr. Hotel Doctor, are you too old to remember that love is or was, the need to be with and hold in *anguish* what you can't stand alone in yourself and in the other?
>
> Doctor: "Anguish" isn't a word I use.
>
> Woman: It's mine. I use it.
>
> Doctor: I'll give you an injection.

We return to the house where Perla accuses King of infidelity, of having a woman downtown. The two men leave the house for a private talk "in the yard." Simultaneously, there is a scene in which the mother accuses her daughter of being a whore. McCabe gets a pain killer from the bathroom for King and their scene continues.

The younger man tries to make clear his love for La Nina: "I tried whores but I was—impotent with them, because you see King, I have to make love feeling love." McCabe tells King how he became obsessed with Nina and how in their first night of love the daughter called out her father's name during their lovemaking. McCabe then tells King, "Your daughter is pregnant by me."

Periodic off-stage explosions sound during the scene between King and McCabe. King explains the loud noises: "Between here and the downtown is this big wasteland, this hollow. Fog collects in it on steamy nights like this. Everything evil collects in that hollow between the tall building sign and here which is called Crestview . . . Delinquent kids have dug caves in that hollow. Adolescent citizens of the future America have dug caves out there in that rubble, there's several gangs of them divided along what's called race lines . . . All throwin' rocks at each other, fighting with switch-blade knives, each blowing up the other with home made bombs."

King persuades McCabe to give up his firearm, and King gives his general approval to the young man: "You're a man needed here. She will give you the child and you will stay here." King also wants McCabe to promise that he will restore "La Nina" to her former glory as a flamenco dancer. McCabe agrees and King stumbles off alone with the gun: "I have a date with a woman downtown." The act ends as King watches an "apparition" of Nina sweep across the stage, dressed as she used to be, "in an few dazzling moments of flamenco."

Act 3 begins with a short scene between McCabe and Perla in which the mother is told of King's approval. McCabe promises to leave his wife. Perla has a premonition of disaster when she hears that King has left with the gun. They leave in pursuit of King.

The second scene begins with another phone conversation. King has called the Woman from a pharmacy. She speaks to him from the bar. He says, "I called to tell you good-bye." He is obviously in great pain. She begs him to tell her where he is. She will go to him and take him to their room where they both will "wash down all my pills." King hangs up: "Good-bye love . . . *much* loved!" Hysterical, the Woman gives herself over to a drummer, who in a phantasmagoric scene rapes her in the backseat of a cab that deposits her, dress torn, at the place from which King had called her. In the dark we hear a gun shot. When the lights come up we see King lying in the Woman's arms as Nina wails a flamenco chant.

In an epilogue the Woman is seen wandering onto the forestage, holding roses. A final monologue, in stream-of-consciousness style, is a memorial
speech for King: "Dying he made me live.—What strange phone conversations, voices so close, so little distance between us, but no touch except—gifts
of love in rough language: a memory which demands—what? (Nods slowly as
if given an answer) continuing with it somehow, and so I *endure*."

There is an unclear affirmation in this first draft's ending. Somehow the
Woman feels that King's love has given her the strength to go on.

To be sure there are problems in this first draft (revised). The affirmative
ending is neither motivated, clear, nor probable. The abrupt shift from the
hotel and the Woman's concerns in act 1 to King's house and his domestic
situation in act 2 splits the action in two parts making it seem like two different plays. The supporting characters of Perla, Nina, and McCabe are underdeveloped, occasionally verging on the comic. Nina is constantly eating and
has become fat, McCabe is a hysteric, and Perla is too much the long-suffering
wife without any dimensionality.

The political/criminal aspects of the play are kept totally in the background. They never intrude upon the world of the Woman or King except
in the most peripheral way. No immediate crises occur from Scout Master's
threats. The world of the Red Devil Battery Corporation relates more to the
Woman's past than to the present situation.

The strongest element in this first draft is the beauty of the relationship
between King and the Woman. Their scenes in act 1 have a sexual and poetic
power that is unique in Williams' writing. It is one of the few depictions in the
Williams' "oeuvre" of a reciprocal love affair that is both sexual and emotional.
No division exists here between the body and soul and Williams seems to be
affirming the possibility of a mature sexual love between a man and a woman.

This uniqueness is partially due to the Woman's sexual assertiveness. She
goes after King without any inhibition. Nor is he put off by her sexuality.
They can't seem to get enough of each other. Their love and desire is expressed in the most candid, "rough" language Williams ever used. This blunt-
ness in language is accompanied by a request for complete nudity of the two
principals in key moments. Neither the language nor the nudity is in any way
gratuitous. This is a passionate love story of two middle-aged characters who
find in each other an escape from everything that makes their lives trapped,
desperate, and sordid. It is not young romantic love; experience has taught
the characters something. Their love is expressed in the frank terms usually reserved for modern novels by writers such as D. H. Lawrence or Henry Miller.
Williams' depiction of this kind of love on the stage is both courageous and
path breaking. One reads the draft wondering if the characters could really say
and do "those things" on the stage.

Important theatrical conventions remove the play from realistic theater, making the play "presentational." First, there is great use of a Mexican mariachi band that functions both as characters and as a musical accompanist to the action. They often become fantasy figures existing in King's mind, commenting upon and underlining key moments. Similarly, the apparition of Nina as a flamenco dancer appears occasionally as a symbol of King's dreams and ambitions. Both devices embody King's need for honor and his personal ambitions of "glory." The phone conversations, not tied to logical location nor even using "prop" phones, are another device that give a dream-like hallucinatory quality to the play.

The Red Devil Battery Sign opened and closed in Boston in the summer of 1975. The play never reached New York, nor even Washington D.C., the second city on its pre-Broadway tryout tour. Only one other Williams play had ever closed out of town. It was Williams' first Broadway play, *Battle of Angels*, that also closed in Boston, that most Puritan of American cities. That had been in 1940. Thirty-five years later history repeated itself.

The story of the planning, rehearsals, and preview period of *The Red Devil Battery Sign* is a true horror story, evidence of the near impossibility of producing a serious play in the commercial theater. If by the late 1980s Broadway was no longer regarded as a creative originator of theatrical art, the *Red Devil* "story" is a key example of that arena in its death throes. Unfortunately, an important play was nearly consumed in the Götterdämmerung. The story, mostly untold, also shows very clearly the kinds of commercial considerations that militated against good productions of Williams' difficult late work.

David Merrick optioned *The Red Devil Battery Sign* in 1973 prior to the Broadway production of *Out Cry*. It is curious that Williams allowed Merrick to renew the option after *Out Cry* or that Merrick wanted to continue it. It is even stranger when one remembers that Merrick had produced the ill-fated *Kingdom of Earth*, insisting that it be retitled *The Seven Descents of Myrtle*. Merrick had also produced the disastrous Tallulah Bankhead production of *Milk Train*. The Williams/Merrick relationship is a curious one: a continuing record of feuds and make ups, on again, off again fidelity.

Bill Barnes, Williams' agent during most of the seventies, has explained Merrick's continuing support of Williams in this period as a result of an affinity Merrick felt for Williams the man. They had both come from St. Louis and were the same age. Merrick considered Williams a great playwright, and he desperately wanted to produce a Williams "hit." However, it was Merrick's decision not to bring *Red Devil* into New York. It may have been a wise decision given the unreadiness of the production, but it may also have been Merrick who was most responsible for that lack of preparation.

After *Red Devil* closed, Ed Sherin, the play's director, wrote a bitter article describing his experience. Meant for publication in the *New York Times*, the monograph, entitled "A View from Inside the Storm," was never published. Sherin was dissuaded from its publication by producer Alexander Cohen, who presumably felt the article might damage Sherin's career. The article was sent to Williams, and Williams later showed it to me. Sherin has consented to use of the article in this book to shed light on the traumatic experience. In my 1987 interview with Sherin, the director commented, "I would be pleased if the salient points in the article were made known."[3] The article is one-sided and influenced by failure, but it is a clear depiction of many of the problems involved in mounting the first production of this difficult play.

In 1975 Tennessee saw a production of *A Streetcar Named Desire* in London that favorably impressed him. Directed by Ed Sherin, the production starred Claire Bloom as Blanche. As a result of this *Streetcar*, Williams gave *Red Devil* to Sherin to read. He hoped the director would want to direct it in New York. Williams also wanted Claire Bloom (with whom he had "fallen in love") to play the Woman. Sherin loved the play and considered it one of Williams' "most important plays," a play "about the decaying morality of our country and the entire western world."[4] It is clear from Sherin's statements about the play that the social/political potential of the play excited the director as much as the human love story.

Many human and practical problems combined to make *Red Devil*'s pre-production and rehearsal period a nightmare. Sherin never trusted David Merrick, nor did he want Merrick to produce the play. "I felt that David Merrick hadn't the patience, understanding or compassion to produce this particular work."[5] Sherin persuaded Williams to insist that Hillard Elkins coproduce the play. Elkins, admired by Sherin, had produced *Streetcar* in London and was the husband of Claire Bloom. When Bill Barnes, emissary from Williams, told Merrick of Williams' insistence on Elkins joining as coproducer, Merrick became furious. A war between producers was imminent before the play ever went into rehearsals.

Also, Sherin did not really believe Bloom was right for the role. It *is* difficult to imagine Claire Bloom, a refined and rather "cold" actress, playing the Woman as originally conceived. She was, however, Tennessee's most recently loved leading lady. He insisted on her. Still, Sherin was dubious. "If Claire were to do it, I felt we would need at least a month of work prior to rehearsal, the most positive and nurturing environment during rehearsal, and several weeks out of town before coming to New York."[6] Anthony Quinn was signed to play King and all agreed he was ideal for the role.

Originally Sherin had been led to believe that Merrick would not renew his option and thus Elkins would produce the play alone. Merrick never did so. "My gut feeling was to pull out as director," Sherin said, but he so loved the play that he stayed on. He felt it would be "a great commercial as well as artistic success."[7]

Eventually, two other producers, Robert Colby and Doris Abrahams, were added, bringing the lineup of producers to four. This practice has become common as plays have become difficult to finance. The problem, of course, is that frequently the producers disagree, especially if a show is "in trouble." A play's production needs one point of view from a director who is strongly supported by a producer who agrees with the director's vision of the playwright's play. That is the ideal. The chances of such support occurring with *four* producers is extremely improbable. Also, given Sherin's attitude toward Merrick and Merrick's attitude toward Elkins, there was little hope of a harmonious production team. Egotism, as well as commercial considerations, was an obvious liability.

Because of contract hassles between Merrick and the director and the actors, contracts were not signed until late in the spring of 1976. "The plan of action became the [then] unprecedented one of rehearsing in May and opening in New York in August." Also, because his personal contract "was not signed until mid-March," Sherin did not begin work with Williams on rewrites until late in March.[8]

The work with Williams seemed to go well. Sherin wrote of this time, "Six days with Tennessee in Key West were among the happiest and most fulfilling I have spent in the theatre. We were working together in calmness and warmth, making great strides toward clarifying the play." At the end of their time together Sherin felt the play was still not ready, "too long and diffuse," but he also believed that its problems could be ironed out in rehearsal with the actors and the playwright.[9]

Sherin did not have his month of prerehearsal work with Claire Bloom "since her contract wasn't completed until ten days before rehearsals began." Part of the problem, according to Sherin, was that "Merrick constantly harassed Elkins by questioning the terms of the agreement with Bloom."[10] As Claire Bloom's husband, Elkins was obviously put in a vulnerable position in his bargaining with Merrick.

Another problem was the scenic and lighting design for the production. Tony Walton, originally hired as set designer, created a design that met Sherin's specifications, "a one-unit set with the lighting grids suspended over the stage." It was a spacious, versatile set, an open space in which "the play would be revealed in space and light simply and poetically."[11]

Red Devil with its multiple locations, not unlike an Elizabethan play, requires a versatile design. In addition to many location changes, the set and light design must accommodate expressionistic changes in the characters' psychology as well as make an overall statement about the play's social/political context.

Thirteen days before rehearsals were to begin, Walton showed a model of the unit set to the producers. According to Sherin, Merrick hated the design, stating that it was "not for a Broadway production with his name on it." (One must remember that Merrick was most famous for producing large musicals with lots of scenery.) Another designer, Robin Wagner, was hired who designed something that included many moving pieces. But, says Sherin, the "set work was not explored with sufficient care" and "modifications were required to simplify scenic transitions."[12] When the production opened in Boston, the production was marred by clumsy, lengthy set changes in an already long play. According to Williams' agent, Bill Barnes, the scene changes elicited laughter from the audience.

Similar problems arose over the obviously important lighting design. Sherin had originally wanted Richard Pilbrow but Merrick "blocked all meaningful efforts to get Pilbrow." Jules Fisher was Sherin's next choice, to which Merrick apparently responded, "He never works for me. He exaggerates the importance of lighting and wants too much money." Merrick hired Marilyn Rengal "who had never lighted a Broadway play."[13]

The mariachi music gave insurmountable problems. The American Musicians Union would not permit real Mexican musicians to play. The few American mariachis who could be found could not read the composed music written by producer Robert Colby, who was also a song writer. The problem was made more difficult by the fact that the musicians had to act in the production as well as play their instruments. Sherin wanted the musicians in rehearsal from the beginning of the four-week period to ensure that they would be integrated into the production. Without notifying Sherin, Merrick cancelled the call for the musicians to join rehearsals from the beginning. "This move of Merrick's (made to save rehearsal salaries for musicians, which are higher than actors) caused untold hardship during the critical last two weeks of rehearsal, when painful hours were spent rehearsing mariachi musicians rather than working on the play."[14]

Further, there were enormous acting problems. Claire Bloom and Anthony Quinn had very different approaches to their roles and "their acting styles were not mixing well." Bloom seemed wrong to many, and at one point Faye Dunaway and Gena Rowlands, as possible replacements, were flown in to watch early previews. In early rehearsals Quinn and Bloom had fought with each other. One of Sherin's victories was to make them vow to "never give up on each other."[15] By the time the play opened, it was rumored that the two had become romantically involved.

But "the show must go on," and the play opened as advertised. Wrote Sherin after the fact, "On June 14 at its first preview performance, an amateurish, ponderous, inaccurate, and incomplete production was presented to the Boston public as Tennessee Williams' 'The Red Devil Battery Sign.'"[16]

Kevin Kelly of *The Boston Globe* called the play "a mess," blaming its failures on the "desperation of the play's plotting."[17] Eliot Norton of the *Herald-American*, while feeling the play was not ready, found "decided virtues in the script and characters."[18] The *Christian Science Monitor* called the play a "cause for rejoicing," stating that Williams' ability for "creating a haunting theatre piece" had "not left him."[19]

According to Sherin, the play improved greatly during its first week. Rewrites were inserted at the start of the second week and the company rallied. Anthony Quinn was particularly well received by audiences who began to give the actor standing ovations at his curtain call.

Merrick, at first, agreed to keep the show going but later reneged, claiming all support money for the production was spent. Closing notices were posted without notifying the director, and the show closed on Saturday night June 28. Bill Barnes has said that after the play closed, David Merrick personally burned the sets, insuring that the production could not go on.

During the time of his troubles, late in rehearsals, Sherin spoke with Zelda Fichandler, producing director of the Arena Stage. They had worked together many times and evolved Sherin's successful production of *The Great White Hope*. "We spoke of the nurturing and tenderness that new material requires and of the consummate faith everyone connected with a new play must have, not only in the regional theatre but on Broadway as well. For a new play, like a new life, is extremely vulnerable, requiring the most considerate handling."[20] This "nurturing" had not happened on *The Red Devil Battery Sign*, and not only had a play been poorly served, but one of America's great playwrights could not even get his play produced in such a way as to be fairly judged or even seen. In his article, Sherin, writing the day after closing, remarked, "the after taste is so bitter it is difficult to bear."[21]

How many factors contribute to the success of a stage production! How difficult it is for all elements of a production to come together in a unified concept of a director who understands a play. How much more difficult when nonartistic matters, commercial hawkers, and ego problems unwittingly contribute to theatrical chaos. Only those who have experienced the heartbreak of an unrealized stage production may fully understand. It is enough to make theater artists abandon their vocation.

Of course, judgments on productions are not necessarily judgments on plays, but very few American plays ever resurface once they have failed in a

Broadway production, especially if they closed out of town before reaching
New York. Nor do regional theaters ordinarily undertake such plays. There
have been no American regional theater productions of *The Red Devil Battery
Sign.* Foreign productions, yes, but no other American productions. The fear
of failure is so great in our theater that few producers or companies are likely
to take on production of a play once it has failed. Thirteen years after its initial
failure, *Red Devil* was finally published. It took that long for the onus of the
original production to wear out a little.

The problems inherent in the revised first draft of *Red Devil* were never
resolved in Boston. There wasn't enough time. However, several trends may
be discerned in the rewrites for this production. Because of Claire Bloom, the
role of the Woman evolved in a different way. Most of the rough language
was eventually cut and there was no total nudity.

There was an attempt to integrate the Perla/Nina world of King into the
first act. A scene between Perla and King as well as a phone call to Nina in
Boston was added to the first act. Also, McCabe was introduced in the first
act in a tense love scene with Nina in which her pregnancy and the fact of his
marriage were clearly stated.

A threat to the Woman was made more specific by a hotel manager in the
employ of the Red Devil Battery Man (no longer Scout Master). The Woman
receives an anonymous telephone call, is told not to see her "daughter," and
is also urged to leave the country. The last moments of the play remained
confused with the final speech of the Woman seeming anticlimactic as well as
unclear, the stylistic changes in the writing unprepared for and "unsignalled"
earlier in the play.

One of the main perceived problems in the script was its enormous
length. The play ran over four hours in Boston. The first act alone lasted two
hours while the third act was relatively short. Length of play has become an
issue in the commercial theater despite the fact that many of the greatest plays
in world literature are well over three hours long. Using length of playing time
as a criteria, *Hamlet*, as written, would probably not be produced on Broadway
if it were a new play today. Too many agents and producers take it as axiomatic that long new plays are poor plays for our contemporary theater. Cutting
becomes a solution to most problems when a play seems in trouble.

One wonders how the play would have evolved if Ed Sherin had been
able to develop the production the way he wanted, given ample planning and
rehearsal time. In our 1987 interview Sherin stated, "No American director
over the last twenty years has been able to do the late Williams plays in the
way he wanted. There have always been outside non-artistic influences."
Asked if he had plans to do anymore late Williams, Sherin answered, "I'm not
going to do much theatre anymore. I've had my heart broken too often in the

American theatre. It doesn't interest me a hell of a lot. The audiences don't interest me a hell of a lot."[22]

Almost immediately after the closing of *Red Devil* in Boston, Williams rewrote the play for a production in Vienna, Austria, at the English Theatre. Presented in the following January (1976), the play became more political and angry. Doubtless, Williams' experience with American commercialism in the Boston production of *Red Devil* contributed to the anger of the rewrite.

The major differences in the rewrite include much more importance on the presence of the Red Devil Battery Corporation, more exposition of the Woman's past, and an enormously theatrical and unexpected new ending that sets the play against an apocalyptic vision of America's future.

Characters are added, Crew Cut and Griffin, who are present in the hotel specifically to spy on the Woman Downtown. The danger to the Woman increases and the stakes get higher. It is strongly suggested that the Woman's husband was involved in the assassination of Kennedy and other various horrors throughout the world. The Woman's initial meeting with King is less a sexual pickup than a seeking out of protection from the eyes of hotel spies. "Please, help me upstairs. Penthouse B!—I need seclusion and rest."

In her expositional "explanation" scene, the Woman tells King of her collusion with corruption: "I was hostess to monsters! . . . Oh, they trusted me to take their attaché cases with the payola and the secrets in code, and WHY NOT? WASN'T I PERFECTLY NOT *HUMAN TOO?*" The word "human" becomes enormously important in the play. Williams is obviously making a statement about what it means to be "human."

> Woman: You you here here—
>
> King: What are you trying to say?
>
> Woman: HUMAN!
>
> King: Oh—Hmm Yes, I'm—
>
> Woman: HUMAN!
>
> King: You say "human" to me like something special about me. A living man is—
>
> Woman: Yes! Human! To enter my life something is special, this day, this night, this place, suddenly—*you*—human! Here!

This halting language, inarticulate stammering seeking expression, is typical of much of the play as if the characters in finding language find their humanity.

The love affair, a contrast to the life the Woman has known before, develops in much the same way as in the earlier versions, if with less "rawness."

The Woman does not drink as much as in her earlier incarnation; she is also less sexually aggressive. The character is more nervous and neurotic.

The scene in which the Woman explains her past to King may be the single longest expositional scene Williams ever wrote: She reveals that she was born the daughter of a state senator on a "huge ranch in West Texas isolated as madness!" Her mother died at her birth, and she was raised by the Indian mistress of her father along with a half-sister, "their ill ill-legitimate child." Wolves howling in the night are a haunting memory of her childhood. She "learned English from leather-bound books in my father's library." Misunderstanding her first menstrual period, she thought she had a "unique disease" and locked herself in her room for three days. "Father dispatched me to a home for disturbed children." Later, she was presented to society and suffered a breakdown, "sudden collapse, crack of nerves."

Recovered, "partial," she reentered the social scene "eyes fixed on chandeliers to keep from screaming." She met her future husband, "this apparently perfect counterfeit of a man." The description of him makes clear his interests: "Outward was dazzling disguise of inside genocide monster—Batteries, what a disarmingly modest title for this deadly complex of interests, investments in oil and mineral countries South and far south east—energy still untapped in strategic locations!" Once married, the woman saw how this industrial complex wielded power in the world. She ran from her husband to a godfather, Judge Callister, when she discovered a "design for surrendering a democracy to rule by power complex."

In the Vienna version of the play, there is a scene between Judge Callister (her protector in the hotel) and the Woman in which the Judge arranges for the Woman to escape the hotel, fly to Washington DC, and testify before a Senate committee against her husband. The play has become more of a "thriller" with actual danger and real physical threat. It has also become more melodramatic.

The King-Perla-Nina scenes are somewhat cut but follow the same confrontations and resolutions with King permitting McCabe to stay. McCabe is given more humanity, relating him thematically to the play's major concerns:

McCabe: My life before I met Nina was vacant as that—vacant . . . (Gestures toward the wasteland.)

King: Dump heap?

McCabe: Yes, empty, empty. Emptiness filled with violence! Oh, I tried to occupy, to satisfy myself with statistics: Statistics on buyer-consumption response to promotion commercials. I *said* that I'm a trained, well-trained computer is what I said! Programmed to be not human! But—I am! Human!

King receives calls at home from the Woman as before, but now she is frantic with the news that Judge Callister has been shot and she will not be going to Washington. Frightened for her life, she is desperate to see King:

Woman: They've killed him, the Judge, they've confiscated the papers! Comprende? And I am alone here tonight!

King: That much money talks and when it talks, there's no answer.

Woman: Oh, yes it talks, money talks, not heads, not hearts, not tongues of prophets or angels, but money does, oh, money hollers, love.

King: I think your Master of Hacienda with his Battery Sign and his secrets has money and power enough to—obliterate all life on earth, generals, rulers, presidents—and, Woman Downtown—yours.

The last scene of the play moves the play in a different direction. The Drummer who brings the Woman to the dying King no longer rapes her. Rather, he tears off her dress and takes a photograph of her in the company of King. He is obviously in the employ of the Red Devil Battery Man and is collecting evidence.

King shoots the Drummer and then collapses. He does not shoot himself but dies from his general condition. At this point an extraordinary coup de théâtre takes place, an eruption of potentially hypnotic power: "A fantastic group enters. These are the wild denizens of the Hollow: They seem to explode from a dream and the scene with them. The play stylistically makes its final break with realism. This break must be accomplished as if predetermined in the 'mise-en-scene' from the beginning, as if naturally led up to startlingly but credibly."

The group is marked with "streaks of dirt on their faces, bloodied bandages, scant and makeshift garments." At first the gang terrorizes the Woman, but then an older "boy-man," obviously their leader, intercedes. Identified by the name Wolf, this leader speaks a kind of guttural language: "Ahgah, nada! Leddums lone wid is nigguls." An extraordinary moment then occurs, which is strangely reminiscent of the last moments in *A Streetcar Named Desire*:

(Something in his harsh voice rouses the WOMAN DOWNTOWN from her crouched, moaning position over KING'S dead body. WOLF'S eyes are on her face, demented with grief. Her eyes meet WOLF'S. Her head is thrown back, teeth exposed as a she-wolf snarling. A moment, then WOLF nods and advances to her; lifts her to her feet; she offers no resistance. In his supporting hold, she recognizes or senses something rightly appointed as her final fate.)

Woman: Yes, you. Take me. Away.

A short epilogue in the Vienna version shows the Woman as a member of the gang. We hear recorded voices of policemen as they search for a sight of the strange wolf woman. Explosions are set off and flares go up as the gang blows up the Red Devil Battery Building. The curtain falls as we hear chants of "burn, burn, burn" from the gang and the Woman.

The English Theatre in Vienna has a small stage and the director of the production used a multiplicity of slides to set the play with a minimum of furniture and props. The slides also commented upon the action in a Brechtian fashion; pictures of current events, worldwide atrocities, and relevant images of public figures continually gave the play a political context. The play, performed in English, featured the Welsh actor Keith Baxter as King and an American/Austrian actress, Ruth Brinkman, as the Woman. The production was successful with a sold-out run and a highly adulatory response from Austrian and German press.

Writing in the *Frankfurter Allgemeine*, Germany's largest national newspaper, Hilde Spiel called the play "one of the most thrilling tragedies of love and fate in all Williams' work."

> The accusations of a tendency to be carried away to heightened states of consciousness as a result of alcohol and other stimulants are here revealed for the rubbish they are as if O'Neill, Fitzgerald, or Hemingway had written any the worse for the same reasons! At all events Williams has seldom worked more precisely, seldom produced more effective entrances or more pointed dialogue. To be sure it's possible to regard all this as cheap effect. Compared to the anaemic effusions of certain contemporary dramatists it may give that impression. But in this case excess is transfigured into compactness, quantity into quality.[23]

Spiel finished her review speaking of the importance of the play that "crystallized the central theme of his *oeuvre*": "the struggle within the net of desires, lusts, fears and neuroses, a net in which he himself is also caught, the struggle for a purer, truer, and more humane world."[24]

The larger-than-life theatricality of the play seems to have excited the German press and public: "In scenes thrillingly dramatic and beautifully lyrical, Williams unfolds all his unbroken mastery. His dialogue is powerful and true to life, he is never afraid of strong theatrical effects which at first may seem trite; he knows no theatrical taboos. This is no burnt out Tennessee Williams but a blazing torch illuminating the very core of life."[25]

Doubtless, the reviews reflect a certain desire on the part of Austrian and German critics to instruct America on its blindness to one of its great artists (a kind of cultural one-upmanship). Also, the apocalyptic image of America projected by the play may at that time have been better appreciated by non-Americans. The play is perhaps too close for comfort, too negative for Americans to accept. There is, however, a certain validity in the following critical observation that cannot be denied: "Europe as a whole is more likely to understand what he is trying to say than the USA. The play itself could only emerge from contemporary America which is no longer a melting pot but the battle-field of counter-forces. An America which is no longer the economically saturated 'God's own country,' but rather a state in which the trash heaps and the debts tower high, a crater-scape of crises, scandals, a state in which the signs of decay of civilization grow from day to day."[26] This description rings frighteningly true, if perhaps a little vengefully. Germany and Austria, defeated by the United States in World War II, veterans of their own apocalypse, may have the experience to recognize the signs of national corruption. They certainly seem to welcome an adventurous and innovative theater that speaks of political as well as personal issues.

As a result of Keith Baxter's participation in the Vienna production, and undoubtedly partly because of his excellent press as King, the English actor became an important champion of the play. He was largely responsible for the London production of the play, which opened at the Roundhouse on June 8, 1977, and was later transferred to the Phoenix Theatre in the West End. Codirecting the play with David Leland, Baxter repeated his role of King with Estelle Kohler playing the Woman. Maria Britneva, a close friend of Williams, repeated the role of Perla, which she had also played in Vienna.

The script was essentially the same one used in Vienna. The response of the British press was mixed, less enthusiastic than the continental response, but good notices were won from some of the London critics. Calling the play "the author's most powerful play in years," Herbert Kretzmer of the *Daily Express* went on to describe the play's special world: "The effect is to create an atmosphere of hallucination. We are given a nightmare picture of a world ruled or threatened by unidentified conspirators, where sudden violence is commonplace, where grief and disease receive little pity, where men live in chronic dread and howl in city canyons like coyotes at the moon."[27]

Peter Lewis in the *Daily Mail* called the play "Tennessee Williams' most substantial new work for many seasons and it reestablishes his cunning grip on an audience's fear and compassion." However, he also wrote that the play was "self-indulgently long and some irrelevances and over written melodrama cry out to be cut."[28]

Bernard Levin writing of the "bleak and merciless" script also found the production and play effective: "A dark, haunting, and coherent play as strong as anything he has written except his very best . . . The play is almost entirely successful on its own terms; I have to add that it offers no comfort, no refuge, and no ultimate truth."[29]

In England, the most controversial aspect of the play proved to be its political implications. As a perceived new consideration in Williams' work it sparked the most lively debate. Benedict Nightingale writing in the *New Statesman* criticized the play for its depiction of a "vague conspiracy": "Williams has, I suspect, imbibed more Watergate than is good for his sense and stability. He was high on Haldeman, crocked silly on Nixon, when he wrote this woozy, scattered, deeply paranoid melodrama, its lack of grasp over its subject proved, if further proof be needed, by its tendency to collapse into cliché."[30]

Nightingale seems influenced by American critics in his use of connotative words hinting at personal problems: "imbibed," "high," "crocked," "woozy." But his main point is interesting. Nightingale insists that Williams is at his best in plays like *The Glass Menagerie* when he describes characters who are "cut off from the world outside."[31]

Other critics saw in the political aspects of the play a retreat from a tragic vision to a more simplistic view of man as victim. Calling the play "three hours of confusion," Victoria Radin applauded the love story aspects of the play: "as long as we're in the pink satin hotel bedroom Williams has us in his power." But she thought the play fell to pieces in its political implications: "I cannot believe that Williams is now shifting the responsibility for human unhappiness from the individual to society." [32]

Irving Wardle writing in the *London Times* understood Williams' intent to create "a public nightmare" but questioned the intellectual content of that vision. He saw important questions of cause and effect as obfuscated in the play: "whether the two lovers are victims of the state or their own paranoia."[33] He might have enlarged the question to ask if the characters are victims of accident, fate, the state, their own natures, or society. Such questions are vital in all discussions of tragedy.

In most tragic situations, combinations of factors contribute to a character's "downfall." It is difficult to ascribe a tragic outcome to any single factor. That is part of the mystery of tragedy, the subtle way in which inside and outside forces conspire to destroy human beings. However, the possibility that characters are largely the victims of social causes generally removes those characters from the realm of tragedy since social conditions are subject to change. Victims of social conditions are not universal, not victims for all time of the human condition. A changed society might change their fate. For that reason, political drama more often than not in its advocacy of change (and implied belief in the possibility of change) seldom works as tragedy.

An even more serious charge was leveled at Williams by Ted Whitehead, who saw the playwright's "political illumination" as the outgrowth of a serious psychological tendency toward sadomasochism. "In *Red Devil* it's as if Tennessee Williams had finally found a political justification for embracing the primitive and violent forces which have always attracted and repelled him."[34] An intriguing criticism, the same charge might be leveled at many artists who depict violence. The modern filmmaker who condemns war with beautiful and violent images of war may in some recess of his psyche be half in love with war. However, is it fair to impugn motives that are subconscious? And don't all human beings have the same subconscious attractions? May we ever condemn anything without in some way participating in the thing we condemn?

Many of the English critics raised interesting questions in their notices of *The Red Devil Battery Sign.* Americans may envy what seems a high level of critical discourse as well as the fact that single reviews do not seem to decide the commercial fate of productions in England. Partly this is due to the large number of newspapers as well as an independent public that attends the theater for a lower price than American audiences in New York. In the case of *Red Devil*, the English audience did not support or attend the production. The West End production closed within a few weeks of its opening. In part, this may be due to an increasing division in England between the production of serious plays at state-supported institutions like the Royal Shakespeare Company and commercial productions in the West End, which are increasingly less theatrically adventurous. Audiences do not expect to see "heavy" contemporary drama in the West End unless a star actor or actress appears in the production. However, at least in England, *Red Devil* was seen in the theatrical capital of the nation. Such was not the case in the United States.

It is also interesting to compare the less enthusiastic English response to the Austrian/German reception of the play. The difference seems to come out of cultural differences as well as differing theatrical tastes. Very few German or Austrian playwrights have been popular in England. (Schnitzler is a possible exception.) The German romantics, expressionists, or Brecht have never had much acceptance in Great Britain. (On the other hand the German and Austrians have adopted Shakespeare as their own.) The English theater, apart from Shakespeare and the Elizabethans, has in general been most comfortable with plays that take place in living rooms and adjacent areas. Wilde, most of Shaw, Pinter, Orton, Coward, Restoration comedy, and Chekhov all locate their plays in specific, usually realistic, worlds in which the drama may threaten the social fabric but seldom erupts to destroy it.

German/Austrian drama, on the other hand, is often sympathetic to rebels, criminals, and *poètes maudits.* Goethe's *Goetz von Berlichtingen*, Schiller in *The Robbers*, Buchner's *Woyzeck*, Wagner's *Tannhäuser*, Brecht's *Baal*, and Wedekind's *Lulu* all come readily to mind. Destruction and apocalypse, generalized public visions of social evils, are a distinguishing feature of much German literature and drama. In this sense, *Red Devil* is Williams' most Germanic play. It seems, then, that criticism is subject to national characteristics as well as the relative individual taste of a particular critic. More cause for critics to admit the lack of absolute values in their criticism.

The most recent production of *The Red Devil Battery Sign* took place in Vancouver, British Columbia, in 1980. Keith Baxter may have been instrumental in arranging the production since he played Hamlet in Edmonton the year before *Red Devil*'s production. The play was cut severely for this production (probably by Baxter), and it is curious that Baxter did not repeat his role of King. The production was directed by Roger Hodgman and featured Richard Donat as King and Diane D'Aquila as the Woman.

The Vancouver production is most important because it is this cut script that was finally published by New Directions Publishers in the spring of 1988. Baxter's responsibility for this edition is made clear in a letter to Tennessee on July 25, 1979, in which the actor wrote the playwright suggesting certain changes in the play. Baxter is very careful in his remarks.

25th July 1979

Dear Tennessee,

Here then is the "Red Devil" with my suggestions and cuts. I send it to you with some apprehension for I know how touchy *I* should be were I you. But I comfort myself that you know how much I love you and believe in the play, and that anything I have done to the script is offered with respect and affection.

Baxter's suggestions for cuts were done "to take time out of the play," "achieve clarity," and "heighten the dramatic structure." The actor felt the audience's response to the Woman would be improved by cutting some of her "surplus hysteria" in early scenes. Two later scenes were elided, taking out a blackout to indicate a passage of time. The blackout had represented King's sexual failure with the Woman, a result of his being "turned off" by her hysteria. In Baxter's version they never get to the stage of undressing. Judge Callister's scene was cut entirely. Baxter reminded Williams, "You always disliked it," referring to the cut scene. Its "information" was reported to King by the Woman. McCabe and Nina's early scene was excised, as was the scene between Perla and the Woman, which had grown considerably in the Vienna production. In Vienna, Perla discovers who the Woman is, and the Mexican woman is given a real confrontation scene. In Baxter's version, Perla and the Woman never meet. "The worst of all," as Baxter wrote in his letter, was the suggestion that the epilogue be cut. "I believe the play should finish as Woman Downtown joins the Gang. The epilogue scene was always a brute to stage, and *always* seemed superfluous to the audience. The time lapse annulled all tension and the blowing up of the Red Devil Building put too great a strain on an audience's credulity."

Williams assented to all Baxter's suggestions and wrote a note to the actor the same month.

July 1979

Dear Keith,

Your contribution to my last major play as leading man, brilliant director, and editor surely entitles you to an exceptional reward, a salary suitable to it, as well as my own inscription to you something like "My dear friend Keith Baxter has unsparingly given his talents as male star, and as director, and as advisor and editor. It is fitting that this 'third' production of 'Red Devil Battery Sign' should be inscribed to him." And I think it is also fitting that no time be wasted in now presenting the play under the best circumstances.

Love,

Tenn

The Vancouver production incorporated all of Baxter's suggestions as does the 1988 New Directions edition.

Baxter's cuts and changes are theatrically sound. However, a final version might be better debated if earlier versions, Boston and Vienna, were also made available to the public. It is not certain that Tennessee preferred all the cuts in Vancouver. Nor was he able to work on the published version, which is a posthumous edition. One thing is certain: if Williams had worked on it, the published version would be still different from all the others. There really is no definitive version of *The Red Devil Battery Sign*. It never really found its "inevitability."

There are three basic versions of the play, which will be referred to in this analysis as the first draft revised script, the second Vienna version, and the Vancouver version. Other versions show stages in this general development. The first "raw" version is the most sexual and emphasizes the love story over its political implications. The Vienna version is the most political, the most expressionistic, and the longest. The third version is the most condensed and probably the most playable.

For me, the best production would combine the sexuality and characterization of the Woman of the first draft with the poetic expressionism and more fully developed secondary characters of the Vienna version. I would make some of the cuts in the Vancouver version, but I would not use others. I would also cut Judge Callister since he is an underdeveloped character who exists only for plot reasons that can be accomplished without his appearance. However, I would keep more of Perla, Nina, and McCabe in order to flesh out their characters and make them more understandable. This hypothetical *Red Devil* would be a long play, but long plays are not necessarily poor plays. The important point is to serve the intentions of *Red Devil*, as ambitious a play as Williams ever wrote, rather than an arbitrary time limit. Of course one would also ask for a patient, intelligent, relaxed audience capable of expanding its experience for such a production.

The Red Devil Battery Sign has a complex plot that operates on several levels. The main plot concerns the love story and chronicles the meeting, development, and tragic end of the love affair of King and the Woman. It is clear early in the play that they are "meant for each other." The threats to the relationship are all external to their love: King's impending death, the Red Devil Corporation, King's wife and domestic situation. Each of these threats claims important consideration and obstructs the through line of action. We learn of King's health problem early and watch his deterioration at several stages. This line of action gives a tragic inevitability to the play. The problem is the result of an "accident," not in any way caused by King's actions or the social/political pressures in the play.

The *Red Devil* plot, made more important in the Vienna version, is an obstacle to the main line of action inasmuch as it presents a physical threat to the Woman. The presence of agents in the hotel, the murder of the Judge, the impending Senate investigation, Drummer's threat to the Woman are all plot devices that increase the danger to the Woman. The Red Devil Corporation, of course, is more than a plot device. It is the all-pervasive symbol of the social background against which the love story gains its significance. Even more, it is a general symbol of all that dehumanizes mankind. This plot is only "resolved" in the Vienna production when, in the epilogue, the gang blows up the Red Devil Building. In other versions, the Red Devil Corporation is triumphant and everlasting.

The subplot involving King's family is very minor in the third, Vancouver version. In the Vienna version it is much more important. Perla, in her hotel room scene with the Woman, discovers a picture of King that causes a confrontation with the Woman. Her love for King as well as her strength are clearly shown. In the Vancouver version this scene is cut. Perla never meets the Woman. In the Vancouver version also, the McCabe/Nina plot seems "brought in" late in the play whereas in the Vienna version the problems of McCabe's marriage and Nina's pregnancy are revealed early in the play. Interestingly, this subplot mirrors, in almost Elizabethan manner, the main plot. A married man meets a woman, not his wife, who gives his life meaning. King's acceptance of McCabe in the second act arises out of the parallel in their two situations. It is doubtful if this parallel will be clear to an audience if the earlier scene in the Vienna version between McCabe and Nina is cut.

This is Williams' most "Elizabethan" play with its multiple worlds, sub-plots, violence, and political background. Only three other of his plays have this kind of complexity: *Orpheus Descending*, *Camino Real*, and *Sweet Bird of Youth*. But none of them combines realism, poetry, politics, and expressionism in quite the same way. It is possible that attempts to cut the play too severely only reduce the size of the play's vision. It is a little like cutting the subplots in *Hamlet* or *Antony and Cleopatra*. Audiences may "get home" earlier in the streamlined version, but expansive richness is lost. Other plays by Williams are traditionally well made; attempts to make *Red Devil* so may only diminish its special madness.

The main characters in *Red Devil* are major Williams' creations. King's character is one aspect of the play that remains the same in all versions. He is a successful portrait of a tragic male character in a modern setting. His natural nobility, his honesty, and his attempt to create something beautiful in his life make him genuinely moving. As a musician he is one of Williams' "artist" heroes. Nor is he overly idealized. His temper, his cruelty to Perla, his Spanish machismo help to mitigate his perfection.

The Mexican background of the character makes him a "misfit" in the Texas wasteland in which he has been displaced. It also gives him poetic exoticism. As a Mexican American he is to some extent a victim of American society, but this element is only suggested in the setting of King's home in a suburb ghetto. In all ways King rises above his circumstances. He may have an incestuous affection for his daughter, but more importantly she represents a part of himself as an artist that will go on after his individual death. The possibility that McCabe may destroy that part of Nina is King's greatest fear. The Woman represents a kind of magic in King's life. The discovery of an all-consuming love, even at the brink of his death, gives the play power and elevates the play to tragedy. Fate, accident, life, *not* social repression, destroys King.

The Woman is really two characters, according to which version you read. The character in the "first draft revised" is an interesting and original creation in its vulgar way. In the Vienna version, she is almost entirely a victim. Some of the savage nature of the character was restored in the Vancouver version in which her "wolf" nature is discussed and illustrated. This helps to make her final transformation into a wolf gang member more credible. The Woman must not be too much a lady. Only with King is she humanized.

One of the most original aspects of the Woman is her anonymity. She never has a name. Too much exposition about her past, as was incorporated into the Vienna production, destroys some of this mystery. She is strongest when we only imagine the horrors of her past. In this respect, the third version restores some of her allure by cutting some of the explicitness of her history. The first draft character is still the most original, if less conventionally sympathetic, creation.

Perla, Nina, and McCabe are potentially dimensionless roles if cut too much. It is tempting to cut them because the main action is not really touched by their problems. However, the result of such cutting renders them shadow figures rather than human characters.

Smaller roles function primarily as symbolic figures. Crew Cut and Griffin are threatening establishment types. The mariachis act as a chorus as well as characters in the hotel. They serenade the main characters in emotional moments and create a retinue for King who frequently imagines them when his mental stability begins to disintegrate.

The language in *Red Devil* is alternately rough and elevated. The Spanish phrases and the Spanish cadence give a "romantic" quality to much of the speech. They also give the language a rhetoric that is open to mockery and may seem excessive to some English speaking audiences. One of King's speeches to McCabe illustrates this kind of rhetorical effect:

> Yes. Stay. But then, what? For La Nina? To turn to a slob, gradual like her *madre*, not singing but remembering singing? Too tired to dance flamenco, but remembering flamenco? This girl I made and gave to the world, she what could have stood higher than the new sign on the skyscraper, tallest in Corona, one you see nights miles away. *That*—that *height* for her was my dream, the dream of a man with quick death in his skull, this flower pot of a skull with a flower in it that is cracking the pot. I think you want just your comfort, not her—glory.

The Spanish cadence, rhetoric, and idiom afford Williams an expressive lyricism not usually found in English. Southern American speech often gave Williams the same freedom, but now it is given in the Latin music of the play. Unfortunately, it is an idiom that has often been comically ridiculed by our entertainment industry. Non-Anglo-Saxon cultures have all suffered similar fates before they have been assimilated into our homogenous culture. Nor has Spanish drama ever been popular in the United States. The poetic plays of Garcia Lorca, for instance, are often laughable in North American English productions. They rarely catch the sweep and soul, the duende, of overtly emotional Spanish theater. Williams had no such problem in his obviously loving use of the Spanish idiom. He had used it before in his one-act play *The Purification*, as well as in *Night of the Iguana*, even as he used the Italian accent, language, and melody in *The Rose Tattoo*.

Live Latin music augments the language throughout the play. Williams obviously adored mariachi music and wants its energy and sentiment to permeate the play. He specifically requests one song, "Palabras de Mujer" (Words of Women), as a special song for the Woman. A director would do well to find the appropriate music and then carefully integrate the live musicians into the production. It is part of the "presentational" nature of the play.

The first draft of *Red Devil* was subtitled, "A Work for the Presentational Theatre." Williams later abandoned this appellation but kept many of the presentational aspects of the script. What is meant by "presentational"? The play does suggest a real world; however, it is represented in theatrical devices that "present" the play in a poetic and theatrical manner. The different worlds of the hotel, the bedroom, the wasteland, and King's house all need to invade each other in hallucinatory and cinematic fashion. In the long phone conversations the Woman must at times come in close proximity to King on the stage without their "seeing" each other. There must be no phone wires or even phones to create the reality. Nor are actors enjoined to "mime" phones. They simply speak to each other as if through a telephone.

The Vienna production used slides and very little furniture to create the world of the play. Williams does not call for a Brechtian slide commentary, which the Viennese production used. Possibly that device tips the play too heavily in a political direction. Properly used, however, such a device could give the play the dream-like fluidity it requires.

At the rear of the stage Williams asks for an evocation of the Red Devil Battery power. This element is most poetically described in the stage directions: "We see the city in profile, many windows of tall buildings are catching the light of sunset; they are like myriad candles and they change color during the phone conversation, turning from gold to flame and to ashes of flame and, finally, to dark, with here and there a point of electric light or a touch of neon. On top of the highest tower now is the only neon sign which is visible. It is the RED DEVIL BATTERY SIGN." The vision is of an increasingly apocalyptic conflagration. For the Vancouver production, Williams added a poetic inscription from Hart Crane, "The city's fiery parcels all undone." As in the end of Wagner's *Ring* cycle, Williams wants "Valhalla" to be consumed in flames.

The costumes also contribute to the hallucinatory quality of the play. Mariachis in black and silver costumes and the fantastic looking gang are but two strongly contrasting worlds. The Woman's initial appearance, wearing a light coat of "loose woven cloth of gold," contributes to the special garish night beauty of the play. Almost immediately she throws off the coat and "reveals a stunning Oriental sheath with a delicate dragon design on it." Importantly, the Woman's perfume is *Vol de Nuit* (Night Flight) and the last line of act 1 (Vancouver version) is spoken by King, alone, in his home as he remembers the Woman. He speaks the line "Night flight" as he smells her perfume on his shirt. In a sense, the whole play is a "night flight" and its production must carry the audience on its voyage. A harshly Brechtian production might "politicize" the poetry out of the play. A poetically Brechtian production might accomplish the goal. The play's style is both sensual and epic. It is closer to early Brecht in plays like *Drums in the Night* or *In the Jungle of Cities* than to the later Brecht of *The Caucasian Chalk Circle* or *Good Person of Setzuan*.

Finally, what does the play mean? What is Williams saying? Has he "gone political"? Do the three versions of the play testify to fuzziness in the play's content? Do the different versions say different things?

The play in fact is quite simple. In all versions Williams is asserting the human need for love in an increasingly dehumanized world. *To be human. To stay human. To find one's humanity.* These might serve as "spine" statements of the play's "super objective." The political background, horrible as it is, intriguing as it is, is only a *background* against which the love of King and the Woman is made more precious and important. The Red Devil Battery Corporation is not only external to our lives; it invades our psychology making us less human, less capable of feeling or love. The threat of the corporation represented many of our culture's greatest fears in the late twentieth century; our ignorance of and helplessness before forces which rule our lives and reduce our capacity for human empathy.

Many contemporary events make us suspect that society is run by immoral forces: the Kennedys' assassinations, Martin Luther King Jr.'s murder, the Vietnam War, Watergate, Mafia killings, Irangate, New York City political scandals, the list is long. More and more it seems that society is threatened by secret powerful groups of which we have little knowledge and over which we have no control. One need not be paranoid to imagine there are secret forces that wield power over our lives. One response to such forces is indifference, another is a kind of fascism; moral and emotional numbness or fundamentalism destroying tolerance.

Love in the hollow wasteland, deep passionate, sexual love is a triumph. It is a victory over all that would destroy what is most uniquely human. King and the Woman find such love. Conventional rules of marriage and religion mean nothing before such love. It is the ultimate triumph of the human heart. Deprived of love man turns potentially violent. That is the play's final message. Violence may be preferable to passive numbness. It is at least a human response.

The play's final image, as last envisioned and changed by Tennessee for the Vancouver production, is a prophecy and warning of impending destruction. After the Woman stands joining the gang leader named Wolf, this stage direction is "A flare behind them and a muted sound of explosion in the Hollow. Against its lingering, warning glow, the denizens of the Hollow all advance, eyes wide, looking at us who have failed or betrayed them.

The WOMAN DOWNTOWN advances furthest to where KING's body has fallen: she throws back her head and utters the lost but defiant outcry of the she-wolf. The cry is awesome. There is a second explosion and a greater whiter flare, exposing more desolation. WOLF takes her hand. All are standing motionless. The scene dims out."

In the end, the play becomes a prophecy of our future, if commercial and corporate interests are allowed to destroy human values. Also, Williams seems to be making a statement about the art of our time, the way in which a work's monetary value supersedes all other aspects of the work. It is indeed ironic that the corporate values embodied by the Red Devil Corporation ("money hollers") ultimately worked against the American production of Williams' play. Ed Sherin also saw this connection, ending his article with the following: "I can't help feeling that people like David Merrick represent the very forces in our society about which Tennessee Williams is writing in 'The Red Devil Battery Sign,' and I am frightened that these forces have apparently been successful in keeping this important work from public view. If these forces are already so powerful that they can silence the warnings of our greatest artists, then it may already be too late."[35] Sherin makes an important point. Commercialism creates its own censorship. It is a subtle form of censorship, but no less real than the censorship of more totalitarian states. We insist that the United States enjoys freedom of speech, yet we do not put on many plays in our theater that say unpopular things in an uncommercial way.

However, for all its political relevance *The Red Devil Battery Sign* is not primarily a political play in the most obvious sense. Williams is not writing political theater that exposes a specific social wrong. His vision is more general and all pervasive. It is a poet's response to forces beyond his control. Of course, it may be that the poet is the most revolutionary of all human beings. The poet seeks a change in the human heart as a prelude to all social change. Without such a change the poet can only predict destruction in the most vivid and dramatic images possible.

NOTES

1. Donald Spoto, *The Kindness of Strangers* (New York: Ballantine Books, 1985), 264.
2. Edwin Sherin, interview with William Prosser, December 11, 1987.
3. Sherin, interview.
4. Edwin Sherin, "A View from Inside the Storm," unpublished manuscript.
5. Sherin, "A View from Inside the Storm."
6. Sherin, "A View from Inside the Storm."

7. Sherin, "A View from Inside the Storm."

8. Sherin, "A View from Inside the Storm."

9. Sherin, "A View from Inside the Storm."

10. Sherin, "A View from Inside the Storm."

11. Sherin, "A View from Inside the Storm."

12. Sherin, "A View from Inside the Storm."

13. Sherin, "A View from Inside the Storm."

14. Sherin, "A View from Inside the Storm."

15. Sherin, "A View from Inside the Storm."

16. Sherin, "A View from Inside the Storm."

17. Kevin Kelly, *Boston Globe,* June 19, 1975.

18. Eliot Norton, *Herald-American,* June 19, 1975.

19. John Beaufort, *Christian Science Monitor,* 1975.

20. Sherin, "A View from Inside the Storm."

21. Sherin, "A View from Inside the Storm."

22. Sherin, interview.

23. Hilde Spiel, *Frankfurter Algemeine,* January 5, 1976.

24. Spiel, *Frankfurter Algemeine.*

25. Katrin Kathrein, *Die Presse,* January 7, 1976.

26. Gunther Martin, *Wiener Zeitung,* January 7, 1976.

27. Herbert Kretzmer, "High-Level Plot That Is Hatched in Hell," *Daily Express,* June 9, 1977.

28. Peter Lewis, "What a Vivid Red Devil . . . ," *Daily Mail,* June 9, 1977.

29. Bernard Levin, "Deep in the Heart of Tennessee," *Sunday Times,* June 12, 1977.

30. Benedict Nightingale, "That's History," *New Statesman,* June 17, 1977.

31. Nightingale, "That's History."

32. Victoria Radin, "Wolf-Howls at the Door," *Observer,* June 12, 1977.

33. Irving Wardle, "Public Nightmare in Dallas," *London Times,* June 9, 1977.

34. Ted Whitehead, "Climax," *Spectator,* June 18, 1977, 27.

35. Sherin, "A View from Inside the Storm."

· 8 ·

An Incredible Visit to
Asheville and Beyond

$\mathcal{A}$fter the busy, productive years of 1973–1977 and the commercial failures of *Out Cry*, *The Red Devil Battery Sign*, and *Vieux Carré*, Tennessee Williams' artistic output slowed down. Already in his late sixties, the playwright had summoned all his energies to produce accepted works of art. None had been accepted, none deemed successful, at least not by his countrymen, certainly not by the critical establishment. No new Williams work was produced on Broadway in the years after *Vieux Carré* (May 1977) until *Clothes for a Summer Hotel* (March 1980).

There were some regional theater productions of new plays and one off-Broadway mounting. *Tiger Tail*, a stage version of the film *Baby Doll*, was produced at the Alliance Theatre in Atlanta. Also, *A Lovely Sunday for Creve Coeur*, an original play based on an unproduced film script entitled *All Gaul Is Divided*, was produced in Charleston, South Carolina, at the "Spoleto Festival USA."

Directed by Keith Hack and well received in Charleston, *Creve Coeur* was subsequently presented at the Hudson Guild Theatre in New York City. It was not well received there. John Simon outdid himself in a review entitled "Sweet Bird of Senility": "the kindest thing to assume is that Williams died shortly after completing *Sweet Bird of Youth*, and that his subsequent, ever more dismal plays are the work of a lover of his who has seemed to impersonate him perfectly in daily life, but only very crudely in playwriting."[1]

The relatively low output during the years in the late seventies may signify that the critics were finally getting to Williams. His continual allusion to the critics in interviews during this period certainly supports this theory. Dotson Rader, in his book, *Tennessee: Cry of the Heart*, records Tennessee's reaction to Simon's review of *Creve Coeur*. "The critics always bellow that their reviews don't affect, psychologically, a writer's ability to create. That isn't true.

157

Critics have killed more writers than liquor. They certainly defeated Tennessee. One of the few times I saw him cry was when he read a review about his work by John Simon, entitled, 'The Sweet Bird of Senility.'"[2] It might be argued that Williams' tears were irrelevant. In fact, despite pain, Williams was *not* defeated but went right on writing. There is, however, no question that critical rejection affected Williams' writing and vision of the world.

In some ways, *Clothes for a Summer Hotel* reveals a lack of self-confidence that may be directly attributable to the critical drubbing Williams took over and over in his late years. In using other writers, and in quoting liberally from those writers in his ghost play about the F. Scott Fitzgeralds, Williams may have been protecting himself from the exposure of his own writing. He may have been invoking the dead Fitzgeralds' posthumous popularity as a protective shield.

Yet, *Clothes* is very much a Williams play despite its borrowings. Tennessee used and transformed material from the works of F. Scott Fitzgerald, Zelda Fitzgerald's novel *Save Me the Waltz*, Ernest Hemingway's *A Moveable Feast*, and Nancy Mitford's biography *Zelda* to create his own very personal vision of the Fitzgeralds and friends. He reshaped those borrowed materials for his own very original purposes.

Interestingly, *Clothes* is the only Williams play that uses such extensive research, taking material from other writers. *Camino Real* used well-known literary figures to create its own special world, but it does not actually borrow lines or imagery from other sources. Nor could *Camino Real* in any way be considered biographical. Its two characters based on "real" men, Casanova and Lord Byron, exist in a totally fantastic setting and Williams used little specific biographical material in his depiction of them.

Why now? Why this interest in the Fitzgeralds and Hemingway? Why did they become so important to Williams? They were writers of such radically different temperament. In addition to Byron in *Camino Real*, Williams had used real artists before as characters in plays: D. H. Lawrence in *I Rise in Flame, Cried the Phoenix*, Hart Crane in *Steps Must Be Gentle*, Rimbaud and Van Gogh in *Mr. Merriwether*. But none of these figures serves as the protagonist of a full-length play.

Although the answer to this question is complex and will take the entire chapter to discuss, some answers are immediately understandable. Tennessee identified with both Scott and Zelda—Scott as a famous writer and Zelda as an unsuccessful artist. Both Fitzgerald and Hemingway had been unpopular in their late careers, often mocked by the critical establishment in the years prior to their deaths. They were young commercial and artistic successes who were later in disfavor. Both had suffered emotional "crack-ups." Both were alcoholic and both had sexual problems. In addition, Williams had sympathy for Zelda as someone yearning for artistic expression. Williams' fears of artistic worthlessness, exacerbated by the critics, made him identify with Zelda's lack of success. Also, her emotional problems and especially her confinement in a mental institution had resonance not only for himself but for his sister, Rose, whom Tennessee often saw and used as an extension of his own psyche.

However, Scott as sophisticated bon vivant and the writer of cool classic prose as well as Hemingway as outdoor huntsman and male prototype have very different personae from Tennessee's. In his later years, more often than not, Williams presented himself as a liberated "out-of-the-closet" homosexual who was not afraid to make his private life public. Unlike Fitzgerald or Hemingway, Williams seldom hid his vulnerability and was often accused of wearing his heart on his sleeve. In a way, the Fitzgerald-Hemingway images are a recrimination to the homosexual artist, traditional images of "real" men who can be artists and retain their masculinity. It is all involved with American images of men and artists, as well as homophobia and anti-art prejudice. Williams is defining and justifying himself in relationship not only to Hemingway and Fitzgerald but also to a continuity of American writers who work in a culture that is fundamentally commercial and demandingly heterosexual. It is a culture in which the sexuality of its artists is traditionally suspect.

Williams both identifies with and against Fitzgerald and Hemingway. His identification with Zelda as a victim of male role assignments is simpler to understand but neither is she totally sympathetic. Williams both loves and hates Fitzgerald and Hemingway even as he identifies with Zelda's vulnerability but loathes her destructive jealousy. In other words, his attitude is contradictory, competitive, complex, and rich.

Clothes for a Summer Hotel may be understood on several different levels, and it is this multilayering that contributes to its density as well as its openness to misunderstanding and misinterpretation. The first level is the realistic, the second is "fantastic" (the play as "ghost" play), the third is the play as archetypal psychological struggle, and a fourth is metaphysical or even religious. If this is not enough, the play in its implications contains specific social criticism. It is a very ambitious play and like so much of Williams' late works is as unique as it was misunderstood in its initial production.

The play went through much rewriting before it arrived at its Broadway "prompt book" state in the spring of 1980. But the greatest changes in the script occurred after its Broadway incarnation when it was published first in a Dramatist Play Service "acting" edition and then slightly changed for its New Directions publication later in 1981. Williams supervised the changes for the published versions so we may say that the published versions represent his last wishes for the play.

The basic structure of the play and, just as importantly, its tone and attitude remained the same in all the early drafts that evolved into the Broadway production. As usual with Williams, the early drafts were considered too long for commercial use and much of the initial work consisted of cutting and sharpening the dramatic action.

The revised published versions radically changed the play, added new material, cut much, but also shifted the play's tone and attitude toward its main characters. It is a very different play from the Broadway version and merits special attention. I shall first describe the Broadway version, its critical reception, and then discuss the published version, which to this day has not been produced.

On a realistic level, *Clothes for a Summer Hotel* "seems" to record a visit of F. Scott Fitzgerald from Hollywood, California, to his wife, Zelda, who is institutionalized in an asylum near Asheville, North Carolina. The time is ostensibly 1940, the year of Fitzgerald's death. This visit is an invention of Williams. In real life, Zelda had not seen Scott for a year and a half when he died in Hollywood in 1940. Their last real visit together had been in February 1939 when Scott and Zelda traveled together to Cuba in a disastrous last attempt to save their marriage. That trip had ended with Scott hospitalized in New York for alcoholism and Zelda returning to Highland Park, the name of the asylum near Asheville. Scott's visit to Asheville in the play on the eve of his death is a fictitious event, historically inaccurate, created for artistic purposes. Williams is not writing biography.

All versions of the play have the same basic stage setting and bear the same set note: "The stage is raked downward somewhat from the "mock-up" facade of Zelda's final asylum (Highland Hospital on a windy hill top near Asheville) which is entered through a pair of Gothic-looking black iron gates, rather unrealistically tall. At rise, there are only two other set pieces, a dark green bench far downstage and, just behind it and slightly right stage of it, a bush of flickering red leaves that suggest flames." To this basic set, units and furniture will be added to suggest different locales as the play moves back and forth in time and space. However, all action occurs in front of the ever-present brooding background of the asylum.

In the Broadway script at curtain rise, an impatient F. Scott Fitzgerald is discovered waiting to see his wife, Zelda, on the lawn of the asylum. Williams describes him as "a man with blurred edges, a tentative manner but a surviving dignity and capacity for indignation." Scott is dressed "unseasonably" in a "blue blazer, white flannels" and carries "a panama hat." Zelda will later make much of Scott's "unsuitable" clothes, dressed as he is for a "summer hotel." He speaks to two German nuns: "Are you sure my wife knows that I'm here? When I arrived here at one, three hours ago, I was told that she was in therapy, would I please wait a while. I have waited three hours. Now it is late, I'm not well. Do you understand what I'm saying? I am the writer Scott

Fitzgerald. My wife is a patient here named Zelda Fitzgerald." From offstage we hear Zelda's screaming voice: "Where is my Bach fugue, what has become of my record with my name printed on the cover with DO NOT TOUCH, ZELDA FITZGERALD? I WANT TO KNOW WHO THE FUCK HAS REMOVED MY RECORD?" Scott is shocked at Zelda's language but even more he is worried about her emotional state. He has been led to believe by doctors that Zelda has improved, has had a "remission." Gerald Murphy, an old friend appears. Scott is pleased to see him. Murphy warns Scott that Zelda's "been taking this thing, insulin shock, and the insulin's put a good deal of weight on her." They discuss Zelda's novel, *Save Me the Waltz*:

> Scott: Her writing I have to admit it was really quite impressive. I sent it to Perkins at Scribners, my publishers, you know: I praised it too highly. Now I'm not sure how I feel about her writing.
>
> Gerald: I suppose all professional writers are self-defensive, first, and maybe last.
>
> Scott: But that's all past now, Murph; anyway as it turns out, poor Zelda's book was practically dismissed as a weirdly beautiful but cloudy, indistinct mirror of—
>
> Gerald: Yours.
>
> Scott (flaring): *Well, wasn't it?*

Murphy leaves. Zelda briefly appears but refuses to believe that Scott is her husband: "No . . . no . . . no! An imposter!" She rushes back into the asylum. Murphy reappears. They discuss Sheilah Graham, the woman in Hollywood who is helping Scott rehabilitate himself. The mention of Graham motivates a flashback scene in which Fitzgerald is giving a Hollywood interview on his fortieth birthday. Fitzgerald sneaks drinks as he gives an interview to a young reporter who is obviously goading the older man: "I still seem to be good copy for journalists that delight in chronicling, the fall of, the break, the crack-up of an artist for such an eager public, so many and still so eager, for the chronicle of the decline and decay." The play returns to Scott and Murphy. Once more Murphy disappears as he shouts back a line in a mounting wind: "You and Zelda will be at our dance tonight at the villa?"

Zelda enters with a young intern. She asks the young man for advice in confronting Scott:

> Zelda: How shall I play it?
>
> Intern: Delicately, delicately.
>
> Zelda: Delicacy is not the style of a hawk.

The meeting begins. Zelda is icy and challenging. Scott tries to make normal conversation: "I'm completing a novel." She "plunges toward him and envelopes him in her coat." He retreats and they both fall to the ground. Contemptuously, she mocks herself and him: "Just wanted to see if my present appearance had aroused your sexual longing." He replies that sex was never "the really important thing between us." Zelda snaps back, "What was important to you was to absorb and devour."

Still, Scott is conciliatory. He wants her to take a ring from him to replace the marriage ring she threw away. He calls it "a ring of, of,—a covenant with the past that's always still present, dearest." Zelda refuses the ring: "I don't want it, I will not take it!"

Zelda tells Scott she is still working on her ballet: "Dance, dance, the career that I undertook because you forbid me to write!" Their long scene continues with a discussion of Sheilah Graham in which Zelda makes anti-Semitic remarks. Finally, she evokes happier memories of the twenties "when the world was young as we were and apparently as ecstatic" but the happy memories return her to her desire to dance. She demands that her Victrola be brought out so she can show Scott "the dance I'm preparing for my audition for Diaghilev this—"

Another flashback is evoked, this time a scene including Zelda's ballet teacher Mme. Egorova and the Murphys. Zelda dances a wild pathetic dance as the onlookers try to be supportive but privately despair over Zelda's chances of becoming a ballet dancer at this late time in her life.

Scott returns the scene to 1940, shouting out for hospital attendants to restrain the dancing Zelda: "See her out there? She is dancing for imaginary people, friends in Europe, she is hallucinating that she is in a ballet studio in Paris. Please, it's not endurable! I was informed that she had nearly recovered, flew out from the west coast to make sure and I discover she's more demented than ever, I am selling my talent, I am bartering my life and my daughter's future for this performance on the lawn, this grotesque hallucination."

The scene changes into another flashback. We are in a younger Scott's studio where the writer is hard at work. Zelda tries to speak with him. He snaps at her, "Zelda, you are interrupting my work, you mustn't interrupt my work, I thought that was agreed on, Zelda." She flies back at him, "What about my work." She presses him further and finally he answers her, "Your work is the work that all young southern ladies dream of performing someday. Living with a devoted husband and a beautiful child." Zelda rejects his idea of a role for her, "can't wear that, too confining." He tells her to go care for their crying child. The scene ends with her warning: "I could betray you by taking a lover could I? I could give it a try."

Another flashback grows out of the end of the previous scene. This time we are on a beach on the Riviera in France. Zelda changes into a robe while the Intern reappears and strips behind the two nuns "and reappears in a swim suit of the period." He is now Edouard, a young French aviator with whom Zelda will have what Williams believed to be Zelda's one adulterous affair.

Zelda and Edouard make plans for their assignation behind a "door that's locked and bolted."

> Zelda: With a window facing the sea, open to admit the sea-wind and the wave sounds, but with curtains that blow inward as if wanting to participate in our caresses!

Zelda is elated at the possibility of her betrayal of Scott. The act ends as two dancers perform a pas de deux upstage. An ecstatic curtain line from Zelda anticipates act 2: "And so the appointment is made! The hawk and the hawk will meet in light near the sun!"

Act 2 begins with the hotel love scene between Zelda and Edouard. "The little hotel room is set up downstage from the flaming bush." Scott is seated on a bench on the other side of the stage during the scene. The sexual experience has been wildly erotic for Zelda: "Scott and I always made love in silence. Tonight was the one time that I cried out wildly." Edouard is concerned that Scott may have heard Zelda's cries. Her answer is comically cruel: "How could he, having never heard them before." Edouard tells Zelda he must leave soon, "I am an aviator, that is true passion and it will always take me away." He gives her a photograph of himself. A bird call is heard to which Edouard responds: "Je reviens." Painfully Zelda understands. "I know what you said, you said that you were returning, you said it to the sky, and the bird, not to me."

Dance music fades into the scene. The Murphys' party has begun. The lovers will see each other one more time at the party. Immediately a host of guests in evening dress assemble on the asylum lawn now "strewn with lanterns." Zelda and Edouard come together again. He tells her that he must soon leave. She begins to get desperate: "Is the *secret* called *truth* being overheard by someone or everyone that's hostile to it?" To calm her, she asks him to dance with her. "The orchestra's playing a tango. Please, please take me to the dance floor."

Scott and Murphy enter. The writer is in a shocked state having just received news of the death of the English novelist Joseph Conrad. "We've just lost our only writer with a great tragic sense." Mrs. Pat Campbell, another guest at the party (and a famous English actress), responds: "Oh, that's why I found him so difficult to read!"

Scott sees Zelda and Edouard dancing the tango. He tries to stop the music. Suddenly the guests vanish and we are back in 1940. A Doctor comes out of the asylum to calm Scott's shouting. Scott confronts the Doctor with the fact that a doctor had called telling him that Zelda had been "transformed." He has flown east to find her more demented than ever. While he tries to calm Scott, the Doctor comments on Zelda's writing abilities: "Mr. Fitzgerald, I think you suspect as well as I know that Zelda has sometimes struck a kind of fire in her work that I'm sorry to say this to you, but I never quite found anything in yours, even yours, that was equal to it." Scott complains of "angina" pains: "I'll take a nitro tablet and just rest a bit."

The lights change and the party recommences. Ernest Hemingway and his first wife, Hadley, arrive. Gerald Murphy questions Hemingway on his opinion of Scott, Zelda, and the Aviator. Hemingway replies dismissively: "Zelda's a crazie, Scott's a rummy, so speculation is useless and interest is wasted."

Zelda enters, overhearing Hadley's remark that Scott pushes "Ernest's work harder than he pushes his own." Her response is suggestive and combative: "Is it the attraction of Ernest's invulnerable, virile nature? Isn't that the implication, that Scott is magnetized, infatuated with Ernest's somewhat too carefully cultivated aura of the prize fight and the bull ring and the man-to-man attitude acquired from Gertrude Stein."

An "elegant Black entertainer" begins to sing "Sophisticated Lady." The Murphys remark that the singer is the "latest sensation of the Moulin Rouge" flown "down for one party." While the entertainer sings, a short scene occurs between Zelda and Sara Murphy. Zelda confides that Edouard has left her alone. Growing more panicky, she loudly declares that she has been "abandoned by the young man with whom I've committed my first infidelity to Scott." Scott enters and "claps his hand over Zelda's mouth." She bites him. Seeing the altercation, Hemingway laughingly comments: "Scott had better have a rabies shot."

The singer begins to dance with "an extremely thin Woman with a lovely face." Sara and Mrs. Pat Campbell comment on the dancing. The former is worried about the outcome of her party: "Whenever he [Scott] approaches Ernest I alert the waiters to prepare for a disturbance." Almost immediately Scott and Ernest enter trading slurs at the expense of the black entertainer. Scott, now drunk, turns pugnacious: "What's that milk-choc'late fairy know about sophisticated ladies?" Hemingway eggs Fitzgerald on to cause a scene. Taking the dare, Scott approaches the singer: "HEY! MILK-CHOC'LATE, WANTA ASK YOU SOMETHING! Which gender do you prefer?" The singer "springs at Scott" and knocks him to the dance floor "with one blow." Sara Murphy ushers her guests offstage for a buffet supper leaving Scott and Hemingway alone together.

Their scene begins as a competition, or as Hemingway calls it a *"mano-mano,"* or hand-to-hand, confrontation. Scott wants to talk seriously but Hemingway doesn't want the conversation. "I've always felt that writers should not know each other . . . The competitive element in the normal male is especially prominent in the nature of writers." Hemingway goes on to criticize *The Crack-Up*, articles written by Fitzgerald for *Esquire* magazine: "What did they give you for exposing the pusillanimous side of you, Scott? Did it fetch a worth-while price? . . . Christ, when will you learn, if ever, that a man should at least behave like one in public . . . Perhaps you don't know the hypocritically pitying response to those pieces, especially the last one about the loss of capacity for any genuine feeling. 'Poor Scott, poor son-of-a-bitch, really finished.'" Fitzgerald's defense is touching and obviously pertinent to Tennessee Williams: "Lots of writers have cracked up in the past and lots will in the future and those in the future will read the book and know that another writer has been there before and come back."

The conversation turns to Zelda and her destructive effect on Scott. Hemingway interrogates: "Is she still trying that trick on you, that you're not equipped well enough to satisfy her?" At one point Scott puts his hand on Hemingway's shoulder and Hemingway snaps, "Take your hand off me Scott!" Scott responds strongly, "Christ! Have you really implied that I desired you sexually, Hem?" They come to an impasse, can get nowhere, exchange no comfort with each other. The scene ends when Hemingway prophesies (recounts?) Fitzgerald's manner of death. "I lacked the Ivy League Gentleman's predilection for dropping down dead on a Hollywood columnist's carpet." (This last comment will become clearer once I have discussed the "ghost" level of the play.)

Reeling from Hemingway's revelation Fitzgerald falls down shouting out at Hemingway: "DON'T NEED YOUR ASSISTANCE. Have acquired a certain facility for falling and getting up unassisted." Hadley rushes onstage. Hemingway ends the scene cruelly and conclusively: "Better tell someone that Scott has hit the carpet that's how our writer's duologue has ended."

The last scene belongs to Scott and Zelda. Approaching the subject of his death, Scott warns his mad wife: "Zelda, I may die soon—I didn't want to tell you but—If it suddenly happens, don't be." He wants her to be prepared and not too disquieted when the event occurs. She says she won't be. "Extinction is one of the few credible things." No sympathy, no comfort, no reconciliation. She tells Scott he has turned into a hack writer accepting only deception as a means of survival. Zelda asks one last request. Will Scott get her a private room? She is kept in a barred room with an incontinent old woman who is in a catatonic state.

A short scene with Zelda's doctor turns into a "future" scene in which Zelda's death is described to Scott. She will die in a fire in the asylum locked in her third floor room with five other women. Scott asks if Zelda can have a different room. The doctor asks if Scott can afford it. He cannot. Scott makes another request. "Could my wife and I spend a night together in a hotel room?" No. "It would be mutually destructive as she is now."

Zelda returns. They share one mutually kind moment:

> Scott: Well, the doctors are encouraged about your—improvement. They're genuinely optimistic for the first time since Switzerland.
>
> Zelda: Where I was first diagnosed as an incurable. How did we fall so far from that high trapeze, our youth?
>
> Scott: Love, were at an altitude that made us dizzy.
>
> Zelda: The winds on this hill top have the velocity of our past lives. We didn't place any bets on much of a future, did we, not in the gambling casinos at Antibes or anywhere else. Such profligacy: privileges of the gods or those born to great wealth.

Zelda forces Scott to look in her eyes and really see her, something she says he has never done before: "Oh, Scott, look at my eyes. See, do you see? They've turned into the eyes of a predatory bird, they're the eyes of a hawk hovering over some doomed creature of the wood or field with talons curved to clutch and tear away from the earth." Could he be her victim? She demands that he tell her what he sees. "Do that, have that remnant of courage! I won't let go till you do." He looks and answers her: *"Your eyes are as you describe them."* As a predator she would destroy him. Has he made her that way?

Visiting hours are over. Scott must leave. Zelda turns into a coy Southern belle mocking her upbringing: "Such a pleasant surprise to find myself still remembered by an old beau." He tries to escort her to the asylum but she pushes him away: "Stay back, let me go, forget me." The iron gates of the hospital slam shut "locking them with a finality." Zelda screams through the bars: *"I'm not your book anymore, can't be your book anymore, write yourself a new book!"* She exits and Scott, "despairing," cries out an earlier line: "The ring . . . a covenant with the past still always present, dearest." Curtain.

Tennessee Williams subtitled *Clothes for a Summer Hotel* "Ghost Play" and all editions of the published play as well as the program for the Broadway production contain a note which to some extent explain his purposes.

> This is a ghost play.
>
> Of course in a sense all plays are ghost plays since players are not actually whom they play.
>
> Our reason for taking extraordinary license with time and place is that in an asylum and on its grounds liberties of this kind are quite prevalent:

and also these liberties allow us to explore in more depth what we believe is truth of character.

And so we ask you to indulge us with the licenses we take for a purpose we consider quite earnest.

This "author's note" is somewhat different in the acting version:

This must be regarded as a ghost play because of the chronological licenses which are taken, comparable to those that were taken in *Camino Real*, the purpose being to penetrate into character more deeply and to encompass dreamlike passages of time in a scene.

The extent to which the characters should betray an awareness of their apparitional state will be determined more precisely in the course of a production.

In these notes Tennessee does not really explain all that he is about. His "justification" for the use of ghost characters is sketchy. Also, *are* all the characters to be considered ghosts? Perhaps he means that the play is written by a ghost (himself). Remember that John Simon had "generously" suggested Tennessee was dead. Also, it may be recalled that Tennessee's preopening Sunday piece for the *New York Times* on the occasion of *Vieux Carré* was entitled, "I Am Widely Regarded as the Ghost of a Writer." Ghosts are a major obsession of Williams in the late plays: *Vieux Carré* and *Mr. Merriwether* as well as *Clothes for a Summer Hotel*.

For all the subtitle's ironic connotations, we must take Williams' note as being "quite earnest." "Liberties" of madness are revelatory. The play will take chronological licenses (as well as license with real events). The purpose is psychological "truth of character," not the truth of external events nor a linear depiction of reality. Importantly, Williams' discussion of the characters' "awareness of their apparitional state" posits a major fact of the play. All its characters *are* ghosts; they are dead. They have died before the play begins.

All characters in the play seem to understand this "fact" except Scott. Hemingway's revelation to Scott in one of the play's climactic scenes tries to make clear to Fitzgerald the fact that he is dead. Whether or not Scott understands this is not clear.

Throughout the Broadway version of the play, characters broach the subject of their death (or Scott's death) only to be warned by a ringing bell signaling that they are treading on dangerous ground. This convention is set up by the Intern (Edouard) who acts as a kind of master of death ceremonies. The same Intern prompts Zelda to confront Scott in the first scene:

Zelda: You'll come to my assistance when I need you?

Intern: Yes, when my turn comes. Now go on.

Zelda: Why should this be demanded of me now after all the other demands? I thought obligations stopped with death!

Intern: Remarks like that will be answered with this: (A Bell Rings.) Go
on, go, he's waiting.

In Williams' ghost world it seems that death is as difficult to face after the fact
as it was before.

The device of the ringing bell was used consistently in the Broadway
production to remind the ghostly characters (and the audience) that the
characters are dead. But, it also warns the ghosts (characters) that this fact of
death must not be revealed to Scott. For some reason, Scott is not supposed
to be told that they and he are dead, and any discussion of death broaches
a dangerous subject. Presumably Scott must discover this "fact" for himself.
The ringing bell, later discarded by Tennessee in the published versions, was
an attempt on the playwright's part to give dramatic tension to this fantastic
ghost level of the play.

Practically and theatrically the ghost device allows the play to go from
past to future events in the Fitzgeralds' lives, making all time "present." Williams may dramatize many different happenings in the Fitzgerald story without
being a slave to chronological events.

As a ghost play, *Clothes* belongs to limited tradition of plays that use
similar devices: *The Ghost Sonata, Outward Bound,* and *No Exit* come readily
to mind but also Giraudoux's *The Enchanted,* even Noel Coward's *Blithe Spirit,*
and the last act of *Our Town.* These "fantasy" plays all create pictures of the
afterlife, imagined ideas of death. In all of the works, visions of death serve to
illuminate the playwrights' vision of life this side of the grave.

Although it is not clear, one could say that F. Scott Fitzgerald's confrontation with the ghosts of his life represents a kind of dying "flashback"
in the play. With both Zelda and Hemingway, Scott remembers impossible
relationships and, especially, with Zelda confronts his own possible culpability
in the creation of her madness. The action of the play may be the moment
of Scott's death, his life passing before his eyes, the moment of his extinction.
This moment becomes elongated into a full-length play in which Fitzgerald
tries to resolve the major conflicts of his life, in which he tries to make peace
with his ghosts.

Of course, since Zelda can see her death, and future events past the time
of Scott's death, the play is bigger than Scott's individual consciousness. The
play shifts focus from Scott's to Zelda's world as if the two ghosts could spiritually commingle; as if they were two parts of a single consciousness that are
nevertheless strangely separate.

Williams is not obvious. He will not show the play simply as Scott's dying moment. The play has more resonance than that but it *is* one of the levels on which the play may be experienced.

A third level of the play is that of archetypal psychological struggle. The male/female combatancy is a Strindbergian death-lock struggle for supremacy between individuals, but it is also a dramatization of a struggle that exists *within* every individual between the male and female parts of his/her personality. Williams suggests this interpretation in the Scene when Zelda interrupts Scott's work:

Zelda: Well, there is equality in us there; savagery equal, both sides.

Scott: Zelda, we are *one* side, indivisible. You know that by God, you'd better know that since I've staked my life on it that you'd know it and—respect it!

In this interpretation, the play is a Jungian dream in which the male (animus) side of the personality seeks unity with its female side (anima). In the play this effort only meets with rejection and permanent schism. Williams had dramatized this kind of psychological struggle before in *In the Bar of a Tokyo Hotel* and *The Two-Character Play*. It is one of his major obsessions in the late plays and even occurs many places where it may not at first be obvious.

Williams, in *Clothes*, is continuing this kind of bipolar, bisexual characterization, seeing male and female as having distinct characteristics that war within all human beings. In a sense, the play is a Jungian therapy for Tennessee and the play in essence is a self-portrait in which different characters represent different aspects of the playwright's psyche.

In no way does this imply a criticism of Williams. Possibly all art is therapy and self-portraiture. James Joyce's idea of the artist as someone detached and separate from his art object is probably a fiction, an image of the artist that tells us a great deal about James Joyce. Self is inescapable in art. At best one may hope for a multiplicity of "selves" within the single artist to give the work variety and scope.

On another level, the play is metaphysical metaphor. The ghost nature of the play is more than a dramatic device. As the late play of a man approaching his own death, the play contains not only thoughts of death but symbolic fantasies of the "beyond." In symbolic terms, the play is a religious statement, one that offers little consolation. What we know of death is what we know of life. Death is an eternally continuous replay, a performance of past sorrows and joys with no resolution. The view is vaguely Oriental, combining aspects of reincarnation with karmic penance. However, nirvana does not seem to be a possibility. Christian ideas of guilt and an eternal hell strongly assert their influence.

The play, then, exists on all these different levels and the levels interact so that it is impossible to read or understand the play on any one level alone. Just when the play starts to make sense on one level, something else is suggested. Because of these interacting levels a performance of the play is nearly impossible, certainly difficult. Stressing one level of interpretation over another unbalances the play and is necessarily incomplete. At times the play is realistic, at times it is fantastic. Sometimes the struggle seems between two real people yet Scott and Zelda are two characters who may function best as symbolic polarities. Finally, the play is wrapped in a miasma of death and unreality so that it is both real and unreal, sane and mad, representational and presentational, a true event and symbol of the unknown. The play is a nightmare to the would-be dramatic categorizer.

Even as the play on one level represents Scott Fitzgerald's attempt to reconcile the present with the past, so the Broadway production was an attempt to create art by using successful elements from the past of the major artists involved in the production. *Clothes for a Summer Hotel* reunited Tennessee Williams with Jose Quintero as director and Geraldine Page as Zelda Fitzgerald. They had all worked together in 1952 on the off-Broadway production of *Summer and Smoke*, a reputation-making event at the Circle in the Square Theatre. Produced after the unsuccessful Broadway mounting of *Summer and Smoke*, the off-Broadway production gave credence to the play as well as wide publicity to the talents of Quintero and Page and in large part was responsible for their subsequent careers. The production of *Clothes*, then, was a reunion of talents that had nourished each other in earlier years. As such, it was good for publicity and a talisman for future success.

Michiko Kakutani, writing for the *New York Times*, did a series of three articles on the production: one on the first rehearsal on January 1, 1980; another previewing the play's New York opening on Tennessee's sixty-ninth birthday, March 26, 1980; and a postproduction article written several months after the play's closing. The last article, entitled, "Williams, Quintero and the Aftermath of a Failure," stimulated a letter to the editor from Harold Clurman and a final letter from Tennessee Williams.

The story of this production is by now familiar in its pattern of rehearsal problems and critical negativity. Above all, it is a sad story—sad because it is the story of Williams' last Broadway production and because it was an "end-of-an-era" production, produced in the manner that had created Williams' early successes. The ritual of out-of-town tryouts on a play that has not been successful either in England or in several regional theaters virtually disappeared from Broadway in the 1980s, and *Clothes* may have been one of the last casualties of that system. As in the play, all attempts to recapture the past were disastrously disappointing. In a sense, the experience was a ghost production of a ghost play.

From the start, all was uneasy despite public proclamations of faith in the play. All said the play was too long. Page wanted another rewrite before rehearsals began. She was also unhappy with Kenneth Haigh as Scott Fitzgerald. She had wanted her husband, Rip Torn, to play Scott. But Tennessee had refused to have Torn, stating to friends that the actor had once assaulted him at a party. Nor was Williams absolutely certain that Page, now considerably overweight, could play the love scenes of a younger Zelda in which the actress had to appear as uncovered as possible.

Initial statements on the play's meaning are not illuminating when read in retrospect. Quintero in Kakutani's first article stated that the play was most concerned with *survival*. "In Tennessee's work, it is always the question of survival."[3] Granted, Tennessee was an extraordinary survivor; however, *Clothes* is a *fantasia* on death in which none of the characters survive. In fact, they're all dead to begin with. Page's interview statement sounds closer to the play's real spirit: "The play is a wonderful kind of puzzle of reflecting mirrors."[4] Upbeat publicity comments aside, the play is in no way a hymn to survival.

The play's rehearsal period was impossibly short: twenty-four rehearsal days before opening for its first tryout performance in Washington, DC. As in *Red Devil*, financial problems bugged the production. Kakutani reported on these in her second preopening article:

> Having set an initial budget of $400,000, the producer Elliott Martin had managed to persuade the financier Donald Cecil, Columbia Pictures, and the Schuberts to help with the financing, but the money was not completely in until the fourth week of rehearsal and even then, matters were not legally settled until the Friday before opening night in Washington.
>
> Several members of the company complained that their first paychecks had bounced and certain plans for costumes had to be curtailed for lack of funds.[5]

The producer, Elliott Martin, much to his credit, tried to give the play a first class production. The ultimate staging was generally praised; but the problems involved created tension that did not help the play in rehearsal.

Another important problem added to the tense situation. More and more, in his late career, Tennessee absented himself from rehearsals, especially when tensions mounted and problems seemed insoluble. This had also been true during *Red Devil* when during the culmination of problems with Merrick, he had flown to Rome. Now, with the play in Washington, after receiving poor reviews, Tennessee seemed incapable of massive rewrites "on the road."

He abandoned the production in its tryouts after cutting the play as much as he thought he could. "The script needed my attention but New York was cold and depressing and I ran away to Key West. Anyway, there are just too many imponderables in a production: does she or doesn't she know her lines? Can they be heard in the balcony? The fights over the cost of a certain light. And it's so difficult to have everything held upon the delicate thread of a woman's nerves. The writing is so much fun it's what you live for, but the production well, it's a wonder you live through that."[6] Surely these are the words of an aging and battle-scarred veteran of the Broadway stage. There is no dishonor in age but the energy and nerves needed to survive the pressures of the commercial theater had taken their toll.

As in most late Williams Broadway productions, tension was created because the play was a weapon for reestablishing Williams' tarnished artistic reputation. This was what Tennessee most wanted. Quintero was also aware of the "proving" nature of the production. It was more than another play. The pressure to be successful was even greater than usual. And, of course, the production was a gesture against "devouring Time." Said Quintero: "In working with Tennessee and Gerry again, you're really confronting the past again and you're terrified you won't be able to meet the demand. And this show seems particularly charged because it hits at a particular stage of age for all of us—Tennessee is no longer young, Gerry is not, I am not. When you're much younger, there is at least the thought of so many other chances, but when you think of, say, Tennessee now how many other chances for a first-class production will he have?"[7]

In the end, in Chicago, Williams returned to rewrite the play: "For the next week and a half, he and Mr. Quintero met every morning in the playwright's hotel room, reading possible cuts to one another, discarding the repetitious, the dull, the irrelevant, and writing new transitions . . . In all, over 45 minutes were removed. For the actors, it meant learning new cues and new blocking. For Quintero, it meant restaging almost the entire show."[8]

A study of the early and later drafts of the play, pre-Broadway, generally reveals a sharpening of the dramatic focus in the rewrites. In the earliest drafts one has the feeling that Williams put the characters together and let them just talk at each other. Digressions abound. Tennessee genuinely seems to have fallen in love with the Fitzgeralds' story. The play began as a compendium of their lives. The Broadway script tried to define the dramatic conflict more specifically. Unfortunately, in stressing the conflict between the characters, some of the characters' dimensionality as well as audience sympathy may have been lost.

Of all the many negative reviews Williams received for productions of his late plays, none are so overridingly sad as those received by *Clothes for a Sum-*

mer Hotel. Many reviews had been crueler, more vitriolic, more self-serving. But the reviews for *Clothes*, in what many must have guessed might be Williams' last Broadway play, show the critics almost reluctant to be vituperative. "Is this, then, at last, Mr. Williams' 'Indian Summer' play? Has his evident affinity for Scott and Zelda culled out his old talents, his delicacy and depth and strength? Does this play, born out of his own artistic decline, give evidence that the decline has finally been arrested. No. Alas, and dammit, no. Not by a long, sad chalk."[9]

Even Clive Barnes, a champion of late Williams, could find little good to say about *Clothes for a Summer Hotel*. While recognizing that "the structure of the play is as in a dream," Barnes could see no overall form to the play. "Williams has failed to shape it into the special surrealistic coherence that even a dramatic fantasy must have." Even sadder, Barnes, like other critics, found the play's writing itself to be disappointing: "Much of the writing is almost defiantly flat and banal, as if Williams were embracing bathos in an attempt to create a cold reality in a picture postcard world."[10]

John Simon said of the play that there was a "curious text book quality to much of the writing." And overall, while Simon called the play "not embarrassing," he found *Clothes for a Summer Hotel* to be an "unfocused, meandering, unnecessary play." Noting the source material of several books, Simon added, "Almost everything of interest and value is contained in one of those books and is better in its original form."[11]

Howard Kissel, in *Women's Wear Daily*, saw the play's subject matter as loaded with liabilities. "If the play were not about celebrities, perhaps Williams might have put the material in closer focus. As it is, he has too many opportunities for digressions . . . [Williams] treats the central character Zelda, with little sympathy, though her situation has a certain poignancy . . . Her affecting, ingratiating moments are few. For the most part she whines. She nags Scott or torments him. It is hard to find her tragic or even sympathetic."[12]

Brendan Gill in the *New Yorker* furiously castigated Williams for a false picture of the Fitzgeralds. Gill, feeling called upon to "bear witness to the mischief that has been done them," called the play "false body snatching" using "scraps that are coarse, inaccurate, and gushingly illiterate." Seeing the play as an attempt at biography, Gill, admitting his personal knowledge of Fitzgeralds' circle of friends, was full of "vehement dismay" at Williams use of his friends and acquaintances.[13]

As usual, Walter Kerr was most thought provoking in his criticism of the play but also most damning: "The most distressing thing about [*Clothes*] is the fact that Mr. Williams' personal voice is nowhere to be heard in it." Finding the play with "no growth, no change, no flow of life," Kerr wrote that the performers as well as the play allowed for no "personal contact between this

Scott, this Zelda . . . Estrangement, remoteness seem total." Insightfully, Kerr identified one of the play's greatest difficulties: "Mr. Williams hasn't arrived at a defined attitude toward either of his unhappy artists."[14] Kerr, always a classicist and Aristotelian, wants the play to feel one way, to be one kind of play. But the late Tennessee's attitude is more complex.

Harold Clurman in his review called the play "well written," but wondered, "Why are we not moved nor genuinely interested?" Clurman's answer is disconcerting: "There seems to be some disconnection now between Williams's inner self and his creative practice. His craft remains but the feeling is no longer spontaneous, no longer, that is, inspired by newly refreshed sources of his being . . . Habit and skill have replaced Williams' original compassion and the deep-seated need of his soul." Summing up his observation of the play's problems, Clurman wrote, "There was too little heart at the center."[15]

It is almost axiomatic in the theater that artists are not supposed to publicly react to poor reviews. This time, however, Williams as well as Quintero broke silence and made known their anguish in the last of Kakutani's three articles. *Clothes* had been the bitterest of all failures. Williams commented to Kakutani, "I had a greater emotional investment in this one, you know. I'm 69 years old and I thought this was my last chance to do a play on Broadway. But it didn't work, it just didn't work."[16] So strongly had Williams wanted *Clothes* to succeed that he had put twenty thousand dollars of his own money into keeping the play running after the reviews came out. This was something he had never done before.

Tennessee blamed the failure on "insufficient time, insufficient money, and improper casting." He particularly felt that Kenneth Haigh as Scott was miscast. Feeling betrayed by his friends and coworkers who had praised the play, he complained, "All I heard was how beautiful it was . . . People should tell you what is wrong with a play before they rush it into production." For Williams the experience has been sobering, giving him a new understanding that Broadway was no longer a possible avenue of artistic expression: "It's just a marketplace where middle-aged men get their jollies looking at Ann Miller. People go for the wrong reasons now—for escape, for entertainment. The whole New York scene has changed enormously. I think Albee put it very well, 'Broadway has become like the strip of Vegas.' I feel old, but I don't feel as old as Broadway—Broadway has become senile, not I."[17]

Vowing to leave for Australia with "one or two American actresses," Tennessee gave vent to his pain and anger: "I think I've been expelled from America, and I'm no longer in the mood to take it."[18]

This public expression of emotion left Tennessee open to criticism and ridicule. Harold Clurman wrote an "appalled" letter to the *New York Times* in reaction to Tennessee's comments in Kakutani's interview. Chiding Williams for his ungenerous comments about the actors and producers, Clurman also called Williams' plans for Australia "very close to a disgraceful joke." Clurman's main point, however, is more important. The commercial theater, he writes, has always been a place where people go "for escape, for entertainment": "When, by and large, have they not on Broadway especially? The commercial theater (as well as the regional and off-Broadway theaters) has always been that way everywhere except where institutional, subsidized theaters exist." Clurman reproves the Broadway artists who "cry out in 1980 against the commercial theater" calling them "absurdly innocent" and "ignorant of the history of our stage." He asks Tennessee and "colleagues" to "maintain their self-respect and artistic pride."[19]

Clurman states that his "reproval" is not addressed to Williams and Quintero as individuals. "Their statements are reflections or echoes of an unnecessary manner of thinking about the arts—especially the theater in terms of receipts, publicity, prizes, awards, interviews, which are equated with excellence. This devastating attitude not only cripples a host of artists, but inflicts many of the reviewers, and the largest proportion of the audience. It is a corruption that goes deep—deeper than just the theater."[20] This last statement is worthy of Clurman, cofounder of the Group Theatre and author of *The Fervent Years*. But it also forgets years of much artistic Broadway excellence, say 1920 to 1960, in which great theater did originate on Broadway in a commercial setting outside any state subsidy. Also, it would have been generous of Clurman to be more understanding of Williams' lashing out. He might have tempered his dismay with more human understanding of the way things are said in the heat of emotion. Nevertheless, Clurman accurately puts his finger on Tennessee's "Achilles heel." Williams' desire for approval and commercial success was a deep need. This is perhaps a foolish need, but it is also a very human failing, especially in artists. It is a weakness certain to cause pain especially in an artistic endeavor. Of course, Clurman never quite absented himself from the commercial arena, on occasion enjoyed the fruits of commercial success in artistic projects. Probably what bothers Clurman most was Tennessee's lack of stoic control in expressing his pain.

Tennessee responded to Clurman's letter in a more reflective, even humorous mood: "I've said more than once that it is possible to retire from a business but not from an art. Certainly in my case this has affirmed itself repeatedly." The playwright called his remarks in Kakutani's article "the invariable shock and anger that any non-masochistic being feels when subjected to punishment of a cruel and unusual nature." Williams further stated that his nerves were "an integral part of my equipment as a writer" and that the "fire and sense of violent drama" in his plays were the product of those writer's nerves.[21]

Tennessee did not go to Australia. Rather, he almost immediately rewrote *Clothes for a Summer Hotel* after its Broadway closing. He had no promise of another production, but the play was to be published in an acting edition for Dramatists Play Service, and Williams used the opportunity to extensively rework the play. There was a concerted effort on Williams' part to make his characters more sympathetic, and most of the play's changes were to that end.

Right from the beginning of the revised play, we see a less demanding, more patient Scott. The rewritten play begins thus:

Sister One: If you are tired of waiting—

Scott (cutting in): Yes, I am tired but I will continue to wait as long as she keeps me waiting.

Zelda's first offstage voice is no longer strident. We hear her practicing her ballet: "Un, deux, pliez, un, deux, pliez." Prior to confronting Scott, Zelda admits to the Intern that she is "afraid." And upon meeting Scott, Zelda no longer attacks him in a mockery of lust. Their initial meeting is gentler and more possibly conciliatory:

Scott: Don't be so standoffish, let me kiss you. (He goes to Zelda and kisses her in a detached manner.) I would describe that as a somewhat perfunctory response.

Zelda: And I'd describe it as a meaninglessly conventional gesture to have embraced at all after all. (He draws back wounded: she smiles, a touch of ferocity in her look.) Sorry, Goofo . . . It's been so long since we've exchanged more than letters . . . And you fly back tomorrow? We have only this late afternoon in which to renew our acquaintance.

The play is cut even more. In his brief first scene Gerald Murphy comments, "It will be over in—(looks at wristwatch) one hour and forty-five minutes." He is referring to the play's length as well as Scott's interview with Zelda. Scott's scene with the critical journalist is cut as are the death reminding ringing bells. Tennessee is obviously trying to make the play an acceptable commercial length.

However, he does add an important monologue for Zelda in which, alone on stage, she tries to express what Williams in a stage direction calls "the desperate longing" of the "insane to communicate something of their private world to those from whom they're secluded." In this stage direction, Williams further tells us that this speech is enormously important in order "to win the audience to her inescapably." But he is also aware that his words may not fulfill their purpose. "The present words given her are tentative; they may or may not suffice in themselves: the presentation performance must."

Zelda: There's something I—(Wind sound up: drowns her voice: then subsides.) But the winds, the winds, this continual lamentation of wind as if (Wind sound rises again and subsides.) they were trying to give one single tongue to all our agonies here.

Neither Zelda nor Tennessee can quite find words to express the perhaps inexpressible experience of insanity. He uses sound effects of the wind instead of words, wind drowning out words, to express Zelda's frustrated attempts at communication.

The Zelda-Edouard scenes remain the same, as does the structure of the play. The play is still a ghost play with the possible interpretation that Scott has died that day and does not know it. The suggestion, however, is even more subtle. It is only occasionally hinted at, for instance, in the scene at the party between Zelda and Sara Murphy.

Zelda: Do you think Scott's arrival means that I'm not alone?

Sara: He's had a shock, someone's death.

Zelda: Oh, has someone informed him that he's a—?

Sara: I'm not sure who it was. (Lowers voice.) Please be careful, Zelda!

The play's thematic concern with gender and the possibility that the play is interpretable as a symbolic struggle of male/female polarities is clearly discussed in the rewrite. In one scene Zelda calls Scott "prettier than me." Scott is offended at the remark and rebukes her.

Scott: You know as well as I know what it disparages is the virility of . . . (Takes another drink.)

Zelda: Oh, but that's so established in your case. And even if it wasn't— know what I think?

Scott: Never.

Zelda: I think that to write about women, there's got to be that, a part of that, in the writer, oh, not too much, not so much that he flits about like a—

Scott: Fairy?

Zelda: You're too hard on them, Scott, I don't know why. Do they keep chasing you because you're so pretty that they think you must be a secret one of them?

The suggestion of repressed homosexuality in Scott is made even more explicit in the Fitzgerald/Hemingway scene. Critics who were offended at the suggestion that Fitzgerald and Hemingway might be "closet" homosexuals would care even less for this new scene. However, it is a much gentler and more tender scene with revealed softness, even in Hemingway.

> Scott: It's said of both of us that we always write of the same woman, you of Lady Brett Ashley in various guises and me of—
>
> Hemingway: Zelda and Zelda and more Zelda. As if you'd like to appropriate her identity and her—
>
> Scott: And her?
>
> Hemingway: Sorry, Scott, but I almost said gender. That wouldn't have been fair. It's often been observed that duality of gender can serve writers well.

Tennessee is posing a theory of art in this scene as well as dramatizing an imaginary confrontation between these two literary friends (rivals). Hemingway continues, "You know as well as I know that every goddam character an honest writer creates is part of himself." Scott replies, "We do have multiple selves as well as what you call dual gender."

The scene goes further in making very clear a sexual tension between Hemingway and Fitzgerald.

> Hemingway: You had the skin of a girl, mouth of a girl, the soft eyes of a girl, you—you solicited attention. I gave it, yes. I found you touchingly vulnerable.
>
> Scott: These attributes, if I did have them in—
>
> Hemingway: You did have them.
>
> Scott: And they were repellent to you?
>
> Hemingway: They were disturbing to me.
>
> Scott: Why?
>
> Hemingway: I'd rather not examine the reason too closely.

Scott pursues the question, noting Hemingway's depiction of homosexuality in certain of his works. Hemingway, as ghost, changes the subject to his future death, "blasting my exhausted brains out with an elephant gun." His reason for suicide is chilling especially as written by Williams at this point in his career: "I chose to blast my brains out for no reason but the good and sufficient reason that my work was finished, strong, good work, all done—no reason for me to continue." Scott's final remark unites Hemingway to him and also to Zelda as fellow human exiles: "I suspect that you were lonelier than I and possibly even as lonely as Zelda." Hemingway mutters, "Fuck it," and brusquely crosses out singing snatches of a song that has earlier been identified with his last wife, "Miss Mary."

In the final scene, Zelda approaches Scott with appreciation for his suffering. She tells the Intern, "It's incredible how, against appalling odds, dear Scott achieved a Christly parallel through his honoring of long commitments, even now to me, a savage ghost in a bedraggled tutu, yes, it's a true and incredible thing."

Despite his "softening" of the major characters, Williams keeps the last scene hard and unreconciled. Zelda confronts Scott with his fear of death: "Why were you afraid to? The sentence is imposed—there's no appeal, no reprieve!—Don't be so gutless about it." Scott becomes increasingly agitated, dizzy; "he clutches hold of the bench." Zelda takes his wrist.

> Zelda: Where's your pulse? I can't feel your pulse.
>
> Scott: Never mind.
>
> Zelda: Somebody has to point out to you these little physical symptoms, not to alarm you but—
>
> Scott (exploding involuntarily): You've pointed out to me nothing I haven't observed myself.

The scene is both a death scene and a recognition scene, both of his death and the failure of his relationship with Zelda. This is as clear as Williams ever gets with the through line of action that defines Scott's confrontation with his death. The greater recognition seems to be his understanding of the total failure of his marriage: "The mistake of our ever having met! The monumental error of the effort to channel our lives together in an institution called marriage. Tragic for us both. Result slag heap of a dream." Zelda agrees. "Something's been accomplished, a recognition painful, but good therapy's often painful."

She starts to retreat into the asylum. But Scott still cannot let her go. As in the Broadway version, Zelda screams out at him after she has gone behind the bars: "I can't be your book, anymore! Write yourself a new book!" Scott's last lines remain almost the same: his lines about the ring as a "covenant with the past, still always present, Zelda!" Only the last word is changed from "dearest" to "Zelda." There is no letting go of nor escape from Zelda. She will always be present.

Tennessee added an interesting stage direction that reinforces the play's lack of resolution: "Scott turns downstage; his haunted eyes ask a silent question which he must know cannot be answered." What is the "silent question"? There are so many possibilities. But the one that makes the most sense would seem to be "Will we ever find peace?" No answer.

It is clear that Tennessee, in this rewritten published version of the play, is taking to heart the remarks of some of the critics, especially Walter Kerr and Harold Clurman. They had complained of a lack of warmth, "heart," in the play. Williams' famous compassion seemed absent in the Broadway version. The published version tries very hard to make Scott and Zelda more sympathetic.

Several points must be made about the critics and Tennessee's reaction to them. First, Tennessee was obviously anxious to improve the play, and he obviously believed the play would be improved by making his characters more sympathetic. In describing the love-hate relationship of the Fitzgeralds, the play may have initially stressed the hate. While not removing the hatred, the published version is careful to show love on both sides while recognizing the irreconcilable nature of the Fitzgeralds' relationship. In this sense, the published version is an improvement on the Broadway script.

The problem, however, is more difficult. The Broadway play was crueler, more frightening. But cool plays are not necessarily inferior plays. More than one critic (Brecht, for example) has often complained of "sentimentality" in American drama. Strindberg's couples seldom show sympathetic kindness in their to-the-death love battles. And it is precisely this uncompromising cruelty that gives Strindberg's plays their power. The Broadway *Clothes* was closer to Strindberg in its depiction of love-hatred. It was more frightening. The published version, softer but not sentimental, has more variety of tone and makes the characters more traditionally sympathetic. They are two different plays with two different attitudes to their characters. The first is more hateful and horrible and possibly more powerful. The second is more compassionate, possibly more moving. More terror in the first, more pity in the second.

However, what is debatable is the critics' assumption that compassionate plays are necessarily better plays. There are many great plays that fill us with more horror than compassion: *The Bacchae, Medea, Hedda Gabler, Dance of Death, Troilus and Cressida, Coriolanus, The White Devil, The Duchess of Malfi.* Critics should not dictate the way an artist should feel about his subject, and an artist should not take critics' words as gospel.

In rewriting *Clothes* to make its characters more sympathetic, Williams betrays a lack of self-confidence in the way he feels about this characters. But because his feelings are mixed, containing as much admiration as hatred, the rewrite is an equally valid, if different, play.

It would be interesting to see if the published version of *Clothes* would be more successful with an audience. One suspects that it would be. To this date, however, there have been no productions of *Clothes* using either the Broadway version or the published script.

None of the critics really understood *Clothes for a Summer Hotel.* Virtually no critic recognized the possibility that Scott might be dying or already dead and that the play records his moment of death. The implications of the ghost play were either avoided or ridiculed. The play was often described as plotless, and yet there are two lines of action that the play follows. The first is Scott's attempt to attain a reconciliation with Zelda. The second is Scott's journey toward his personal death. These arcs of action and Scott's growing understanding are the ways in which the play moves. This movement in Scott toward a realization of his mortality and his utter failure with Zelda make him the protagonist and consciousness of the play. Zelda suffers but she does not change. She understands at the beginning what Scott must learn in the course of the action.

Another major critical misunderstanding was the way in which critics wanted Williams to give insight or depth to the famous characters portrayed in the play. The play is not an attempt at biography. Unlike many plays and films that recount (with relish) the destruction of famous artists, this play uses the mythology of Zelda, Scott, and Hemingway to make a statement about relationships and reality. The truth of character is not specific but is archetypal. Williams has no particular psychiatric understanding of the special problems of Scott and Zelda. He uses the "idea" of Scott and Zelda. By the time Tennessee wrote this play, the Fitzgeralds had become cultural icons, representatives of certain universal types and cultural problems. They were beautiful; they were damned. Scott is an archetypal figure of the great self-destructive writer who never fulfills himself. He was also charm personified. Zelda is a mythic example of the beautiful woman who goes mad through the frustration of her potential, a victim of a male-dominated society. Likewise, Hemingway is by now a mythic figure of troubled masculine assertion.

Our gods are our celebrities, especially the ones who have died. Performers most often enter this pantheon: Marilyn Monroe, James Dean, Elvis Presley, Frances Farmer. Some writers attain the same status. Of all American writers, Fitzgerald and Hemingway most clearly achieved this kind of fame. All of them represent more than their works. Their lives make them cultural figures, representatives of deep-seated dramas in the national psyche. Over and over the pattern is the same. Glamour, success, sexiness, money, victimization, self-destruction, and finally death—this is the pattern of greatest national interest. Our gods most often die young.

Something in this pattern speaks to our fantasies and our fears. As the Greek playwrights used the gods for dramatic purposes, as Shakespeare used dead kings, so Williams, true to his culture, uses dead artists as his archetypal characters. Williams' use of the Fitzgeralds represents a "deconstruction" in the same way that Andy Warhol used Marilyn Monroe's image in his silk screen paintings. His work says more about our culture than it does about Monroe. The truth of Monroe was not important to Warhol, but the culture's *idea* of Monroe is very important.

To accuse Williams of being false to the actual facts of the Fitzgeralds' lives or his characters in lacking psychological complexity totally misunderstands Williams' intentions. It does not matter that Shakespeare's Richard III is not historically accurate or that Brecht's Galileo is not psychologically subtle. Moliere's Don Juan is different from that of Mozart/Da Ponte or Tirso de Molina or Errol Flynn or his real life model, Casanova. Williams' Fitzgeralds are *Williams'* creatures, not themselves. It is more expanding to try to understand what an artist is doing than to tell him what to do.

The dialogue in the play *is* at times "textbookish." Characters sometimes sound less like human beings than "ideas" of characters. But much critical comment on the language is based on criteria of dramatic speech for the realistic style. These characters are ghosts with pressing needs. They go right to the issues that are torturing them. As ghosts they even imitate ideas of themselves. Speeches are sometimes heavily significant, repetitious, or even platitudinous, as if heard in an echo chamber. Voices come from echoes of characters rather than from realistic flesh-and-blood people. May not Williams invent his own ghost language?

Nor did any of the critics point out the lush poetic speeches that express Zelda's sexual awakening with the Aviator, Edouard. Granted the language is rich, but except perhaps to the most dietary of tastes, it is also beautiful. Zelda speaks with a sensual imagery appropriate to her unleashed pleasure: "The champagne is still cool as the counterfeit moon and I am cold without you. Return. Come back to bed. We haven't slept together, only made love. These are words. Words are the love-acts of writers. Don't turn. I love your back. It's sculpted by Praxiteles and even in the moon wash, it's copper gleaming. Except for the groin which is dark with imagination."

An interesting comparison may be made between Zelda Fitzgerald's and Tennessee Williams' writing, revealing both Williams' attraction to Zelda's writing and their difference. In the Broadway production and in all early drafts, Zelda has a long reminiscence about New York in the 1920s. The speech is a paraphrase by Williams of a descriptive paragraph in Zelda's novel, *Save Me the Waltz*. Here is Zelda's original:

> Vincent Youmans wrote the music for those twilights just after the war. They were wonderful. They hung above the city like an indigo wash, forming themselves from asphalt dust and sooty shadows under the cornices and limp gusts of air exhaled from closing windows. They lay above the streets like a white fog off a swamp. Through the gloom, the whole world went to tea. Girls in short amorphous capes and long flowing skirts and hats like straw bathtubs waited for taxis in front of the Plaza Grill; girls in long satin coats and colored shoes and hats like straw manhole covers tapped the tune of a cataract on the dance floors of the Lorraine and the St.

Regis. Under the somber ironic parrots of the Biltmore a halo of golden bobs disintegrated into black lace and shoulder bouquets between the pale hours of tea and dinner that sealed the princely windows; the clank of lank contemporaneous silhouettes drowned the clatter of tea cups at the Ritz.[22]

It is easy to see what Tennessee sees in this descriptive piece. It creates a mood with idiosyncratic details against a cultural context. The writing is not unlike some of Tom's speeches in *The Glass Menagerie*, tinged as they are with irony and sensuality. Here is how Tennessee used and changed the piece as Zelda's reminiscence in the play:

Vincent Youmans wrote the music for those twilights just after the war. They floated over the city like a deep violet wash and through the dusk the whole world went to tea, girls in amorphous capes and long flowing skirts and hats of delicate straw, waiting for taxis in front of the Plaza Grill, girls in long satin coats torn out of the shimmering sky. They tapped the tune of cataract on the dance floor of the Lorraine and St. Regis. Under the somber parrots of the Biltmore, a halo of golden bobbed hair disintegrated into smoky gray lace and orchid shoulder bouquets. Oh, it was all, all youngness; Lillian Lorraine would be drunk as the universe, the cosmos, on top of the New Amsterdam by midnight and football teams breaking training would scare the waiters with their intoxicated antics in the Fall, yes muscles that strained the seams of their tuxedos and dress uniforms caught you about the waist, tight, tighter and on your soft, slender belly you felt the urgency of the question their bodies—implored.

Both pieces have been quoted at length to show Tennessee's clear debt to Zelda but also the difference in the two writers. Starting with "Oh it was all, all youngness," the speech is all Williams, building the speech to its climactic conclusion. Zelda is more ironic while Tennessee creates a sensual rhapsody. Zelda continually undercuts her sensuality with odd word choices.

The speech was cut from the published editions. This is a shame as it is one of the few lyric moments in the play that reveals the beauty of Zelda's youth. That beauty adds poignancy to Zelda's fall, creating as it does the whole jazz age in one lovely memory.

Possibly Tennessee was embarrassed by his absorption of Zelda's work. Walter Kerr in his review of the play specifically noted the beauty of this passage. "Though there are occasional echoes of the real thing (after World War I the music of Vincent Youmans 'floated over the city like a deep violet wash') the finest playwright of our time has spent his evening trying hard, much too hard, to sound like other people."[23] It is ironic that Kerr chose this passage, paraphrased from Zelda, as the "real thing." Zelda's ghost must have enjoyed the joke. But, of course, it does sound like "early" Williams and that is what

Kerr really enjoys about it. Also, note in that one quoted line how Williams changed Zelda's original: "floated over" as opposed to "hung over" and "deep violet wash" as changed from "indigo." These changes alter the tone of the piece and create a sexier, more dramatic memory. Also, Williams creates a whole coda that takes the speech beyond Zelda's intentions.

Other words and ideas are borrowed from his source material. For instance, Zelda's description of herself as a hawk comes from Ernest Hemingway's *A Moveable Feast*: "Zelda was very beautiful and was tanned a lovely gold color and her hair was a beautiful dark gold and she was very friendly. Her hawk's eyes were clear and calm."[24] In Williams, Zelda says of herself, "Delicacy is not the style of a hawk." She refers several times to her "hawk eyes."

Williams must have consciously appropriated the other writers. Perhaps it was done out of fear of his own waning powers, but he really need not have feared. At its best, *Clothes* reveals Tennessee able to speak his own voice, however influenced that voice may be and regardless of his use of the other writers.

All versions have *Clothes* have enormous potential for poetic theatricalism. The "mock-up" asylum in the background should only suggest a real building. The iron gates, the flaming bush, the raked stage all reveal a playwright able to create a special world through stage pictures as well as words. The Murphy party with lanterns and streamers and twenties costumes all create a beauty that is especially poignant because of its presence on the lawn of an asylum.

Costume, likewise, is used by a playwright able to make symbolic statements with purely theatrical elements. Scott is inappropriately dressed in light "clothes for a summer hotel." His touching appearance bespeaks a faded elegance totally at odds with the play's darkness and therefore oddly moving. Likewise, Zelda's initial appearance in a bedraggled ballet tutu is grotesque but also sadly beautiful.

As in most late Williams, the leading roles are enormously difficult. Zelda is a particularly difficult role to cast since the actress must appear as her younger, more beautiful self in certain scenes. At the beach, in the bedroom, and at the party there should be an evocation of Zelda's extraordinary beauty that makes her present state more tragic. She must not look "like a gypsy moth that's been put through a shredder" as Walter Kerr described Geraldine Page's appearance in the play.[25] Of course, the actress must also have great emotional resources, and Page was obviously cast for those abilities.

Nor is Scott an easy role to cast or play. Far less flashy than Zelda and given fewer "arias," the actor must combine style, charm, and an inner life that suggests unexpressed suffering, repressed pain. Kenneth Haigh, an Englishman, was cast, according to producer Elliott Martin, for his sense of style. "Few American actors seem to have that sort of thing," said producer Martin in a press release announcing the casting of Haigh. It's not easy to find actors who communicate sophistication and inner agony. But surely there are American actors who could be found. Scott Fitzgerald was almost quintessentially American, an innocent from Minnesota with manners and wit. That is a very different thing from a world-weary English style.

What is the theme of *Clothes for a Summer Hotel*? What is Tennessee saying? The play's vision? The task of simplifying a play into a single statement is nowhere more impossible than in this play. Of all Williams' plays this one may be the most mysterious. Of course the entire ghost play is symbolic. Some of the meaning is clear while much of it is elusive. The play's "topics" include relationships, death, time, eternity, gender, art, and the artist. Just a few subjects! But what is Williams' point of view?

Artists are predatory. They use themselves and others. But they are also a privileged class of people, given a gift by fate. Zelda's exclusion from the class of artists is her most painful torture. The only other escape from life is madness, and she has taken that path.

Relationships as a source of salvation are doomed to failure. The love relationship is seen as intrinsically allied to hatred and "use" of the other. Lovers destroy each other, and that's all that can be said about love. Lovers are "enemies."

Relationships are further complicated by gender problems. Artists contain mixed genders that allow them to create male and female characters, but it is further suggested that the male/female struggle for supremacy between individuals also occurs within single individuals. Furthermore since we have both male and female within us, no single relationship with another can satisfy all our needs. The bisexual nature of human beings makes satisfaction impossible. This problem is most obvious in artists but is also implicitly true for all.

In *Clothes for a Summer Hotel*, Williams suggests that both Hemingway and Fitzgerald had a homosexual component in their natures, which, while totally repressed, caused both men to be remote and unfeeling, as well as tortured. Interestingly, part of Zelda's problem is that she does not fit into the role model of wife and mother that Scott and society insist she play. Sex roles, gender generalities are strong social influences that constrict the individual. All the characters are wearing the wrong clothes. Clothes for summer in winter. None of their "roles" really fit. All choices make our lives incomplete.

Life is a ghost play, a performance, a dream, madness. In this play and in all his late work Williams repeatedly uses metaphors that suggest the insubstantial, ephemeral, unknowable, unreal nature of our lives.

All time is present, past, and future. The play embodies a "relativistic" vision in its dramatic depiction of time as simultaneously past, present, and future. One is reminded of T. S. Eliot's beginning to his *Four Quartets* and its discussion of the nature of time:

> Time present and time past
> Are both perhaps present in time future,
> And time future contained in time past.
> If all time is eternally present
> All time is irredeemable.
> What might have been is an abstraction
> Remaining a perpetual possibility
> Only in a world of speculation.

What "might have been" is a continual source of torture to the Fitzgeralds in *Clothes*. Zelda "might" have been a dancer. Scott "might" have written the great American novel. They "might" have loved each other without cruelty.

The play is also obsessed with death and is an end-of-life retrospective vision. Just as Scott tries to make his peace with his past, Williams, in his late sixties, is looking back at his life and considering its truth and value. More than merely a dramatic device or metaphor, the ghost nature of the play is an imagining of life after death, a rumination on death's possibilities, a Dante's inferno imagined by a twentieth-century atheist who still has a religious impulse and need. Williams bases his vision of eternity upon his vision of life. It is the only thing he knows. Hell is a continuous reenactment of past pain, a performance by madmen. Little but pain is real; perhaps some remembered sensual pleasure. Ghosts are doomed to repeat past performances in a long run that never closes. It is all "incredible." Zelda expresses the play's overriding vision in the last scene in a speech that was added to the published play:

> The incredible things are the only true things, Scott. Why do you have to go mad to make a discovery as simple as that? Who is fooling whom with this pretense that to exist is a credible thing? The mad are not so gullible. We're not taken in by such a transparent falsity, oh me, what we know that you don't know—(She is now facing the audience.) Or don't dare admit that you know is that to exist is the original and greatest of incredible things. Between the first wail of an infant and the last gasp of dying it's all an arranged pattern of submission to what's been prescribed for us unless we escape into madness or into acts of creation.

Madness may not be much of an escape since it forces one to see more clearly the incredibility of life. *Clothes for a Summer Hotel* may be Tennessee Williams' final statement on the nature of reality. It is a horrifying vision, a tragic vision. But like all tragic visions, it is also full of awe and wonder. It is a vision of life as incredible.

NOTES

1. John Simon, "Sweet Bird of Senility,"*New York*, June 26, 1978.

2. Dotson Rader, *Tennessee: Cry of the Heart* (Garden City, NY: Doubleday, 1985), 55.

3. Michiko Kakutani, "'Ghosts' of the Fitzgeralds Rehearsing under the Watchful Eye of Williams," *New York Times*, January 8, 1980.

4. Kakutani, "'Ghosts' of the Fitzgeralds."

5. Michiko Kakutani, "Williams and Quintero Build a 'Summer Hotel,'" *New York Times*, March 23, 1980.

6. Quoted in Kakutani, "Williams and Quintero Build a 'Summer Hotel.'"

7. Quoted in Kakutani, "Williams and Quintero Build a 'Summer Hotel.'"

8. Quoted in Kakutani, "Williams and Quintero Build a 'Summer Hotel.'"

9. Julius Novick, "Ungreat Scott," *Village Voice*, April 7, 1980.

10. Clive Barnes, "'Clothes' Needs Some Tailoring," *New York Post*, 1980.

11. John Simon, "Damsels Inducing Distress," *New York*, April 7, 1980.

12. Howard Kissel, "Clothes for a Summer Hotel," *Women's Wear Daily*, March 27, 1980.

13. Brendan Gill, "Body Snatching," *New Yorker*, April 7, 1980.

14. Walter Kerr, "The Stage: 'Clothes for a Summer Hotel,'" *New York Times*, March 27, 1980.

15. Harold Clurman, "Theatre," *Nation*, April 19, 1980.

16. Quoted in Kakutani, "Williams, Quintero, and the Aftermath of a Failure," *New York Times*, June 22, 1980.

17. Quoted in Michiko Kakutani, "Williams, Quintero, and the Aftermath."

18. Quoted in Kakutani, "Williams, Quintero, and the Aftermath."

19. Harold Clurman, "Theatre Mailbag," *New York Times*, July 13, 1980.

20. Clurman, "Theatre Mailbag."

21. Tennessee Williams, "Tennessee Williams Replies," *New York Times*, August 3, 1980.

22. Zelda Fitzgerald, *Save Me the Waltz* (New York: Scribner, 1932).

23. Kerr, "The Stage."

24. Ernest Hemingway, *A Moveable Feast* (New York: Scribner, 1964), 186.

25. Kerr, "The Stage."

• 9 •

Through the Dark Door

Will Mr. Merriwether Return from Memphis? occupies a curious position in Tennessee Williams' work. Written in 1969, the play has never been published and was not performed until 1980 in Key West, Florida, where it was the opening production of the Tennessee Williams Fine Arts Center. This occasion is described in the introduction to this book. As the director of that world premiere production, I have spent much time thinking about the play and have grown steadily fonder of the work. Perhaps flawed, the play is nonetheless unique, beautiful, innovative, and moving, when understood.

Mr. Merriwether was apparently rediscovered by Tennessee in the late seventies. He had put the play away after showing it to Audrey Wood, who according to Tennessee, was not encouraging about the strange play. Jay Leo Colt, the director of the San Francisco production of *The Two-Character Play*, and briefly a secretary to Tennessee, says he found the manuscript in a cardboard box when Tennessee was moving into his Manhattan Plaza apartment in the late seventies. Colt was enthusiastic about the play and tried unsuccessfully to interest several off-Broadway groups in the play. Tennessee showed the play to me in the fall of 1979. He was fearful that the play was not worthy of production but was curious as to my reaction. I was impressed with the play's wild theatricality and thought it would be exciting on stage.

A play in two acts and eleven scenes, *Mr. Merriwether* is composed of brief, dream-like scenes and encounters. The play begins "in situation," and the situation remains the same throughout the play. A young widow, Louise McBride, lives alone with her daughter, Gloria. Before the play, Louise has had an affair with a young boarder, a drummer, Mr. Merriwether, who has gone to Memphis to better his career. Before leaving, he promised to return to Louise. Each night Louise puts on a white lace dress and sits at a long table

188

anxiously awaiting the return of Mr. Merriwether. At the start of the play, Louise is discovered seated at the table. Gloria, her sixteen-year-old daughter, sits opposite her.

The set is a unit white box, which, through the addition and subtraction of a few furniture pieces, becomes different locations in the course of the play: "For all interior scenes of the play the setting is a white room with two enormous windows that look out upon clear evenings in Spring. Illogically, between the two windows, is a curtained doorway: the curtain is purple-dark with little glints of silver and gold thread woven into it." Scenes are revealed and ended by the rise and descent of a full proscenium scrim curtain "designed as an abstraction of wild roses and clover."

Another important element of the set is a "crescent shaped runway outlined with light bulbs when in use." This vaudeville runway is used from time to time as actors "walk or dance out on it."

A long table, "parallel to the proscenium," is set in the white room at curtain rise. The table is always present when the room represents Louise's home. Williams very specifically describes this table and its covering. The table has "a cover which is delicately checkered in pastel colors and it bears a collection of articles, selected and arranged as if for a painter's still-life. There are chairs at either end of the table, one pale yellow and the other pale blue."

At curtain rise, Louise and Gloria sit "as silent and motionless as figures in a tableau for several moments." Offstage, we hear a banjo playing a ragtime tune "as if at a distance." Finally, Louise rises, selects from the table a "black lace fan sprinkled with bits of iridescent metal." The scrim lifts to allow her to move downstage. She steps upon the "runway projected from under the set" and speaks over the banjo to the audience "as if continuing a revery":

> Today I prepared his room for his return. And today an old Gypsy woman came to the door. "Ask me the question most important to you." she said, and I said to the Gypsy: "Can I expect Mr. Merriwether to return from Memphis tonight or tomorrow or?" The Gypsy said—it wasn't exactly an answer— (distant banjo: a Gypsy tune) "He will never forget you." No, not an adequate answer. His life was mine, mine his. I bought some little sachets of dried flowers and herbs from the old Gypsy woman and put them in the back corners of Mr. Merriwether's chiffonnier.

Louise returns to the room. Gloria gently questions her: "You're still dreaming that Mr. Merriwether is going to come back from Memphis?" Louise changes the subject, refuses to consider the possibility that he will not return. She then interrogates Gloria: "I suppose you're going to the library tonight?" It is revealed that every evening, "dressed for a warm night on the equator," Gloria goes to the library where she meets boys and often then goes "to an excursion steamer with ten or twelve boys" who escort her to the "dark upper deck." Gloria's response is simple: "Mother, I think it's a little too late to pretend that we're conventional people."

Louise warns Gloria of "early fire," again drifting into a private dream world. She tells her daughter the story of meeting Gloria's father. During the speech Gloria leaves the stage. Louise is left alone with her memories and does not notice her daughter's departure:

> At a dance, once, the dance-floor was out-doors,—a storm came up suddenly. A lantern, a paper lantern was blown from—tumbled across the— flamed up as it touched my dress, burned the hem of my dress, burned my ankles. I screamed, started to run. A man caught hold of me. "Stop! Stand still!" He put the fire out with a bowl of punch! (Laughs.) I still screamed. He picked me up in his arms and carried me into the house. There were slices of orange on my burned, wet dress. The room, I think it was dark. He picked the orange slices off my dress that I had been, oh, so proud of, and then he rubbed an ointment, a salve, on my ankles. The room, it was his bedroom. It was light first, "Quiet, quiet!" he kept whispering. He locked the door of the room. He turned the lamp down. The man—dead, now—was your father.—Be careful of early fire!

Nora Waddles enters through the upstage curtained door. She is a "plump little woman of fifty," and has brought Louise a bowl of strawberries and cream. Louise confides her worry over Gloria to Nora. She feels she is "not a competent mother." Neighbors have told Louise of the boys who follow her daughter like "male dogs tagging after a female dog in heat." But Louise doesn't know what to do "and life does have to be handled or it gets out of hand."

Nora's advice is to "forget it tonight." She suggests "an apparition to distract you, honey." It seems the two widows regularly receive apparitions of an evening for their entertainment. Nora is particularly accepting of and sensitive to their presence. "Tonight, ow, they're moving tonight. There's a fresh wind blowin' too." The two women sing a summoning song of incantation:

> TURN NOT BACK, GO ON, GO ON
> ALL THE WORLD'S YOURS TO ROAM.
> IT ISN'T STRANGE AND SINGULAR
> TO SEEK AND FIND NO FINAL HOME.

An apparition of Vincent van Gogh appears, entering through the curtains. Van Gogh is strangely quiet. Louise asks, "Is there anything we can do for you?" He answers, "Thank you but there's nothing a living person can do for an apparition except to receive him." Louise and Nora do not know who he was. Van Gogh tells them he was a painter and "the only thing I want is light again and paints and brushes." They hold a lamp up in front of the painter but he can see no light. "It's foolish of me to suppose that my apparition could see anything but dark . . . The usual dark of an apparition's vision." Leaving unsatisfied, the painter gives Louise and Nora a directive: "Remember that light is a treasure of incalculable value. Whether you paint or not." He leaves. The two woman have been chilled by the visitation. Louise remarks, "It's turned cold in the room," and she exits for light sweaters.

Alone, Nora addresses the audience explaining how the apparitions give comfort to her loneliness: "Ow, I wouldn't part with my apparitions. I know I could. I know I could. I know I could keep them out by mental resistance to them, but I wouldn't do that, no, poor creatures, they feel nothing I guess and think nothing I know but sometimes they'll have a bit of conversation with you and that I like since I live alone on a field of clover and wild flowers like dear Louise."

When Louise returns Nora relates a fascinating bit of gossip: "You know there's a good deal of leprosy in this town?" Nora begins her leper "aria." It's a ghoulish story, a long tale full of enjoyably grotesque details. "The families afflicted with members afflicted by the disease of leprosy, keep the members IN OLD EMPTY CISTERNS, that's how they hide 'em from daylight, but at midnight, out they come from the old empty cisterns to receive their rations and congregate with each other."

Is this story true? Possibly. Is Nora mad? Possibly. The story comes to a conclusion, which has its own crazy logic:

> The backyards along Bella Street have all big trees, all big shadowy trees, and under the trees, in the shadows of 'em, the lepers not too far gone, they commit fornication together, by the balls of himself, that they do, they retire to the shadows of the big pecan and oak trees an' there the young lepers, some y'know, are comparatively not old, they fornicate together in the shadowy yards of Bella Street, and this, hear this, oh this is a thing to be told, some of them bear children which are born in the cisterns without attendance by a doctor or mid-wife and not a cry from them in childbirth since everything must be quiet to keep the secret, y'see.

This run-on speech serves little purpose in the plotless play. It is a "turn" by a performer, full of bizarre fun and grotesquerie. The reality of these lepers may be questionable but in a world where apparitions visit widows anything may be true. What are lepers anyway but social outcasts and pariahs, eccentric members of society? In a sense, every character in the play is a "leper."

Nora bids Louise good night. Remembering Van Gogh's eulogy to light, Louise decides to leave the lamp on all night. She exits, her voice trailing off: "I'll hurry to bed, since Mr. Merriwether isn't apparently going to."

Scene 2 is a monologue delivered by Gloria in front of the scrimmed curtain. She speaks directly to the audience, expressing her yearning and attraction to the opposite sex: "Yes, I wear light dresses. The school rooms have been so warm lately, and the boys I suppose it's their age that makes their bodies fill the rooms with a sort of warm, heavy muskiness in late Spring. It's not offensive to me. It's a natural thing, as natural as the pollination of plants and flowers." Her young life is filled with a kind of wonder informed by her awakening sexuality: "The air seems to hum. A piece of chalk seems almost too heavy to hold, yes, actually, I'm not exaggerating." At the end of the scene Gloria exits into the library.

In the library (scene 3) the Librarian attacks Gloria for her behavior with the boys "at the big dictionary." Gloria is rescued by a Youth who is described as "romantically handsome and dressed in white shirt and trousers." The Youth also "speaks with a stammer." Gloria leaves the library with the young man as the Librarian sputters in rage.

In scene 4, another vignette scene, Louise is seen in a "pin spot" of light holding a "telephone of the period." She is trying to call Mr. Merriwether in Memphis. The telephone operator has trouble understanding Louise. "Would you say that louder, please." The scene has the quality of a bad dream in which one attempts a nearly impossible task. Finally Louise nearly shouts, "I said I wanted to speak to Mr. Merriwether." The voice replies, "Mr. Merriwether has asked not to be called after midnight." Desperately, Louise cries out, "It's necessary!" A male voice comes on. It is Mr. Merriwether. "Hello? Hello. Who is it? I said, who is it, who's calling?" Louise cannot answer and hangs up the phone "as if it might cause an explosion." As the scene ends, Louise cautions herself: "Don't follow. Don't call. There's nothing to do but wait, with fox-teeth in my heart."

Scene 5 takes place in the white room, which now represents an English classroom. Miss Yorke, Gloria's English teacher, praises an essay by Gloria and asks the young girl to read her paper aloud to the class. It is an essay descriptive of a geology field trip "to look for fossils." Gloria describes how, with the assistance of the handsome Youth, she found and chipped fossils out of a rock quarry: "Two of them were fossils of ferns and three were fossils of very early and primitive kinds of organisms that existed in water millions and millions of years ago, you might say an incalculable time ago in the oceans and seas of the earth, which at that time were steaming like tea-kettles."

Gloria reads on, describing how she began to "cry and tremble" in the presence of the fossils, "for some reason that I can't analyze and explain." The boy took her home where she showed the fossils to her mother: "Oh mother, look at these rocks, these little fossils on them. They give us evidence that there has been life on this earth for more time than we are able to estimate."

Gloria says she still does not understand why she cried. Miss Yorke helps her. "I believe I can tell you why the fossils disturbed you. They made you think of how transitory things are. In their living state." A "Voice from the Wings" asks, "What is transitory?" Miss Yorke replies, "Things that pass, things of brief duration." Gloria "makes a gasping sound." She starts to tremble again. Miss Yorke asks for someone in the class to "take Miss McBride to the streetcar." The "Romantically Handsome Youth" steps out of the wings. He will take her. They exit. Miss Yorke lectures the class. "The lesson to be learned from Miss McBride's theme is simple in a way and difficult in a way. I think it is that we must dare to experience deep emotion even though it may make us cry and tremble." Miss Yorke dismisses the class, "not for several million years, just till tomorrow." The scene dims out.

The Youth and Gloria come onto the projected runway. Gloria consoles the Youth over his stammering. She tells him that he should say to himself, "There's no boy in the school or in the town of Bethesda that's handsome as I am." Shyly the boy rejects such vanity. Gloria continues, "I want you to feel confidence in yourself. There's no light in the house. We're sitting in the middle of a field of wild flowers. There's no one to see us. Would it shock you if I took off my dress so it wouldn't be stained by the clover if we lay down in the clover?"

The boy is frightened. "I've had no experience at what you're suggesting." Gloria answers, "I didn't think you had any but I think you ought to have some." She slips out of her dress and advises him to take off his clothes "to avoid stains." She runs off. A banjo is heard in the distance. The boy calls out for Gloria. Behind the scrim, she calls out, "Look for me. Find me. I'll be invisible to everyone in the world except to you." He follows her voice as the scrim rises to admit him to the darker upstage regions.

Three crones enter for a bizarre vaudeville turn. In Irish brogues they identify themselves as the Fatal Sisters. Gross old hags, eating sausages and drinking from a jug, they stitch the fate of mortals on their sewing looms. Part mythic "Eumenides," part comic "Norns," they oversee and describe Gloria's seduction of the Youth. The head crone makes the pronouncement that ends the scene: "Hush a minute, sister. Yes. In a field of wild flowers, the lovely young girl has imparted a tender knowledge to the boy and he'll stammer no more."

At the start of scene 8 Louise "comes out of the purple dark curtains." She takes the iridescent fan from off the table. "She stands holding it a moment against the bosom of her white dress as if waiting for a signal to move."

The runway is lit up and the banjo begins to play. "Louise nods as if the signal had been given." She then begins to cross the runway in a dance-like fashion. "There are several pauses in which she turns to the audience with a gesture of the fan and a smile that has a slight touch of defiance in it. Each time she pauses, she lifts her summer white dress above her white slippers."

The dance is part Japanese Kabuki with its fan and runway *(hanamichi)*, but also part refined striptease. By the time Louise arrives at the other end of the runway, two stage hands have removed her table and replaced it with a "desk and several white chairs." Two female "dummies" sit on the left side of the desk. Nora enters. Louise sits in the chair next to her. They discuss their apparitions. Louise remarks that all her apparitions have been tragic. She hopes to receive a saint, especially "Saint Francis of the Flowers."

A French Club Instructor enters. He is "disconcerted to find only four of our members in the room." The Instructor speaks several French phrases, which he asks the ladies to translate. A fifth member, Mrs. Biddle, enters. The Instructor reiterates the purpose of the club: "all of us should know that our club existed for two things, the study of the French language and the confession and purgation of what is troubling our hearts."

The Instructor refers to the dark doorway that "*represente l'elemente de la mystere dans la vie.*" He asks Louise to translate: "The dark doorway behind us represents the element of mystery in our lives."

Next, the instructor asks, "Who has something to confess?" Louise rises and starts to speak but she cannot. She begins to cry. Nora then makes a confession. Yesterday she made a dinner for two even though her husband has been dead for twenty years. Louise rises again and starts to speak: "*Meme dans un reve.*" With difficulty, she finally finishes her sentence: "*Meme dans un reve on peut souffrir.*" Mrs. Biddle translates this as "Even in a dream one can suffer." But there is more. Louise continues: "*Meme dans un reve on peut souffrir l'angoisse d'une separation.*" Nora translates: "Even in a dream one can suffer the agony of a separation."

It is now the Instructor's turn to make a "difficult confession": "In the town of Bethesda I have had the indiscreet habit of going two nights a week, after midnight, to the Greyhound bus station for the purpose of making the acquaintance of, of some youth in the military services of the country who are so often in transit." Civil authorities in the town have told the Instructor to remove himself "from Bethesda before midnight." He has his suitcase with him. He will go to Memphis. Louise says, "Memphis is as far away as a memory of—a dream." The Instructor bids them adieu and "lifts his suitcase as the lights dim." End of act 1.

The second Act of *Mr. Merriwether*, having only three scenes, is short. Because of this it should probably be played without intermission. At the beginning of scene 9 (act 2, scene 1), Louise and Nora are seated at Louise's table, invoking apparitions.

The poet Arthur Rimbaud, seated in a wheelchair, is pushed through the curtains by his sister Isabelle. Unknown to either Louise or Nora, Rimbaud gives a precis of his life and career as a poet who gave up poetry at the age of twenty: "Poetry *merde*! a thing for cafe degenerates! Identify me as a man who traded in ivory and fire-arms in Aden on the Red Sea." In spite of the fact that he is dead (and even as an apparition paralyzed from knee cancer), Rimbaud wants to return to Africa. He needs paper and pencil so Isabelle may write his former employer: "They know me. Trust me. I was excellent as a trader in ivory." Before he can dictate a letter to Isabelle, Rimbaud drops off into a kind of coma. Isabelle wheels her brother off through the curtained door.

Chilled by the apparition's appearance, Nora tells Louise that she will return tomorrow. Louise's answer is strange and disoriented: "You're always welcome, Nora. But give me a call on the telephone first because it's possible that tomorrow a friend of mine who's staying a while in Memphis might return to . . . What's the name of this town?" Nora advises Louise to go to bed. Louise delivers a final line after Nora's exit: "The possibilities of the possibilities are *sans fin*. Translate. Endless."

Louise is once more seated at her table at the top of scene 10. Nora enters immediately and sets a cake on the table. Louise becomes agitated. "There's no such thing as a vacant spot on the table." Her table is like the composition of a painting in which the spaces between the objects, "plastic space," are as important as the objects themselves.

Eleanor of Aquitaine has appeared to Louise. Her description of the apparition betrays a worsening in Louise's mental condition. She jumps up suddenly. Nora asks what is wrong. Louise answers, "REST-LESSNESS." This reply prompts Nora into a reverie of memories of her late husband, Cornelius Waddles, "run down by a beer truck on a business trip to Milwaukee." Breathlessly, Louise thinks she may have heard something outside: "I didn't hear his car but the sound of it may have been lost in the sound of your voice. Excuse me. Go out a window." Louise exits. Nora refuses to leave. "I'll go out nobody's window."

The next encounter is one of the strangest in the play. "A fantastic creature, female, enters the white room." It is Mrs. Eldridge, the richest woman in town. Her appearance is extraordinary: "Her sleeveless gown is Oriental, or pseudo-Oriental. Arms, hands, face appear to be lacquered, to be covered with a glittering wax. Little silver bells are attached to her fingers and her jewelled arm bracelets so that her motions make a musical sound. Sometimes, to emphasize a point, she raises her arms and makes the bells tinkle louder." The driver of Mrs. Eldridge's "Phaeton" has had a "seizure." She has stopped at Louise's house for help. "My Phaeton has stopped on the road in front of your house not because of any technical difficulties but because the chauffeur has had some kind of a seizure. I cracked him over the head with my cane. And there was no response so I suspect he——"

Mrs. Eldridge looks out the windows and sees the bright lights of "Tiger Town," which light up above the set of Louise's house. "Tiger Town" is the black section of town where bars abound and Mrs. Eldridge makes nightly forays. "Your house has a fortunate location. Through the right window I can see Tiger Town and the lights of the Bar Apache where I'm expected."

Louise offers to call a taxi. Left alone with Mrs. Eldridge, Nora gives the fantastic woman a piece of her mind: "A black man with a razor is what you're out for and in for, surely." Mrs. Eldridge hisses at Nora and rings her silver bells. Louise returns. A taxi is on its way. Mrs. Eldridge thanks her and exits: "I'll wait outside in the field of wild flowers, to lift my heart to the sky with expectations that have never once failed me."

After Mrs. Eldridge leaves, Louise suggests that the strange woman may have been an apparition. "No," says Nora. Esmerald Eldridge is the "richest woman in the town she disgraces." She has had her face lifted five times. No longer able to get an effective face lift, Mrs. Eldridge "has herself covered with glittering wax." Nightly, she goes to Tiger Town where she picks up some unfortunate young black man. "She wheels him away to her mansion, and he's never the same after that. His youth is confiscated, his youth is drawn out of him like blood drawn out by leeches or a vampire bat." Louise feels some sympathy for Mrs. Eldridge: "It might be, it could be, that she is waiting for someone, or something, somewhere."

Scene 11, the last scene of the play, begins as all the scenes in act 2 have begun and also the way the play began: Louise is seated at her table awaiting Mr. Merriwether's return. She is holding a glass of iced tea, which she distractedly pours back into a pitcher. The "moon appears serenely through one of the huge windows." Nora enters "bustling through the dark door with a bowl of something." It is *blancmange*, which Louise translates as "white magic." Louise is very remote, preoccupied, quite indifferent to her surroundings. "You shouldn't bother to bring me anything, Nora. I have no appetite, I have no sense of taste." Nora fears Louise would prefer it if she didn't visit her any longer. Louise remarks, "If you didn't come over, nobody would come over." Tentatively, Nora suggests that Louise might "take in a new boarder." Louise resents the suggestion: "I am not a promiscuous woman."

Louise lifts and opens the iridescent fan from her carefully composed table. She erupts in anger calling the fan *"Savage!"* Her resentment toward Mr. Merriwether pours out: "After the nights between us, how could he accept a position to separate us!" The fan is thrown to the floor "like a challenging gauntlet." In a moment there is the sound of an approaching car that abruptly stops outside. Louise and Nora hold their breath. And then: "Mr. Merriwether steps through a window with a daisy between his teeth. He is an immoderately handsome man in his middle thirties. He is all in immaculate white except for a polka-dotted tie of unusual size." Louise and Mr. Merriwether are joyfully reunited. Their meeting is almost operatic:

> Louise: You've returned from Memphis?
>
> Merriwether: Don't you see I'm here?
>
> Louise: For just a visit or for a longer time?
>
> Merriwether: I've come back to stay. That is, if my old room's vacant.
>
> Louise: All the house was vacant till you returned.
>
> Merriwether: I would have returned from Memphis if I'd had to crawl on my belly over brimstone. I wasn't cut out for a sales manager at a desk in an office. I was made for the road.
>
> Louise: Because of the wild blood in you.
>
> Merriwether: And the wild blood in you.

Nora rushes off to see if Louise has something "in her medicine cabinet." Merriwether rushes to Louise's chair, which he kneels before. "She touches his throat, his hair, his face as if she were blind." He picks her up in a "rapturous embrace." She tells him she was about to follow him to Memphis. He replies, "Isn't it better this way? Me returning from Memphis?" She answers: "Yes, yes, it's better. It's a mistake, a useless mistake, for a woman to follow a man. He's a bird, the shadow of a bird, his home's in the sky, he rests on you for a moment. Then he's gone and after that, look for him in the sky. Try to follow him there. In his wings' hurry, the hurry of his wings, he takes your body but scarcely speaks your name."

Merriwether asks if his "old room's waiting for me." She answers rapturously, "My life is waiting for you." At this moment, the "Banjo Player springs through one of the enormous windows and strikes up a ragtime piece." Louise dances around the room summoning Mr. Merriwether to join her: "Let's do a fantastic cake-walk to celebrate your return from Memphis."

Louise's table lifts off the ground, flying up above the stage. "Gloria and 'the Romantically Handsome Youth' enter. The two couples do a fantastic cake-walk around the room. Fantastic it is, but there is a barely perceptible touch of sadness in it. They suddenly leap out of the windows, followed by the Banjo Man. Nora returns to find the room empty and the music distant."

Alone, Nora decides "it is necessary to invite an apparition." A male apparition appears "in a stick-candy striped silk shirt and pale grey trousers of a dandified cut." It is Cornelius Waddles, Nora's dead husband. He compliments her on her cooking and cheerfulness during his life adding, "You showed no sign of knowing what you must have known: that I was not just sometimes unfaithful but unfaithful all the time." Nora feels a chill, puts on a sweater and plaintively asks, "Cornelius, why were you unfaithful to me so much?" He laughs and whistles the ragtime tune played by the distant banjo. "The two couples return through a window followed by the Banjo Man." Nora and Cornelius join the dancing couples. The white room is filled with "delicate rainbow colors" as the curtain falls on the dancers.

It was during the planning of rehearsal period of *Will Mr. Merriwether Return from Memphis?* that I worked most closely with Tennessee Williams. As a premiere production Williams took more careful interest in its production than in other of his plays mounted at the Fine Arts Center during my directorship.

During the same period Tennessee was involved in preparations for *Clothes for a Summer Hotel*, which was also in rehearsal. However, Tennessee was most interested in the production of *Merriwether*. His suggestions at rehearsals were few, but he was an appreciative audience. If he had something to say it usually came after rehearsals in the form of a note or letter. Few people realize how reticent and shy Tennessee was in dealing with people. He would often hold things back, and then when they finally came out, the release was sometimes explosive and dramatic.

The two areas of greatest controversy in the *Merriwether* production were the design and casting of the production. These were vitally important areas to Tennessee, and he spent much time discussing these aspects of the production. He was naturally concerned that with our limited resources we be able to produce his play professionally. To be sure there were problems.

For the production I had invited two professional designers to Key West to insure a beautiful mounting of the play. They were Peggy Kellner as set and costume designer and Michael Orris Watson as lighting designer. I had worked with both before and knew them to be talented professionals. Peggy had worked for many years as the head costumer at the Old Globe Theatre in San Diego and was head of the costume department at the University of Arizona. I had known Michael Watson at the Virginia Museum Theatre where I had worked in the early seventies. During the period of *Merriwether*'s production, Michael was master teacher of lighting at the North Carolina School of the Arts.

Peggy came to Key West with a gorgeous design of a luxurious Victorian home. While it was beautiful, I feared it was not right, both too grand for Louise's house and not what Tennessee had described in his script. It was also a very realistic design and would not permit the many scenic changes with facility.

Peggy and I showed Tennessee her design. His response was strong. "This is very nice but it is not what I wrote. Can you read?" He then picked up a script, and from his bed (the conference was in his bedroom) he read his stage directions describing the white room. "That's what I want and that's what you will do." No more said. Peggy went back to her room and exactly drew up what Tennessee had described. With good nature she remarked, "It's all right with me. It's much easier." Tennessee's response to the drawing was approving, "Yes, that's right."

Peggy was allowed more freedom in her design of a scrim curtain, which became a proscenium-width fan painted with roses and clover. When lit from behind, the fan framed the white room and tableaux were visible "inside" the fan. We had built a forestage over the orchestra pit to allow more intimacy in the cavernous theater so we could not build the required runway around the orchestra pit. However, the downstage area was lit with "runner" light bulbs that lit up at special moments when Mr. Merriwether returned. Tennessee was amenable to this adaptation. In the end he was very approving of the physical production.

The major point is that Williams as a dramatist is very visual and most specific in his requests for certain effects. These requests, even at times calling for specific colors or shapes in furniture and props, may at times seem unimportant or trivial. They *are* important.

Tennessee was an amateur painter, and his paintings are often like stage settings. A bold colorist, he loved vibrant colors and he also loved pastels. Above all, he adored white. In all his plays white costumes abound. Blanche is more than the name of his most famous female character.

Interestingly, Tennessee's request for a white box set predates Peter Brook's famous use of the white box in his 1971 production of *A Midsummer Night's Dream*. Of course, no one knew of Williams' innovation since the play was hidden away. Peggy Kellner's desire to make Louise's room more interesting by making it less of a box represents a traditional response of designers to box sets. In this case, as in Brook's *Dream*, the box was a poetic symbol, an empty space representative of several locales, a space of the mind. One should respect Williams' visual requests. They have meaning.

The casting of the play was the most difficult element in our production. Tennessee was most concerned that *Mr. Merriwether* be given a "professional production." As financed by Florida Keys Community College, the operating budget for the theater was very small. Much money had been spent to build the center and little was left for operating expenses. I thought I could afford two Actors Equity guest artist contracts for the roles of Louise and Gloria or possibly Nora. Roxana Stuart was cast in the role of Louise. Tennessee had praised her work in *Suddenly Last Summer*, *Eccentricities of a Nightingale*, and *A Streetcar Named Desire* and he wanted her from the start.

Having worked in Key West before with the Greene Street Theatre, I knew there was much excellent local talent that could be used in the production. Auditions for the play were first held in Key West. All the smaller roles were cast there with interesting types and good actors. Tennessee attended all final auditions.

Our biggest problem was the casting of the daughter, Gloria. She needed to seem about sixteen and project natural sexuality, sensitivity, and intelligence. Also, she had to be technically secure as an actress in order to handle her long monologues. We really had no one young enough with all those qualities who could also be believable as Roxana's daughter. Roxana was in her early thirties so the actress really needed to be a teenager.

When Tennessee and I expressed our frustration over the casting of Gloria, a friend of his urged us to see an actress from Houston. Tennessee liked the idea that the actress was "professional." The young actress would fly to Key West and audition for us at her own expense. How could we refuse to see her?

In a few days, I went to Tennessee's house to hear the young woman read. In no way was she right for Gloria, an unspoiled small-town girl of the early twentieth century. Also, her reading convinced me that she did not have a feeling for the poetry of the play. But Tennessee roared with laughter and said she was "perfect." I was miserable.

The following day I pursued Tennessee to the Pier House Restaurant where he was surrounded by an entourage of friends. I explained my unhappiness with the actress. But Tennessee was adamant. He would withdraw the play if she was not cast. We signed the Houston actress to an Equity guest artist contract.

In the meanwhile a friend recommended a young actress named Melissa Leo who, with her red hair, was even supposed to look a little like Roxana. She was willing to jump on a plane and fly to Key West at her own expense and do the role for no money.

Since I had no Gloria for the first week of rehearsal, I told this young actress on the phone that she could understudy the role and fill in for the crucial first week of rehearsal. She agreed. Upon her arrival in Key West I was delighted with Melissa. She was a perfect Gloria—a fresh young talent, the right age, beautiful, sensitive, and a talented actress.

On the evening of the Houston actress' scheduled arrival in Key West, Tennessee saw a rough run-through of the play with Melissa Leo. After the run-through, Roxana went up to him and said, "Wasn't Melissa lovely?"

Tennessee answered, "Yes, she is beautiful and, of course, she must play the part."

What is the point of all this? Obviously Tennessee could be influenced by friends and his entourage. He was enormously vulnerable and in need of support from his circle of friends. But when something was really important nothing stood in the way of his desire to get what was right for a production. He was also capable of admitting himself wrong. He also supported those he felt to be right. Friends were never as important as his work.

This drive for excellence manifested itself one more time when, one week before the opening of the play, Tennessee demanded that the actress playing Nora be replaced with a professional actress. I flew to New York and recast the role with the help of Tennessee's then agent, Mitch Douglas. The actress, Naomi Reisman, helped carry the production and was amazingly proficient in one week of rehearsal.

None of this was the way a new play by Tennessee Williams should have been produced. Money, money, always money dictated a minimum of professionals and only three weeks of rehearsal. A better job could have been done if there had been less pressure. Later, Tennessee regretted that he did not have time to rewrite the play. His preoccupation with *Clothes for a Summer Hotel* prevented such work.

Most people were pleased with the "event," but there were whisperings about the play. Most scathing was the local Key West review, which in the small community became something of a cause celebre. In a review entitled "Send Mr. Merriwether Back to Memphis," Jim Tucci of *The Key West Citizen* wrote a review that may have spoken for a large segment of the audience. He called the performance

> A play that makes you think. Unfortunately, you think you just made it through the "Twilight Zone."
>
> "Will Mr. Merriwether Return from Memphis?" Yes, and none too soon. One wishes however, that the return had occurred midway through the play which was already encroaching upon eternity at halftime.
>
> Perhaps the best description of the play is "strange and bizarre." The play came across as a combination Tennessee Williams, "Saturday Night Live" and "Real People." One had difficulty finding a thread of continuity in the play as the action changed rapidly.
>
> All of this seems to have had one purpose it made the audience wonder what was going on.[1]

Perhaps the wisest thing is to let Tucci's review speak for itself. Doubtless he reflected the confusion of much of the audience.

Christine Arnold of the *Miami Herald* wrote,

> It is an odd play, an entertaining play, an amusing play, a flawed play, all of those. It isn't likely to have much life beyond the inauguration of the center; it is a poor relation to Williams' classic works of the 1950s. But its intrinsic joyfulness somehow seemed right for a happy night.
> The mixture of the crass, the genteel, and the absurd makes for a play that is sometimes confusing but never boring. The final mood is one of happiness pierced by the melancholy sound of a banjo, a contradiction that is pure Williams.[2]

This review somewhat restored the company's hurt pride, which was almost healed by an article in *Time* magazine. Really more of a news item than a review, T. E. Kalem's article did manage to say some interesting and complimentary things about the play as well as the production:

> Among Williams' work this play most nearly resembles *Camino Real*. But it is more pensive and muted, a violin to *Camino Real*'s trumpet. Like *Camino Real*, *Mr. Merriwether* laces together reality and fantasy, the romantic spirit and the appearance of actual cultural heroes of the past, such as Van Gogh and Rimbaud, here presented as "apparitions." In episodic fashion *Mr. Merriwether* embraces the four major concerns that have spurred Williams' dramatic imagination: loneliness, love, the violated heart and the valiancy of survival . . . Director William Prosser makes sensitive contact with the inner spirit of the play and considering that the company is a mix of amateurs and professionals, the result is creditable.[3]

A telegram from Tennessee thanked me for my work and asked me to "convey my deep thanks to every member of the cast and other artists involved in this most gratifying production." All of this publicity pleased the college. It was a heady, fantastic time. The play closed after eight performances and has never been done since.

Will Mr. Merriwether Return from Memphis? in its poetry and theatricalism, does resemble *Camino Real*. But unlike *Camino Real*, the world of *Mr. Merriwether* is at times recognizably "real" while other times filled with the supernatural and the fantastic. Is there any rationale to the division between the real and the fantastic? Are there any organizing schemes to the play? Any through line of action?

At first acquaintance the play seems a brief musical idyll, characters held together by mood and images. Upon closer investigation, the play reveals a structure that mirrors the disintegration of the mind of its central character, Louise McBride. In *Mr. Merriwether* the only plot question is the one of the title, and as the play develops we seem to be faced with an impossibility. It seems clear to us that Mr. Merriwether will never return. We watch Louise McBride in the process of a nervous breakdown, a disciplined mind cracking before the impossibility of its strongest needs and desires. The alienation of her world is suggested at the play's start and increasingly grows as the play progresses. Nora is a fellow traveler into Louise's world of dreams, apparitions, and dislocation. However, Nora is more pragmatic and seems more adjusted to the strange. She will survive whatever life throws at her. Louise is more fragile. For both Nora and Louise, apparitions are necessary opiates, a kind of saving grace of the imagination. But Louise needs more.

In the play we meet a variety of lonely eccentrics, sensitive souls. As the play progresses, the characters become more and more fantastic until the audience moves away from a clear separation between the real and the unreal, people and apparitions. This, of course, is exactly the point. This confusion in the audience mirrors the fragmentation of Louise McBride's mind.

The climax of the play, Merriwether's fantastic return, explodes the play in several ways. A play that has become increasingly desperate suddenly becomes joyous. The play ends with a celebration. But the possibility that what we are witnessing is a final release into madness somewhat mutes the celebration. Like the endings of *Tartuffe*, *Threepenny Opera*, and *Madwoman of Chaillot*, the outrageous improbability of a happy ending casts a cynical pall over the reality of the events. The end of the play is very light and joyous. Mr. Merriwether has returned from Memphis. Or has he?

Characters in *Merriwether* represent responses to the mystery of life and are themselves manifestations of that mystery. Nearly all the characters share an anguished loneliness; all are waiting and incomplete. Gloria is the one exception to that frustrated group. She represents freedom and unabashed sexual response that celebrates life's mystery. Yet, she too, is frightened before the fossils that remind her of her own transitory life.

Nor do the apparitions represent any kind of solution. They are themselves searching—wandering impulses looking for completion. They seem to be looking for answers from the living as much as the living look to them for help.

The characters in the play are neither detailed nor psychologically rich. They are all simple immediately recognizable types. Importantly, they represent a spectrum of ages from the young Gloria to the older Mrs. Eldridge. All want sexual fulfillment. Sex is a part of the greater mystery and perhaps our closest direct contact with life's mystery. There is a possible ecstasy in life reached primarily through sexual experience. There is the suggestion that without ecstasy, life is not much worth living.

While *Merriwether* deals with familiar characters and themes from Williams' early work, lonely frustrated eccentrics and sexual salvation, the play is different in its epistemological emphasis. In this play Williams moves beyond portraits of psychological frustration to show how personality colors perceptions of reality. Also, adventurously, Williams embodies those perceptions on stage in theatrical images. We are no longer outside of Blanche DuBois, but rather inside as realities change and dissolve. Louise McBride's alienation is experienced directly by the audience in image and language. Things happen with no simple motivation, and it is a world in which anything can happen. The possibilities of her possibilities are indeed endless. Dreams become reality when reality becomes too difficult to bear.

Williams does not romanticize the world of apparitions and the imagination. Louise, in her French club confession, gives voice to the play's most bitter vision: "Even in a dream one can suffer the agony of a separation." Separation seems to be the natural state of both man and apparitions. Reunion is a consummation devoutly to be wished. Mr. Merriwether, like Jim the gentleman caller in *The Glass Menagerie*, represents "the long delayed but always expected something that we live for."

The language of the play is both rich and fanciful as well as spare and incomplete. Language itself is a kind of eroticism that gives ease to loneliness. Nora's rattling ghoulish fascinations represent this kind of sexuality transformed into language.

Speeches also are "numbers," or vaudeville turns. Throughout the play characters directly address the audience and characters seem continually aware of the audience. Characters often feel a need to entertain both the audience and themselves. Louise's speech about "early fire," her fan dance, Nora's leper speech, Gloria's speech about young boys, the entire "Eumenides" scene are entertainments. They are "time passers" during the waiting process of life.

Louise's language is often hesitant and incomplete. She occasionally speaks in strong enigmatic ways: "The name of the fan is savage." There is a privacy in her imagery that puzzles and intrigues. At times her suffering finds expression in striking images: "There's nothing to do but wait, with fox-teeth in my heart."

In many ways *Mr. Merriwether* is a masque in which language is only one component part of the total effect and perhaps not the most important. Equally important is the visual component of the play: sets, lights, costume, and dance. Music, too, as in the masque, plays a vital part. The bare white room with its windows and dark door, the single table parallel to the curtain line—these all create an unreal threshold world that takes the play out of the "real" world while leaving one foot behind. Louise's position at the table creates a ritualized pose that begins many scenes. At times Louise may seem like a manikin. The curtain acts as a revealer and separator, almost arbitrarily manipulated by unseen operators. The fan of the curtain is echoed by the fan on the table.

Realities within realities, as in reflecting mirrors, lose one in images within images. None claims precedence. None is more real than others.

Also important in the play's theatrical imagery is the garish world of Tiger Town occasionally evoked throughout the play as a contrast to Louise's white room. Tiger Town, in addition to being Mrs. Eldridge's destination on her nightly trips, is evoked through a recurring theatrical device that Williams explains in a production note at the start of the play:

> At carefully spaced—not too frequently—intervals in the play a scrim should mask the white room and two or three negro couples should dance out of the wings and perform a cake walk to the ragtime music of the banjo. Of course the banjo should be louder than during the dramatic scenes. Lobes of light above the "thrust" stage should spell out "Tiger Town."
>
> Perhaps the couples should sing, perhaps not. Underlying the gaiety of the dancing should be something of a different nature and I don't know how to define it except by saying it should correspond to Louise's comment about the iridescent fan removed from her table "The name of the fan is savage."

Tiger Town obviously represents a sexy Dionysian world, a neighboring area to Louise's home. It promises pleasure but it is also threatening and "savage." In our production this element was most difficult to achieve. The cakewalk dances tended to be musical comedy numbers. Finally, I decided to try the dance numbers "dead pan" without smiles or facial expression. This device worked rather well, giving the dancers a sepulchral appearance despite their activity and the music. They became "apparitions" themselves. Dressed in garish colors, the cakewalk dancers offer a strong contrast to the many characters wearing white.

White is certainly Williams' favorite color and a major symbol in his work. Actually white is both the absence and container of all color, suggesting purity and sterility, transcendence and death. Nor was Williams the first artist to use white symbolically. Melville's chapter on "The Whiteness of the Whale" in *Moby Dick* is an interesting correlative to Williams' use of whiteness: "Is it that by its indefiniteness it shadows forth the heartless voids and immensities of the universe, and thus stabs us from behind with the thought of annihilation, when beholding the white depths of the milky way? Or is it, that as in essence whiteness is not so much a color as the visible absence of color, and at the same time the concrete of all colors; is it for these reasons that there is such a dumb blankness, full of meaning, in a wide landscape of snows—a colorless, all-color of atheism from which we shrink?"[4]

While a dominant white overrides all in the play, there are requests for specific colors that stand out. The two chairs at Louise's table are "pale yellow" and "pale blue." Nora and Louise put on pink and blue sweaters. A "dusky blue" fills the white room when its lamp is turned down to invite apparitions. The forestage is lit "violet and rose" for Gloria's monologue to the audience. The Librarian wears a "pink linen" dress. A bunch of marigolds sits on Miss Yorke's desk. The fan is "iridescent." Mr. Merriwether wears a "polka-dot tie of unusual size."

It would be helpful for directors and designers of Williams' plays to study Williams' paintings. They are most influenced by the expressionistic paintings of Vincent van Gogh. More than any other painter, Van Gogh seems to have made a strong impression on Tennessee. One remembers how in *A Streetcar Named Desire* Williams describes the Poker Night scene as having the "lurid nocturnal brilliance" of "Van Gogh's billiard parlor at night." Of course, Van Gogh's palette was often softer, more pastel. One thinks of his room at Arles, paintings of white irises, certain pastel self-portraits. The lurid Van Gogh and the pastel Van Gogh are both present in *Mr. Merriwether*. They represent two worlds often concurrent in Williams' world. It is altogether fitting that Van Gogh should be an apparition in the play.

The requested music for the play is also specific. Williams wants a solitary banjo to supply the play's musical score. The banjo can be plaintive and moody as when it underscores Louise's waiting and longing. It can also become raucously celebratory as when it accompanies the Tiger Town Dancers and the final "fantastic cakewalk." Both moods are necessary to the play.

There is a great deal of dancing in the play. The Tiger Town Dancers, Louise's fan dance, the final cakewalk. In a way, the love scene between Gloria and the Youth is a pas de deux. The Fatal Sisters dance on and off. All of this reinforces the dream-like atmosphere of the play. The director must choreograph much of the action. Indeed, the scrim and lights need to "dance"—changes timed to music. Everything needs to flow. It is not unlike a musical or ballet in its elements.

The play aspires through all the elements of theater to a place where the theater resembles other art forms, forms less rigorously subject to objective criteria of realism. Using music, dance, painting, and poetry, *Mr. Merriwether* creates an almost total dream world. One asks of it what it "means" at one's peril and to the possible diminution of the play. What does a Balanchine ballet mean? Or a painting by Pollock? Or a late Beethoven quartet? Williams, in *Merriwether*, seems to want the theater to "mean" in the way those other art forms "mean." The play seeks the freedom of poetry, music, painting, and dance. Like *Waiting for Godot*, basically plotless, *Merriwether* is a situational "waiting" play. Yet it does have form and an organic structure that is unique to its own needs.

The scenic, musical, and dance components of *Mr. Merriwether* are, of course, symbolic elements in the play. And many of these symbols dominate the play: the white room, the dark door, the carefully arranged table, the fan, apparitions, Tiger Town, the cakewalk, and finally Mr. Merriwether himself.

Symbols are perhaps better left unexplained. After all, they contain possibilities and contradictions, dichotomies and paradoxes. However, certain explanations are easily forthcoming. The white room may be the mind containing within it the possibility of several worlds. The dark door is an entrance-way to the beyond, the subconscious, the mysterious unknown. It may also be a symbol of the female vagina, an entrance to strange adventures. The carefully arranged table represents the ordering, rational mind that demands that everything be in its proper place. Chaos is unbearable on the table. The table will fly up into the air and disappear in the final moments of the play. The savage fan seems to be another symbol of sexual desire, female genitalia, savage in its demands, incapable of control. Tiger Town is unbridled sexuality. It alluringly and threateningly beckons. The cakewalk dance represents final satisfaction, fulfillment, unity of the dancer with the dance. Mr. Merriwether is both sexual fulfillment and a life partner, loneliness escaped. He is God and Godot, and perhaps he is Death.

Much of the symbolism is sexual but for Williams, sex is our greatest earthly connection with the universe. Williams' alliance with D. H. Lawrence is most clear in this view of sex. Sex is our contact with, our acquaintance with, the divine. Our best knowledge of life's mysteries comes through our sexual experience. Repression or deprivation of sexual fulfillment represents mankind's greatest alienation and separation from the divine.

In *Night of the Iguana*, Shannon tells Hannah Jelkes, "We live on two levels . . . the realistic and the fantastic level." After *Iguana*, Williams was no longer content to have characters tells us about the "fantastic" level. He wanted the audience to directly experience this more difficult-to-express level of reality. During rehearsals of *Mr. Merriwether*, I asked Williams why he felt artists turned more toward the fantastic as they grew older. His answer was simple: "Because the world becomes more fantastic as you grow older. I can't go on writing realistic plays anymore, I can't!"

Williams' movement toward the fantastic, the dream-like, is perhaps most clearly parallel to the plays of August Strindberg's late career. Strindberg's introduction to *A Dream Play* could serve as an introduction to many late Williams' plays.

Everything can happen; everything is possible and likely. Time and space do not exist; on an insignificant basis of reality the imagination spins and weaves new patterns: a blending of memories, experiences, free inventions, absurdities, and improvisations.

The characters split, double, redouble, evaporate, condense, scatter, and converge. But one consciousness remains above all of them: the dreamer's; for him there are no secrets, no inconsequence, no scruples, no law. He does not judge, does not acquit, simply relates; and as the dream is usually painful, less frequently cheerful, a note of sadness and sympathy for every living creature runs through the swaying story.[5]

This description is fascinating as an analog to Williams' late plays. Always in late Williams, one feels the presence of a consciousness "above" the play, which, of course, is that of Williams. The "dreamer," Strindberg's term for himself, is a perfect description of this "character." Also relevant to Williams' vision is Strindberg's assertion of the "painful" nature of the dream. One remembers Louise McBride's enigmatic statement: "Even in a dream one can suffer."

Will Mr. Merriwether Return from Memphis? is essentially a play about illusion and reality. In the play Louise and Nora receive apparitions to fight their loneliness. As the play progresses we are unable to determine whether their visitors are apparitions or real people. Is Mr. Merriwether real? Williams refuses to answer this question. However during rehearsal Tennessee privately expressed his feelings to this director that Mr. Merriwether is quite as real as anyone else in the play.

NOTES

1. Jim Tucci, "Send Mr. Merriwether Back to Memphis," *Key West Citizen*, January 25, 1980.

2. Christine Arnold, "Tennessee's Dreamy Play Hits the Right Note," *Miami Herald*, January 26, 1980.

3. T. E. Kalem, "Apparitions and Cakewalkers," *Time*, February 4, 1980.

4. Herman Melville, *Moby-Dick* (Berkeley: University of California Press, 1979), 197–98.

5. August Strindberg, "An Explanatory Note," *A Dream Play*, trans. Walter Johnson (New York, W. W. Norton, 1973), 19.

• *10* •

In the Old Country

*A*fter *Clothes for a Summer Hotel* failed on Broadway, it became clear to Tennessee Williams that Broadway was no longer a possible home for his plays. It was at this time that he turned to regional theaters and seriously began to submit his work for production outside New York City. Williams had few acquaintances in regional theaters. The growth of the regionals had occurred apart from his experience. To many of the theaters he was a legend, and his earlier plays were produced as modern classics. But there was little interest in his recent work. Most regional theaters seemed to accept New York's critical opinion of Williams' later work. It was easier to deal with the early accepted plays than to take chances. Williams was treated with the respect given to great "dead" playwrights when he was actually a struggling writer trying to get his plays on.

There were a few exceptions to the general attitude. The American Conservatory Theater in San Francisco premiered *This Is* in 1976. The Alliance Theatre in Atlanta, Georgia, produced *Tiger Tail* in 1978. The Vancouver Playhouse produced *The Red Devil Battery Sign* in 1980, and in 1981 the same Vancouver theater mounted Tennessee's "free adaptation" of Chekhov's *The Sea-Gull*, which he entitled *The Notebook of Trigorin*.

Williams' best experience at regional theaters probably occurred at Chicago's Goodman Theatre under the artistic leadership of Gregory Mosher. It was here that *A House Not Meant to Stand* was developed over a period of eighteen months (November 1980 to April 1982), and three productions of the play were given. In Chicago, Tennessee was given the chance to see his play before audiences in three different stagings, and the play changed in response to those stagings. This is an experience that is almost unique in the American theater.

In the summer of 1980 Tennessee Williams was in Chicago with Gary Tucker, a young actor/director. They had met in Atlanta during the Alliance Theatre production of *Tiger Tail*. Tennessee had seen a production Gary directed of his one-act play entitled *The Frosted Glass Coffin*. Gary had also worked for several years in Chicago and hoped to interest some Chicago theaters in projects he wanted to direct of Williams' work. Gary's ambition and chutzpah were a good antidote to Williams' shyness. Greg Mosher recalls that Gary called him in Chicago. "I got a phone call from a Chicago actor/director [Gary Tucker] whom I had not known when he was working in Chicago (we weren't there at the same time.) He said, 'Hi. I'm working with Tennessee Williams. We'll be in town. Would you like to have dinner?'"[1] Mosher met with Williams and Tucker at the Ambassador East Hotel. "Gary did most of the talking." The young man offered some new one-act plays to Mosher, which he hoped to direct at the Goodman. Among the plays were *The Chalky White Substance, The Traveling Companion,* and *Some Problems for the Moose Lodge.* Mosher was most impressed with the black humor in the last play and suggested it might be combined with some earlier "late" Williams' one-acts, *A Perfect Analysis Given by a Parrot* and *The Frosted Glass Coffin* in an evening entitled "Tennessee Laughs." The bill of one-acts was subsequently produced in November of 1980 in the Goodman Studio Theatre directed by Gary Tucker.

Some Problems for the Moose Lodge begins (as do all subsequent longer versions entitled *A House Not Meant to Stand*) with the return of Cornelius and Bella McCorkle to their home in Pascagoula, Mississippi, after they have attended the funeral of their son Chips in Memphis. It is quickly made clear that Chips was a thirty-one-year-old gay alcoholic who was turned out of the house by his father. It is an act that Bella, the mother, has never forgiven. Now in their seventies, Cornelius and Bella suffer from a catalogue of physical ailments that restrict their mobility. Cornelius has arthritis and pancreatitis, and Bella is grotesquely obese and consequently has high blood pressure.

At the house when they arrive, their younger, unemployed son Charlie introduces them to his pregnant fiancée, Stacey. Stacey is a "bawn-again Christian" who enjoins the family to prayer and salvation. In the course of the one-act play Bella receives a letter from their daughter, Joanie, who is presently in a mental institution. In the letter Joanie asks the mother not to tell Cornelius where she is as she fears Cornelius will permanently commit her.

The one-act play largely deals with the revelations of skeletons in the family closet. There is a rising tension between Charlie and Cornelius that erupts when Cornelius calls Charlie's fiancée a "Jesus freak of a whore." (Prior to this climax, Stacey had erupted in orgasmic "tongues.") Cornelius calls the police. Cornelius and Charlie take their fight outside the house with Stacey following. In an offstage fight Charlie hits his father and breaks the old man's dentures. A police officer hauls everyone off. He will take them to the town's "Moose Lodge," where hopefully friends will solve the family's problems. Left alone, Bella begins to hallucinate and talks to her imagined younger children. She is visited by a neighbor, Jessie, who becomes concerned when Bella collapses. Jessie calls a doctor. Upon arrival, the doctor tells Bella she must diet or "it's just a question of time." The doctor leaves. Bella makes peanut butter and jelly sandwiches for her remembered children. She muses, "Maybe the Moose Lodge will straighten everything out." As the play's lights dim out, Bella "sensuously spreads the bread with jelly."

The one-act play is an incisive dissection of a troubled American family. It's as if the roof were removed from a seemingly normal family, exposing the hatred and loneliness within. There is little plot to the short play, but a blackly humorous anger holds together the portrait of this family obviously headed for extinction. Both Cornelius and Bella are apt to die soon. Charlie and Stacey offer small hope for future generations. Not much develops in the course of the play. We simply see below the surface of the family until little is left but hatred, madness, and death. All of this works within a slightly cartoonish situation comic framework. A reference to a norm of television comedy is probably intended, a kind of Southern Archie Bunker world in which the family's hostility though comic cannot finally be dismissed as comedy. The play has a bitter aftertaste, a sadness born of lost love and missed opportunities.

The first expanded version of the play, retitled *A House Not Meant to Stand*, restructured the material from the one-act into a two-act play and added several plot lines to the basic situation. One of these plots concerns Cornelius' quest for lost money that he believes was given Bella at her grandfather's death. Cornelius wants to run for public office in his small town and needs the lost "Dancie" money to finance his campaign. In this first full-length version, Cornelius is given much more to do. He becomes an obsessed Don Quixote madly addressing diatribes to the audience as his political constituency. He rails at the contemporary world like an aging Jeremiah.

A second parallel plot line involves the McCorkles' neighbors, Jessie and Emerson, who are expanded as major characters. This plot line follows Jessie's commitment of her husband, Emerson, to a mental institution. It is hinted that Cornelius has similar plans for Bella.

However, the most important feature of the increased plotting in this first rewrite is the dimensionality given to Cornelius' character. He is a monster but one to whom the playwright gives some sympathy and understanding. Cornelius' cruelty is more understandable, more human in the earlier full-length version. One moment in the first full-length version particularly suggests this "rounded" approach. At one point in the first full-length version Cornelius attempts to make some "contact" with Charlie.

Cornelius: When your health goes your patience goes with it, Charlie, you don't present a likeable side to your character anymore.

Charlie: Pop, I cain't remember you presentin' any other side of you than I—

Cornelius: Son? Don't, don't I mean DON'T!

(It is important that this appeal seem authentic.)

At another point in the action in this version, a plant in the audience questions Cornelius on his progressive liberalism and claims of support for "minorities, underprivileged, and abused."

Plant: How can you make such a claim after the mean-minded attitude you showed toward your dead son that was gay?

Cornelius: You must never judge a man's heart by despicable things said at the end of endurance. List "atrocities" of the San Salvador, Guatemala murdered young blacks—WHERE IS GOD IN THESE TIMES OF IN-IQUITIES PAST ALL CREDENCE?

After the first full-length "studio" production of the play, again directed by Gary Tucker, Gregory Mosher decided to stage another production of the play. This time it would be on the Goodman Main Stage. Another director, Andre Ernotte was hired to direct the play. Ernotte had directed Harold Pinter's *Betrayal* in a successful Goodman production the year before. Mosher has insisted that the change of directors did not imply any criticism of Gary Tucker but was to give Williams another view of the play.

Ernotte's approach to the play was more theatrical and less realistic, and this approach is reflected in the final script. This theatricality was particularly evident in the play's emerging new structure. For instance, Jessie's character was introduced early in the action planting the possibility of Emerson's commitment. Stacey's entrance was saved for the end of act 1 as a possible plot complication. The structure is less accidental, the style less naturalistic. The play became more of a performance piece with characters directing many lines to the audience. The play also became darker and crazier, as well as more blackly comic. The social implications of the play are suggested in a surreal way. This final version is a unique work in the Williams' canon, an unbeliev-ably cruel play that is also wildly comic. It is this version that I shall describe in detail, not only because it represents Williams' later thoughts on the play, but also because it is the most "different" and original of the two full-length versions. It takes Williams further away from the conventional theater of his time and is the more adventurous journey of the two expanded versions.

The set for this final *House*, as well as in earlier versions, is the McCorkle residence in Pascagoula, Mississippi. The time is "late December of this year." The house is in a state of "dilapidation . . . which is a metaphor for the state of society." Throughout the play, the house will be continually described as literally falling apart. The set must have several specific playing areas: "a small entrance hall, a living room with rain-streaked and peeling wall paper and a dining-room masked by a transparency." The dining room will be frequently used, often by Bella as she aimlessly wanders throughout the house and into the kitchen. The audience, of course, may see simultaneous actions in the living and dining areas. In addition, a "stair-case ascends to a landing on which there is a withered palm in a cracked jardiniere." The house suggests a vast emptiness as well as decay and dilapidation. It is realistic and metaphoric, sad and funny.

The physical appearance of the characters continues this sad-comic vision. Cornelius and Bella are both described as overweight and should both have a slightly grotesque appearance. "The upper frame of Cornelius is slight in comparison to his distended abdomen . . . Bella's way of walking suggests more weight than the actress needs to carry." One of the play's running jokes is Cornelius' continual list of physical complaints. It must not seem easy for the characters to get around the house. Movement is difficult and perhaps painful.

Upon entrance Cornelius immediately remarks that he wants to have a "showdown" with Bella over a "certain cash reserve that's in your possession." He turns on the Christmas lights, which have been carelessly strung around the entrance way without benefit of a tree. Bella cries out, "Not the Christmas lights!" She is obviously still grieved at the loss of her son, Chips. The lights remind her of the telephone call informing her of Chips' death. "I took up the phone. Said 'Chips? Is that you, precious?'—Then came on this strange, this hard, cold voice. 'Are you Mrs. McCorkle?' I was scared by the voice—had to set down by the phone.—'Yes, what?' Man said, 'I'm afraid I got some bad news for you, Mrs. McCorkle. I'm your son's roommate. Just come from the hospital. He is in a deep coma and the doctor admitted it wasn't likely that he'd get through the—'" Cornelius finishes her sentence: "Night. I know and he didn't." Cornelius launches into a generalized diatribe against gays, blaming Bella for his son's homosexuality: "Yeh, that's how they all are, concerned only with self and their dissipations, disgusting practices . . . You encouraged it Bella. Encouraged him to design girls' dresses. He put on a yellow wig and modelled himself. Something—*drag* they call it. Misunderstood correctly by the neighbors." Cornelius insists that Chips' homosexuality was inherited from Bella's side of the family, the Dancies, who were well known for "sex confusion and outrageous public behavior."

Jessie, the McCorkles' next-door neighbor, enters. She has recently used inherited money for "cosmetic surgery," which she believes has made her look younger. Warning Cornelius of her husband Emerson's plans to start a motel chain (called the Nite-A-Glory), Jessie informs the McCorkles that she intends to take "legal action" against her husband, whose plans for the motels are proof of his mental instability. She directly addresses the audience: "You know, Emerson Sykes is fifteen years my senior and is gone into a senile dementia of a sexual nature."

Following Jessie's exit, Bella defies Cornelius with knowledge gained from Jessie. "Jessie Sykes told me that you'd told Em that you thought I was gone in the head and had to be removed." It seems that Cornelius and Jessie both have plans to have their mates committed. Just as Em wants Jessie's money for his X-rated motels, so Cornelius wants the hidden Dancie money to finance a futile political campaign. Old age has brought no pacific acceptance to these veterans of marital battles. They are all in a hurry to discard each other. Only Bella seems free from schemes. But, as a woman of heart, she is totally ineffectual.

We hear voices from upstairs. A woman's voice calls out "CHARR-LEE." Cornelius tells the audience that his son Charlie's "got him a woman up there." Charlie enters calling back to his girlfriend whom he identifies to his family as "Stacey, my steady in Yazoo City!" Charlie asks his mother if the funeral went "off all right." Cornelius answers, "Yeh, perfect. Grave dug. Body interred." Bella exits intending to make Charlie and Stacey some food.

Left alone with Charlie, Cornelius tries to enlist his son's aid in his attempt to discover where Bella has hid the Dancie money. He tells Charlie the story of how Bella was in the death room with her grandfather where he believes the dying man gave "a big wad of thousand dollar bills, a least a coupla hunred thousand dollar bills" to Bella. He is sure Bella has hid the money somewhere in the house. Charlie has no sympathy for his father. He will not help him, "for you to blow in runnin' for Congress with no pancreas, Pop, an' hobbling on a stick?" He blames his father for the loss of his brother and sister. "Too late to butter me up with that 'Son' crap. Man had three children you don't acknowledge a one. Chips was my brother, Joanie's my sister, you're no relation to me."

Reentering the room, Bella in confusion calls Charlie by Chips' name. She falls onto the sofa and "the scene freezes for a moment or two." Coming to, she complains of "terrible stawms" in her ears. Bella then returns to the kitchen where she has left an omelet on the stove. Charlie asks his father how much the house is worth. "What would it be worth if we was obliged to sell it when you, if you ever after you're."

There is a knock at the door. Emerson, "an old man about the age of Cornelius stalks in." He is an old friend of Cornelius and "dressed in rubber boots and hunting clothes." Emerson is also a brother of Cornelius from the Moose Lodge. He complains about his wife, Jessie, who has "come into some money from her older brother who finally died." Cornelius confronts his friend with what he considers foolishness in taking out a loan at 20 percent interest to finance the Nite-A-Glory Motel. Furious, Emerson tells Cornelius that his finances are none of Cornelius' business. The argument gets hotter as Cornelius accuses Emerson of dishonesty in business dealings in order to secure past loans that ended in declared bankruptcy. Charlie cautions the two men to control their tempers and volume of voice. Bella is becoming more and more distracted. At one point in the dining room she "picks up a candelabra and staggers about the table, gazing around with an air of disbelief and loss past enduring."

Stacey calls out for Charlie to bring a suitcase upstairs. Cornelius reacts with sarcasm: "You're being paged by your Yazoo City import. Tell her there's an embargo against her kind here in my house."

Charlie, in anger, returns to Bella seated in the "weirdly candle-lit dining room." She is "staring about in a bewildered way." Charlie asks, "What are you lookin' for Mom?" Bella answers, "Life, all the life that we had here!" The mother asks Charlie to return "five chairs to the table." Charlie leaves to get the extra chairs from out back in a wood shed.

Bella wanders into the living room "holding the black and silver speckled candelabra." Cornelius asks her if she is looking for something. Her answer is vague and self-absorbed: "Heavy, heavy hangs over the head or the heart—and what shall the owner do to redeem it . . . !" Charlie returns to the dining room with more chairs. Bella asks for a picture of "Gramp's and Grannies's Gold Anniversary Picnic, summer of 1930" to be rehung on the wall where it used to be. Charlie says he "noticed it in the woodshed." He goes out for it. Cornelius, overhearing Bella in the dining room, comments to Emerson, "I'll need some witnesses to her condition to git her removed and I count on you to stand by me." Emerson's answer, ironic in view of the play's subsequent action, is one of the play's few humane moments: "I couldn't stand by you in putting that woman away no more'n you stand by putting me away or me stand by putting you away. There's too much putting away of old and worn-out people. Death will do it all. So why take premature action?"

Charlie brings in the photograph, which sparks a series of reminiscences for Bella. Cornelius cannot resist making remarks about the Dancies. He says that Grannie Dancie (in the photograph) is "grinning like a possum eating shit." Bella, turning her back on Cornelius, cries out, "That man is full of hate as the Dancies was full of love!" Sarcastically, Cornelius rejoins, "and moonshine money, that's what the Dancies were full of!"

Incensed, Bella orders a cab, enlisting aid from Charlie (calling him Chips). Charlie pushes his father into the living room, declaring, "I am putting Pop out!" Before they can stop her, Bella, "thrashing about" and "knocking things over" in "delirious passion," runs out of the house. Outside we hear "driving rain and an approaching car." Stacey's voice from upstairs yells out, adding to the cacophony: "*Charlie, is something going on down there?*" There is "a loud screech of brakes. Charlie rushes out. Cornelius hobbles after." The door is blown shut. Alone in the living room, "Em moves about in confusion 'til his attention is focused on the appearance of Charlie's girl-friend Stacey. She has descended to the landing, holding before her a large and fantastic beach towel that shields her body from view from shoulders to knees. The faded towel is patterned with beautiful, stylized creatures of the sea: fan-tail fish of many colors, seahorses, crustaceans, shells, etc. Her face has an ingenuous wide-eyed charm." Finally making her first appearance on stage at this climactic moment, Stacey speaks the curtain line that ends act 1: "Sounds like a disturbance goin' on down here." There is a black out that punctuates the understatement.

The action of act 2 follows immediately. It is a grotesque scene in which Emerson makes sexual advancements to Stacey. Calling the young woman "honey" and "baby," the old man brags about his financial investments, "his voice quivering with the hunger that possesses some of the elderly for the young and lovely." He informs Stacey, "I take a thing by injection called depo-testosterone once or twice weekly along with one thousand units of Vitamin E to keep my virility up."

He offers Stacey a hundred dollar bill, which he always keeps "in my pocket just in case I should happen to run into a beautiful young lady in re-duced circumstances." Stacey becomes hysterical: "This sounds like you are mistaking me for a *whore!*" She screams and Em falls down, "seized by a slight cardiac attack." He fumbles in his pocket "for nitro-glycerin tablets which he spills." He "falls to his knees to recover a tablet and puts it in his mouth."

Bella and Charlie reenter the house. She is "wildly dishevelled . . . sug-gesting an element of nature." Bella has barely avoided being hit by a car, which swerved to miss her. Charlie locks his father, who is wildly knocking at the front door, out of the house. Emerson admits Cornelius after Charlie exits. Cornelius enters looking like an "outraged bedraggled old monster." He launches into a generalized diatribe to the audience about the threat of nuclear destruction: "Sinister these times. East West—armed to the teeth. Nukes and neutrons.—Invested so much in every type of munitions, yes, even in germs, cain't afford not to use them, fight it out to the death of every human inhabit-ant of the earth if not the planet's destruction opposed by no one."

Emerson exits upstairs for a much needed "pee." He cautions Cornelius about the presence of "a bad-tempered woman" in the house. The phone rings after Em has exited. It is Jessie informing Cornelius that she has sent over two men to observe Em's behavior, to take him away, and "commit" him. Cornelius calls it a "highly irregular procedure" but wants "no involvement." Almost immediately two men arrive who tell Cornelius "we have been instructed to observe Mr. Sykes a short while before we remove him." The strangers cross into the dining room.

Emerson returns from upstairs. Almost immediately he notices the "strange young men." He calls out for his gun. From the darkened dining room the anonymous men ask for Emerson to "step in here a minute." Reluctantly Em advances into the dining room whereupon the young men quickly usher the old man out the back way through a kitchen door. Charlie confronts Cornelius over his lack of help to his old friend. Charlie believes that Jessie has had Emerson "removed" to get him out of the way for someone younger. Charlie calls his father "as mean as a junk-yard dawg."

Cornelius decides this is the time to confront Bella over the Dancie money. He calls her in. Bella vaguely denies there is any such thing as Dancie money.

> Cornelius: Off and on I've asked you this before, but now, you in your condition and me in mine and the roof of this house and every wall of the house threatening to collapse before we do, the question is too urgent *not* to call for an *immediate* answer.
>
> Bella: Question is?
>
> Cornelius: Concerning the Dancie money. It's time now you told me, don't you think so.
>
> Bella: Dancie?
>
> Cornelius: Yes, Dancie
>
> Bella: Money?
>
> Cornelius: *Yes!* Money!

She denies there is any Dancie money. Cornelius begins to holler at Bella: "NOW FOR THE LAST TIME TELL . . . WHERE THE HELL YOU HID IT BECAUSE I SWEAR IF YOU DON'T THIS GODDAM HOUSE, EV'RY TIMBER AND EVERY SHINGLE OF IT, IS GONNA FALL, YES, WILL COLLAPSE ON YOUR HAID, MINE, EVERY, ALL UNDER IT, IT IS NOT GONNA *STAND!*" Charlie stops his father, "Why, you DISGUSTING CHEAP OLE—" Cornelius raises his cane to strike Charlie. Bella "cries out in terror, staggers off: Crash in kitchen." Charlie grabs his father's cane and throws it away. There is a clap of thunder and lights go off. This theatrical moment undercuts the drama with nature's elements participating in this comically orchestrated climax.

Stacey's voice calls out as she creeps downstairs in the dark. The lights pop back on, and Stacey is clearly seen for the first time "clasping her hands over her belly, protuberant with late pregnancy." Cornelius sees her, "jaws falling open in astonishment." Charlie introduces Stacey to the family, informing them that they will marry the next day. Cornelius is not pleased. Stacey says she will help Bella out with the house. She looks at a photograph of Chips and tells Bella of her sympathy for gays: "They used to flock into the Late and Lively, where I was employed as a waitress befo' my engagement to Charlie, yais, boys like this come in there when the bars closed fer our ninety-nine cent breakfast of aigs, sausage, grits, and biscuits, haws-biscuits with sawmill gravy and with chicery coffee. I made acquaintance with them I sympathized with their problems."

Stacey is a "bawn-again Christian" who brought some of her gay acquaintances to Jesus. Almost immediately she launches into an evangelical sermon seemingly possessed by the Holy Spirit. She wants to "save" the McCorkle household. "Let's pray for peace in this house which is attacked by demons! All together pray with me!" She starts to speak "in tongues." Cornelius is beside himself: "Shutterup. Goddam it." Stacey collapses "as if arrived at orgasm." Bella worries that the young woman may lose the baby in labor. Cornelius calls the police who arrive immediately. Cornelius informs the officer: "We just got back from a fam'ly fun'ral in Memphis when we discover our other one, Charlie, had brought a pregnant lunatic in here in our absence."

The argument proceeds outside. We hear bickering voices. Cornelius continually insults Stacey finally calling her a "Jesus-freak of a whore!" Charlie hits his father, "a yell of pain." Cornelius screams out, *"Broke my dentures."* A second police officer suggests, "Before he files claims against my friend Charlie here, why don't we stop by the Moose Lodge. My Dad's there tonight. This thing can all be—" They haul Cornelius, Charlie, and Stacey (crying "Keep praying") off in the police car.

Bella is left alone in the house. The following actions motivate the last moments of the play:

> For a few moments she sits there as if senseless. Then her eyes focus on a small bottle of sedative pills that were given her by Dr. Crane after she fell on the street. She lurches forward to remove it from the low table that fronts the sofa: clumsily and exhaustedly gets it open and spills contents on table. Collects several and puts them in her mouth; is unable to swallow; notices a beer bottle on the table and washes the pills down with a

beer . . . Apparently the beverage hasn't displeased her. She takes several more swallows. A synergistic reaction occurs. Gradually the apparition of Chips becomes visible behind the transparency of the dining room. THE APPARITION stands motionless for a while before Bella lifts her clear, deeply innocent eyes to him.

Chips' apparition keeps saying the word "clock."

Jessie enters. She is curious for a report on Emerson's removal: "Emerson Sykes' removal to Foley's—was it violent, Bella?" She tells the audience, "His removal to a closed ward at Foley's was all that was left to do." Jessie notices a letter Bella has been clutching. It is from Bella's daughter, Joanie. Curious to know its contents, Jessie convinces Bella to read it aloud to her. "You got to know the contents and the sooner the better." The letter reveals Joanie's fate. Bella reads aloud:

> Dear Mom, don't commit me. They can only hold me ten days without your permission or Pop's. He would give it I know. But I know you wouldn't. All I had was a little nervous breakdown after that sonovabitch I lived with in Jefferson Parish quit me and went back to his fucking wife . . . That black motha, he quit me without a dime. Honestly, I was much better off at Miss Lottie's where I last was, would've gone back there but the place shut down because Miss Lottie stopped paying off somebody to keep it open and it was election time. Well, Mom I know you got lots of problems of your own. Cheer up. That's my philosophy always. I swear I'm okay, never felt better in my life, so if you get papers, refuse to sign them and say nothing about this to Pop. I'll get back on my feet, can either return to Miss Lottie's or get my old job back at the Pizza King on the highway. I know the manager can't wait to get me back there. So don't let nothing upset you, things will work out for the best. Love, your little Joanie.

Jessie consoles Bella as best she can. "Yes, it contains some terrible details, but she does say she never felt better in her life."

A knock is heard at the door. A man says he is a "police officer." But Jessie is not so sure. A sex fiend has been on the loose in the area. The man identifies himself as Pee Wee Jackson, a police friend of Charlie's, who is trying to get a deposition from Bella in order to save Charlie from going to jail for the assault of Cornelius. Bella is very vague but she does manage to say, "Cornelius McCorkle's only intr'est is money to run for office . . ." The policeman says he can use that statement in Charlie's defense. He rushes off hurriedly in spite of Jessie's efforts to distract his attention once she has seen that he is an attractive young man. After Pee Wee's exit Jessie delivers an "interior monologue" to the audience.

What a handsome and sexy, what a strapping young man that boy we used to call Pee Wee has grown into. Now that the children are grown and gone away, I see nothing wrong in looking at attractive and vigorous young men such as Bruce Lee Jackson or Spud, that young Irish waiter at the Dock House. Do you? I always give Spud a good up and down look and since my rejuvenation, he returns it, and, of course I slip him an extra tip as I leave . . . I'm sort of put out with Mary Louise Dean that she's had him first, but then she had her rejuvenation first, too . . . I didn't have mine till I saw how hers turned out. Miracle.

Bella seems to have finally understood the significance of the message "clock" from Chips' apparition. She asks Jessie to look behind a clock on the mantle piece, which has been loudly ticking throughout the play. Looking inside the clock, Jessie finds a yellow envelope, which she gives to Bella. The envelope is filled with money. Bella starts to breathe heavily and complains of a "terrible stawm" in her ears. Jessie retrieves the money from Bella, putting it in Bella's hand bag. There is a tussle between the two women for the bag of money. Jessie finally secures the money from the failing Bella and "stuffs it down her negligee." Bella "sprawls back as if lifeless on the sofa." Jessie rushes off for a doctor.

Alone, Bella hears the sound of childrens' voices "projected over house speakers with music under." She wanders into the dining room and lights the candelabra. Bella imagines the voice of her black maid Hattie, whom she instructs, "If supper is ready, call the children in, please. Don't let them chase fireflies, they never stop chasing fireflies."

Jessie returns with Doctor Crane. Bella tells the doctor that Jessie "tried to grab my bag from me . . . bag with Dancie Money." Jessie denies the allegation showing Dr. Crane a purse that contains only candy bars. The doctor however notices "a corner of the fat yellow envelope protruding from the top of Jessie's negligee." Dr. Crane takes the money from Jessie and gives it back to Bella. With a "luminous smile," Bella says, "It's mine, not for Jessie, not for Cornelius, for *Charlie's children coming*." Subjective cries of children are heard "enchanting with the lost lyricism of childhood." These sounds build as Jessie protests her innocence and asks the audience, "*Who in this world can you trust?*" Doctor Crane hushes Jessie saying, "Can't you see that the immediate concern is not money." Bella, seated now at the table says "Grace" with her imaginary children. They end together, "Amen." The final action is Bella's expiration as "her head sinks slowly to the failing support of her hands."

The changes incorporated into this final third Goodman version represent a radicalization of the theatricality that had always existed within the play. In the second Goodman production (first full-length version), plot elements (the Dancie money, Jessie's commitment of Em) had been introduced but they were not manipulated nor developed in so climactic a manner. The play finally became a well-made play that heightened the theatrical and "unreal" nature of the play. As in a farce or melodrama, the structuring gives entertainment value.

Also as in farce or melodrama, characters are deliberately kept simple, less sympathetic, more grotesque. In the final version Williams eliminates all moments of possible sympathy for Cornelius. Williams' natural tendency may have been to find moments of Chekhovian compassion for unlikable characters, but the director, Andre Ernotte, seems to have encouraged Williams toward a more classically cruel comedy closer to Moliere or Ben Jonson or Joe Orton. The final play is uncompromisingly free of compassionate moments until the play's end when Bella is alone with her apparitional children. Arnotte's direction accented the play's theatricalism through direct address of all characters, Brechtian lighting, comic "sound effects," and broad acting. It is very clear from an interview during the rehearsal period of Ernotte's *House* that the director very specifically wanted to take the play into a theatrical, larger-than-life direction. His comments to Richard Christiansen in an interview for the *Chicago Tribune* indicate the aims he sought for his production: "This play cannot be a television drama. It's almost like it was written in capital letters. It's a loud play for large audiences, and you have to play against any sentimentality or schmaltzy whining. Otherwise it becomes campy."[2]

To be sure there were differences between Ernotte and Williams. When Ernotte flew to Key West to see Tennessee, the playwright did not see the director for several days. To complicate things further, Gary Tucker insists that Tennessee was very happy with the full-length version Tucker had directed and wanted Tucker left on the project. Tennessee was clearly caught between Tucker, who was his secretary, and Mosher, who wanted Ernotte to direct the final version.

Gregory Mosher was firm with Williams when problems arose in rehearsal over the performance of the actor playing Cornelius in the Ernotte production. Tennessee felt that the earlier actor had been funny and charming while the later actor was unpleasant. Mosher insisted there was nothing wrong with the new actor. "I told him he could go back to Key West or wherever but we were doing the play. We had a contract."[3]

It is fascinating that many of the play's problems stemmed from the character of Cornelius. This, of course, is the name of Williams' own father, the person (along with Williams' brother Dakin) on whom the character is based. Psychologically this late play represents a final confrontation of Williams with his love-hatred of his father and heterosexual male authority. A comically

black treatment leaves little room for resolution or hope of love. It may have
been too painful a possibility.

In the end Tennessee seems to have appreciated Ernotte's firm hand and
vision of the play, although Gary Tucker insists Tennessee always preferred
the earlier, more compassionate version that Tucker had directed. Speaking
with *Chicago Tribune* critic Richard Christiansen after the Ernotte production,
Williams stated, "The production startled me at first. I wasn't prepared for the
stylization. I think the German expressionist treatment was right for my material. I hadn't realized how far I had retreated from realism in my writing. I had
long since exhausted the so-called 'poetic realism.' This, after all, isn't twenty
years ago. I always write to satisfy myself, so I'm not conscious, perhaps, of
the change in my work. Ernotte had never encountered a Southerner before
this play, and he gave the play a general theatrical approach far removed from
Southern regionalism. It needed to be larger."[4] There are merits to both approaches. Unfortunately, neither text has been published. It would be helpful for subsequent directors of this remarkable play to study both versions,
understanding that the play can be more compassionate and realistic or more
theatrical and cruel. Both aspects are present in the play, and both are capable
of being stressed in different productions by different directors.

The critical comments on the play's different versions in Chicago ex-
hibited a wide range of opinion. But, on the whole, they were more positive
than any reviews Williams had received in recent years. Here are some of the
critical reactions to the one act-play, *Some Problems for the Moose Lodge*:

> The three one-act plays that opened Tuesday night in the Goodman Stu-
> dio Theatre under the umbrella title of "Tennessee Laughs" are filled with
> what their author has called "the endured but unendurable pain" of life.
>
> The presence of pain, pain of loss, pain of abandonment, pain of death
> is nothing new to Tennessee Williams. But in this wintry trio it erupts in a
> bleak slapstick that expresses life as a mad, pathetic farce.
>
> This is particularly true in the case of the evening's premiere, "Some
> Problems for the Moose Lodge," which furiously descends on a grotesque
> family torn apart by a horrible, hilarious combination of madness, alcohol-
> ism, sexual perversion, obesity, disease, despair, stupidity, and futility.
>
> The play is a mammoth, mercurial mixture of pratfalls and a pathos.[5]

> [*Some Problems for the Moose Lodge* is] a candidate for rewriting and expand-
> ing as another three-act Williams' classic. [It] ends too abruptly and without
> that soul-cleansing resolution that turns all too familiar human failure into
> shattering drama.[6]

> These are bitter-sweet plays, well-crafted examples of the genre, and for
> the most part delightfully acted; but the bitter rises over the sweet. Worth
> seeing if only to refresh the memory of what a one-act play can be.[7]

Glenna Syse, main critic of the *Chicago Sun-Times* felt that, in *Moose Lodge*, "the great Williams' gifts for compassion, gallantry, artful craft, and lacerating truth only appear in slivers." She wondered if the play represented Williams "become television."[8]

Subsequently, Syse's reaction to the first expanded full-length version of *A House Not Meant to Stand* was by far the most positive review the play received. She obviously respected the play's expanded humanity, and her description of the play reflects an appreciative understanding of the play's world:

> There are termites in the walls in "A House not Meant to Stand" . . . and there are tremors in the tissues of the people who live and visit there. It is a damp, crowded place where dreams have decayed and mildewed.
>
> What is most important is that Tennessee Williams, who turned seventy, last week, is in residence here. He is now part of the Goodman Theatre family and we are glad his muse is in our neighborhood.
>
> It never has been and it never will be a casual muse. He knows his characters like an old hound dog knows his master. And he gives them no cheap solace, few excuses. Naturally they are not your ordinary, jolly little old tribe. They are riddled with avarice, lechery, hypocrisy, vanity, and self-deception. And if you doubt that they are real, consider that you will probably always remember them. They are a composite of the hurts of the world.[9]

Richard Christiansen found the first full-length version "potentially a play of power." Perhaps influencing the way the play was to develop in its final version, Christiansen called the drama "a work of shreds and patches, of dross and substance, a drama in search of a connecting spine and above all a properly surreal tone for its hallucinatory madness. If they are to succeed, they need to bring more madness of mood and more clarity of form to this strange 'House.'"[10] This is exactly what Ernotte and Williams attempted to do in the final *House*.

Glenna Syse was still appreciative of the third version and defended the play as she had done before:

> Yes, some of the natives will get restless. Some will hold a hand to their brow and ask with exasperation, "Who are all these loonies?" But there will be others like me, who will say the gentleman is still a major voice in the American theater. At seventy-one, Tennessee Williams is a canny old hound dog who knows where all the bodies are buried and he is still the best undertaker in the business.
>
> This is no idle reworking. Williams told me that in all his years of writing, he has never given a director such exhaustive notes. And from its many layers, you can see that this is a meticulous honey comb of a story, a complex spider web with a gossamer heart and a granite spine. It's overwritten. It's

too obsessed with theatrics. But it is not old-fashioned. It has its departures from the usual Williams' style. And it reminds us again of how funny the man can be. This is a playwright who has shed his tears, but you know that there's a cackle coming around the next corner.[11]

Christiansen was still also positive, noting Ernotte's contribution, but he asked for even more theatricalism:

Director Andre Ernotte uses stabs of lighting, amplified voices, bursts of music, sudden shifts in lighting, and long arias spoken directly to the audience to break down the naturalism of the theatre and I wish he had done much, much more.

This is a play of freaks and outcasts, and it requires a production that completes the hilarious, horrible madness. It is "The Cabinet of Dr. Caligari" on the Gulf-Coast.[12]

This is in an interesting instance of a critic imagining his own production, who was associated with the play's development from its first production and probably influenced the play's development. From his first review Christiansen had recognized the play's uniqueness:

From its beginnings, Tennessee Williams' *A House Not Meant to Stand* has never veered from its powerful original impulse. Then, as now, it is a loud, harsh, bitter pain-filled shriek at the degenerative process of life . . .

A House Not Meant to Stand now has reached the end of its long road of development at the Goodman. It's not a brilliant exit, but it is not a dead end, either. It has taken us to where Tennessee Williams is today.[13]

Perhaps the most historically interesting notice of the final production was a radio review by Claudia Cassidy, who had first championed *The Glass Menagerie* in her initial Chicago review in the 1940s. No longer writing for a major Chicago paper newspaper, Cassidy in her review for radio station WFMT summarizes her lifelong support for Tennessee Williams. She begins by defining Williams' intentions in the play from his description of the play as a "Gothic Comedy":

If we take the term in the sense of the mysterious, the grotesque, and the desolate, then "A House Not Meant to Stand" is a gothic structure, and southern Gothic at that. But it is Tennessee Williams' southern gothic and it is shrewd as well as bitter, acidly funny as well as sad . . . a rotting house pictured in the playbill as on the edge of an abyss, a kind of metaphor for the human condition inside.

It is indeed mysterious, grotesque, and desolate but whoever said that theater is none of those things? There is here the acute compassion Tennessee Williams has always had for the victims of the world we live in . . . This is not wholly successful but it is, at least to me, fascinating being a play by a playwright.[14]

What a piece of criticism! Cassidy describes the piece, recognizing its own intentions. She tells us what it wants to be. She also respects and understands those intentions as coming from a unique voice. She does not want to change it. She does not want to dictate the function of the theater. She defines the voice as having "acute compassion" and finally, recognizing her own subjectivity, says that it is fascinating "to her." "It is a play by a playwright," no hype, no condemnation.

The third Chicago production went on for a few performances in Miami, Florida, where it played as part of a New World Festival of the Arts in 1982. This festival was planned as an annual event, but it was never subsequently repeated. The Goodman production of *A House Not Meant to Stand* was substituted at the last minute for a new production of another Williams' premiere entitled *Now the Cats with Jewelled Claws*. The latter play, more daring than even *House*, was dropped when finally read by festival director Robert Herman after he had announced its title. *House* drew little attention in the crowded Miami Festival, playing in an old converted movie house to small audiences. *Time* magazine called the play "probably the best thing he has written since *Small Craft Warnings*."[15] It closed in Miami and never went on. The play has never been produced in New York City. And, to date, it has never been published.

There is much plot in the final version of *A House Not Meant to Stand*, but it merits little belief or real interest. The play is more expressive of a series of death rattles than any actions that might change or affect its characters. Even if Cornelius did get Bella's money, we doubt that his political campaign would win. Surely his past record of defeats clearly tells us this. Jessie's move to confine Emerson seems outrageous and farfetched in the way it is casually depicted in the play. It belongs more to a world of bad dreams than to objective reality. The device of having Chip's apparition reveal the money's hiding place to the dying Bella is a coup de théâtre, again more acceptable in a dream than in a realistic play. Therefore, while Williams added conventional plot devices to his one-act, the additions are basically theatrical devices that accomplish his real intent: the creation of a Southern spook sonata, a dream play of old age. The expanded *House* only extends the nightmare, the added plot devices only increase the horror of Williams' vision of old age. At the same time, black comedy is increased and entertainment value is increased. But little of this is believable on a realistic level. The play's truth is beyond those limitations.

In calling the play a "Southern Gothic spook sonata," Williams invokes the modern Swedish playwright August Strindberg. Several times in this book I have noted Williams' alliance in his late plays to the late dream plays of Strindberg. This alliance is most specific in *Clothes for a Summer Hotel* and *Will Mr. Merriwether Return from Memphis?* In *A House Not Meant to Stand* Williams clearly acknowledges his debt to Strindberg in the play's descriptive subtitle. *A House Not Meant to Stand* is more than a generally stylistic analog to Strindberg's *Spook Sonata* (sometimes called *The Ghost Sonata*). Williams' aims in *House* are very nearly the same as Strindberg's in *Spook Sonata*.

The Spook Sonata is a play in which the focus moves from an observation of the outside of a house to a depiction of death and misery inside. In the first scene a young student, Arkenholz, observes a grand house from the outside and envies the wealth and seeming happiness of those who live within. He sees a beautiful young girl inside the house who captivates him. He believes that if he could only win the girl all happiness would be his. He accidentally meets an old man in a wheelchair, Director Humel, who gains admittance for Arkenholz to the house. There Arkenholz attends a ghost supper in which many dark secrets are revealed. The family is really dead, a congregation of living mummies involved in Byzantine hatreds and cruel revenges.

The last scene of the play takes us into the most interior room of the house, a hyacinth room where the beautiful young girl lives and is dying from a strange poison emitted by the hyacinth flowers. Arkenholz wants to marry the young girl, but she tells him it is impossible. All the young are destroyed by a poison mysteriously created by the hyacinths, which symbolize the past of the house and the adults' hatred. The student says, "Imagine the most beautiful flowers are so poisonous, are the most poisonous—why the curse rests on all creation and life . . . why didn't you want to be my bride? Because you're sick at the very source of life." The young girl dies as the play ends and "Bocklin's Island of the Dead becomes the back drop."

It may at first be difficult to see the relationship of *House Not Meant to Stand* to *The Spook Sonata*. In no way does Williams follow Strindberg's plotline. He changes Strindberg's particularly European family portrait to a Southern American one. Williams' characters are American and very Southern, yet the vision of family life is the same as in Strindberg's play: families are prisons of hatred and lost love, and this destroys the young before they have begun to live. Somehow we view this idea as appropriate to a gloomy misanthropic Swede. In an American writer, one so close to us, the idea seems unbearably painful. That this should possibly be true makes it all the more important as a contemporary statement on that most American of all institutions, the American family, the subject and setting of so much of our drama.

Appropriate to a Southern Gothic spook sonata, characters in *House* are oversized, ill, eccentric. This causes a nightmare quality that is both funny and frightening. Time has "bloated" all the characters. It is specifically requested that Cornelius and Bella be overweight. Stacey is very pregnant. Jessie's face is slightly unreal as a result of her face lifts. Emerson is ridiculously dressed as if for a hunting-fishing trip. The physically grotesque quality of these characters is important to Williams' late ironic vision of a "normal" family.

The characters are simple with little dimensionality in the final version. Cornelius is crustier, Bella is daffier, Jessie more self-absorbed, Emerson more lascivious. The movement of the rewrites is away from moments of compassion to a more classic kind of comedy in which characters are laughed *at*, rather than *with*. In this respect, the comedy of *House* is reminiscent of contemporary black comedy.

One could argue that this movement robs Williams of the traditional compassion characteristic of so much of his work. However, the cruelty and theatricality of the final version are appropriate to a spook Gothic play and expressive of a side of the playwright already existent in such works as *The Gnädiges Fräulein*. Cruelty and theatricality were certainly embryonic in the one-act *Some Problems for A Moose Lodge*. In pushing the play further in this direction, Williams emphasized the uncompromisingly nightmarish quality of his play.

The language in *A House Not Meant to Stand* is earthy and funny but less lyrical than the language in many other of Williams' Southern plays. Cornelius speaks the Southern speech of Big Daddy, brutal in its virility: "Grave dug. Body interred." His no-nonsense vocabulary gives him an admirable toughness. Only Bella speaks in lyrical Southern flights, but her sentences are largely abbreviated, breathlessly incomplete. Accusations and insults have become the most customary means of expression in the household, more common than any shared expressions of gentleness.

A listing of increased physical disorders, words that describe diseases, is a major comic device in the play. This language is meticulously detailed, creating as it does a poetry of disorders: cardiac asthma, cosmetic surgery, osteo-arthritis, senile dementia, pancreatitis are a few of the clinical terms that are discussed in this manner. Similarly, drugs to treat the disorders are also named: Tylenol Three, Cotazyme, nitro-glycerin tablets, and Donnatal all appear in the language of these old people, allusions as necessary to the characters as invocations of the Gods' names in Greek tragedies.

In the final version of the play, Cornelius' long political diatribes to the audience were almost completely cut. They lengthened the play and gave dimensionality to Cornelius, something Ernotte wanted to avoid in his production. In the earlier version Cornelius is as much interested in contemporary political problems as he is in attacking his family. Pollution, advertising, the arms race, racism, social problems—all are criticized by the aging liberal.

Similarly Bella in the earlier full-length version is capable of moments of clarity. In the first full-length version of the play, she importantly corrects Cornelius' criticism of the dead Chips' homosexuality:

Cornelius: Lunacy and unnatural love is—

Bella (cutting in strongly): No such thing exists, if it's love. Love is love regardless of who's love for who! This much I've learned out of life! Unnatural? Only hate's unnatural and terrible hurts that hate inflicts on one's hatred!

Williams and Ernotte may have felt this speech to be too polemical, too out of character for the daffier Bella. Yet the point of view informs all of Williams' work as well as this particular play. It may be unspoken, but Williams' compassion never really left him. The characters became less dimensional in the final more nightmarish version of *House*, but it seems evident that it is Williams' (the Dreamer's) wish that the nightmare end. The compassionate side of Williams was never destroyed; it simply became more hidden and possibly more despairing.

Thematically, *A House Not Meant to Stand* is Williams' vision of old age as well as a depiction of American society circa 1982. The interest is primarily on the old, and it is a report from the graveyard looking into the grave. Williams reports what he sees with pain, honesty, and laughter. Statement after statement in the play reflects this preoccupation with old age. Looking at his crumbling house Cornelius says at the play's beginning, "So much living gone on in this place none of it come to much more than thickening of cartilage in the joints." When Cornelius complains of new physical ailments and looks for some explanation of his pain, Bella replies, "Maybe age is the only explanation." Old age as seen in this play is a horrible time and is somehow unjust. Contemporary social values are of no real help. Emerson and Jessie, infected with an illusion of youth's power, can only chime, "We're entering a period of youth!" Emerson hollers this slogan as his rationale for entering the motel business. Over and over, throughout the play, Cornelius is made to face the humiliating truth: "Too many Goddamn afflictions come upon us at this time of life." Perhaps Cornelius' most horrible observation is "There's cases in which continued existence is not desireable." Of course, he is planning to do away with Bella when he says this, not contemplating his own suicide. He still thinks he will run for public office after Bella is gone. It is easier to see truth for others than for oneself.

Williams sees old age and death in *A House Not Meant to Stand* not only as the fate of individual characters (or himself) but as the state of society as a whole. It may be a kind of supreme egotism to suppose that all civilization dies with the death of a single consciousness, but it is a common (and perhaps forgivable) observation of many in old age that all society seems to be headed toward extinction as one approaches personal extinction.

Williams was not alone in the 1980s in feeling that something was fundamentally wrong in American and Western society as we approached the end of the twentieth century. Williams was expressing a general feeling of Armageddon that existed in writers younger than himself as we faced the "dark march to whatever it is we're approaching." This feeling of doom suggests that death is more than an individual concern of the moment. Something more than individual death seems a distinct and likely possibility. Prospects are particularly gloomy and depressing. As early as 1962 in *Who's Afraid of Virginia Woolf?* Edward Albee had his George read Oswald Spengler's prediction of the West's destruction from *The Decline of the West*: "And the West, encumbered by crippling alliances and burdened with a morality too rigid to accommodate itself to the swing of events, must . . . eventually . . . fall."[16] Of course this attitude and feeling emerged much earlier in twentieth-century European literature in works like T. S. Eliot's *The Waste Land*. Williams in *A House Not Meant to Stand* takes his play's epigraph from "The Second Coming," W. B. Yeats' famous poem written in the early decades of the century: "Things fall apart: the center cannot hold."

It may be that theater generally follows other arts in its ideas, and commercial American theater may be the very last of all arts to accept certain generally accepted universal ideas. Yet within the last few decades it has become commonplace for America's theater artists to contemplate their own destructions as a major theme in their work. The idea seems to have finally entered the mainstream. As recently as September 1987 in *American Theatre* the American playwright David Mamet was expressing this amazingly apocalyptic point of view: "It's true of all other aspects of America. We're at a very difficult time. Our culture has just fallen apart and is going to have to die off before something else takes its place. So whether you say American theatre, or American car production, or American standard of living, they're all in the same boat. Theatre is not an aspect of our civilization to be separated out. It's part of the body politic."[17]

Reports of the death of American (Western) civilization in the American drama are quite often linked with reports of the death of the American family as a cohesive value-giving institution of positive identification in our lives. Indeed it is difficult to think of any American drama of significance since the start of Eugene O'Neill's career that does not play out its crises in a living room in which mothers, fathers, sons, and daughters do not love but rather destroy each other. From *Beyond the Horizon* to *Buried Child*, our plays have used the home's battlefield for their most intense confrontations.

One could say that this was always true and point out Greek family problems in Sophocles, Euripides, and Aeschylus. But in those plays the family battles had social significance outside the family; they mirrored more cosmic disputes. Similarly in Elizabethan drama, domestic tragedy disrupts social values that are nonetheless seemingly unchangeable and fixed. In American drama, little exists outside the family but the isolated self. In American drama, families give all identity and value, and similarly their destruction makes us particularly vulnerable to aloneness and chaos.

This is understandable in a society of immigrants where personal identity came not from social givens but from protective units that guarded against homogeneity and competition—the family. The family has always been an American defense system against outside enemies. Problems within the family cut at our deepest sense of security.

But the family has often needed to die because it also represents the greatest limitation on personal freedom. Families may give security but they also stifle individual expression. Marriage, cruelty, guilt, hatreds are all played out in the limiting atmospheres of responsibility and lessening joy. The answer seems to be escape, but there is nothing outside as Tom so painfully learns in *The Glass Menagerie*: "Oh Laura, Laura, I tried to leave you behind me but I am more faithful than I intended to be!"

Throughout this book I have resisted the temptation to read Williams' late plays in reference to his family and personal life. Too often biographical interpretation is limiting and obvious. Of course, Amanda and Laura are in some part based on Tennessee's mother, Edwina, and his sister, Rose. Having said that, we have really said nothing. It does not help us to understand *The Glass Menagerie* to know the biographical facts of Williams' life. It does not illuminate or enlarge our experience of the play. In order to do that we must *feel* with *Menagerie*, overcoming those aspects of the play that separate us from the play's experience. Biographical criticism too often dismisses and pigeonholes a work of art. Ultimately, what a critic is trying to do is to make a work of art more accessible to an audience by opening the work's experience up, to make it more universal. Biographical interpretation too often stresses those aspects of an artist's life that separate the work from others. It may separate the audience from an experience if background experiences are different. One must always look for the universal link in a work of art.

However, having said that, it may also be said that certain personal impulses resulting in some of the special circumstances of one's life often serve as the particular impulse for a work of art. It is obvious that *House Not Meant to Stand* was born of Williams' relationship with his father, Cornelius. Interestingly, however, the character is also an amalgam of his father, Cornelius, and his brother Dakin, who several times unsuccessfully ran for political office.

However, it may be safe to say that the play records Williams' feelings toward the overtly heterosexual male elements in his family, father, and brother. But what it records is no simple attitude. The portrait of Cornelius contains love and hatred, anger and affection. It may also be that Williams most identifies with the dead homosexual son, Chips. The father's rejection of his dead son and his homosexuality in the play obviously had personal meaning for the playwright. All his life Tennessee suffered from what he perceived was his father's childhood disapproval of his son's lack of masculinity. It was an idee fixe. As late as 1982 in a *Miami Herald* interview, Tennessee related details of boyhood humiliation from his father that made clear that even in his seventies, Williams had not resolved his feelings toward his father: "My father was quite homely. I thought. I was terrified of my father. Oh God. [He laughs.] He used to call me Miss Nancy—but yet he did love me. He wanted to make me like his father. He thought my mother was making a sissy of me and he resented that terribly."[18] *A House Not Meant to Stand* is both an asking of love from the father as well as an act of vengeance upon the father for his lack of love. Both things were probably true. Did Tennessee love his father? Yes. Did he hate him? Yes. Did he need him? Yes. Could he escape him? No.

Perhaps nowhere is this ambivalence more clearly expressed than in an article Williams wrote shortly after his father's death in 1980. Entitled "The Man in the Overstuffed Chair," the article is really an autobiographical reminiscence of his father. The overstuffed chair of the title stands for Williams' father; it was his throne, his retreat from family tensions.

> A psychiatrist once said to me, You will begin to forgive the world when you've forgiven your father.
>
> I'm afraid it is true that my father taught me to hate. But I know that he didn't plan to, and terrible as it is to know how to hate, and to hate, I have forgiven him for it and a great deal else.
>
> The best of my work, as well as the impulse to work, was a gift from the man in the overstuffed chair, and now I feel a very deep kinship to him. I almost feel as if I am sitting in the overstuffed chair where he sat exiled from those that I should love and those that ought to love me.[19]

This father/son paradox—the amalgamation of the father into the son; the son becoming the needed, hated father at the same time he needs and rejects his own son—that Oedipal drama may be the source of *House* as well as the impulse behind much American domestic drama, from *Death of a Salesman* to *Buried Child*. It is a mythic drama, tragic and universal, occurring in O'Neill, Miller, Albee, and Shepard. Williams' homosexuality does not lessen the drama—but only aggravates and gives fuel to the struggle in a different way. Without a son to pass on the struggle, the homosexual artist perhaps faces annihilation more painfully. He makes his art his offspring, his record of the mythic process. Approval for that art becomes an obsession almost as if social acceptance might give the artist an acceptance the father never gave. What is remarkable in Williams' case is that he was able to withstand so many years of critical censure, so much lack of approval. He was hard, as tough as he was vulnerable. But he never stopped wanting his father's love and forgiveness. It may have been the greatest impulse in his life and art.

Williams' offspring was art, his record of the mythic struggle between every father and son, be the son-father struggle hetero-hetero, hetero-homo, or homo-hetero. Heterosexuality does not remove any of the participants from the struggle. It only gives different ammunition to the combatants. Williams' need for love and approval from his father could be the need of any heterosexual artist.

In the end, love and hatred are not resolved, only recorded. The two full-length versions of *A House Not Meant to Stand* stress different aspects of the same relationship and feeling. One impulse is compassionate, the other more contemptuous. One wonders if Tennessee ever reached the state of consciousness where approval from his father was not necessary. Could he ever make himself his own father? Was he ever able to make himself a secure father to his children, his art? Probably not.

In American drama, the loss of family means the loss of all value, all sureness, as well as the loss of all limitations. Families are both necessary and impossible. Without them we are parentless children and childless couples awaiting some ill-defined end. Abandonment may have become our most common experience. With a loss of continuity, we have lost our past and future. We are an unsuccessful experiment. We are literally awaiting demolition, a "house not meant to stand." With a great roar of laughter, because it is the most logical emotion, Williams laughs at his and our deaths, at the same time that he rages and cries out "*NO*" to death's dominion.

NOTES

1. Quoted in Richard Christiansen, "The Pain, Risk and Tumult of Staging Williams' New Play," *Chicago Tribune*, May 9, 1982.
2. Quoted in Christiansen, "The Pain, Risk and Tumult."
3. Gregory Mosher, interview with William Prosser, December 10, 1987.
4. Quoted in Christiansen, "The Pain, Risk and Tumult."
5. Richard Christiansen, "'Tennessee Laughs': Emotions Run Amok in Pratfalls, Pathos," *Chicago Tribune*, November 12, 1980.

6. Sam Lesner, "Williams' Play Has Potential," *Booster Newspaper*, Week of November 14, 1980.

7. *Chicago Free Weekly*, November 21, 1980.

8. Glenna Syse, *Chicago Sun-Times*, November 12, 1980.

9. Glenna Syse, "Tennessee Williams' 'House' of Tremors and Quiet Terrors," *Chicago Sun-Times*, April 2, 1981.

10. Richard Christiansen, "'House Not Meant to Stand' Needs Madness and Clarity," *Chicago Tribune*, April 3, 1981.

11. Glenna Syse, "Williams Does It Again with 'House.'" *Chicago Sun-Times*, April 28, 1982.

12. Richard Christiansen, "Tennessee Williams' Freak House Is Doomed by a Weak Foundation," *Chicago Tribune*, April 28, 1982.

13. Christiansen, "Tennessee Williams' Freak House."

14. Claudia Cassidy, radio review, WFMT, May 2, 1982.

15. Gerald Clarke, "Sweating It Out in Miami," *Time*, June 28, 1982.

16. Oswald Spengler, *The Decline of the West* (New York: Knopf, 1934).

17. David Mamet, *American Theatre*, September 1987.

18. Quoted in "The Private World of the Key West Playwright," *Miami Herald*, May 16, 1982.

19. Tennessee Williams, "Preface: The Man in the Overstuffed Chair," *Tennessee Williams Collected Stories* (New York: New Directions, 1985), xvi.

· 11 ·

On the Beach

$\mathcal{I}$n the fall of 1981, the *Paris Review* published a long interview with Tennessee Williams by Dotson Rader. It was one of the last in-depth interviews he gave. In it Williams discusses his then current work and mentions two plays—*In Masks Outrageous and Austere* and *Something Cloudy, Something Clear.* It was these two works that most concerned Williams until the time of his death in February 1983. They are, as far as I can tell, his last major works.

As was often the case with Williams, both plays had their germ of idea in earlier works and both were worked on at various times as he simultaneously worked on other projects. *Masks Outrageous* went back to a short story entitled "Tent Worms," which was written in 1945, although not published until 1980. The first draft of the play *In Masks Outrageous and Austere* (as it was entitled in that draft) dates back to 1970, according to a play script in the research department of the Lincoln Center Library (Billy Rose Collection). The setting of *Something Cloudy, Something Clear* on the beach at Provincetown suggests a very early one-act play called *The Parade.* Dating from the early 1940s, that play is about a young writer who discusses his sexuality with a young female friend whom he cannot love in a heterosexual way. Though enormously different, *Something Cloudy, Something Clear* still bears a relationship with the early play. Interestingly, both plays describe their protagonist as waiting for a "parade" in his life. That Williams returned to this early symbol in his last play is typical of the way he used material throughout his career.

During my years in Key West (1979–1983) Tennessee often discussed *Masks Outrageous* as well as *Something Cloudy, Something Clear* and allowed me to read both plays in manuscript. He always described them as "major works."

Masks Outrageous was given one mounting on the "other stage" under the title *Gideon's Point* at the Williamstown Festival Theatre during the summer of 1981. It was not a production that pleased Tennessee nor was it well received by local press. The play has never been produced anywhere else. The last draft of the play, from the years 1982–1983, as submitted by Luis Sanjurjo, Williams' last agent, was entitled *Masks Outrageous* and bears the note "edited by Gavin Lambert" on its title page. It is not clear exactly what Gavin Lambert contributed to the play since the final play is essentially the same play that was presented in Williamstown. Presumably, Tennessee showed the manuscript to Lambert, asking him for help on the play's structure. Williams was especially insecure in later years about his ability to structure a play successfully. Williams may have turned to old friends for help.

In the *Paris Review* interview, Williams described *In Masks Outrageous and Austere* as "bizarre as hell":

> It's about the richest woman on earth. Babe Foxworth is her name. She doesn't know where she is. She's been abducted to Canada, on the east coast. But she doesn't know where they are. A village has been constructed like a movie set to deceive them. Everything is done to confine and deceive them while her husband is being investigated. Babe is really an admirable person, besides her hypersexuality, though that too can be admirable. I think it is! It's a torture to her because she's married to a gay husband who's brought along his boy friend. I think it's an extremely funny play.[1]

Masks Outrageous (the play's last title) is probably the *most* outrageous version of the play. Over the years the play became more nightmarish, going from a basically realistic play with some fantastic overtones to becoming one of Williams' most outlandish creations. Given the current critical attitude toward Williams' late plays it is doubtful that *Masks Outrageous* would be well received by the critical establishment. It is also doubtful that it would be popular with a wide audience, as the play combines bizarre characters, dark humor, and exorbitant theatricality. It is, however, one of the last works of a great writer, a play of rare imagination and poetic sensibility.

Both first and last drafts of the play, radically different in tone and style, merit attention. The first draft of *Masks* is not unlike the early draft of *The Milk Train Doesn't Stop Here Anymore* in both its wealthy central character and in her change of heart. Similarly, the changes in the rewrite versions of *Masks* reveal the playwright's movement to a more negative, despairing central vision, one distrustful of all human motives. I shall describe the play as it exists in its first draft and then describe its more "bizarre" final form.

All drafts of the play place its action on the "sundeck of a summer cottage on a northeastern coast": "The sundeck is backed by a great picture-window, so full of reflections, from a sun which it faces directly, that the interior of the cottage is invisible till near the end, when some white angularities, bone-like, of summer furniture may be seen. This mirror of reflections, projected from behind should be influenced by the palette of Monet and should change gradually, from a subdued gold at the beginning to a fading, violet at the end—" At curtain rise Billy and Jerry are seated on the deck at a table which "has been set up outside: there is beautiful crockery, crystal, and a baroque silver candelabra." It is clear that the two men are lovers. They are soon joined by Billy's older wife, Babe, who is already inebriated. Babe senses the affection between the men. Her drinking accelerates and she bitchily goads her younger husband. Billy tries to control her drinking and begs Babe not to create a scene. He is not well and Babe cruelly hints at serious problems in his health.

> Billy: I'm not well Babe . . . To endure night after night of fending off bar-room brawls isn't why I came here.
>
> Babe: No, no, you're not well. Don't understand why after such a remarkable successful—surgical—removal of that benign little tumor—or wasn't it just a lesion?—in your left lung, Billy, that cough hangs on as it does.

Billy turns angry and tells Jerry to "give her all she wants—she'll fall asleep at the table—we'll have our walk on the beach."

A mysterious female figure dressed in hat and veils appear. Called Matron, she is Babe's neighbor who lives next door "in an invisible house." Matron has a mentally retarded adolescent son named Playboy who continually masturbates under a beach slicker and says nothing but "coo, coo." Throughout the scene with Billy and Jerry, Matron cautions Babe against losing her temper. But Babe cannot resist her attack on Billy noting his "mind blowing beauty" that hides "animal cunning, avarice, and perversion." She tells him that "being desperately lonely I bought you at an exorbitant price." Babe confronts Jerry, "What's your price over mine?" Jerry's answer is simple. "This," he says as he "presses his shoulder to Billy's and places a hand over Billy's hand." With a "terrible outcry," Babe hurls her "jewelled eye-glasses" across the table at Jerry. The lenses are shattered. In anguish, Babe "clasps her face in her hands." Matron's voice "softly but audibly" intones, "Babylon. Oh Babylon." The lights fade out on the first scene.

Scene 2 begins the following afternoon. Billy and Jerry, seated on the sundeck, are joined by Matron and Playboy. She is trying to control her retarded son who wants to go to the lighthouse. Matron is vehement. "No, no, no. Mama will be very angry if you ever go back to that lighthouse." It seems that unnamed persons in the lighthouse "abuse" Playboy and give him gumdrops in return for sex. Playboy obviously enjoys the abuse and wants to return for more. Matron is horrified. She tells Jerry and Billy, "I think the abuse of mentally afflicted young people is a revoltingly immoral thing" but she also notes that "the crustacean heart has become the fashionable heart nowadays."

Alone, Billy reveals a letter to Jerry that states that Babe's father has died. He also tells Jerry that he is maneuvering to take control over Babe's money with the ploy that Babe, since her stay in a "rest farm," is incompetent to manage her fortune. Hearing Babe's offstage voice, the two men leave. Babe enters and sits on the sundeck.

She is practically blind after having lost her glasses the previous evening. She asks her maid, Peg, to find an extra pair of glasses, but all Peg can secure is an opera lorgnon through which Babe surveys the scene as she drinks martinis from a silver thermos. The previous evening is discussed with Peg, and Babe reveals to her maid that Billy is dying of cancer. "They did cut into him, Peg, but then they discovered that the cancer on the lung was too close to the heart for it to be surgically removed so it's still there, still active and spreading and poor Billy does not suspect this." Babe plans to tell Billy the truth after she has spoken with her doctor. Matron, who has entered quietly and overheard Babe, enjoins her not to tell Billy: "It would be savage of you."

There is a brief scene in which Babe talks to her doctor on the telephone. The scene starts as a phone conversation with Dr. Symse seated downstage and becomes a two-person vis-à-vis scene when the doctor unmotivatedly and unexpectedly walks onto the sundeck and sits with Babe. He advises against telling Billy of his illness: "Even in this time of moral collapse, a sort of moral blindness to each other, some of us can hold onto decent feelings, offer some mutual comfort."

Matron returns to the sundeck. She and Babe discuss "moral collapse in our time." Matron drops the letter Billy has left on the table. Babe reads it but it only seems to amuse her, "as for Billy's control of my estate that's a laugh." The scene is interrupted when Matron sees Playboy running down the beach.

Matron: Oh, Lord, he's headed back to the lighthouse again.

Babe: For what?

Matron: Gum drops, little cellophane sacks of gum drops, in return for permitting himself to be—sexually abused.

Matron tells Babe she will run after Playboy with a Polaroid camera to collect evidence against the abusers. She runs off in the direction of the lighthouse crying out, "My God, what Babylonian vice. It must be exposed, prosecuted, the limit." Babe is alone as "clouds pass over the sun" and the scene ends.

At the beginning of scene 3 Matron reports back to Babe. "The sounds were cries of pleasure, my son's, and the others were grunts of orgiastic wantonness." Matron is afraid her husband will have the boy "put away." Babe comments, "If this were theatre, I'd think this was a metaphor for the idiocy of existence." Babe defends Playboy's lighthouse pleasures. "It appears that your son has discovered in this lighthouse the complete, the unlimited gratification of his—carnal desires, innocent animal pleasures of the flesh."

Playboy's pleasure awakens in Babe the need to satisfy her own desires. These desires are further fanned by the appearance of Joey, her maid's boyfriend, who is described as the "strapping, stud type." Babe tells Matron that "he's fair game for any pursuer," and she approaches the young man as "paper torches are reflected flickeringly in the picture window."

Babe's attempt to seduce Joey comes to nothing when it is interrupted by Peg's entrance. In a fury Peg resigns her job and tells Babe off: "We're already engaged and he's not one of you showfers from Newport that you use for a gigolo." Defeated, Babe comments to Matron. "My God—Deprivation continues—no relief." Matron suggests to Babe that she use an escort service called "Cavaliers for Milady" to satisfy her needs. Depressingly, Babe faces a future of bought love.

Jerry returns from burning tent worms off dying trees. He and Babe trade confidences. Babe reveals to Jerry her aching loneliness: "When I have fallen in love, and I have several times you know, with persons of both genders and in the case of Billy, with someone containing them both,—then afterwards, sooner or later—not always as in the case of Billy—I've found it to be an intensely lonely feeling—a feeling that left me lonelier than before." Babe recognizes that in spite of the fact that she has been a person with "several potential gifts," in the end she has only her "criminal amounts of personal wealth." All that her money has given her is the "disgusting old practice of buying persons for pleasure—bondage." Jerry says that "buying something is sometimes worse than stealing, more deeply immoral." They discuss Billy's health. Jerry is aware that Billy is dying. Babe generously tells Jerry, "I think that the soul is very loathe to quit the body when it's finally found its—*true*—love." Babe announces that she wishes to go for a swim and exits. Billy joins Jerry on the sundeck. They have an affectionate moment, Billy telling Jerry, "The youth of a man is like a summer place."

Matron comes on. She has found Babe's white beach wear in the sand without a trace of Babe. Apparently Babe has disappeared into the sea. Billy sees that Babe has left her jewelry on the table. The last image of the play is a light on Playboy who "advances to stage center, just below deck, his hand jerking inside his slicker, a light spot on his idiotically smiling face."

The final draft of *Masks Outrageous* keeps all the same characters from the earlier drafts but represents an about-face in its final attitude to the possibility of human love. Every element of the play is crueler and the atmosphere of the play is pervaded with a paranoia that is totally justifiable on the part of all

its unloving characters. Jerry is a scheming adventurer. Billy feigns ill health
in order to avoid physical contact with Babe. All the characters are being
watched by mysterious characters called Gideon One, Two, and Three who
act as guards and spies.

None of the main characters know where they are. Billy, Babe, and Jerry
have been spirited to an unknown seaside location in order to have security
checks. The Gideons work for a large corporation called Kudsu Chem, which
controls all of Babe's money. An atmosphere of ominous insecurity is established at the beginning of the play when Gideon Two tells Billy that Jerry is
particularly suspect.

> Gideon Two: I'd advise you to keep an eye on the kid, Mr. Foxworth.
>
> Billy: Why?
>
> Gideon Two: He's one of the reasons we've got to use such carefully
> screened communications.
>
> Billy: I don't understand.
>
> Gideon Two: Security at Kudsu Chem rarely takes more than a couple of
> days to check out anyone's exact identity, but *his*—oh, boy! It's still almost
> as obscure as it was in the beginning, six months ago.

Billy has a private line to the chairman of the board, a higher-up named Kennelsworth, whom he now calls. Over the phone he asks his contact why they
are where they are. "Gideons hustled us into a car. We drove to a private airport—were hustled onto a private plane—landed at another private airport."
Kennelsworth cannot (will not?) answer Billy's questions.

> Billy: Surely in our position—
>
> Kennelsworth: Positions change. Not known from one day to the next.
>
> Billy: Even yours? Chairman of the—?
>
> Kennelsworth: All positions change. Kudsu Chem is a very great conglom-
> erate, Billy. Very complex, very intricate. I could be sitting here right now
> and no longer have my position—yet have no idea I'd lost it.

At this moment in the phone conversation (Kennelsworth is in a spotlight), a
hit man, Gideon Three, appears behind Kennelsworth who quickly tells Billy
he is sending him a letter which will explain more. The phone conversation
is interrupted by Gideon Three, who intimates a sexual relationship between
Billy and Kennelsworth. "Was it just a social occasion when he followed you
upstairs to a room, where you waited in the dark, whistling Dixie?" Kennelsworth is suddenly attacked. Gideon Three quickly strangles him. Spotlight

out. On the sundeck Billy holds the phone. Gideon Two appears and makes a sexual overture to Billy. Billy rejects the offer.

In the next scene Billy and Jerry discuss their bizarre situation.

Jerry: That drive they took us on this afternoon—*unbefuckinglievable!*

Billy: Both roads stopping at the end of one street town with fake stores.

Jerry: Fake hotel, fake bar, fake everything.

Babe makes an entrance with regal aspect, "covered with important jewels." She moves with "ceremonious care to her place at the head of the table."

The dinner scene is similar to the earlier draft and also ends with Babe hurling her glasses at Jerry. And Matron, as in the first draft, also mysteriously appears on the scene with her veiled face and silently intones, "Babylon. Oh Babylon."

In scene 2 Billy has received the letter from Kennelsworth stating that Babe's father has died and that he is watching out for Billy's interests at Kudsu Chem. Billy tells Jerry that his interests are Jerry's interests.

One of the Gideons suggests that Jerry take a ride into town for kerosene to burn off tent worms, which are infesting the shrubbery around the house. Jerry reluctantly acquiesces. Babe has entered and observes the scene through her opera lorgnon. Left alone with Gideon One, she is given a small revolver.

Matron and Babe share a scene in which Babe discovers and reads Kennelsworth's letter to Billy. "My name only husband is planning to take control of the three-billion dollar trust fund set up by my father!" In this final version of *Masks Outrageous*, Matron makes a sexual pass at Babe who rejects the offer. Matron describes Babe as "a person who's at heart a victim of great Puritanism in combat with . . . a wildly licentious nature." The scene ends, as in the earlier draft, with Matron rushing after her son, Playboy, who has run off to his stolen pleasures in the lighthouse.

In scene 3, Matron (as in the first draft) reports on the lighthouse adventures of her son. The scene in which Babe makes advances on Joey, Peg's boyfriend, follows. As in the first draft, Peg deprives Babe of her pleasure. Matron appears once more. They discuss Billy's illness, which Babe says is a ruse to avoid sexual contact with her. (He is not dying of cancer as in the earlier version.)

One of the strangest scenes in the play (and perhaps in all of Williams) follows when a giant black man enters up the aisles of the theater with an Interpreter. The black man is Mac, Matron's husband and Playboy's father. He hurls obscenities at Babe demanding to know where his son is. Interpreter speaks for him, "Mac is looking for woman next door and her son. She calls it Playboy. Mac calls it Albino." Babe refuses to help Mac or the Interpreter. Apparently Mac is looking for Playboy in order to put him away. The Interpreter says, "Freaks must be put away. Will take action to put Albino away!" Mac and the Interpreter are finally scared off by Babe, who fires shots after them.

At the end of scene 3 Playboy enters and "comes up to Babe and hands her a small cellophane wrapped bag." The cellophane bag contains bullets. Babe appreciatively receives them. "Bullets! For my revolver. Just what I wanted. How did you guess?" The scene ends as Babe reloads her revolver.

Scene 4 begins with a conversation between Babe and Jerry. Jerry has returned from a boating trip in which Billy was nearly drowned, mysteriously thrown overboard. Babe hints at an insidious interpretation of the events. She continues the scene by suggesting that Jerry visit her bedroom later that evening. Jerry wants to leave the mysterious place but that does not seem to be a real possibility.

Matron comes out on deck. She is trying to escape Mac, who is pursuing her in order to put Playboy away. Babe questions the truth of Matron's story. It is possible that she and Mac are actors hired by the Gideons for a theatrical performance. But no. Babe decides Matron's panic is genuine. It seems that life has become too fantastic to understand. "All my life I've been travelling toward a frontier. Now I've crossed. The frontier of the impossible—things I imagined without ever imagining they could really exist. Momentous moment." Babe says that she will shelter Matron and Playboy from Mac whose growls are heard in the distance.

A phone call is placed to Babe's doctor, Lester Symes. Dr. Symes confirms Babe's suspicions that Billy is not really ill, that his "tests revealed no lung or other problems. Billy is everything you suspected, sweetheart." Symes goes on to propose marriage to Babe. Babe's response is sardonic, "If God's not already dead, Lester, he must have dropped dead this moment—laughing." A Gideon appears behind Lester and fires a bullet into his skull.

When Billy reappears Babe cradles him in her arms. "Let me hold you just a moment, Billy, before I go to God's funeral." She "gasps and suddenly claws at Billy's face." Interrupting this moment a loud growl is heard offstage followed by wails from Playboy. Matron enters with Playboy. She has confronted Mac and scared the monster away.

Babe tells Billy and Jerry she is going for a "nude dip in the ocean." Flashes of northern lights accompany her exit. Left alone with Jerry, Billy fingers Babe's jewels, which have been left on the table. He notes that her engagement ring is missing and accuses Jerry of stealing it. Jerry takes an emerald ring from his pocket, confirming Billy's suspicions. He throws the ring at Billy and exits into the house. Inside, Gideon One aims a revolver at Jerry and fires. Jerry falls. Gideon Two comes on the deck and aims his revolver at Billy. Suddenly Peg, Babe's maid, enters the scene and says, "Let me." She fires at Billy, who falls to the ground. Matron is heard singing a few snatches of Liebestod from *Tristan and Isolde*. Playboy appears and runs off the other side of the stage. Matron runs after him. "He's escaped again." The last vision of the play is of Babe in the ocean and reflected in her picture window "apparently nude and wet." Playboy appears just below the sundeck "staring at Babe." He croons "Coo." "Babe stretches her arms like wings as the lights flicker brilliantly." The play ends. The evolution from *In Masks Outrageous and Austere* to *Masks Outrageous* reveals the romantic turned cynic with a vengeance. Tennessee in the two plays goes from the early draft with its evidence of love and selfless action to a world of total self-interest in which no one may be trusted. The subtle change in the play's title reveals the same shift in attitude. The titles come from an Elinor Wylie poem that Tennessee has used for a source:

> In Masks outrageous and austere
> The years go by in single file,
> Yet none of them deserved my fear
> And none has quite escaped my smile.

On the title page of the first draft Williams quotes this poem. In the final draft no mention is made of the Wylie poem nor is it quoted directly. I think Williams does not want us to think of the Wylie poem with its fearless smile. Nor are any of the masks any longer austere. They are only outrageous, and it is this vision of outrageous masks that is the most important aspect of the new play.

One may wonder about the change in Williams' vision. Why this merciless cynicism? Does anything warrant such distrust and pessimism? The key to understanding this attitude may lie in the circumstances of Williams' life in its last ten years, and while normally I would eschew such comment, the connection of distrust that necessarily arises from "bought" love is obvious and inescapable in discussing this play.

Tennessee Williams was an enormously romantic and sensual man who required in his life love and sexual satisfaction. As he grew older he often fell in love with younger men and often bought sexual favors from hustlers. He also was an unpractical man who needed assistance in his everyday chores such as correspondence, laundry, and bill paying. Quite often he had a young male secretary who served in a business capacity. But Tennessee was sometimes romantically drawn to such secretaries, and occasionally these male secretaries became lovers. Since these young men were officially hired and paid, they were never quite free to respond naturally to Williams. Often they feared him. And, of course, he had reason to distrust their motives. Naturally the young men were also attracted to the glamour of Williams' life. For many of these young men, nearness to Tennessee was the closest they would come to fame or greatness. They traveled, they met famous people. But did they love him? Was their love sincere? This is the question that tortured Tennessee throughout much of his late life. It was the source of much of his tortured questioning of reality. His cynicism grew out of the frequency with which he was (in his eyes, perhaps) betrayed by young companions, yet he never stopped needing love. And he never stopped trying again. Of course he was foolish in picking unlikely candidates for returned affection. But one does not always choose where one will love. Friendship will not suffice. In Tennessee's case, love was often foolishly offered. Ignorance of the other's truth and disappointment in love made him little wiser but infinitely sadder and rather angry. This anger may be seen in *Masks Outrageous.*

Of course Williams' cynical attitude comes from the specific situation of the famous, successful, aging homosexual, but is anyone sure of the love in his or her life? Even the most conventionally married person may feel a possible hypocrisy of marriage late in life and wonder if he really knows his partner after many years of marriage. The consequences of this question are too horrible for most, and so the question is not often asked. One need not be gay to question love's sincerity. All people may suspect the truth of the supremacy of outrageous masks, unquestioned lies, and bought love as the basis of many relationships. But that way lies madness.

This madness expresses itself best in fantastic twists and turns of the plot in the final *Masks Outrageous.* The play has become a crazy fun house in which characters go up passageways never knowing what is real and what is reflected glass. Even the set, with its reflecting window, does not look directly at nature. Everything is seen in reflection. Danger lies everywhere and anything can happen since no one can be trusted. Love is unlikely in such an environment yet the characters still pursue it.

Masks Outrageous is also an investigation of the consequences of a death of God and the concurrent death of the possibility of ethical action. Babe's description of unreality may be taken as a common twentieth-century experience. "These last few years, I've frequently had the feeling I'd wake up and find everything—dissolved. The way you wake up after a dream." In this play Tennessee Williams seems to feel that ethical judgments are irrelevant and impossible. This may be his most frightening suggestion. Babe makes this point clear. "Does such a thing as individual guilt or even collective guilt truly exist in our world? In a world outside dreams and fiction. In my time and experience—both considerable—no. Apocalypse is now and before and to come. So-called vice, satisfaction of flesh, brute or innocent, something, same . . . You can't deny it. I can't anyway."

Finally, this play as it evolved describes a terrifying if comically mordant world. If God were truly dead, if moral choice and ethical concerns were total illusions, if reality were completely shattered and anything was possible, then outrageous masks would indeed be our total experience.

The characters in the play have turned into cruel ciphers. They are masks hiding little but self-interest. One suspects that something may have once been behind Babe's mask, but now that, too, is dead. Only the surface is left but even the surface is fake. Greed and sexual appetite are all that remain of human faces. Only Babe's ironic intelligence and sardonic wit raise her above the others. Playboy, the idiot, is the most sympathetic character in the play.

The language in the play is clipped and largely unlyrical. Irony is the dominant tone. Metaphors abound and they are self-consciously employed by characters doomed to see all of their existence as a metaphorical trope.

Jerry: What do they call those caterpillars?

Billy: Tentworms. We had some one summer back home. They're a blight on vegetation like decay on human beings.

Babe: Decay?

Billy: Age or disease.

Babe: One or the other can't be avoided. They come to all of us.

There are some beautiful theatrical poetic effects in the play. The beach setting and especially the large reflecting window at the rear of the sundeck create an atmosphere of constantly changing light. These lighting effects, northern lights, shifting skies, and passing clouds, contribute beauty to the constantly changing, ephemeral world. The sound of offstage ocean waves and stretches of silence similarly contribute to the fluid atmosphere.

Richly suggestive, *Masks Outrageous* may at first seem confusing and arbitrarily odd, an absurd situation stretched beyond any possible credibility, innumerable metaphors for the illusive nature of reality. And it is all of those things. To audiences of rich theatrical taste it might prove an exciting experience, a vicious carnival of the imagination.

Something Cloudy, Something Clear was Tennessee Williams' last "new" play produced in New York during his lifetime. Given one production at the off-off-Broadway Jean Cocteau Repertory Theatre, the play was not generally appreciated for its value. It was rather summarily dismissed and had no strong champions. However, *Something Cloudy, Something Clear* is Tennessee Williams' last major play, and one wants to consider it as it is a beautiful elegiac play of a master in full control of his artistic powers. It also represents an artist maturing in several of his most consistent obsessions and themes.

Clearly autobiographical, the play may still be understood without reference to Tennessee Williams' life as the portrait of an artist looking back at a turning point in his life. The play, like *Vieux Carré*, is an artist's memory play in which one moment in September 1940 is seen as the fulcrum of a life, which looks both backward and forward in an attempt both to make sense of his life and to expiate the past. The details of the play are specific to Tennessee Williams, but the action of the play is universal. One need not be Tennessee Williams to seek expiation for past deeds. The play's most searching question from an aging heart is the query, "What in all my life was real?"

The play is set on a realistic beach that poetically evokes more than a few days in September 1940. Williams' description guides the designer in his wishes:

> A time and sunbleached shack on dunes rolling upward like waves of pale sand-colored water, occasionally sparsely scattered with little clumps of light green beach-grass. The large windows have no panes, the front and side walls are transparencies and there is no door, just the frame. Part of the roof is missing. Adjoining this somehow poetic relic of a small summer beach house is a floor, a platform, all that remains of a probably identical beach house that was demolished more completely by storm. Shimmering refractions of sunlight from the nearby sea play over this dream-like setting.
>
> The setting itself should suggest the spectral quality of a time and place remembered from deep in the past: specifically from a time forty years later.

Seated in tableau on a box behind a typewriter is a "still unsuccessful young playwright" named August. He begins to move when a beautiful young man, Kip, enters. August tears the writing out of his typewriter calling it "Outline for—*shit*." A young "also apparitionally lovely" woman enters. Clare carries a wicker basket. She is following Kip, who discovers the bare platform next to August's shack. "Floor of some blown away beach shack and the floor's intact, it makes a perfect dancing platform." Kip is a young dancer. August comes out from his shack and is obviously interested in Kip. He takes a portable phonograph and a bottle of rum out from under the platform of his shack. He exits back into his shack "and immediately starts to write like a man possessed." Clare, having noticed August, asks Kip, "Was that real? Did that really happen?"

Kip and Clare discuss August, whom they met the previous evening. Drunk, August had stared at Kip all evening. They also discuss Bugsy, Clare's boyfriend, who is coming that day to collect Clare. The two (Kip and Clare) do not want to be separated, but they both need protectors who will take care of them. Kip has a suggestion. "Maybe one person could keep us both. We could be two kept for the price of one." Clare notes that she is expensive to keep because of a need for "insulin, periodic hospital stays that get longer." But she dispels any somber thoughts. "Let's try to absorb this light—and face dark later."

They discuss August as a possible protector. Clare will approach the young writer—investigate the possibilities. She enters August's shack. The writer is happy to have his work interrupted. They talk about August's writing. Clare tells August that writers should be like Van Gogh and Nijinsky who "refused to make concessions to bad taste and yet managed survival without losing their minds."

Clare asks if Kip might use his neighboring bare platform as a rehearsal space. She tells him Kip is her brother (untrue). August offers her a drink of rum, which she declines. "I have diabetes." August tells Clare he remembers having seen Kip the previous evening, but Kip was obviously not interested in his attentions. August also tells Clare he picked up a "much less attractive object, a merchant sailor at the bar." He explains, "It's also very lonely out here at night."

The play briefly shifts reality to the future:

Clare: You have a strange voice.

August: Are you sure you can hear it?

(He is winding up the portable phonograph.)

Clare: It isn't as clear as it was that summer.

August: Forty years ago, Clare.

Clare: I feel light headed. Is it a *déja vu*?

August plays Ravel's *Pavane pour une infante defunte*. He tells Clare he has played it all summer on his silver victrola. Clare remarks:

Clare: Dead princesses don't remember their pavanes on your silver victrola.—Is it as bad to die when you're young as Kip and I were and even you were that summer? Tell me. You've lived to discover an answer.

August: To live as long as forty years after the ecstasy of—It's enough to reconcile you to exile, at last, to the dark side of the moon or to the unfathomably dark hole in space.

Clare tells August to "play it straight, play it not like it was a summer long past but as it was then." The play becomes more "realistic," as it was then.

Outside, Kip stumbles on the platform where he has been dancing. Suddenly the play shifts focus. A Nurse wheels in "the memory of Frank Merlo," and a short scene follows between Frank and August. Frank is obviously sick. August describes the moment of Frank's death: "I waited till finally, when he was turning blue, the oxygen tank was wheeled in and attached to the transparent tent in which he would die that night." Clare brings August back to September 1940, telling him Kip has gone for a swim to clear his head. She suggests that Kip give August a massage later that night to relieve his nerves. They discuss August's eyes, one of which is clear and one of which is cloudy. Clare finds August's clear eye "very appealing." Another young girl, Hazel, enters. She calls out "Tom? Tom?" Hazel's apparition confesses to August (Tom) that she "loved girls" but married Tom McCabe. Similarly, August confesses to Hazel that he "crouched at a hole bored in a cubicle in the boy's section of the Fowler's pool to watch the—naked boys shower." Hazel's apparition drifts off. August remarks, "Life is all—it's just one time, it finally seems to all occur at one time." August tells Clare that Hazel will later die in Mexico City of "liquor and pills." He feels guilty that he will later fail Hazel when she will return to August at a time when he will be with Frank. His cloudy eye represents a "side of my nature that's been hitherto obscured a little.—A streak of savagery in me connected with." August confesses: "I'm a morbid and decadent son of a bitch."

Kip enters and asks August to play the silver victrola again. He wants to dance outside to the Pavane. Clare tells August that Kip needs "someone to keep him when he goes back to New York." She also tells August that Kip is an illegal alien from Canada who is trying to escape from the draft. She loves Kip but is not *in* love with him and cannot protect him. He has been impotent with her, and she is "sexually precocious" needing a more vigorous lover for her satisfaction. August asks Clare how Kip feels about him. She says that Kip likes him but cannot satisfy "his amatory demands." August says, "I would want to sleep in the same bed with him and hold him all night in my arms while he slept."

Clare leaves and Kip reenters. August suggests that Kip return to New York with him after a "negotiation of term. I'll give you this for that." Kip goes off to think about it. He does not want to have sex with August but may have to submit in order to survive.

A drunken Seaman from the previous evening enters and demands that August pay him five dollars for last night. Finally August pays the Seaman in order to get rid of him. A helicopter drops mail from overhead. August tells Kip that he is awaiting option money on his new play and that he, like Kip, is broke. A telegram comes telling August that his producers, the Fiddlers, are arriving that afternoon to collect rewrites on the play, which will be produced that fall on Broadway.

The Fiddlers (Maurice and Celeste) enter. August bargains with Maurice Fiddler and reveals his business acumen. He will give over the wanted rewrites when he has gotten the remainder of his advance money.

Caroline Wales, the actress who will play the lead in August's play, enters. She makes a tentative pass at August and, when the Fiddlers have departed, speaks a line from August's play. "There's something still wild in this country, this country used to be wild, the men and the women were wild and there was a wild sort of sweetness in their hearts for each other." Caroline leaves vowing to make the play work for August.

Clare enters with Bugsy. He is a mobster but Clare will leave with him. After a short scene in which Bugsy declares his hatred of "faggots," they go. Alone, August calls out for Kip. The Seaman enters instead. They discuss the previous night when the Seaman would not let August perform certain sexual acts, but tonight the Seaman will let August "fuck me for a fin and another drink." August says, "We've made a deal this time." They rise from the platform and the lights dim out. End of part 1.

Part 2 begins with an outraged Actress (clearly Tallulah Bankhead) storming onto the beach for an angry confrontation with August.

> Actress: There you are, you drunk little bastard! What was it you said I did to your goddamn play?
>
> August: I said you pissed on my play. You performed a classic role in the style of a transvestite in a drag play.

The apparition disappears as Kip enters. The dancer tells August that Bugsy has been violent with Clare. He wants August to be kind to her. Clare knows the "exigencies of desperation." "Clare and I are the ones that are in a vulnerable position. You and Bugsy have power, not us." August tells Kip that he makes him shake. Kip offers to give August a massage. August, clearly bargaining with Kip, asks what if he becomes sexually aroused? Once more Kip leaves in order to think the situation over. August remarks, "His voice, it sounded almost panicky. Was I that terrifying, forty years ago?" Kip returns and tells August of his difficult life, of Clare's rescuing him from starvation. He makes clear his destitution and desperation. August takes hold of the young dancer's arms and asks, "Will you accept my instructions?" August tells us "he could have easily broken away but he didn't." End of scene.

The lights come back on and it is the following day. Clare enters. August tells Clare that Kip does not feel well and indicates that he and Kip have made a bargain. She is distressed at Kip's appearance: "He looked like a whipped dog, dragging his feet back in the shack." Clare calls August a "complete Hun." Later, alone with Clare, Kip tells her that he has let August use him and that they must submit to their fates, he to August, and she to Bugsy.

But they will all have a final picnic together. Clare tells Kip she "will die later this year." Kip says, "This is our last day together." Kip will "mix a salad and heat the chowder. Perhaps if I convince him of my domestic skills, he could value me for that."

Alone with August, Clare tells the playwright that Kip is a dying young man: "You've noticed how short his hair is, just barely enough to cover the scar on his head where a piece of his head was removed last Fall at the Polyclinic Hospital in New York. It was a blastoma, the most malignant of all." August asks her, "Couldn't we all live together? For a while." Clare says, "Yes, but purely, cleanly. I'll not have you use him again like a whore."

A telegram from August's producers drops out of the sky. They love the rewritten script and await August's arrival in New York. August remarks, "Life—it's a lovely clear evening." Kip says, "This is our last evening together." August kisses Clare "again and again on the mouth." Kip kisses her "sweetly and delicately." Continuing this ceremony of farewells, August touches Kip "along his wide throat." "Child of God—you don't exist anymore." August makes a final speech as the lights dim:

> See how light the sky is? Light as clear water with just a drop or two of ink in it. Note to end on? How did it go, that bit of Rilke? The inscrutable Sphinx?
>
> Poising forever—the human equation—against the age and magnitude of a universe of—stars . . . The lovely ones, youthfully departed long ago. But look (he points) very clearly here, here while this memory lives, the lovely ones remain here, undisfigured, uncorrupted by the years that have removed me from their summer.

Something Cloudy, Something Clear is a simple play. While the action has occurred in the past, the audience, as in *The Glass Menagerie*, becomes involved in the play's events as if they were occurring in present time. The plot centers on August's seduction (extortion) of Kip, the destitute dancer. August will give his protection in return for sexual favors. Kip's acceptance of the terms of the agreement is the climactic moment of the play.

Flashbacks, flash-forwards occur the way the mind works. Incidents suggest other incidents occurring at different times until all time seems concurrent. But all the memories related in this evocation of love relationships are somehow marked by incompletion and guilt. The important action of the play is the evocation of past memories by an unseen consciousness (August in the future) for the purpose of expiation. Finally, the play, like *Vieux Carré*, is an act of love and appropriately ends in a ceremony of farewell kisses.

The play is also a self-portrait. August is an obvious recreation of Williams at the age of thirty. Significantly, the Swedish playwright August Strindberg is invoked as an alter ego and soul mate. Strindberg is appropriate both for his dramatic experimentation and stormy personal history.

To Williams' credit, the self-portrait is unsentimental. August is seen as a tough negotiator, a lover with a poetic sensibility, an appreciator of beauty but also a strong man who pursues his desires. August takes advantage of the weakness of others to get what he wants. He "buys" both the Seaman and Kip. Yet we never doubt his sincere love of Kip nor the dedication to his art.

August's divided nature is symbolized in his two eyes, one cloudy and one clear. His is a recognizably split human condition, both kind and manipulative, caring and selfish. August is a protector but he also needs sexual satisfaction and will use others for that end. Other characters in the play participate in this same split although some are more clearly corrupt (the Fiddlers and the Seaman) while others are more pure (Kip). Clare, a hustler, is able like August to operate in the corrupt world. Her selfless love for Kip coexists with her own attraction to Bugsy. August's love for Clare is perhaps more pure than his love for Kip since it is devoid of sexual desire. The play as memory is a loving memory of Clare as well as of Kip.

Something Cloudy, Something Clear concerns itself with most of Williams' major themes. It is a culminating work replaying his lifelong obsessions. These may be called time and memory, reality and fantasy, loneliness, survival, sex and love, the pure and impure divided nature of man, and the ever present reality of death. These are, of course, life's major questions and in no way reveal an artist with limited concerns. It is puzzling that so many critics have accused Williams of having a limited thematic repertory. It is true that Williams concerns himself with these themes repeatedly in his work, but this is not so much as "rehash" but as a confrontation with ultimate questions that can never be answered. Williams concerns himself with the great tragic questions. They are the ultimate concerns of any great drama and any great dramatist.

In this play Williams seems to have reached a clearer understanding of time, one in which it is seen that "all time occurs at once": "Life is all—it's just one time, it finally seems to occur at one time." This observation, one to which Williams has been moving in his late plays, has serious implications for the drama. All drama presupposes a conception of time that is represented in a playwright's dramatic structure. A progressive conception of time is most clearly representable in the theater as an event that occurs over the length of an evening. An understanding of time as simultaneous and ever present cannot clearly be represented in the drama except through the use of symbol. It presupposes a mystical understanding beyond the simple dramatization of time as linear. *Something Cloudy, Something Clear* suggests this greater understanding—an experience that is in effect a Zen satori. The play aims at a religious experience similar to August's epiphany. It aims to be a revelation occurring within time, which suggests a greater understanding outside time.

In a way this is Williams' most spiritual play, one to which he has been moving in all the plays of his late period. The calm acceptance of the play suggests a final forgiveness. It is very positive and, by inference, a religious play.

In the end, the love of *Something Cloudy, Something Clear* counteracts the cynical despair of *Masks Outrageous*. That these two final plays represent two contradictory attitudes should not be surprising. In effect with these two plays Williams is seeing with the two eyes described in *Something Cloudy, Something Clear*. *Masks Outrageous* is seen with the cloudy eye. It describes a world of greed, lust, and human distrust. *Something Cloudy, Something Clear* is seen with the clearer eye. It suggests both love and possible forgiveness. Both visions are true; both are necessary for an accurate and complete picture.

Interestingly, both *Masks Outrageous* and *Something Cloudy, Something Clear* are set on beaches that look out at the ocean. By implication this setting suggests a final vision, an ultimate look, a resting place. I believe that Tennessee knew these two plays would probably be his last works. In their concerns and contradictions they suggest a last testament. Whether we choose the anger and irony of *Masks* or the peace and love of *Something Cloudy*, the ocean reflects ourselves back to us. It is a place to end.

NOTE

1. Tennessee Williams, quoted in Dotson Rader, "Tennessee Williams: The Art of Theater No. 5," *Paris Review*, Fall 1981.

· 12 ·

Forgotten Things Remembered

$\mathcal{C}$omparing previous chapters to a list of titles of late Williams' work I realize how incomplete my description really is. The depth of the work has been shown but the breadth has still not been adequately suggested. In defense I would say that the works previously described seem the most important ones of this amazingly prolific writer and also the ones most needing critical illumination. The styles described have shown the variety of the work, but there is more to be said. Mention must be made of other works.

How many titles! They seem to have no end. And what suggestively alluring titles: *The Latter Days of a Celebrated Soubrette*, *Tiger Tail*, *The Eccentricities of a Nightingale*, *The Wild Horses of the Camargue*. In some cases the plays are rewrites of earlier plays. *The Latter Days of a Celebrated Soubrette* is a cut version of *The Gnädiges Fräulein*. *Tiger Tail* is almost a word-for-word stage version of the film *Baby Doll*, which, in turn, was based on two one-act plays, *27 Seven Wagons Full of Cotton* and *The Unsatisfactory Supper*. Despite its genesis in familiar material, however, *Tiger Tail* merits attention as a producible and stage-worthy adaptation.

The Eccentricities of a Nightingale is a much-changed version of *Summer and Smoke*. It cuts the Spanish characters of Rosa Gonzales and her father thus eliminating the climactic drama of the shooting of John's father. It also adds an important character, John's mother, Mrs. Buchanan, who becomes a strong adversary of Alma. And finally, most importantly, it adds a scene in a hotel room between John and Alma prior to the actual consummation of their frustrated romance. In *Summer and Smoke*, Alma and John never get that far. *Eccentricities* is perhaps less melodramatic and more probable, but it is also less theatrical. However, the emphasis on John's mother as an Oedipal figure robs John of some of his attractiveness as Alma's fantasy figure. The fact of

252

Alma and John's sexual encounter lessens Alma's tragedy. I confess that this is a romantic preference. Producers should carefully consider *Eccentricities of a Nightingale* as a viable, perhaps more honest play than *Summer and Smoke*. Both *Summer and Smoke* and *Eccentricities of a Nightingale* have assets and problems, but they are both stage worthy and should be considered for production. Tennessee often said he preferred *Eccentricities of a Nightingale*, but that may have been because it was the last version and the less well-known.

The Wild Horses of the Camargue is described in Donald Spoto's *The Kindness of Strangers* as a play about an older man who keeps a younger man captive. This description comes from an interview Tennessee gave to *Gay Sunshine*. To my knowledge the play has not materialized, yet it may be among Williams' papers not yet released by his estate. More treasures may be revealed once the contents of Tennessee's personal papers in his late years are made known.

Of all the post-*Iguana* Williams plays, *Small Craft Warnings* received the best New York press and even enjoyed an off-Broadway run of several months at the Truck and Warehouse Playhouse. The run was perhaps somewhat extended by Williams' appearance in the role of Doc late in the run, but the play's relative success was also due to its general accessibility. *Small Craft Warnings* is in the tradition of other American barroom plays, including *The Iceman Cometh*, *The Time of Your Life*, and *No Place to be Somebody*. This subgenre permits freedom from the necessities of plot considerations and offers the playwright a chance to introduce characters who do not necessarily further the central action. Color and atmosphere are substituted for plot and story elements, and these elements keep our interest even while nothing seems to be obviously "happening." It is the perfect setting for an emerging absurdist sensibility. People just pass time in bars. In fact bars are a refuge from the world of events. As in other plays of this type, Williams introduces us to a collection of characters, each of whom makes the bar a kind of home. The characters are united to each other by their aloneness, homelessness, and need for personal confession.

Small Craft Warnings is an expanded version of the play *Confessional*, which had its premiere in Maine at the Bar Harbor Summer Theater in 1971. In *Confessional*, Williams uses the convention of direct character address to the audience. Characters come center stage and in a circle of light tell their problems to the audience. In *Small Craft Warnings* the monologues are more integrated into the setting. Occasionally lights will dim and a light will come up on a character as he reveals his thoughts, but the character does not come "front and center" nor does he directly address the audience. The other difference between *Confessional* and *Small Craft Warnings* is that the action starts earlier in *Small Craft Warnings*.

Briefly described, the central action of the play concerns the conflict between Leona and her "stud" boy friend who can no longer bear the demands of his "meal ticket." At the beginning of *Small Craft Warnings*, Bill comes into the bar seeking refuge from Leona. He enjoys the attention of Violet, another denizen of the bar, who has recently been thrown out of her apartment. Violet fondles Bill under the table. Leona enters looking for Bill. She sees Violet's attentions and attacks her, sending Violet into the bathroom. *Confessional* begins at this point.

Small Craft Warnings is notable for its collection of characters, the quality of the writing, and Williams' compassionate affection for his bar habitués. Leona is an original Williams creation. Living in her small trailer and working at a beauty parlor, she is a tough, loud lady with a kind heart who pulls up her roots and hits the road whenever her personal life is too painful. Her most cherished memories are of a dead gay brother, and she continually plays a sentimental violin solo on the bar's jukebox in memory of him.

Violet, the other female character in the play, is equally memorable. Described by Williams as a "water plant," she is a destitute drifter who gravitates to male protectors for brief sexual encounters. "Her eyes are too large for her face, and they are usually moist: her appearance suggests a derelict kind of existence; still has about her a pale, bizarre sort of beauty."

One of the most interesting characters in the play is a gay character named Quentin, whom Williams describes as having a "quality of sexlessness, not effeminacy" whose "face seems to have been burned thin by a fever that is not of the flesh." Quentin enters the bar with Bobby, a young man he has picked up. The evening has not gone well. In a beautifully written monologue, Quentin describes his personal pain: "There's a coarseness, a deadening coarseness, in the experience of most homosexuals. The experiences are quick and hard, and brutal, and the pattern of them is practically unchanging. Their act of love is like the jabbing of a hypodermic needle to which they're addicted but which is more and more empty of real interest and surprise." The character of Quentin is not someone whom the gay liberation movement would offer as the portrait of a happy, well-adjusted homosexual. Yet neither is he an inevitable portrait of the gay man. Almost in contrast to Quentin, Bobby is a fresh young man who is open to life's experiences. Williams seems to offer Bobby as an emerging gay consciousness even as he honestly portrays Quentin's jadedness. Both portraits complement and correct each other.

A Lovely Sunday for Creve Coeur is a touching and funny play about dreams and hopes. Set in a small west-end St. Louis apartment during the "middle or late thirties," it is a seemingly "small," realistic play with a cast of four women. The action of the play occurs on a Sunday afternoon on which Dorothea (or Dotty), a high school civics teacher, exercises as she awaits a telephone call for a date from Ralph Ellis, principal of the high school. Bodey, Dorothea's German roommate and friend, wants Dotty to go on a picnic with her and her twin brother, Buddy. Bodey hopes they will become romantically involved. Dotty is not interested. She has had one romantic encounter with Ralph Ellis in his Flying Cloud automobile during a rain storm, and she is hopelessly in love with the handsome young man. Bodey hides a Sunday newspaper from Dorothea, which announces Mr. Ellis' engagement to a young society debutante. She is terrified of the effect the article will have on Dotty.

Into the apartment comes Helena, a high school colleague of Dotty who wants to entice Dotty into sharing a fashionable apartment. It is also obvious that Helena is aware of the engagement announcement, and she is anxious to see if Dotty has seen the newspaper.

The play comically pits the snobbish and predatory Helena against the lower-class, uneducated Bodey as they vie for the possession of Dorothea's friendship. An undercurrent of unexpressed lesbianism runs through the play. Adding to the play's comedy is the periodic appearance of Miss Sophie Gluck, Bodey and Dotty's mentally disturbed upstairs neighbor. At various moments in the play Miss Gluck, who has recently lost her mother, despondently and sobbingly throws herself into Bodey and Dotty's apartment. The madness gets out of hand when Helena tries to eject Miss Gluck off Dotty, who has fallen onto the floor as a result of Miss Gluck's physical expressions of grief.

The action of the play comes to a climax when Dorothea accidentally sees the newspaper article announcing Ralph Ellis' engagement. In a moment of Chekhovian understatement we understand that Dorothea's dreams have been shattered. She will go to the picnic with Bodey. Her dreams will not be realized, but she will go on.

At the time of the off-Broadway production of *A Lovely Sunday for Creve Coeur*, several critics castigated Tennessee Williams for letting the audience know early in the play's action that Ralph Ellis was going to marry another woman. They regretted the play's lack of suspense. They suggested that the audience knew the play's outcome too early.

Yet it is precisely the audience's knowledge of this frustrated outcome that makes the play so sadly absurdist in its depiction of the impossibility of Dorothea's romantic ambitions. We, along with Bodey, know that Ralph Ellis will not call Dorothea. This knowledge makes her anticipation of his call all the more pathetic. While realistic with its apartment setting and action, the play is a near relative to a more absurdist dramaturgy, which uses wilder, more symbolic images. The excessive freakishness of Miss Gluck along with certain aspects of the set, point the play in this direction. "Attempts to give it [the apartment] brightness and cheer have gone brilliantly and disastrously wrong and this wrongness is emphasized by the fiercely yellow glare of light through the over-size windows which look out upon vistas of surrounding apartment buildings that suggest the paintings of Ben Shahn: the dried-blood-horror of American urban neighborhoods.''

Interestingly *Creve Coeur* bears a strong similarity to a television drama Tennessee Williams wrote in the mid-fifties. This earlier work, entitled *All Gaul Is Divided*, was posthumously published in 1984 and offers a fascinating comparison to the later work. In an author's note attached to the published television drama *All Gaul Is Divided*, Williams describes how he found the manuscript of *All Gaul Is Divided*, which had been lost. Apparently, *Creve Coeur* was written independently of the forgotten *All Gaul Is Divided*. However, both plays relate the same basic incidents in very different ways. "Recently I decided to thoroughly clean out the files of old manuscripts in my New Orleans apartment, files which had long been in storage. Many surprising items surfaced through this proceeding, of which I suspect that *All Gaul Is Divided* is the most fortuitous. The screen play rectifies the major defect dilemma of the recent play; the giving away of the 'plot' in the very first scene. In this initial use of the material, the denouement is saved till the last few minutes of the final scene." In this note Williams seems to accept the majority judgment of the critics of *Creve Coeur*. He sees *Creve Coeur* as having a "defect." Yet he also unconsciously pinpoints one of the most important differences in his early work, full of "youthful spontaneity and of true freshness," and the later work, which is no longer interested in a dramaturgy of surprise. Simply put, the late Williams plays are not interested in questions of plot, and it is this very lack of plot concern that marks one of the major differences in the early, commercially successful, critically well-received plays and the later, more experimental, darker, more ironic plays.

Plot may be the strongest tool of a playwright interested in audience approval. Spontaneously used, it is more than the manipulation of a story's incidents to give maximum suspense. In a good plot the audience hopes for a fortunate outcome of a sympathetic protagonist. Plots are the province of the young (or naive) who still believe that life may turn out well. Older, more ironic persons (artists) seldom believe in the possibility of such good fortune. They know in advance that the game is rigged and that little ends well. Good plots seldom interest older artists, who come to see happy endings as impossible outcomes. At some point most older artists (human beings?) cease to believe in the possibility of a happy ending. This crisis of faith predicts the death of plot as a possible tool in the older writer's arsenal.

While not commercially practical, the "giving away" of the plot in *Creve Coeur* in its first scene is not an artistic defect. It is rather the honest expression of an older vision of reality in which human hope is seen as a pathetic and amusing illusion. *Creve Coeur* is different from, not inferior to, the younger *All Gaul Is Divided*. Late works with their disregard for matters of plot are less likely to be popular works of art. The knowledge that little turns out well does not have a large nor accepting audience.

One of the most moving works from the late Williams oeuvre is a long one-act play entitled *I Can't Imagine Tomorrow*. This play was written for Kim Stanley and was first produced as a television play featuring that formidable actress. The play recently resurfaced in a performance of Williams one-acts entitled *Ten by Tennessee* directed by Michael Kahn. It is a great play but because it is a one-act play and because it comes from the late period, it has not been generally recognized for the wonderful work it is.

A play for two actors, it recounts the visit of one friend to another. The two characters, simply called One and Two, are a dying woman (One) and her painfully shy friend (Two). The visits are a nightly ritual in which the two friends play cards and eat together. Life has become increasingly difficult for both of them. One is in so much pain that she has trouble climbing the stairs to go to bed, and Two has been unable to talk to the students at the high school where he teaches. It is clear that they are the only friends each has. The woman is seriously worried about what will happen to the man when she dies. He is terrified of the changes life inevitably brings. She badgers him and insists that he must meet new people. The play's subtext is clear even though it is never mentioned that One is dying.

The play has absolutely no plot. Nothing significant happens during its action. Things are getting worse for the two characters, but they will continue until the end. What makes the play so beautiful is the unstated love of the two characters, their great care for each other.

There is an important monologue in the play that the woman speaks while Two is offstage in the kitchen. Written as a soliloquy, it is given in a specially lighted area that isolates the character from her surroundings:

> Dragon Country, the country of pain, is an uninhabitable country which is inhabited, though. Each one crossing through that huge, barren country has his own separate track to follow across it alone. If the inhabitants, the explorers of Dragon Country, looked about them, they'd see other explorers, but in this country of endured but unendurable pain each one is so absorbed, deafened, blinded by his own journey across it, he sees, he looks for, no one else crawling across it with him. It's uphill, up mountains, the climbs very steep; takes you to the top of the bare Sierras.

I Can't Imagine Tomorrow was published in a volume of plays that Williams emblematically called *Dragon Country*. The volume included, among other plays, *In the Bar of a Tokyo Hotel* and the plays that comprise the *Slapstick*

Tragedy. Dragon Country is a metaphor for the psychic location Williams in-habits in so many of his late works. A place of pain and isolation, it stands as a symbol of the most despairing of psychological states. The voyage through Dragon Country seldom abated for Williams in his late career.

Although it has been published (in volume 7 of *The Theatre of Tennessee Williams*), no one to my knowledge has produced *This Is the Peaceable King-dom or Good Luck God.* This is an understandable situation due to the play's large cast as well as to the nature of the cast. The play requires thirteen actors plus extras. More than half the characters in the play are patients in a nursing home, and a good professional production would require a large number of convincing character actors. It is also a possibly "offensive" play that chronicles an actual nursing home strike that occurred in New York City.

Another aspect of the play's potential offensiveness derives from the char-acterization of several Jewish characters in the play as well as the play's frank discussion of ethnic types. Saul and Bernice are a brother and sister who are visiting their mother who neither speaks nor moves except to eat. Because of the strike in the nursing home the patients have been left on their own, and Saul and Bernice have come to the nursing home to feed their mother. A look at some of dialogue in the opening moments reveals the play's "problem" as well as its black comic tone.

> Bernice: Saul, you know how often she's got to be changed now like a baby. You know she's incontinent, don't you?
>
> Saul: Be careful what you say.
>
> Bernice: I said it in English. Mama would not understand it except in Yiddish.
>
> Bernice: MAMA! YOU HEAR ME, MAMA?
>
> (Mrs. Shapiro [Mama] turns her tremulous head slightly toward Bernice.)
>
> Mrs. Shapiro: Anh?
>
> Bernice: Where's your teeth, Mama, what's become of your teeth?
>
> Saul: She does not understand and couldn't answer if she did. Why don't you ask Miss Goldfein, the nurse I pay extra to give Mama special attention, what's become of her teeth?
>
> Bernice: It is not *you* that pays extra, it is *us* that pays extra and Miss Gold-fein is out on strike with the others.

Other characters in the play include two very elderly Southern types, Ralston and Lucretia, who have a loving relationship with each other. There are also a couple of elderly black men who continually roar obscenities. A television crew films the elderly victims of the strike. A middle-aged Westchester county-patron type brings shopping carts of food to the hungry old people in the nursing home with the help of her chauffeur. A riot breaks out when food is spotted. A "Strange Voice" over the loudspeaker continually repeats "This is the Peaceable Kingdom" as pandemonium breaks out in the wards.

During the time between scenes 1 and 2, Mrs. Shapiro dies. Ralston tries to comfort the incontinent Lucretia, who wishes herself dead. The play ends as Saul and Bernice intone a Hebraic hymn, Lucretia calls out for God's help, and the voice repeats over and over on the loud speakers, "This is the Peaceable Kingdom, this is the Peaceable Kingdom."

Despite its large cast and the possibly "offensive" nature of *This is the Peaceable Kingdom*, it is a powerful play and would be moving in the theatre if there were a theatre courageous enough to undertake its production. It could be produced in the same evening with several other plays Williams wrote about old age.

The Frosted Glass Coffin may be the most moving in this genre of "old-age" dramas. Set on the "street facade" of a low-priced Miami hotel for the aged, the play shows several old folks who spend their time waiting for the Dixie Mammy Kitchen, a cafeteria across the street, to open so they may go for their meals. The five old characters are simply called One, Two, Three, Mr. Kelsey, and Mrs. One (Betsy). One has started a petition against the rising prices at the Dixie Mammy Kitchen. Two doubts the petition will have much effect on the management. They watch the breakfast line form. One of the ladies collapses in the line. One remarks, "In our age bracket you're living in a glass coffin, you just barely see light through it." He continues to discuss old age: "In some cases the conversation consists of almost nothing but one-syllable questions like who, what, what, where? The silent question is WHEN. The silent meaning of it is: when do I go? There's no one to answer that question, if it was asked out loud and mighty damn few would have the guts to ask it if there was." They discuss the death the previous evening of Mrs. Kelsey. Both One and Two thought Mr. Kelsey would die first since he was much more ill and required more continual care than his wife. But Kelsey has survived his wife. One says: "You know, it's not so surprising that Winnie went first of all, because old Kelsey has crossed that age limit where the human body, all it functions and its processes are so slowed down that they live a sort of crocodile existence that seems to go on forever. The question is what to do with him." Mr. Kelsey appears from the hotel. He does not answer a greeting from One. "Tapping each step before him with a cane," the old man stops when he reaches the walk "uncertain which way to turn." Finally sitting in a chair, he remains "motionless, expressionless."

One and Two discuss the relationship between aging women and men. One suggests that women are secretly pleased when the doctor gives their husbands negative medical reports. Mrs. One (Betsy) enters. She tries to take Mr. Kelsey to breakfast. Mr. Kelsey does not respond to her. Together the three old people slowly exit on their way to Dixie Mammy Kitchen. Kelsey is left alone on stage. The final stage direction is powerful: "Kelsey raises his cane and brings it down hard on the pavement: the light begins to dim out to a crepuscular pallor. Kelsey closes his cataract-blinded eyes and opens his jaws like a fish out of water. After a few moments, a sound comes from his mouth which takes the full measure of grief."

Lifeboat Drill is the most comic of Williams' old-age plays. Its characters, Mr. and Mrs. E. Long Taske, are an "ancient couple, nonagenarians" who are "afflicted with practically every geriatric problem." They are in their first class stateroom on the Queen Elizabeth II. Mrs. Taske wants to discuss a separation with her husband: "I will take the Madison town house, if, if, IF, I said IFF! you will install elevator, expense of."

A Steward and Stewardess bring their breakfast trays. Giggling, the Steward informs them that the lifeboat drill has been cancelled. (This is obviously to spare the old couple the difficult participation in the drill.) Left alone, Mr. and Mrs. Taske read the instructions for the lifeboat drill, which includes a description of life jacket procedures. They deal haphazardly with the life jackets as they quarrel with each other. Finally they end in total disarray: "With the life jackets hanging on them loosely, they sway forward and backward in grotesque profile, panting, gasping, clutching each other, hanging onto the ends of the beds."

Little more than a dark joke, *Lifeboat Drill* could have a place on a bill of three one-act plays about old age that might include *This Is the Peaceable Kingdom* and *The Frosted Glass Coffin*. These plays have never been produced together. In fact only *The Frosted Glass Coffin* has been produced at all, in Workshop Productions both at the Alliance Theatre in Atlanta and at the Goodman Theatre in Chicago. In Chicago it was on a bill of one-acts entitled *Tennessee Laughs*, which also included *Some Problems for the Moose Lodge*, the first version of *House Not Meant to Stand*. These plays are an important part of Williams' late work, a part almost totally ignored and unknown. Taken together they reveal a richly comic vision of old age, mordant yet loving.

This Is (An Entertainment), written in 1974 and produced at the American Conservatory Theater in San Francisco in 1976, has never been published. It is a big work, ambitious and maddening, difficult to grasp yet intriguing and theatrical. A play in eleven scenes, it dramatizes the miserable marriage of a wealthy Count and Countess who madly indulge themselves while a revolution rages outside their window. A satire on the rich, the play is also a philosophical vaudeville demonstrating the inability of anyone to live "in the moment." A look at the first scene illustrates the play's unique style.

Taking place in a "room with a moonlit balcony over a lake," the Countess sends her children out to play. She ignores the attention of her ailing husband, reads mystery novels, and contemplates assignations with her chauffeur. Breathless lines move the manic play at an exhausting clip as the Countess addresses the audience:

> He's into munitions, you know. Big shot, dot the i. This year struck it rich, saturation bombing profitable for how many orphans and widows did you make with pacification of, oh, yes, terribly peaceful in Ping Pong, compliments of Daddy, nothing disturbs the moonlight but the whimpers of maimed infants. So naturally Daddy is a little fatigued, needs vacation by lake, recuperate for future pacifications, must be relieved of marital obligations by surrogate spouse, conveniently discovered at wheel of Hispano when I sat up front to anticipate the road signs, yes, I anticipate sign kilometres away, being continually a moment ahead of the moment, excitement sometimes made me mistake the gear shift for the chauffeur's third leg, so to speak, oh it was an exhilarating drive through the mountains, children squealing, nanny squawking, daddy gasping the rarefied atmosphere, and chauffeur, well the gear-shift was well-lubricated.

Eventually the Count is cuckolded and he appears in the play wearing antlers. The revolution is successful and the hotel where the Count resides is invaded by the revolutionary forces. The Countess takes the general for her lover. They enjoy a short nearly idyllic moment before the Countess is given an escape pass by the General. Near the end of the play the General describes the life of the passing decadent class: "This is how they lived: for entertainment, indulgences which obscured the decline of vigor, time's a remorseless assault on . . . irremedial attritions: a theme exhausted by romantic poets inspired by laudanum and carafes of, frosted glasses of . . . heroic dreams of spirit transcending Death, sometimes with the heroic flush of consumption beneath arranged curls."

This Is (An Entertainment) may seem to some to be undisciplined, disjointed, and self-indulgent. On the other hand it is hard to see how it differs from the work of many experimental European writers of the twentieth century. James Joyce, Jean Genet, Eugene Ionesco, and Jean Cocteau, among others, are its natural cousins. Poetically it is written in a stream-of-consciousness style capturing the cadences of both Hart Crane and even Allen Ginsberg. It is hip and it is intoxicated, perhaps even written under the influence of drugs. It is also Tennessee Williams at his most unbridled. Unnerving as it is, the work should not be thrown out or forgotten. Someday, somebody may do a perfectly coherent production of the play, and it may even be enjoyed for the manic entertainment piece it aspires to be.

Tennessee Williams was attracted to revolution during the late sixties and early seventies, but his attraction was more poetic than practical, more erotic than programmatic. *This Is (An Entertainment)* reflects this attraction as do several other plays of the seventies. Of these works, *The Red Devil Battery Sign* is the most complete and important but several others are also worth attention, notably *A Monument for Ercole* and *Demolition Downtown*.

A Monument for Ercole seems to have been written in the early seventies. It was linked as a play to *Demolition Downtown* by Tennessee, and the two plays were to be presented as one evening called *Of Babylon the Fall*. They were never produced, but *Demolition Downtown* was published first in *Esquire* in 1971 and later as part of volume 6 of *The Theatre of Tennessee Williams*. *A Monument for Ercole* came to my attention along with several other unpublished and unknown Williams manuscripts as part of a pile of plays generously given me by Peggy Fox at New Directions Publishers. To my knowledge, it is an almost completely unknown and unnoted play.

The play is set in the office of a recently executed Latin American president during the first moments of a revolutionary victory. Ercole is the brother of the revolutionary force's general. He is a drug-taking poète maudit who ironically enjoys the services of the ex-president's manicurist while he terrorizes a couple of Americans who have been captured while boating in near waters. The man is named Tre and the woman is called Jan. Ercole shoots himself up with drugs from the ex-president's private stash even as he makes eyes at Tre. Jan protests Ercole's behavior and language. Ercole tells his cohort guard, "Violence of speech offends the chick and the chico. It's superior upbringing. Delicacy of it, y'know. With complete acceptance of saturation bombing . . . Civilians, old and infants, incinerated by napalm—the blood's gone out of their face at the mention of that. It's not supposed to be talked about or known but the world stinks with it. It's the big fart of the world anesthetizingly powerful in its stench." Ercole quotes Rimbaud, "Now, I should experience nothing but the luxuries of Babylon, sacked and burning," as he tries to seduce Tre. Both Jan and Tre are stripped. Jan is forced to wash Ercole. Tre manages to acquire a gun, but he is too afraid to use it. Ercole molests Tre, jerking the boy's jaws open: "Ah, ah, ah, say AH. I want a good look at the perfect young cuspids in thy little pink cave. Say it, open wide and say AH. Never mind, see. Impeccable pink satin entrance to the invisible lower internals of the orifice for the in-take that transfer it to the output though the lower orifice in the natal cleave, you know between the Jesus, what a perfect pair of young buns, protecting the natal cleave and the exit." Getting drunk on champagne and high on drugs, Ercole raves on about "The Big Lie." It is "the lie that the kingdom of Babylon is built on." At a climactic moment when Ercole gives Jan over to his black guard and he is about to rape Tre, a door opens and a "bearded young man in guerilla uniform" enters. It is Ercole's brother. He calls Ercole a degenerate and has him taken out by guards. Jan and Tre are also led off. The brother will raise a "monument for Ercole. Clean, simple. Not a trace of corruption." We hear gun shots offstage. The play ends as the brother eulogizes the dead Ercole.

Monument for Ercole seems not to have been rewritten or revised. The manuscript is obviously a first draft with cross-outs. One wonders why no more work was done on the play. Was Williams discouraged by others to drop the play or did the playwright lose interest in the savage play? Excessive and overwritten, the play exerts a strange masochistic power with its raw language and brutal action. The play is also fascinating as an extreme expression of a violent strain in Williams' complex nature, especially as it is coupled with political radicalism informed by realistic despair over the efficacy of political action.

Demolition Downtown, a one-act play, takes place in a wealthy American suburb. Revolutionaries have seized the city and are bombing downtown buildings. Offstage we hear dynamite blasts. Mr. and Mrs. Lane discuss possibilities of action as the blasting gets closer. They will try to conserve gas and food. Their little girls have returned from Sacre Coeur convent school, where they have been molested by revolutionary guerrillas. The Lanes are joined by their next-door neighbors, the Kanes. The two families discuss the possibility of escaping: "Going up to the mountains by the Sunny Peak Road." The men go off to get their cars ready. Women hear their daughters singing the "marching song of the guerilla forces." Mrs. Kane's reaction to the girls is fearful: "We can't stop them, you know. Children are creatures that know without knowing, they instinctively know without thinking or knowing, and I think that they know, well *know* that they know that siphoning gas out of one car is not a true solution and salvation. And, oh, they know we're not old, we're just a lot older than they are, and a generation gap is now a—wide—perpendicular—chasm!"

Mrs. Kane confides in Mrs. Lane her secret plan. Under her heavy coat she is naked and plans to leave Mr. Kane. She will offer herself to the rebels. "My plan is to go downtown in this plain gray coat and find the headquarters of the general and somehow get to see him . . . Get him to see me. Open my coat and say 'Take me.' I'm counting on his being ravenous for a woman which I think is likely. Before they took the city, they lived in mountain caves, and the general's still a young man."

Mrs. Lane likes Mrs. Kane's idea. They will leave together. As the play ends the two husbands return to an empty house. In the distance the wives are singing the revolutionary hymn.

This play is a wicked joke, a deliberate attempt to epater le bourgeois. One can hear Tennessee's cackling laugh as he wrote it. There was without question a mean streak in Tennessee Williams that occasionally revealed itself in the plays. He had a strong bad boy impulse that loved to shock. His enemies were quick to note and chastise this streak while his defenders usually smiled and tolerated it.

No play embodies Williams' mean streak more completely than *Kirche, Kutchen [sic], und Kinder*. Williams' subtitle for the play, "An Outrage for the Stage," is definitively apt. At one point in rehearsals with Eve Adamson who directed the play at the Jean Cocteau Repertory Theatre Williams called the work "a doodle of a play." Actually there is a good deal more in it than doodling.

At rise of curtain "a suspiciously healthy, handsome and powerful looking Young Man" is seated stage center in a wheelchair. He is wearing a costume of the "kind commonly worn by young male hustlers." A few moments after the curtain rises Miss Rose enters wearing "a heavily veiled tall hat resembling a lady's hat of Victorian vintage." She goes to a "gilded mock-up of a pipe organ" and begins to play.

The young man begins his opening monologue:

> A man constructs about him his own world as the chambered nautilus constructs about it those delicately iridescent chambers which are its dwelling—its place of retreat and refuge—and then is obliged to occupy it till he's evicted by the expiration of his lease on personal existence. But I when my time's run out will leave behind me this single chamber now visible to you, ordered as I'm best able to my convenience, and taste, and protection. Pro tem. All is pro tem. And my dear friends, if you get that into your heads, why them, I say, your heads are not totally vacant.

It seems clear that Tennessee Williams is describing himself and his work in relation to his own life and death. The young man goes on to describe the room he sits in as his "Kirche" (Church). It is a box set with three walls, each of which is painted a different color. He tells us that the blue wall is "sentimental" and the opposite red wall is "violent." On the red wall is a red light that lights up when the door is approached. The upstage wall is yellow. Through a window in this wall one can see a daisy. At night the daisy is "mysteriously retracted" to be replaced by a "fragrant night blooming vine." The young man refers to the invisible fourth wall as "unbesmirched by vulgarities."

The young man begins a sly strip tease but then stops and introduces his wife who is in another room called the Kutchen (Kitchen). She is the "daughter of the Lutheran minister of the island known as Staten." She is a slatternly woman in dress and behavior. Her father, the Lutheran minister, enters. He says nothing but is dressed in black and carries an umbrella. The Wife says outrageous things to her father, talking to him about his new girlfriend, Miss Haussmitzenschlogger. "She maybe don't take the cake in the beauty contest department, but Dame Gossip tells me she giffs wonderful head between hymns while you're preaching a sermon." The Wife goes on to mash a black banana on her father's face. She then intimates that he murdered her mother by pushing her off the Staten Island Ferry.

The Wife enters the Kirche with a big axe, which she intermittently wields at her husband. She asks, "What are your plans for the future, if any." Prior to her entrance we have seen the young man out of his wheelchair, so we understand that he is not paraplegic.

A very old woman comes on. She is pregnant, the aforementioned Fräulein Haussmitzenschlogger, "knocked up by your Papa who rapes me before and after church service and at choir practice back of the organ." Ninety-nine years old, she talks to the young man and offers to give him "a good blow job, personal, private." The young man tells her, "Madam, you are a lost soul in a lost world." The first scene blacks out.

The Kinder (Children) enter. They are two tall adolescents "of opposite gender." The boy wears "a scanty blue serge sailor-suit." The father instructs his offspring in whoring. They are advised to go out into the world to seek their fortune. "Hereafter always remember that your daddy conveyed to you all worldly knowledge he ever knew: limited, yes, but it will suffice."

In the last scene of the play the children return beaten and bedraggled from their venture into the city. They have been unsuccessful at hustling. The father decides he will once more have to leave his room and go out into the city "to compete for the hotlicker award given by a John who lives in the Plaza Hotel and whose hobby is duck watching." He gets out of his wheelchair and as he leaves the room he tells his offspring, "Yes, it appears that I must now face and accept the old male responsibility and prerogative of providing a living for himself and household." End of play.

It may be that Tennessee never wrote anything so unrestrainedly capricious. Yet the obscene cartoon still says something. In this portrait of the artist as hustler, the father must get out of his wheelchair and go back to his life of hustling. All life is sham and hustling is the only reality. This "doodle of a play" may well be Williams' most scathing comment on the professional theater and his own determination to continue with his hustling career. Actually it is also a pretty funny charade in the tradition of Alfred Jarry, a Genet-like naked ass to the world, an "up yours" to his audience, which is totally outside any American tradition and, yes, quite a lot of fun. Outrage can be a healthy act. Williams had a strong urge to defecate on the institution of marriage. Normalcy occasionally needs offending. *Kirche, Kutchen and Kinder* offends with panache.

Now the Cats with Jewelled Claws is a two-scene lyric play of strange beauty. It was announced as a world premiere for Miami's First International

Festival of the Arts yet was later withdrawn when it was finally read by the producers. It is just as well that *Cats* was withdrawn. Such an odd play would not have been well received by Miami's audience. The play has been published in volume 7 of *The Theatre of Tennessee Williams* and may be appreciated with the other fugitive works that comprise that courageous volume.

The play is set in a restaurant without walls, an open space with only a luncheonette and a few tables. Purple drapes hang upstage looking out on a mostly deserted street. "Through the window, we can see (on a canvas backdrop) the marquee of a cinema." Two middle-aged ladies, Bea and Maude, meet for lunch and exchange non sequitur inanities. An outrageous queen manager sings a song and dances around them. Two attractive young motorcycle-type hustlers arrive and discuss their relationship. One does not want the other to perform tricks without him. The other goes into the men's room for a quick blow job from the manager. The two leave. We hear their offstage motorcycles. Scene 2 continues the women's conversation. A "shattering crash" is heard outside. One of the women reports on the outside scene. "One of the motorcyclists came a cropper—his brains scattered on the street." The surviving young man "staggers blindly through the door." The two ladies exit. They shove and knock into each other outside. "Then there is a sound like the roar of an ogre in the sky." Bea and Maude part, "screaming, running." The waitress resigns her job. The surviving young man retches and "plunges" into the men's room. The Queenly Manager advances downstage, recites a poem.

> And now the cats with jewelled claws
> glide down the wall of night
> softly to crouch with bated breath
> and glare at all below,
> their malice on each upturned face
> descending pure as snow.

The entire play has been a preparation for the recitation of this poem. Life is malevolent and totally unpredictable. The odd dance of a play ends as the young man comes out of the men's room and asks the Manager who he is. The manager answers, "I am your future. I'll introduce you to it. Shall we go?" They exit through the revolving doors. In this final moment we recall the earlier conversation between the two young lovers and how the dead lover warned his friend that one day the other might end up going with queens like the Manager. The play ends.

Not much can be said about this mood-piece play. It has a lurid attractiveness, rather like a piece of atonal music or a Paul Cadmus drawing. It is a small chamber work. Little seems to have fettered Williams' imagination. It is also amusing that he would have offered the play to the Miami festival. I don't think he meant to be malicious but was in fact rather naively innocent in offering his writing to producers. He seemed to have little feeling for the appropriateness of particular works. A play is a play is a play.

There are in fact a whole series of short poetic plays, odd little works of several pages, that emerged rather frequently from the playwright's typewriter during the last years. One can imagine these plays being written in short bursts of insomnia. Again intriguing titles abound. *The Chalky White Substance* is an apocalyptically poetic play in which a young man, Luke, "sits on the precipitous verge of a chasm over what is presumably a dried up bed." He is visited by his aging lover, Mark, who tells Luke that he will betray him. There is nothing to be done. A strange chalky white substance covers all before it.

Steps Must Be Gentle is a poetic duologue for two characters who represent Hart Crane and his mother, Grace. They stand behind lecterns at opposite sides of the stage and speak across the stage to each other. Hart is dead and Grace calls to him. They recriminate each other with past pains but also seek some truce in their relationship. At first Hart feigns cool indifference to his mother's voice, but as the play progresses it is obvious that they are tied to each other in a love-hate relationship that death cannot end. The play is really poetic music for two voices that reveals a deep sympathy for the pain of dead poets and their necessary betrayals.

A Cavalier for Milady is a touching and amusing fantasy play. The play is set in a fashionable New York apartment. At its beginning two older ladies, Aida and Mrs. Aid, are dressed for an evening on the town with younger men from an escort service. They leave behind Aida's daughter Nance who is an emotionally disturbed young woman. Dressed in a child's party dress, Nance is obviously in her own world. Aida and Mrs. Aid leave Nance with a "baby sitter," who makes sarcastic comments on the situation. During her mother's absence Nance receives a visit from the apparition of Vaslav Nijinsky. She begs him to make love to her, but Nijinsky is not of the flesh. Aida and Mrs. Aid return, delightedly remembering their escorts and happy trysts in the bushes of Central Park. The baby sitter flees in angry dismay. Nance finds her mother's card from "Cavaliers for Milady." Once her mother and friend have left the stage, Nance calls the escort service and asks them to send her an escort cavalier that looks like Nijinsky. She exits into the night as the play ends.

The Traveling Companion concerns itself with an older man and a young hustler. The hustler refuses to sleep in the bed with the old man but is convinced to do so when the old man promises to buy the hustler a dreamed for guitar.

Sunburst dramatizes the terrorization of an older woman by two young hustler-type thugs. *The Youthfully Departed* concerns itself with spirits united after an automobile accident. Even after death they are fated never to join each other. *The Lingering Hour* (perhaps Williams' very last play) describes a piazza in Sicily where tourists watch an exploding Mount Etna that promises to destroy the world.

These short plays are the product of a great artist's imagination, and as such they are important. One can picture Williams ripping off many of these plays the way Picasso tore off his late pen and ink drawings. Perhaps they were not meant for production. Perhaps they are not worthy of production. I do not know. But they were the necessary expression of a writer who wrote instinctively and continually in an ongoing relationship of his uncensored psyche with the world. If one would want to really know Williams, one would want to know *all* of Williams.

It should be clear by now that I have a special affection for the unconventional and the estranged, the different, and the fugitive. For some reason I delight in complex works that dramatize paradoxes and unresolved difficulties. Perhaps they seem more honest than plays with conclusions and resolutions. "Late" plays of great playwrights more often contain this kind of beauty than do their earlier works. Occasionally they are willful and perverse. But late plays connote more than a mere definition of time or chronological description. "Late" suggests a tolerant way of looking at the world, a dislike of labels, and a welcoming of contradictions.

There is, I believe, a discernible pattern in the dramas of great playwrights who produce a large body of work over an extended period of time. The late plays of almost all major playwrights mark a turning away from plot to matters of theme and poetry, less concern with "realism" and more with metaphysics and epistemology.

Rules are broken late in great dramatists' careers. Plot, exposition, psychology are often forgotten in preference for metaphysical and spiritual mysteries. Psychology becomes less a matter of cause and effect than a record of the "transformations" humans can effect, sometimes with no explanation given at all.

Pervasive symbolism marks the late plays of many great playwrights: Sophocles' *Oedipus at Colonnus*; Euripides' *The Bacchae*; Shakespeare's *The Winter's Tale* and *The Tempest*; Ibsen's *The Master Builder*, *Little Eyolf*, and *Lady from the Sea*; Shaw's *Too True to Be Good* and *Back to Methuselah*; and, of course, Strindberg's *The Ghost Sonata*, *A Dream Play*, and *To Damascus*. Unanswered questions abound in these plays, fantastic events replace "real" happenings and characters are often mysterious and capable of strange powers. Oedipus ascends the heavens in a miraculous apotheosis in *Oedipus at Colonnus*. Dionysus razes temples in *The Bacchae*. A statue comes to life in *The Winter's Tale*, and in *The Tempest*, perhaps the most fantastic of all plays, the magician Prospero gives up his powers in order to become merely human.

There is no real contest in *The Tempest*. Prospero does exactly what he says he will do. We never suspect the success of Trinculo and Stephano's plot to overthrow Prospero. Indeed, this subplot is almost a mockery of a plot device. The real action in *The Tempest* occurs within Prospero, in the movement from revenge to forgiveness within the single man. There is an acceptance, indeed, a giving up of power that suggests an acceptance of his impending death. The movement has been internal; if you wish, it has been spiritual.

Of all modern playwrights, perhaps August Strindberg most clearly reveals this turning away from the drama of external events to the dramas of the psyche. In his "dream plays" he firmly asserts that the dramas of the outside world are nothing compared to the battles that can occur within a single individual. At the time Strindberg wrote these plays, there were many who saw the work as the product of a disturbed mind and therefore dismissed the plays as in some way "diseased." Dramas of the soul, of the psyche, easily lend themselves to charges of privacy and inaccessibility. There is often the negative suggestion that artists like Strindberg use their art as personal therapy. Yet, the question persists. Did Strindberg's mental problems impede him from seeing clearly, or indeed is it possible that his "illness" permitted him to see certain aspects of life more clearly than others?

The question is obviously pertinent to a study of the late plays of Tennessee Williams. Strindberg has been made more palatable with the passage of time. His personal rages and the wounds he inflicted on others are not remembered by any still living. The personal memory of Tennessee Williams by many alive, indeed, his own *Memoirs*, refresh a distaste for behavior unacceptable to a middle-class majority. But still the question persists and is valid: Is the art (of artists like Strindberg and Williams) the product of illness, or is the illness perhaps a result of living with an almost intolerable vision? Can we really dismiss art produced by what is considered by some to be a "sick mind"? Totalitarians of all persuasions have repeatedly tried to do so. Of course, much that we value in art would have to go: Van Gogh, Rimbaud, Caravaggio, Lewis Carroll—the list is endless. One may insist that art is always produced in moments of lucidity during returns of the artist to sanity. Yes, but would those moments of lucidity have produced those works of art without their artists' periodic journeys into madness, despair, and chaos? For many modern artists their works are reports from the abyss by travelers who have returned to tell us of their journeys, journeys most of us are too frightened or too fortunate to have to make. Modern artists tell us that different worlds hide behind the paper-thin covering of everyday reality, worlds no less real though hidden to many.

Many may see no personal connections in these visions to their own lives, especially if their lives are simple, with few questions left unanswered and personal security firmly entrenched. The late plays of the various dramatists I have mentioned have never been popular works, with the possible exception of *The Tempest* and perhaps Strindberg's *Dream Play* in his native Sweden. But even *The Tempest* is not at the top of the list of Shakespeare's most popular plays, and the Strindberg dream plays have not exported well.

Late plays are also notoriously difficult to produce. How does one theatrically represent the apotheosis of Oedipus? What does Dionysus look like? How are Ariel and Caliban to be cast and costumed? Ariel, who is spirit, is possibly not representable except in cliché terms. Caliban too often looks like a celebrant from a costume ball. He must be frightening yet capable of poetry.

Beyond the scenic, costume, and lighting difficulties, where does one find actors with the intelligence as well as the inner resources to project dramas that are basically internal? To play *Oedipus at Colonnus* an actor of extraordinary presence must be found who in his every word can make you feel his years of suffering. Similarly Prospero's transformation, his conversion, can only be played by an actor of enormous power, voice, and bearing who has experienced or at least understands the hatred of revenge and the peace of forgiveness. Most importantly, actors must be found who can communicate inner lives, the subtext of characters who have lived extraordinary lives. For it is in the subtext of these plays that the real dramas occur.

Behind this book's description of Tennessee Williams' output in the years following *Night of the Iguana* lies the firm conviction that a great artist has a unique voice that may be heard in all his work. Whatever he does is interesting because it comes from him. It cannot *but* be of interest. That is not to say that every work of a great artist is equally important. However, critical judgments are so notoriously subjective that it is the job of the scholar to protect all the works of a proven artist for future generations in the understanding that future generations may have different critical judgments.

One must try not to be obsessed by the critics. In the end they probably do little harm although they certainly give pain. The real problem is that critical opinion may stop productions and publication, as has happened with Williams. I cannot believe this will last. In the end all the work will be known, and good productions may some day reveal the plays' virtues.

How one longs for an adventurous theater that stages more than the same familiar works! Of course, one would always want to see *A Streetcar Named Desire*, especially with great actors in fresh productions, but how much more exciting would be a good production of *Clothes for a Summer Hotel*.

The reasons why we do not have such a theater are too depressingly well-known to be discussed here. American society is in such need of total help in all areas that our theater seems of low priority. The theater can only benefit or be harmed by all that happens in our nation at large. One must resist the temptation to discuss the effects of unbridled free enterprise. But behind bad art lies bad economics and business, and behind bad economics and business lie shattered value systems. Our best artists, like Williams, have said that repeatedly but few listen to them.

In the future, it may be that the twentieth century will be seen as one of the greatest periods of art man has ever known. This seems a highly likely possibility. Many have already called that century the most horrifying of all time. Along with the remembered horror will be some inexpressibly beautiful works of art. Ironically, some are beautiful *because* they express the heartbreaking sorrow, the aching cruelty, the split, the contradiction of our lives. Seen with distance the most painful art of our time may not seem so painful. How wonderful that time and beauty can subsume pain! Maybe the future will reveal us to ourselves more clearly. For now we are like Chekhov's Three Sisters at the end of his play. We grasp each other as we listen to receding music and cry, "If we only knew, if we only knew."

Surely among the remembered future works will be the plays of Tennessee Williams. Which ones will be most favored we can only guess. In the face of the future's laughter, let us not be too sure of our present judgments. Let us be generous to our artists, admit the precedence of art over criticism and of life over theory, and, above all, let us be humble in our value judgments both in art and in life.

Index

About the Author

William Prosser was a theater director and teacher. He studied at Williams College, Purdue University, and the City University of New York where he earned a Ph.D. in theater in 1977. He taught directing at the University of Arizona, Virginia Commonwealth University, and Florida Keys Community College before joining the faculty of Brooklyn College in 1984 where he headed the graduate directing program. During his tenure at Florida Keys he became the founding director of theater at the Tennessee Williams Fine Arts Center. At the center's opening in 1980 he directed the world premiere of Williams' play *Will Mr. Merriwether Return from Memphis?* written eleven years earlier as Williams was mourning the death of his lover Frank Merlo.

Prosser's professional directing credits included the 1973 world-premiere performances of *She Who Would Be He*, by Rosalyn Drexler. He also directed at the Woodstock Playhouse in Woodstock, New York, and at the York Theatre Company in New York City. Before his death, he directed professional productions of five other Tennessee Williams plays: *Vieux Carré*, *Sweet Bird of Youth*, *Night of the Iguana*, *A Streetcar Named Desire*, and *Suddenly Last Summer*.

He was married to the actress Roxana Stuart from 1969 to 1981. They had a son, Bertram. In 1984 he became the companion of Eric Stenshoel. He died in 1991 of complications from AIDS.